D0358822

ABRAMOVICH:
THE CHELSEA DIARY

ABRAMOVICH:
THE CHELSEA DIARY

HARRY HARRIS

JOHN BLAKE

Published by John Blake Publishing Ltd,
3, Bramber Court, 2 Bramber Road,
London W14 9PB, England

www.blake.co.uk

First published in hardback in 2004

ISBN 1 84454 048 0

All rights reserved. No part of this publication may be reproduced, stored in a
retrieval system, or in any form or by any means, without the prior permission in writing
of the publisher, nor be otherwise circulated in any form of binding or cover other than that
in which it is published and without a similar condition including this condition being
imposed on the subsequent publisher.

British Library Cataloguing-in-Publication Data:

A catalogue record for this book is available from the British Library.

Design by www.envydesign.co.uk

Printed in Great Britain by CPD, Wales

1 3 5 7 9 10 8 6 4 2

Text © Harry Harris 2004

Papers used by Blake Publishing are natural, recyclable products made from wood
grown in sustainable forests. The manufacturing processes conform to the environmental
regulations of the country of origin.

All pictures © Stuart Robinson / *Daily Express* except where indicated.

To Poppy and Linda

Acknowledgements

My personal thanks to Roman Abramovich's Moscow-based PR John Mann, Peter Kenyon's PR, Stuart Higgins and Jon and Phil Smith at First Artists' Management, who represent Claudio Ranieri. Also, Jean Carlo Galavotti who is UK correspondent for *Gazetta dello Sport*. At Blake Publishing, thanks to editors Nigel Matheson and Alex Perry and project editor Lucian Randall. Special thanks to Bill Bradshaw, sport editor at the *Daily Express* and Neil Sullivan, the *Express* sport picture editor.

Contents

The Chelsea Cast

Abramovich, Roman – Russian billionaire and new owner of Chelsea FC

Barnett, Jonathan – Football agent who represents players such as Kieron Dyer and Ashley Cole

Bates, Ken – Chelsea's controversial chairman and major shareholder prior to Roman Abramovich's takeover

Berezovsky, Boris – Russian billionaire and one-time business partner of Roman Abramovich

Birch, Trevor – Chelsea's chief executive before Roman Abramovich took over

Buck, Bruce – A partner in a law firm that acts for Roman Abramovich in the takeover who becomes a Chelsea board member when Eugene Shvidler stands down

Creitzman, Richard – Roman Abramovich's personal adviser and also head of corporate finance at Sibneft

Duran, Lino – Former Venezuelan referee who was the main backer in a rival bid for Chelsea headed by Mel Goldberg

Goldberg, Mel – Lawyer, whose clients include Paul Gascoigne, and head of a Venezuelan consortium that put together a rival bid for control of Chelsea

Harris, Keith – Chairman of Seymour Pierce, Chelsea's financial advisers prior to the takeover

Kenyon, Peter – Chief executive at Manchester United who replaces Trevor Birch as Chelsea chief executive after the takeover

Mann, John – Spokesman for Roman Abramovich and Sibneft

Mellor, David – Ex-MP and friend of Ken Bates who was involved in introducing a rival takeover bid for Chelsea

Schechter, Stephen – A financial consultant brought in by Ken Bates when Chelsea's debts hit a critical level

Shvidler, Eugene – Close ally of Roman Abramovich and president of Sibneft, his Russian oil company

Sibneft – Russian oil company, one of the largest in the world, owned by Roman Abramovich

Smith, Paul – Appointed to be temporary chief executive by Peter Kenyon while he was on gardening leave

Taylor, Paul – Property developer who, introduced by David Mellor, was a rival bidder for Chelsea

Tenenbaum, Eugene – Close ally of Roman Abramovich and in charge of his worldwide investments

Tkachenko, German Vladimirovich – Russian politician and friend to Abramovich who also owns Russian club Sovietov Krylya.

Zahavi, Pini – Influential football agent involved in many of the biggest player transfers and also a key player in setting up Roman Abramovich's deal to buy Chelsea

INTRODUCTION

June 2003–May 2004

A YEAR AT THE BRIDGE

From the glory, the tears of joy at beating Arsenal in the Champions League quarter-finals, to the misery of tactical blunders against Monaco in the semi-finals, this has been an historic season for Chelsea. Had it not been for Arsenal going the whole Premiership season without a defeat, it is conceivable that Chelsea would have won the title.

This has been a remarkable season in every possible way, with Chelsea totally transformed from 'potential' champions to realistic contenders. But Roman Abramovich's pot of roubles has so far failed to bring any silverware and, in the eyes of new Chief Executive Peter Kenyon, that amounts to failure, given the expenditure on players. This more than anything has necessitated the inevitable replacement of Claudio Ranieri by new coach Jose Mourinho.

On reflection, Chelsea have enjoyed an exhilarating European campaign, including their first win over Arsenal in 17 attempts in the Champions League quarter-finals, and a battle for their first title in nearly 50 years.

They also finished above the mighty Manchester United in the Premiership with a larger haul of points than that managed by the 1955 Championship side, not forgetting a breathtaking 4–0 win in Rome against Lazio in the Champions League qualifying stages.

Ken Bates stepped aside after nearly 22 years in charge at the Bridge and in the following months Chelsea began to consider themselves part of English football's elite, alongside Arsenal and Manchester United. They are clearly set to be a powerhouse of European football. Abramovich's personal fortune of £7.5 billion means that Chelsea will not be satisfied to remain where they are.

Numero Uno is the desire. Move aside, Real Madrid, Juventus, Bayern Munich, Barcelona and Valencia. Even Real's mighty Florentino Perez has been usurped as the master player in the transfer market. No star is beyond Chelsea's financial reach.

There is now every reason to look forward to the club's centenary with optimism. Plans are already in place for Chelsea to mount an even more impressive bid next season. Speculation about possible transfers has as much impact as the arrival of new players at the Bridge and levels of expectation have gone through the roof. There will be another influx of world-class stars, this time of even higher quality.

For all the hype surrounding the tortuous uncertainty for Ranieri, his glaring 'Tinkerman' errors in Monte Carlo vindicated the decision made by Abramovich's inner circle to dispense with his services; the Italian was ultra-cautious so often, then dramatically over-adventurous against 10-man Monaco. Publicly the coach, who thought it was inevitable that he would be replaced by the current regime, was always dignified, his broken English and self-effacing style making him popular to the bitter end.

Having progressed further in the Champions League than both Manchester United and Arsenal, Ranieri had much to be bullish about. With increased gate receipts and matchday income, the Champions League cash flowed: £19.8m for Chelsea compared to £19.4m for Arsenal and £19.15m for Manchester United. Ranieri concluded, 'Mr Abramovich did not ask me to win a trophy for him but I was one hour away from getting the chance to do exactly that. I can hold my head high because this special group of players and I have done a very good job for Chelsea. My way is to try to improve every year. This season we have done that so next season there must be improvement again.'

I think second place in the Premiership and the Champions League semi-final is a fair return for the investment made in players. If you had said we'd achieve that at the beginning of the season, then everybody at Stamford Bridge would have been happy.'

Sven-Goran Eriksson, the man once courted as his replacement, praised the Italian for his club's performance and the way he has handled all the speculation over his future. The England coach said, 'I think he is used to this [speculation]. He is Italian and every day in Italy there are rumours. I think he is handling it very well.'

Arsene Wenger said, 'It's a bit ridiculous for Chelsea to be second in the Premiership, to reach the Champions League semi-finals and for people to call it a failure. But that is football nowadays. This season has shown that you can't buy success. There are big clubs waiting 50 years to win the championship, clubs who spend as much as we do. When you make mistakes by buying a lot of players who don't settle, it takes time to get over it. Because you can't just sell them on, you end up carrying those mistakes for several years. Chelsea don't really have that problem as they can afford to forget the mistakes of the previous year and change the team every year. At some point, you'd imagine they might get it right.'

Even Sir Alex Ferguson defended Ranieri, 'The man has shown great integrity and nerve and he has made his team play. I believe they have had a successful season. I felt for them against Monaco because they could easily have been 4–0 up at half-time.'

Peter Kenyon thanked the players and staff for their efforts but did not praise the manager. 'I'm on record on this and you should look at what John Terry said. He as club captain feels the players have failed. I've been around enough footballers who've thrown away their runners-up medals because they're not proud of them. Finishing second in the league and reaching the semi-finals of the Champions League is a good achievement and thanks to everyone involved in that, the players and the staff. We've had a good season but are not where everyone at Chelsea wants us to be. We want to do better than this next season and better than that the season after.'

The future occupies the thoughts of Chelsea fans, as the whole nation – indeed, Europe itself – awaits the next wave of signings. Goalkeeper Petr Cech and PSV's young strike sensation Arjen Robben, pinched from under the nose of Manchester United, were snapped up in the course of the season. Robben became the 13th signing of Abramovich's reign, taking the owner's spending on players alone to £134m. That is on top of the £60m for the shares to take the club private, plus £100m worth of inherited debt.

Heysel, Hillsborough, Bosman – events that change football are rare and to them can be added the arrival of Abramovich in SW6. The new owner doesn't conform, refusing to wear a tie on matchdays, performing 'high fives' with his Russian pals when 'his' team score and ordering takeaway sushi from plush Mayfair restaurant Nobu to enjoy in his £10m executive box (which he prefers to the boardroom and directors' box).

Who would have imagined that the club that once, unknowingly, was a breeding ground for National Front recruitment would end up being owned by a Russian Jew? For all those who criticise an owner who 'wants to buy' silverware, there are others who wish Abramovich had bought them instead – certainly Spurs after the Russian's meeting with Chairman Daniel Levy and definitely Aston Villa, whose Chairman Doug Ellis commented, 'If Mr Abramovich had come in the summer, I would have been a hell of a good listener. I would have learned Russian in a flash. When you are talking about the kind of money he has invested in Chelsea, anyone would listen.'

The day they were told that Abramovich had bought Chelsea is one that few people connected with the club will ever forget. Frank Lampard recalls, 'I was in Vegas on holiday lying by a pool last summer and Rio [Ferdinand] rang and said that there was a Russian taking over Chelsea. He told me this geezer was really rich and was going to buy everyone and I was a goner, but I took no notice. A week later, I came back and it was all true.'

As a succession of midfield stars were either bought, lined up or speculated upon, Lampard knew he had a defining season ahead of him. 'I said to myself, "You can either look for another club, or become a better footballer and play every game." I decided to become a better player.' Lampard finished second in the Football Writers' Footballer of the Year awards (beaten to the top by Thierry Henry).

Perhaps the biggest saga within the soap opera was the courting and pursuit of Eriksson. The England coach was disappointed he was treated 'almost like a traitor' after it was revealed he had met Peter Kenyon. Although he eventually signed a contract extension with the FA, the Swede was heavily criticised for considering Kenyon's advances. 'Of course, you would do it differently, looking back,' he admitted. 'I'm happy that these discussions are over, but it's very difficult for me to understand that you are treated almost like a traitor if you listen to another job [offer]. In a democratic world, you should be allowed. I've always said that I'm going to stay in the job and I'm still here.'

Eriksson is confident the controversy has not affected his relationship with the fans. He said, 'If you are a football manager, you are judged on results. What is strange about rumours saying another manager is coming into a club? For Claudio Ranieri, it is not a problem. It is normal life. If you can't handle the pressure...'

At the height of the speculation, Tord Grip, Eriksson's trusty aide, urged his manager to make a decision about his future. Grip, who has known Eriksson for more than 30 years and is his assistant with England, was a key figure in the decision to agree a new contract with the FA rather than go to work for Abramovich. The 66-year-old Norwegian said he told Eriksson that he should quit England immediately if that was what he wanted and not wait until the summer of 2004 and the European Championships in Portugal. Eriksson first met Abramovich in July 2003, just days after the takeover, and had further discussions with Kenyon.

'It was necessary to do something,' said Grip. 'We couldn't go on as we were; it was not good for us, the players, the FA – no one. I said, "If you are thinking of going away, you should have done it before. Now it is settled and we are fully focused on the European Championships. I would say, though, that Claudio Ranieri has handled it all very well.'

FA Director of Football Trevor Brooking admitted that Eriksson was 'a little surprised by the ferocity of it'. Asked whether he groaned when he saw the photographs of Eriksson meeting Peter Kenyon to discuss the succession to Claudio Ranieri at Chelsea, Brooking laughed. 'There'll always be issues when everyone has an opinion and asks, "What on earth is he doing?" You need to deal with it as effectively as possible, so it doesn't become a saga. It mostly came from Chelsea. When I came here everybody was saying, "What's happening to Sven?" To me it was clear-cut. He had two years left on his contract, so there wasn't too much concern. I thought, "Let's wait and see what happens at Euro 2004." But of course, with the Chelsea speculation, the momentum gathered and in the end you had to quash it.'

While there is little disputing Eriksson's managerial qualities, the FA was forced into an inflated contract, paying out ten times the salary, for example, of Jacques Santini, the coach of France, probably the best team in Europe. They are also England's first opponents in Euro 2004. 'In the end it was between Mark [Palios] and Sven to sort out those details, but the fact there was so much speculation and interest from major clubs tells you it was probably worth fighting to keep him. If you speak to the players, you'll hear they're delighted. If Sven continues to be successful then speculation will crop up again – that's inevitable.'

While many still believe the hand of Eriksson was evident in a number of Chelsea's signings, Abramovich himself was often left bewildered when Ranieri revealed his line-up before a game. Maybe it was all down to serious lack of communication. The problem was that Ranieri's command of English left a lot to be desired... and Abramovich did not speak a word. Once the Russian was shocked when told that Baba was playing at left-back – because 'Baba' in Russian means 'grandmother'. The confusion ended when it was pointed out that 'Baba' is Celestine Babayaro's nickname.

But the tinkerings were far more confusing for the players and the fans, who craved a team with sparkle as well as the capacity to win. It finally all went pear-shaped in Monte Carlo. Abramovich had one of his three luxury yachts parked in the harbour and his team had a golden chance of reaching the Champions League final.

It was, potentially, a winning hand for Chelsea. The score was 1–1 when Monaco went down to ten men in the second half – then Ranieri had a brainstorm. He didn't have the players on the bench capable of improving the team's chances, yet his introduction of Veron, Huth and Hasselbaink diminished rather than enhanced the performance of the team. Veron was not fit, while Huth and Hasselbaink both ended up in roles to which they were seriously unsuited.

Chelsea lost 3–1. Afterwards, the players turned on Ranieri, behind his back.

In general, though, the players liked their boss, despite his eccentricities. Hasselbaink was bemused one time when Ranieri marched into his hotel room and ripped the television connection from the wall to ensure his player would not stay up all night. 'He's a bit mad at times, but you'll enjoy him,' confirmed Damien Duff.

Hasselbaink has made no secret of his problems with Ranieri. 'There have been a few difficult times when it was hard for me to keep quiet. I knew it wouldn't be right to make a big deal of it. I talked to some of the players about it, especially Marcel Desailly, he knows just what to say. He keeps you calm. There were three moments when I was left out – against Newcastle, Liverpool and Stuttgart. The worst was Liverpool. We were having a meal at the ground when the team was announced. I wasn't even on the bench. That's when you explode inside. I wanted to just get out of there, but I did what I normally do and went to the dressing room with the squad. I always read something before a game and I so sat there with a book open. But I didn't read any of the words, I just stared at the page.

'I watched the game from the tunnel and afterwards I had a talk with the manager. I said what I felt. He didn't say anything. I didn't feel it was fair, but I felt better afterwards. I don't know if that meeting affected my relationship with him. I used to be much closer to him before this season. It is very good to have competition; it keeps you on your toes. But you have to have fair competition and I don't think it has been fair all the time. I stuck in there and didn't say a lot and kept on working, and I am happy I did that. I wanted to do what was best for the team.'

Tony Cascarino, who spent three seasons with Chelsea, watched Ranieri conduct a training session. 'The thing that really struck me was how much things had changed since my time at the club. I kept seeing Andy Townsend driving into the car park ten minutes late and Vinnie Jones telling Ian Porterfield where to get off when he suggested a session of weights. I thought, "My God! That wouldn't have happened with this guy in charge."

'I saw him shouting at Marcel Desailly – a World Cup-winner – and he was ordering him around like an army grunt. You would have sworn they had lost 5–0 the day before. He was so hands-on it was unbelievable.' Marcel Desailly thanked Ranieri for what he achieved and gave a warning to the new man that the Italian will be a hard act to follow. At the Laureus World Sports Awards in Estoril, Desailly said, 'It looks like the chairman wants to change the manager. They've decided to say, "Thank you, Ranieri, for all you've done," and to say goodbye. He made small mistakes like everyone else, including the players, but did a good job.

'The reality is that Chelsea definitely have to win the Premiership title next year and go further than the semi-final in the Champions League otherwise there will be big trouble. We must have someone in charge who is clever, who must understand that he will have some famous and great players in the squad and that it's a heavy, heavy job. There's now a lot of pressure. We have built the foundations under Mr Ranieri and now we must start to win things. There is no excuse.'

Next season will be a big season for the club. The Roman Empire's first full season has been packed with intrigue, awash with roubles and it has shaken English football to its very core. The behind-scenes conflict, the players' true feelings about Ranieri as well as the public comments are intricately documented in this detailed diary. Every match is analysed, each of Ranieri's team tinkerings is scrutinised, and every emotion is relived from one of the most amazing seasons ever in the Premiership, indeed, in the history of the game.

This book details the full season from the perspective of Abramovich, Ranieri, the players and the fans. Abramovich has transformed Chelsea. Now fans wear 'Chel$k*' T-shirts and baseball caps, give the Russian owner a standing ovation at every home game and favour Cossack music over old favourites such as 'Blue is the Colour'.

But second is not good enough for Abramovich. The Russian billionaire went into the Chelsea dressing room after their failure to reach the Champions League final and promised, 'Next time it will be different.'

The players have mixed feelings after all the disruption. Jesper Gronkjaer said, 'It's not black or white. We've achieved quite a lot this year. We've moved a few steps forward as a club even though so many new players came in. But at the end of the day you look for silverware and we haven't got any.'

Emotions were best summed up by John Terry. Initially he insisted, 'We said at the start of the year that it would take time to improve. For many years, it's been Manchester United and Arsenal in the top two, so it would be good to put an end to that.'

Then he added, 'It's not good enough. Even before Roman Abramovich took over, everyone wanted to win things and I'm no different. I want to win trophies – firstly the league title and secondly the Champions League.'

Next season, everybody at Chelsea will be taking steps to ensure his dreams come true...

Harry Harris, Surrey,
June 2004

June

The remarkable story of how Roman Abramovich came to buy Chelsea began in March 2002 when the Russian was introduced to football agent Pini Zahavi by German Vladimirovich Tkachenko, owner of Russian club Sovietov Krylya and an influential member of the Council of the Russian Federation, their equivalent of an MP.

Abramovich's passion for football had been activated when he went to the 2002 World Cup finals in Japan and Korea. But he first set his heart on owning a club when he sampled the atmosphere of a Champions League tie between Manchester United and Real Madrid at Old Trafford and thought seriously about buying United.

As an agent, Zahavi had been involved in many major United deals, including the lucrative transfers of Rio Ferdinand from Leeds United for £30m and Juan Sebastian Veron from Lazio for £28.1m. Through his multitude of contacts at Old Trafford, Zahavi had arranged tickets for Abramovich in the directors' box, but no one at the quarter-final of the Champions League that night recognised the unfamiliar face watching the Real Madrid game.

As a favour to the Israeli agent, Blackburn Rovers manager Graeme Souness, another of Zahavi's many friends, contacts and business associates, had picked up Abramovich from Manchester airport and taken both the Russian and Zahavi to Old Trafford. When Souness later spotted Abramovich's features plastered all over the national newspapers the day after he bought Chelsea, he was straight on the phone to Zahavi.

Oddly enough, it was Ferdinand who chauffeured Abramovich back to the airport after the game. One of the passengers in Ferdinand's car was his four-year-old brother from his mother's second marriage. The boy loves to sing and, throughout the journey to the airport, he had Abramovich joining in the songs.

The game between Manchester United and Real Madrid had been inspiring, a proverbial feast of football. England captain David Beckham had controversially been left on the bench by Sir Alex Ferguson but he came on and scored twice in United's 4–3 second-leg victory. The Spanish club still progressed 6–5 on aggregate.

Abramovich says, 'It was a very beautiful game and I realised I couldn't pass it by. That's when I decided I really wanted to be involved in football. The whole atmosphere got to me. On the way back to Moscow, I couldn't stop thinking about it. So I said to my people, "Find me a football club." I looked at ten clubs in England, of which four were "possibles".'

On Wednesday, 23 April a meeting took place between Jonathan Barnett, Zahavi and Chelsea's then-chief executive Trevor Birch. Barnett represents some of the country's leading players, including Kieron Dyer and Ashley Cole, and he is highly influential in some of the big transfers and player contracts. 'Jonathan is a nice guy and a friend of mine and he afforded an introduction for me to Chelsea's managing director Trevor Birch; he has good connections in the game,' says Zahavi.

Lunch took place at Les Ambassadeurs Club, Park Lane, where they enjoyed a convivial meal paid for by Zahavi. Barnett explains, 'I arranged lunch on behalf of Pini to meet Trevor Birch, who wanted to discuss some players he wanted to move out of the club. The conversation got round to Chelsea's precarious finances, and Trevor mentioned that Chelsea were in need of money and quickly. Pini said he knew somebody.

'It all moved on from there. There were several meetings, or conversations, between Pini and Trevor. Pini and Trevor had their own agreement over commission, and I had an agreement with Pini. It would not be uncommon, would it, for agents such as Pini and myself to be on a commission for this sort of introduction?'

Clearly the Zahavi-Birch-Barnett meeting was the catalyst for the Abramovich takeover, but the issue of commission has since become contentious. Zahavi tells me, 'We discussed players, and Trevor wanted to know if we could help move some of his players out of the club.'

Because Chelsea were burdened with one of the most expensive wage bills in English football on top of debts estimated at £90m, it was imperative to unload surplus playing staff as discreetly as possible. As lunch progressed, it became clear that Chelsea's financial problems were worsening and that, while the aperitif was about the players, the main course was to do with whether Zahavi had sufficient worldwide contacts to find a suitable buyer for the club.

The well-connected Israeli knew Spurs fan Philip Green, billionaire owner of Bhs and the Arcadia group of stores. He might be persuaded to invest in a club, but through his connections in Russia, Zahavi also knew Abramovich would be keen. Zahavi says, 'I made a point of asking Birch whether he was talking on behalf of Bates and the board. He told me he was. After the lunch, I said to Birch to give me a couple of days.'

In fact, it was more than two weeks later when Zahavi called Birch to inform him that he had somebody who was interested. The delay was because Abramovich had looked at Spurs first, and then examined the feasibility of buying either Manchester United or Arsenal. 'Listen I have an interested party,' Zahavi told Birch.

Ferdinand and Zahavi travelled to Moscow for a working holiday. There, Zahavi had the opportunity to discuss with Tkachenko the possibility of involving Abramovich in a takeover deal. A shortlist of clubs was drawn up, which comprised Lazio, United, Arsenal, Tottenham and Chelsea. Abramovich first met with Spurs chairman Daniel Levy to discuss 'general issues', and the question of whether Levy would be interested in selling his shares arose. Levy confesses, 'Yes, we did have a meeting at his request because he wanted ENIC's perspective on the European football market. It is important to note, however, that at no time did we discuss, either then or subsequently, his desire to acquire a Premiership club.'

Any deal was difficult because it would have been a problem to buy out both Levy's shares and the 13 per cent still in the possession of Sir Alan Sugar. However, Levy later received a telephone call from Zahavi, who made a more formal declaration of intent, asking whether he would be keen to sell and at what price. Levy made the mistake of asking far too high a price for the shares – £50m for 29.9 per cent of the club which he valued at £150m. At the time, the share price was 18p, valuing the club at just £20m. Ironically, a further appointment was made for the day after the announcement of the Chelsea takeover. In the event, there was no need for that second meeting, in fact no need to even cancel it!

SUNDAY, 1 JUNE

For 18 months, Ken Bates has been wrestling with the precarious finances of Chelsea Village and the need to pay back the £75m Euro Bond that helped fund the project. There are three key problems which have led to a cashflow crisis requiring major refinancing: the slow build-up of business for the hotels and restaurants; the interest repayments on the bond which are set at a crippling rate of 9 per cent; the annual cost of player salaries which comes to £50m. Bates is running out of time to pay the rapidly-approaching £23m bill, even though it irks him that he is sitting on £165m worth of assets.

MONDAY, 2 JUNE

Bates examines the possibilities of 'securitisation' with Schechter and Co Ltd, who organise facilities for clubs and who were consulted when the FA ran into its own cashflow difficulties. Stephen Schechter proposes a £120m securitisation deal when the debts reach a peak of £99m. The deal will be secured by advance season-ticket sales for the next 25 years and will clear all current debts, leaving £26m in the bank.

Chelsea will be able to pay off the £5m outstanding loan to the Harding Estate, pay off Multiplex (the Australian construction company currently rebuilding Wembley), who are owed £12.5m on the West Stand at the Bridge, pay off the £75m Euro Bond issued in 1997 and meet cashflow obligations, with £5m to be paid to Barcelona for the transfers of Emmanuel Petit and Boudewijn Zenden. With £26m in the bank, Claudio Ranieri will still have his pick of some of the best international stars. Chelsea's securitisation would have been by far the biggest in football.

While Bates is confident of a deal going through, he declines to sell Jimmy Floyd Hasselbaink to Barcelona whose £6m offer he describes as 'derisory'. Eidur Gudjohnsen's agent is agitating for a pay rise, while defender William Gallas has an escape clause that needs to be addressed – with Arsenal sniffing around. Meanwhile, Trevor Birch travels to the States in the hope of buttoning down a rescue deal, but time runs out

Faith in football clubs' securitisation deals has faltered and Chelsea could become victims of what has happened at Leeds United, where investors had their fingers so badly burnt. Another option is an investment by the Californian Pension. Schechter introduces the pension fund known as CalPers (Californian Public Employees' Retirement System) as an alternative to securitisation. The injection of funds would be formidable but a condition of their purchase is that Bates has to 'retire' and the company would put in their own people to run the Chelsea Village complex, football club and all.

TUESDAY, 3 JUNE

The prospect of Californians describing Chelsea Village as a 'great lee-sure investment' fills David Mellor, ex-MP and friend of Bates, with dread. Mellor decides to act and introduces Paul Taylor, chief executive of Rotch, a London-based property company, to Bates. Mellor tells me, 'I had every faith that Paul Taylor, in the long run, would become the new Ken Bates.'

Mellor does all he can to achieve that aim and is only thwarted at the very last minute. The Taylor proposal is an immediate £10m injection of cash, a loan set against the Sky TV income due in August, as a prelude to the purchase of a stake of up to 29.9 per cent.

Taylor will utilise his banking and City connections to refinance the club with a further injection of £25–30m in the first three months. The Taylor proposal gains boardroom acceptance and is going ahead, with him purchasing 30 million new shares – raising the total number of shares to 200 million – plus a part of Bates' holding. The offer comes in at 25p a share, some way off the 40p per share offered by a rival consortium led by London-based lawyer Mel Goldberg.

WEDNESDAY, 4 JUNE

The Goldberg-inspired offer is even higher than the 35p that Abramovich will eventually bid. Little wonder that Bates would love Goldberg to get his client's act together. But Bates feels the Taylor-Mellor proposals are a far more realistic proposition. Birch is worried. He comes to the conclusion that the financial predicament is far more serious than he had at first diagnosed, and that the Taylor deal would mean waiting for a major refinancing programme. The club does not have much time left.

THURSDAY, 5 JUNE

Dermot Desmond, the owner of Celtic who has shares in Manchester United, has made it clear that he feels his club as well as rivals Rangers should be involved in the Premiership. That is not going to happen, so he is keen to invest in Premiership clubs. He is interested in acquiring shares below the 10 per cent threshold that is acceptable if he is to retain his controlling interest in Celtic.

Over convivial dinner and lunch dates with Bates, many suggestions are put forward but little of substance comes of them. In the end, Desmond would probably not have been content with a 10 per cent stake and negotiations don't develop too far.

FRIDAY, 6 JUNE

For three months, Goldberg has been in talks with Bates on behalf of a Venezuelan-backed investor. Bates has never quite been convinced by talk of a 1920s German bond and how it would release funds. Goldberg, an Arsenal fan, is keen to come on the board and oversee the investment.

The Venezuelan consortium offer is to buy 29.9 per cent of Chelsea shares for

£25m, with Bates diluting his shareholding. There are three names on the 1920 German bond – a former Venezuelan referee and two female pensioners. It turns out the pensioners have no plans to be part of the consortium to buy Chelsea. One of the 70-year-old ladies lives in Norwich, the other in Germany.

Although German bonds from the 1920s are regarded as 'junk bonds', this one has been authenticated by the Federal Reserve Bank of the United States and Citibank are acting on their behalf. With part-ownership of the German bond, the offer from the Venezuelan ref and his consortium comes in at 40p a share, at a time when the shares are trading at under 20p, making it a tempting bid for a minority stake. Best of all, they do not want to run the business, merely to invest in it.

SATURDAY, 7 JUNE

Mellor and Taylor know they have competition from Goldberg's consortium, and vice versa. Neither, however, knows anything about the Russian connection until it is too late.

Goldberg tells me, 'We were two days away from completing a deal and I knew there was another party involved, but Ken Bates wouldn't tell me who it was. I suspected that it was someone connected to the Rotch group and I had an inkling that they were close to a deal to buy 15 per cent of the shares for £10m. But we were going ahead with the purchase of 29.9 per cent of the shares for £25m. Yes, we were two days away from completing the deal; due diligence was holding the contracts up. We knew we were in competition with someone from Rotch, but what we didn't know was that the Russian would come along and blow us all out of the water.'

Lino Duran turns out to be the Venezuelan and, together with two others, holds a meeting with Bates. Goldberg says of Duran, 'He likes English football I took him to Chelsea and he loved the Chelsea Village complex and he wanted to replicate the concept in three or four different South American countries and, in return, offer first option to the best South American players. The deal didn't come to its conclusion quite quickly enough; we met Ken about ten days before Abramovich completed his deal... '

MONDAY, 23 JUNE

Two weeks later, an 8.00am meeting is arranged with Birch at the Marble Arch flat of Zahavi. The value of Chelsea Village shares is languishing below 20p and Zahavi wants to know the price required to buy the club. Birch demands 40p a share, but concedes that, if Zahavi's man is serious, the price would be negotiable.

Zahavi passes on the information to Abramovich in Moscow via a call to his friend German Tkachenko. The call is returned with a request for a meeting to conclude a deal.

THURSDAY, 26 JUNE

Stamford Bridge is the venue as Birch meets the Russian delegation of Abramovich, Tkachenko and Eugene Tenenbaum. Birch keeps Zahavi fully updated about the talks by telephone. No one has any doubts about Zahavi's pivotal role in the deal, which takes all of 20 minutes. They break up at 11.30am and decide to go out to lunch to celebrate. Birch is teased by the Russians that they are there only for the free lunch! Later that day, Zahavi receives a call from Birch. Could Roman meet his chairman, Ken Bates? Through Tkachenko, Zahavi persuades Abramovich to delay his flight back to Moscow in order to meet Bates. The meeting is arranged at the Dorchester Hotel – Zahavi won't be attending as the deal has already been done.

At 7.10pm, Bates marches along the narrow corridor, past the cloak room and on to the plush Dorchester bar, haunt of the rich and famous, to greet Abramovich and his entourage. Bates and Abramovich drink Evian water and nibble the delicate finger food on offer. Forty-five minutes later, they shake hands on the deal. If the strain of the past few days and weeks is taking its toll, Bates is hiding it well. When he later returns to his penthouse at Chelsea Village, he confides in his wife, Suzannah, that it is time to hand over the reins at Chelsea after 21 years. This confession is not without tears as he flops exhausted into the huge, comfortable sofa opposite his giant plasma TV screen set in the wall.

FRIDAY, 27 JUNE

Abramovich, personal adviser Richard Creitzman and Eugene Tenenbaum, who runs the Russian's worldwide investments, meet with Chelsea's financial advisers along with stockbrokers Seymour Pierce at a hastily arranged meeting at Chelsea Village.

Seymour Pierce chairman Keith Harris has seldom seen a deal go through so speedily. He tells me, 'It was breakneck speed. I have never experienced anything as quick as this. I thought the deal to buy the *Express* by Richard Desmond was quick, but we had to raise the money.

'We arrived on Friday afternoon, around 4.00pm, and were told of the meetings the previous day. It was all relatively straightforward; the finances were in place and verified by Citibank who knew Abramovich from deals in Russia, so I had no problem with them.'

Estimates as to the fee for his advice on the Chelsea deal suggest a cool £1m for his firm, in which he owns a 20 per cent stake. Looking back, Harris now says, 'This deal has lifted the shadow over the entire football industry. Everyone was down, forecasting gloom and doom and suddenly it all looks a bit brighter. Whether or not more Russians will end up owning football clubs over here is an interesting point, but Abramovich has shown he is deadly serious with the welter of player purchases and that can only encourage others to follow suit. As for all the accusations that it is a toy, well, anyone who commits to something like half-a-billion dollars is hardly playing at it. That shows commitment in my book.'

Harris suggests that Abramovich snubbed Manchester United because it would have cost £700m to take over. Harris says, 'There was a great deal of research done by him and his advisers before going for Chelsea. He looked at a number of Premiership clubs. They were Manchester United, Arsenal, Spurs and Chelsea. He chose Chelsea for a host of reasons.

'Why not Manchester United? If you think of the sums of money involved, United are the most successful financially. They would have cost £650–700m. That's a huge chunk of change. He paid £60m for the shares outstanding at Chelsea. But buying the company meant assuming responsibility for the debts and that was another £80m. So he got Chelsea for £140m.'

Although the debts were £90m, there were reserves of £10m so Harris is right to put the real figure at £80m. 'As for United, what can you do with them, how can you improve them? At Arsenal, you would have to spend to buy and build a stadium. You have all those problems and it would be expensive. Spurs have spent on the ground, but is it big enough and in the right place? And how much would you have to spend on the team?

'You look at Chelsea the assets are in place and they have spent a lot developing the ground into one of the best in the Premiership. The infrastructure of the team is good. Sure, there is money to be spent but the backbone is strong. Only time will tell whether it was money well spent. One suspects this is an investment.'

Bates adds a footnote. 'Abramovich went to United to watch a game but he didn't like the atmosphere. He decided he wanted a club in London and opted for Chelsea as they had more going for them than other teams. We have no problems with stadium redevelopment.'

SUNDAY, 29 JUNE

The foundation stone of Roman Arkadyevich Abramovich's fortune is oil. His personal worth is estimated at £5–8bn. Abramovich hasn't counted it lately. 'It is very difficult for me. I do not sit around all the time, calculating how much I am worth.'

Until 1999, no pictures were published of this intensely-private entrepreneur; he rarely gives interviews, and there is scarcely any TV footage. In person, he is quietly spoken, has an unassuming appearance and seems perfectly comfortable conducting business in jeans, T-shirt and designer stubble.

At the age of 37, he hardly gives the impression of being one of the world's wealthiest individuals. His business empire ranges from aluminium, trucks and hydroelectricity to meat processing and pharmaceuticals. He used to own 26 per cent of Aeroflot, Russia's national airline, but sold his stake to the National Reserve Bank.

Abramovich was born on 24 October 1966 in Saratov, a city on the river Volga. His parents were of Jewish-Ukrainian extraction and came from southern Russia. His mother Irina, known affectionately as Irochka, was a piano teacher. She died tragically at 28 after having a termination because she could not afford another child. Her only son Roman was a day short of his first birthday when she died of blood poisoning in Komi, one of Russia's most remote regions.

Irina's decision was hardly uncommon. Many women chose to have abortions rather than give birth to more than one child during a time of severe housing shortages and poor financial prospects.

Tragically, 18 months later, Abramovich's dad, Arkady, known by the family as Arkasha, was killed after a crane collapsed on him. He was 32. Arkady discovered a broken jib on the crane during a site visit and, as the project was already delayed, he tried to fix it himself. But the jib fell, crushing his legs, leaving him trapped. He died in hospital ten days later of post-traumatic shock.

After his father's death, Abramovich's close-knit Jewish family never considered sending him to a state orphanage. Arkady was the youngest of three brothers and, as Abramovich grew into a young man, he learned from his devoted uncles, Leib and Abram. As Arkady was the only brother to have had a son, the boy's future was especially important to the Abramovich name. He was raised by Leib and his wife Ludmilla and was enrolled in Ukhta City Municipal School Number 2 at the age of six in September 1973.

At the age of 14, he was sent to Moscow, where he shared a cramped, one-room flat with his grandmother, Tatyana, and enrolled at School Number 232. At 17, he failed to get into the prestigious Gubkin Russian State University of Oil and Gas in Moscow. Without a place, which would have allowed him to postpone his compulsory two-year national service, he was forced to join the Army as a truck driver in the artillery detachment. Aged 20, Abramovich returned to Ukhta and enrolled at the town's Industrial Institute where he studied for two years before successfully applying for a transfer to the Moscow Auto Transport Institute, a prestigious engineering school where he studied for a year. It was around this time that he met Eugene Shivdler who was studying at

Gubkin University in Moscow. He has remained a close confidant and partner ever since.

Abramovich started his first company, Ooyut-Comfort, in 1987 while still a student, making plastic toys, dolls and ducks and selling them at the markets springing up around Moscow, as well as dabbling in retread tyres. He became extremely rich, extremely fast, by exploiting the hybrid law of the Gorbachev-Yeltsin transition which allowed companies to trade on the huge difference between Soviet and Western prices for raw materials.

In 1999, he was elected to the lower house of the Russian parliament, the State Duma, for the Russian Far East region of Chukotka, where he was invited to run by the local governor. He also founded the charity Pole of Hope and became a sponsor of a Russian ice hockey team, Omsk Avangard, which came second in the Russian premier hockey league last year.

He met his attractive second wife Irina Malandina, a glamorous former Aeroflot air stewardess, on board a plane. At the time he was married to Olga, a women three years his senior, and lived in a single-room Moscow flat with her and step-daughter Anastasia.

Irina would return from some exotic locations with examples of Western goods and Abramovich copied them in Russia. Since he's become such a great success, Roman and Irina and their five children – Anna, 11, Arkady, 10, who is named after Roman's father, Sonya, 8, Arina, 2 and Ilya, 6 months – have several luxury homes. Irina studied for a law degree when she started her family and enrolled for a doctorate in Fine Arts in Moscow, an affirmation of the couple's growing interest in collecting paintings.

Abramovich lives on a 99-acre walled estate outside Moscow, where they have entertained President Vladimir Putin on numerous occasions. They also own a castle in Bavaria with nearby skiing, one of Roman and Irina's hobbies. Then there is a £10m villa in Nice in the South of France. One of the Russian's newest luxury homes is the 424-acre estate called Fyning Hill, consisting of secluded woodland on the South Downs near Midhurst in West Sussex, once the British bolt-hole for King Hussein of Jordan. He bought the £12m estate more than two years ago from Kerry Packer, the Australian media magnate.

The seven-bedroom house, built in the 1920s, has stabling for 100 horses, two polo pitches, a swimming pool, a tennis court, a clay pigeon shoot, a rifle range, a trout lake, an equestrian centre and a go-kart track. The stables are being converted into a massive £2.5m complex, comprising a bowling alley, gym and indoor swimming pool.

Abramovich has been spotted driving through the locality in a red Bentley and arrives on the estate by helicopter. President Putin is reputed to have flown in for lunch! Abramovich also owns a plush, multi-million-pound apartment in Lowndes

Square, Knightsbridge, and although he plans a more permanent residence in this country, he has said publicly that he does not plan to leave Russia for good. 'I'm most comfortable in Moscow. I spent most of my life there. I like the seasons. But I like the lifestyle in England. It's multinational and multicultural. There are signs that remain from the Empire, and I like that. People are used to dealing with different people. Everyone can feel comfortable there. This also goes for the United States.'

His business life took off when he first traded in oil products using the Swiss-based 'vehicle' company Runicom, now absorbed into his mother company Sibneft. 'I used my own money,' he insists. 'I didn't use state money through bank loans. My most important deals were when I was unknown. Now you have to be a known name to be a success.'

In the early 1990s, Abramovich consolidated the oil business in the Omsk region so successfully that, when the most powerful businessman of that time, Boris Berezovsky, conceived the idea of creating Sibneft, an amalgamation within the oil industry, he made Abramovich his first choice for the board and then head of the Moscow office.

After Berezovsky's exile to London, Abramovich was left in sole charge of his own and his former boss's shares. The web of companies owned by Abramovich is largely controlled by a British-registered holding company, Millhouse Capital, based in Weybridge, Surrey, which is, in turn, controlled by a Cyprus-based organisation called Electus Investments.

So how did he become so wealthy, so quickly? He says, 'I bought a company that was not the largest back then,' – referring to the rapid privatisations of the 1990s that made billionaires of a few supporters of the former President Boris Yeltsin in return for their support in the 1996 elections – 'and it is important to remember that the people who took part then were willing to take a risk and there were all kinds of risks. I was not part of a system that would take care of me, I had to survive. In 1995 [when Sibneft was privatised], $250m was an amount of money that people in Russia couldn't fathom. An apartment then cost $5000.

'Most of these companies were bankrupt, extremely inefficient and poorly run, and it was extremely important to save them quickly because thousands of jobs were at stake. The people who made it were the ones who didn't just sit back and skim money off the enterprises they bought, but instead brought in good management, Western techniques and invested in new technology.'

These days, Abramovich has two yachts, a Boeing Business Jet, enjoys Chinese food and films such as *Straw Dogs* and *Pulp Fiction*, along with the music of a Russian band called Spleen. He doesn't smoke or drink, and describes himself as a 'family man' and 'a Jew first and a Russian second'. He and Irina are considering educating their five children in the UK because the

British education system has 'hundreds of years of educational excellence'.

He also runs the governorship of Chukotka, 4,000 miles away in Siberia. There he has invested millions, building homes, improving schools and public buildings for the area's 73,000 population, mostly reindeer herders and fishermen. He provided the region's first international-standard hotels, supermarket, cinema, a restaurant/billiards hall that brews its own beer, a college, a museum and house of culture, an international-standard medical facility and a fish-processing plant. The list goes on and on, and he is treated like a god there.

Above all, Abramovich represents Russia's new buying power, and his arrival here adds up to the biggest shake-up in the British football industry since the creation of the Premier League in 1992. Manchester United no longer have a monopoly on cash.

MONDAY, 30 JUNE

Crowd favourite Gianfranco Zola is growing tired of waiting for an improved offer. In last-ditch talks with Zola's lawyer, Trevor Birch refuses to budge on a 50 per cent wage cut. 'The differential was so minimal as to be almost irrelevant,' according to Italian sources. But, a mere 24 hours later, money is no longer a problem at Chelsea FC. Step forward, Abramovich, with his promise of more spending to come. 'There are lots of rich, young people in Russia. We don't live that long, so we earn it and spend it.'

David Mellor's mobile phone emits its usual trill as he is enjoying the company of a dozen family and friends in a Thai restaurant on Wimbledon Common after a pleasant day out at the tennis. Bates is calling from his penthouse. Bates informs Mellor that it is time to break open the Dom Perignon – he has just struck a deal with a Russian multi-billionaire and Chelsea are saved.

Not that Mellor could have found a bottle of upmarket bubbly at the local Thai if he had wanted. Mellor says, 'I cannot blame the Chelsea board, or Ken, for taking that deal because you only have to look at the finances involved to see why they did, rather than go in our direction which would have, in all honesty, been applying the sticking plaster to the problem.

'Naturally, I was furious when the Russian tied up a deal, but as it turned out, Ken met the Russian on the Thursday and the whole damn thing was done by the following Tuesday, and nobody knew outside of those involved.'

Mellor adds, 'I don't think it is good in the long run for a football club of Chelsea's standing to be owned by a foreign billionaire, even if he turns out to be an eminent one. There are consequences for football in the broader sense, and ramifications for the Premiership as an international brand.'

The news travels fast. Chelsea Village shares shoot up 40 per cent on their

AIM (Advanced Institute of Marketing) listing, and jump a further 7p 24 hours before the announcement to close at 35p, after Abramovich agrees to buy 84.9m shares from Bates. Dealers note that 270,000 shares changed hands in the day leading up to the late-night announcement when their usual daily turnover would normally be in the low tens of thousands. A total of 1.27m were traded the day before the news broke. The London Stock Exchange, which regulates the AIM, asks the Financial Services Authority to investigate. A hit list is circulated by the FSA of those under suspicion of insider share dealing prior to the takeover, and the names of five individuals and two companies are on it.

July

RANIERI ASSEMBLES HIS DREAM TEAM AS THE SEASON DRAWS NEAR

TUESDAY, 1 JULY

It's announced at 8.00pm that Abramovich has bought Chelsea for just under £60m – cheap enough, yet Ken Bates still can't believe his luck. He tells me, 'Because of what has happened at Leeds, football has become a dead duck as far as clubs getting bank loans and investors interested is concerned.'

Abramovich has acquired Bates' shares for £17.5m, along with those of the five offshore trusts, to give him control from day one with 57 per cent. The next stage will be to bid for the entire company, buying up any remaining shares and de-listing it from the AIM Stock Exchange. Abramovich's company has absorbed Chelsea Village's £90m debts, including the £75m Euro Bond, which is not due to be paid in full until 2007.

Chelsea Ltd, a special-purpose vehicle, registered in England, was formed specifically to buy Chelsea Village, but it is just an intermediate entity. Chelsea Ltd is wholly owned by Isherwood Investments Ltd, a company incorporated in Cyprus, which in turn is wholly owned by Taverham Holdings Limited, a company incorporated in the British Virgin Islands. Taverham will ultimately be owned by Millhouse Capital, a holding vehicle for all of Abramovich's assets, which is registered in the UK and has offices in Weybridge, Surrey. Millhouse shares are all owned by an entity in Cyprus. That's because Russia and Cyprus have a tax treaty that makes the Mediterranean island an attractive place for wealthy Russians to keep their money. In short, everything is owned by Abramovich.

Bates and Birch remain from the old board. The five new board members are: non-executive chairman Ken Bates, in a figurehead role; chief executive Trevor

Birch; Richard Creitzman, Eugene Tenenbaum, and Eugene Shvidler, the president of Sibneft, who has been credited with turning the Siberian oil company into Russia's fifth-largest crude oil producer, making it the primary source of Abramovich's vast wealth and expanding industrial empire.

News travels fast. Claudio Ranieri is driving through France when he is told by Birch that the club had been sold. Eidur Gudjohnsen is out with his two boys in his home town of Reykjavik, Iceland, when he takes a never-to-be-forgotten call on his mobile phone. It is his father, Arnor, telling him Chelsea have been bought by a Russian billionaire. He laughs and gets on with his shopping: Dad has got it wrong again! Then curiosity gets the better of him and he rings John Terry, who confirms it's true. Gudjohnsen recalls, 'I started negotiating a new contract at the start of the summer and was about to finalise things when Mr Abramovich came. Trevor Birch called me and said, "You're going to have to put everything on hold because the new guy wants to come in, have a look around and see what's going on."'

Bates encapsulates what the past 21 years as overlord of the Bridge mean to him. He tells me, 'Fantastic experience, wouldn't have missed it for the world. I have loved every minute of it.'

Bates bought the club for £1 in 1982, but he also took on £1m debts that were crippling at the time. 'I took over when the club had a crumbling stadium, was bankrupt and bottom of the Second Division, and it is great recognition of my achievements that when this guy wanted a football club he looked at Manchester United, Arsenal and Spurs, and he chose Chelsea because we had the most potential. We have a great ground – not necessarily the biggest, but the best – and we have a good team.'

With the sale of the club, Bates' vision of lavish hotels and a banqueting complex in the heart of one of London's most fashionable areas has also come to an end. Abramovich may even decide to offload the extras, as he says, 'If I decide they are burdens, I'll look at other options.'

Abramovich explains why he bought Chelsea. 'It's one of the best teams. We like England because it has the most competitive league in Europe. For me, that was a very important criterion. It's also easier to buy here because many of the clubs are publicly quoted.'

Bates is unperturbed by Abramovich-related jibes – some say that selling out to a Russian will start a trend of overseas 'sugar daddies'. He points out, 'There are several clubs already owned by Scandinavians, while an Egyptian owns Fulham. If there is a trend, and I don't think there is one, it won't have started with this transaction.' Neither does Bates believe that Abramovich will be railroaded into paying inflationary transfer fees. 'This man is a billionaire and hasn't become that by making silly, emotional decisions. It will be evolution, not revolution.'

Bates is either bluffing, or doesn't realise just how much Abramovich is prepared to spend. He goes on, 'This is a marriage made in heaven. Let's be honest about it, I have always had to run Chelsea on a shoestring. We could have continued to pootle along, but if we want to compete with the likes of Real Madrid and Barcelona, then we need more money... Much more money. With Abramovich's financial muscle behind us we can compete on the world stage and that has always been my main ambition – it has been the reason for all my hard work at this club.'

Abramovich won't be on the Chelsea board, as Bates quickly explains, 'He can't come on the board because he is a Governor of one of the Soviet provinces [in fact the Russian province of Chukotka in Siberia] and that precludes him from becoming a director.'

Above all, Bates denies claims he sold just as the club was running out of money. Bates originally asked for 40p per share, but settled at 35p. However, an Abramovich insider tells me, 'He could have bought Chelsea for half the price, but he didn't want to harm the club, waiting for it to go into administration before buying it. He could have got it much cheaper but he is a man of honour.'

Abramovich himself observes, 'It is the right price. I don't feel like I saved the club.'

WEDNESDAY, 2 JULY

At 10.00am, Bates, Abramovich and his aides go on a stadium walkabout at Stamford Bridge. During this, Abramovich insists his motives are simply 'to have fun'. But for such men fun tends to involve winning. 'Buying Chelsea is a way to realise my ambitions,' he says. 'Chelsea is near the top of its league. My message to the fans is I will do everything possible to ensure they enjoy the game as much as me.'

Supporters should be reassured by his record with Russian ice-hockey team Avangard Omsk, which he transformed from provincial also-rans to a leading power in the superleague, with an annual wage bill of $15m. Player salaries approach the levels of those in North America's NHL, even though Omsk is a just a city out on the West Siberian plain.

But Russian Football Federation president Vyachelsav Koloskov is furious that Abramovich has shovelled his cash into Chelsea. He says, 'Russian money should be put into Russian sport for the Russian fans.'

The Mayor of Moscow, Yuri Luzhkov, one of Russia's most prominent politicians, who had previously not always seen eye-to-eye with Abramovich on other matters, agrees with Koloskov. 'They spat on Russia by buying Chelsea. In buying Chelsea for such a huge amount of money, they abandoned the Russian teams which needed support.'

But John Mann, spokesman for Sibneft, answers criticism, by pointing out the fact that the tycoon carefully considered Russian teams before investing abroad. 'He looked at several Russian teams over the last couple of years, but there were no deals available that met his requirements.'

Abramovich also counters objections with a pledge to build new stadiums in Russia, including a state-of-the-art example for £65m in Moscow. In his homeland, there are still suspicions that he wants to move his assets out of Russia and expand his empire elsewhere.

Abramovich insists he is not driven to rule the world. 'Some will doubt my motives, some will think I am crazy. I have no Napoleonic dream. I'm just hard-working and pragmatic. I am realising my dreams of owning a top football club.'

The football industry wonders how long he will maintain his 'hobby'. When asked if he'll be around for at least ten years, he replies, 'It's hard to talk about ten years. Maybe 20 years, 50 years, I see it as a very long-term commitment.' Refusing to disclose the limit on funds he is willing to release to the club, he explains that to do so would push up the price of future contracts.

It doesn't stop journalists sticking their fingers in the wind. It is estimated that Russia's second-richest man plans to spend £150m–200m on players over the following two years. 'I want a team that wins the league and Europe. The goal is to win. It's not about making money. I have many much less risky ways of making money. I don't want to throw my money away, but it's really about having fun and that means success and trophies.'

Asked which players he would most like to buy, Abramovich is quick to mention Thierry Henry. After some discussions with his advisers, he adds, 'I also like Sol Campbell.' Then he remembers himself. 'I'm not going to tell you other players because their price will just go up.' Cue laughter from advisors Creitzman and Tenenbaum.

Abramovich is prepared to pay top dollar to get the players he wants. It turns out he made an amazing attempt to bring Zola back after the greatest player in the club's history signed for Cagliari. Abramovich's representatives twice contacted Cagliari president, Massimo Cellino, who reveals, 'Abramovich sent Zola a fax offering him €4m (£3m) a season. I have seen it with my own eyes – it is all true. He also contacted me by phone via an Italian middle-man, offering me $2m (£1.25m) to tear up Zola's contract.'

Zola refused to 'do the dirty' on Cagliari. 'I think I have made the right decision,' he reveals. 'My reputation with the Sardinian people was at stake, and I knew that they were expecting a great deal from me.'

Elsewhere, goalkeeper Jurgen Macho signs a two-year deal on a free transfer from Sunderland, and John Terry signs a new four-year contract. Bates goes on Chelsea TV to explain the recent momentous events.

A private meeting is held that will make national headlines. Pini Zahavi accompanies Sven-Goran Eriksson to Abramovich's palatial apartment at 39 Lowndes Square, but it isn't until a photographer realises the significance of the pictures he has taken that the front- and back-page story breaks a few days later at a time when Roman's wife Irina goes on a much-publicised two-hour shopping trip to Harrods.

Is the England coach once again thinking of defecting? After all, he had done so before when conducting talks with Manchester United. Zahavi tells me later, 'Sven was never offered the job, and I should know. I introduced Sven to Abramovich a year earlier and they met five times before this meeting.'

If Eriksson can't become manager of Chelsea straight away, there can be no doubting he indicates that he might be available after the European Championship. Their chit-chat also includes his liking for a certain kind of English player, such as West Ham's Glen Johnson, and a foreigner who would always be on his team sheet, Juan Sebastian Veron.

THURSDAY, 3 JULY

For the players, the hard works starts. Training begins at 8.30am with blood assessments and jump tests. Then a feeding frenzy of transfer speculation erupts with AC Milan suggesting they received a €50m bid for Alessandro Nesta. Chelsea sources deny bidding. Abramovich adds to the uncertainty surrounding Ranieri by admitting that he is 'not sure' about him. 'I just don't know. I am going to sit down with him in the very near future.'

Ranieri, in the Stamford Bridge hot seat since 2000, expresses his own fears. 'I don't know anything about these rumours about another manager. But I know the rules of the game and that, when control of a club passes from one man to another, anything can happen. It's the right of the new man to decide who he wants in charge of the team. I don't know Mr Abramovich and I would like to speak to him. At the moment I'm relaxed and continuing to coach my side.'

Having steered the club to the coveted fourth place in the Premiership and into the lucrative Champions League, Ranieri naturally feels he deserves a chance under the new owner. But continued speculation centres on Eriksson, Roma's Fabio Capello and others. Even Sir Alex Ferguson is linked. A surprise name is Graeme Souness. The plot thickens when Ranieri admits he had no idea that Chelsea are in negotiations with Barcelona's Patrick Kluivert. 'I don't know anything about Kluivert, only what's been in the papers. But he is one of those strikers every manager would like in their team. I don't permit interference on the technical side and, if something like that was to happen, my departure is a sure thing.'

FRIDAY, 4 JULY

The new directors are going over the finances. A wish list of players is drawn up as Ranieri takes charge of the morning training session, and then returns in the afternoon to meet Creitzman and Birch to plan Chelsea's strategy.

The list is not short on quality: Wayne Bridge, Glen Johnson, Patrick Vieira, Steven Gerrard, Pavel Nedved, Kieron Dyer, Edgar Davids, Damien Duff, Emerson, Geremi, Juan Sebastian Veron, Claude Makelele, Rivaldo, Ronaldinho, Harry Kewell, Joe Cole, Thierry Henry, Ruud van Nistelrooy, Raul, Michael Owen, Wayne Rooney, Ronaldo (senior, at Real Madrid), Ronaldo (junior, at Sporting Lisbon), Christian Vieri, Hernan Crespo, Alvaro Recoba, Djibril Cissé, Zlatan Ibrahimovic, Andrei Shevchenko, Patrick Kluivert, Adrian Mutu – only the best will do. The identity of the person who has compiled the list is the subject of feverish debate. Was it Eriksson Zahavi Abramovich?

Zahavi and Birch set out to discover the availability and price of various players. Zahavi embarks on a whirlwind tour of Europe's most glamorous destinations: Tuesday it must be Paris; Wednesday, Turin; Thursday, Milan; Friday, Monaco. A spoof email circulates the inner sanctum of the Stamford Bridge hierarchy: 'Now we are owned by a man with £5.4bn, we are in the market to buy just about any top player in the world and the first one he's bought is Emile Heskey.'

The initial problem is to convince a number of the players on the wishlist that Chelsea are about to become a major force within European football. Abramovich takes a 'hands on' approach to new acquisitions, saying, 'This is what the pleasure is all about – to participate in the game and the selection process. The coach will determine which areas are in need of new players. I will participate in that discussion and analysis.'

Zahavi and Birch carry out negotiations for the club, haggling over fees and personal terms until they are agreed in principle. At that point, Birch calls Creitzman. Once Abramovich is happy with each of the deals, Creitzman talks to Tenenbaum who controls access to Abramovich's funds and who acts as Abramovich's interpreter, as well as a key adviser. Tenenbaum releases the funds from one of Abramovich's numerous bank accounts straight into Chelsea's current account. 'Roman isn't actually signing any cheques. It's all sorted by Tenenbaum.' Birch observes, 'The business works at the speed of light now. We tell Roman what it costs, and he sorts it out. Simple as that.

'Last pre-season we brought in only de Lucas on a free transfer and, all of a sudden, we have a menu of the world's best players. It's a dream job. There's such a buzz around the place.'

Creitzman adds, 'There are a lot of discussions with Claudio. Roman knows the players who have come in. He watches videos and goes through cassettes on a lot of players. Agents all over have been sending him cassettes and if Claudio says, "Yes," then they go ahead.' Remarkably, Creitzman is a Barnet supporter who was born and raised in London, educated at Surrey University, before leaving England to work in Moscow where he became part of the new Chelsea owner's business empire. He has been head of corporate finance at Sibneft since 2001 and it was he who prepared the initial report on how the Russian might buy into a football club.

Abramovich makes it plain that money is no object in securing the players of his choice, although Zahavi tells me, 'I won't allow him to be ripped off.' Deciding which players to go for, Abramovich takes a wide range of soundings, not just from Ranieri and Zahavi, or even Eriksson, but also from Russian sports journalists and supporters. 'Their opinion is very important to me. They understand more than the press.'

Abramovich receives a letter from a ten-year-old fan. 'He described the situation in the team perfectly and three of his five suggestions for new players we were already thinking about,' he said. Abramovich is impressed. 'I couldn't even write at that age.'

A new £20m training complex complete with enhanced youth facilities is now affordable. 'I don't believe the model of Real Madrid would fit in the English structure. I see Chelsea between Manchester United and Real Madrid,' the Russian says. 'There is an academy at United that prepares future players. But when you have to make a purchase, you do.'

SATURDAY, 5 JULY

There's a double training session for the players but at lunchtime Gianfranco Zola turns up to say his emotional goodbyes. Bates is taking the brunt of the criticism for losing Zola but makes it clear he has not dealt personally with players' salaries for some time.

Back in town, construction gets under way on the fifth floor of Chelsea's office block inside Chelsea Village for Abramovich's new headquarters.

SUNDAY, 6 JULY

The rumour mill goes into overdrive: talk of Christian Vieri, Wayne Rooney, Fabio Capello and Sven-Goran Eriksson dominates the headlines. Former Real manager

Vicente Del Bosque claims he's been approached to be the new coach. The speculation grows more fanciful by the day.

MONDAY, 7 JULY

Zola holds his farewell press conference at the Bridge and Ranieri is visibly upset. 'We have lost a great player and a great ambassador. It's going to be impossible to replace him in the hearts of the supporters. When the Queen decided she should arrange a dinner for Italians in the UK, Zola was on the list. His loyalty, generosity and technical skills were all put at the disposal of our club and he was a vital leader in the dressing room.'

Zola is asked if he would have stayed had he received an improved offer before 1 July. 'Chelsea made me a better offer on 2 July, when the transaction between the old owners and the new owners happened. That gave me a really bad couple of hours. Unfortunately, it was too late.'

TUESDAY, 8 JULY

Two key meetings are held. Ranieri meets Abramovich in the morning and Abramovich meets the players in the afternoon at the training ground.

Ranieri is very impressed. He instantly knows the new owner will not accept anything but success. 'The meeting lasted one hour in which I told him straight I saw no reason for him to get rid of me. I simply told him the truth, that last season people called us no-hopers but we made it to the Champions League But I also told the new owner it was already in my plans we should do much better this season. He told me and the players he wants to be the top club in Europe.'

Abramovich has a poor grasp of English but can still convey a simple message. 'There are no plans for a change of management.' Yet his words do little to quell speculation that, in time, Ranieri will make way for Eriksson, and that, in turn, will only increase the likelihood of David Beckham joining, should he eventually jet back from Madrid.

Ranieri says the pressure is now on for Chelsea to start winning. 'Throughout my career, I've had to fight on my feet at clubs where situations have been tough, really tough. But at Chelsea with Mr Abramovich, the expectations are now very different and we have to start winning big trophies very soon before getting to the top of European football.'

WEDNESDAY, 9 JULY

New goalkeeper Jurgen Macho twists his knee in training and has to be carried off. A cruciate ligament injury means a new keeper must immediately be added to the list of potential recruits. Eidur Gudjohnsen and his father arrive as the striker signs a new contract to start in a week. Gudjohnsen observes, 'I'm looking forward to seeing where this is going to take the club.'

THURSDAY, 10 JULY

The squad head off to Roccaporena, Ranieri's favoured training camp in Italy, as the club reach agreement on their first signing. A little-known talent from the East End marks the start of the spending spree.

Glen Johnson signs a five-year contract following his surprise £6m move from West Ham. A right-back to replace Albert Ferrer is sorted. The 18-year-old is 'gobsmacked' to be the first of many new arrivals. Johnson becomes the most expensive teenager in Chelsea's history. 'This is a massive step for me, a big learning curve. This time last year I was still in West Ham's reserve team and now I'm looking at playing in the Champions League. It's hard to take in how quickly everything has happened.'

FRIDAY, 11 JULY

Rumours spread like wildfire. Chelsea are linked with Southampton's Wayne Bridge and admit to having two bids for Blackburn's Damien Duff turned down. Then they move for Real Madrid's Geremi, and express a desire for Christian Vieri.

But in Roccaporena, it's straight down to pre-season work, two sessions a day at 8.30am and 5.30pm. Permanently out-of-favour defender Winston Bogarde hears of a family illness and returns to Holland. In Vienna, accompanied by club doctor Neil Frazer, Jurgen Macho has a cruciate knee ligament operation. The tear is estimated to put him out for six to seven months.

Back in London, Sven-Goran Eriksson denies any interest in taking over at Stamford Bridge. 'I can confirm that I met with Pini Zahavi and the new owner of Chelsea Football Club, Roman Abramovich. The meeting took place at Mr Abramovich's property in London. Due to the intense media profile given to Mr Abramovich's involvement with Chelsea, I accept that this meeting may create unfortunate speculation. Therefore, I would like once again to categorically reaffirm my total commitment to my role as England head coach. I am thoroughly enjoying the current European Championship qualifying campaign and I am looking forward to leading England to success in the future.

'Pini Zahavi and I have been good friends for 20 years, since I was coaching Benfica. As Pini spends a lot of time in London, we regularly meet socially.

Additionally, I have known Roman Abramovich for several months and during that time have also enjoyed socialising with him when he is in London.'

Chelsea officially distance themselves from speculation as Birch leaps to the defence of Ranieri. He declares, 'There is no truth in the rumour we are trying to bring Eriksson to Chelsea. Claudio Ranieri is the coach, has four years remaining on his contract, has just got us into the Champions League and has already had a very positive meeting with Roman Abramovich. Together, we have charted the Chelsea path forward.'

Something Birch does not mention is that it would also cost Chelsea £8m to end Ranieri's four-year Stamford Bridge contract. The bookies remain unconvinced as they slash the odds from 20/1 to 7/2 for the Italian to be the first Premiership managerial casualty. Amid such intense media speculation, William Hill suspend bets at one point. Glenn Hoddle is second favourite at 4/1, and new Fulham boss Chris Coleman is 5/1.

SATURDAY, 12 JULY

An irritated Ranieri criticises Eriksson's naïveté at being caught by a photographer when meeting Abramovich. From the training camp, he says, 'In my opinion, if it is true Sven doesn't have his mind set on this job at Chelsea as he has claimed, then I am willing to believe him. However, that means he was very naïve to let himself be photographed so obviously going into Mr Abramovich's house in London.'

John Mann issues a public declaration of support on behalf of the new owner: 'Mr Abramovich wants to express explicitly his support for Claudio Ranieri as manager. He thinks he's doing a great job and has made sure Claudio knows that.'

SUNDAY, 13 JULY

Chelsea are newly linked with such players as Steven Gerrard, Juan Sebastian Veron, Thierry Henry, Patrick Vieira and Roma's Francesco Totti. Roma immediately block any moves for their Brazilian midfielder Emerson, while Juventus overprice Edgar Davids, even though he only has one year left on his contract. They are even willing to pay Arsenal a world-record £50m for Henry, eclipsing Zinedine Zidane's £46.5m move from Juventus to Real Madrid, but chairman Peter Hill-Wood and Director David Dein make it clear, when Chelsea put the feelers out, that neither Henry nor Vieira are for sale at any price. Hill-Wood tells me, 'I'd be very reluctant to sell at any price, whether it is £50m or £70m. It's only money, after all, and we are trying to build a team here at Arsenal – not destroy one. Henry is simply irreplaceable.'

Vieira is equally untouchable and is about to sign a new £100,000-a-week contract for the Gunners. Arsenal offer Freddie Ljungberg and Francis Jeffers instead – but no way can Chelsea have Henry or Vieira! Meanwhile, Liverpool issue a hands-off warning over Steven Gerrard and Michael Owen.

Chelsea are approached by Raul's agent and quoted an astronomical € 100m (£71.4m), in addition to wages of €12m a year (around £8m). The £100m package is proposed to Chelsea because the striker has fallen out with Real Madrid president Florentino Perez. The player's agent, Gines Carvajal, says, 'Roman Abramovich has made an offer of €100m for Raul and they want to pay him €12m a season, double what he is earning at Real Madrid. FIFA agent Marc Roger, on behalf of Chelsea, asked me if Raul would be interested in entering negotiations for a transfer to Chelsea. I spoke to Raul and he said, "No."'

Roger then admits that he is involved in a deal for Claude Makelele. 'I do not deny that I have been in touch with Carvajal but that was about other matters,' says Roger. 'I am not working for Chelsea.'

Ranieri makes light of some of the more glamorous and outrageous names linked with his club. 'Raul tonight, tomorrow it is Rivaldo,' says Ranieri. 'Maybe Raul must renew his contract.'

Following the morning training session in Cascia, the village next to Roccaporena, the first warm-up game ends in a 12–0 thrashing for the local amateur team. Abramovich seems sure about one Italian, at least! 'I really like Cudicini. He is a great goalkeeper.' He is one of Ranieri's shrewdest buys, a bargain £160,000 from Castel di Sangro.

MONDAY, 14 JULY

Chelsea have signed two new goalkeepers; but Macho is set to miss most of the season, while there are doubts over the quality of Marco Ambrosio, who came from Serie A club Chievo. Rhys Evans, the former England Under-21 keeper, has been released and England Under-20 goalkeeper Lenny Pidgeley has gone on a season-long loan to Watford. Leeds United's Nigel Martyn declines a move down South to back up Cudicini. A third bid for Damien Duff is turned down by Blackburn Rovers.

TUESDAY, 15 JULY

Physio Mike Banks flies back from Roccaporena to oversee medicals for the influx of new players; England masseur Steve Slattery flies out and gets straight to work after dinner. Many players, it seems, are desperate to jump aboard the

Abramovich bandwagon, realising the salaries on offer. Parma's Japanese icon, Hidetoshi Nakata, is one. Following an approach from Leeds United, he tells reporters that the English club he wants to join is Chelsea.

WEDNESDAY, 16 JULY

Real Madrid's Cameroon international Geremi signs a five-year contract in a deal worth £7m, and goes off on holiday. He believes the Blues have the ambition to rival the likes of Manchester United, who were also interested in signing him. He says, 'We could win the Premier League and even the Champions League this season.'

Graeme Le Saux flies back from Roccaporena to become the first big-name casualty of the takeover, shipped off to Southampton with Wayne Bridge going the other way. Saints manager Gordon Strachan makes it clear that no deal for Bridge would have taken place without Le Saux moving to St Mary's. Le Saux moves on a free transfer and also receives a 'leaving present', rather than the reported solution that Chelsea would continue to pay half of his salary. It amounts to the same sum. Chelsea also pay the fees of Le Saux's agent and those of the agent representing Bridge, raising the costs by a further £1m.

Le Saux made more than 300 appearances for Chelsea in two spells, between the two of which he won the Premiership title with Blackburn. He has also played 36 times for England. Even before Abramovich arrived, Le Saux was deep in contract talks which were not progressing very well. He had a year to run and the club were in no mood for improved terms to keep him. 'It didn't come as a shock at all,' Le Saux says. 'I realised it was time to move on. Like everyone who's interested in the sport, I'm looking at what's happening at Stamford Bridge from a general perspective – whether they are going to gel or not, whether it's a risk – although when a man's that wealthy, it's not really a risk.'

His hope is that Abramovich's wealth does not harm the game. 'That's something we will have to find out. We all hope that it doesn't destabilise an already fragile market. It is naïve to say money brings success, because football has a nasty habit of disproving that philosophy. It will be interesting to see what happens but there is no tinge of regret that I am not in there.'

THURSDAY, 17 JULY

Ranieri promises the new Roman empire will stretch across the whole of Europe. Instead of fearing the sack as he takes the Blues to his home city for the first match under new ownership, Ranieri believes the meeting with Lazio is simply the first step to winning the Champions League.

Speaking at their training camp in southern Italy, Ranieri says, 'Throughout my career, I've had to fight on my feet at clubs where the situations have been tough, really tough. I started in football management 15 years ago at the very bottom, but now I think we have the chance to go right to the summit. In my opinion, Mr Abramovich represents a gigantic opportunity for this club and Chelsea have to make the very most of it. Expectations are now very different.'

Another mogul, Italy's Silvio Berlusconi, bought bankrupt AC Milan in Italy's Second Division and turned them into the club that dominated Europe for a decade. Ranieri beams, 'The truth is, everything I see of Abramovich reminds me of Berlusconi when he arrived in football and decided to make Milan great.'

Knowing Abramovich moves in the kind of circles which enables him to loan a personal Lear jet to Real Madrid's Ronaldo so the player could attend Christian Vieri's 30th birthday party in Italy, Ranieri suggests a star-studded shopping list. He observes, 'How much better is it this summer compared to the last one? Last year I put my list to the club and not one of the players ended up joining because Chelsea had financial problems.

'Mr Abramovich has already signed Geremi and I think that is fantastic for Chelsea. I've tried to get him for two seasons without success. I cannot talk about Juan Veron or Edgar Davids, but I will confirm we need a great player in midfield because the Champions League qualifier is right around the corner in August.'

Ranieri has one lingering regret: Zola. 'We were talking about his new deal and told him the "old" Chelsea couldn't afford the extra money he wanted. I had no idea the new owner was coming because it was a secret until the very last moment. Franco had agreed terms and, even though Chelsea made such a good offer under Mr Abramovich, Franco came back and said, "People like us are born to sell dreams and, in Cagliari, they really need me in order to start dreaming great dreams once more."'

Meanwhile, Southampton-born Wayne Bridge, 22, who made his England début in a friendly against Holland in February 2002 and was part of Eriksson's squad for the World Cup in Japan and South Korea, has no regrets about arriving at Stamford Bridge. 'I discussed it with my family and we all thought it was a great move. This is a very exciting time for everyone at Chelsea. I know it will help my international chances to be playing in the Champions League. It also gives you the experience of playing against top foreign opposition week in and week out.

'It was the toughest decision I've ever had to make to leave Southampton. It hurts because I've supported them since I was a boy. But joining Chelsea is a challenge I felt I couldn't turn down.'

FRIDAY, 18 JULY

LAZIO 2, CHELSEA 0

Roman's new empire was never going to be built in a day. Abramovich is in the Italian capital with his wife and children to see just what he is getting for his money and quickly sees why Ranieri wants so many new faces. Seated just behind Bates in the directors' box of the Stadio Flaminio, Abramovich politely refuses all interview requests as he swelters in the evening heat. Lazio's directors – even more desperate for cash than Bates had been a month earlier – queue up to shake his hand.

More than 25,000 fanatical Lazio fans turn out at Italy's national rugby stadium to see a Chelsea team they could face in the season's Champions League. Most seem to be there just to boo Giuseppe Favali, the only black player in Lazio's line-up. But Brazilian winger Cesar is the first to lose his cool, clashing with Jesper Gronkjaer after the Dane's innocuous challenge. Frank Lampard intervenes and is met with a hail of empty plastic bottles from behind the high fences which keep Lazio's infamous 'Ultras' away from the pitch.

For both teams, this is the first game of their pre-season preparations, yet there is an unusually competitive edge. Every other top player is being linked with a move to Stamford Bridge, and those already in possession of the shirts are keen to show they do not need replacing. Young Glen Johnson is given a chance to show his pedigree on the right side of a makeshift defence. Desailly and Gallas are not yet back in training, Terry is rested to protect a strain and Le Saux has flown back to London for talks with Southampton. So it is hardly surprising that the inexperienced Johnson has his work cut out containing superstar strikers, Simone Inzaghi and Claudio Lopez.

The youngster impresses with one last-ditch tackle on Inzaghi, but ruins his good work by then losing the ball to Lopez, whose 25-yard drive is well saved by Cudicini. A minute later, Chelsea go behind when Massimo Oddo crosses low from the right and Inzaghi shakes off Mario Melchiot to score from close range. The Italians should double their lead just before half-time. Celestine Babayaro goes missing as Stefano Fiore delivers another ball which Inzaghi drills wide. No wonder Ranieri wants Wayne Bridge to strengthen the left side of his dodgy defence. Not that Chelsea are much better up front, where stand-in skipper Jimmy Floyd Hasselbaink looks as though he has spent the summer eating his way through his £80,000-a-week pay packet.

The visitors do not manage a shot of note in the first half and Mario Stanic even manages to miss the target with an unchallenged header from Gronkjaer's cross. Three half-time changes by Ranieri fail to turn the tide. Rome-born Cudicini, who played one game for Lazio nearly ten years ago, is given a standing ovation by the fans who unfurl a huge banner proclaiming, 'Welcome, Carlo, you will always be one of us'.

It is more support than the keeper receives from his team-mates. He is left stranded again after 52 minutes when unmarked Dejan Stankovic heads home from Lopez's free-kick. Abramovich does not look happy while Bates shifts uncomfortably in his seat.

Team

Cudicini, Johnson (Kitamirike), Melchiot, Huth, Babayaro (Keenan), Gronkjaer, Lampard, Zenden, Stanic (Forssell), Gudjohnsen (Cole), Hasselbaink (Kneissl)

After the match, Ranieri brushes aside talk that he will be shown the door. As he good-naturedly breezes past the waiting media throng minutes after the match, he quips, 'I know the bookies have stopped taking bets on me.' When asked by a media inquisitor if he finds that situation funny, Ranieri quickly retorts, 'Of course I do. Very funny.'

Back in London, Blackburn Rovers finally accept a £17m offer for the 24-year-old Republic of Ireland winger, Damien Duff, after three bids had been rejected. The bid triggers a get-out clause in his contract. Duff and his adviser Pat Devlin negotiate terms, but the player needs time to think it over. Devlin denies the player is holding out for a move to Manchester United after Sir Alex misses out on Barcelona-bound Ronaldinho.

Duff arrives at the Bridge in a black cab, admitting he has thought long and hard for days over the deal. He confesses, 'This was probably the biggest decision of my life and I didn't want to rush it. I had seven great years at Blackburn and there was no big reason to move. It was just a matter of thinking everything through.'

His pace up front will give Chelsea an added dimension. He says, 'It looks as though great things are going to happen at Chelsea. It just feels right. It is a big, big chance and I can't wait. I have been training with Blackburn reserves and keeping myself ticking over, but I just can't wait to meet up with the lads and start kicking a ball again.'

Before the Abramovich takeover, Liverpool were always regarded as favourites to sign Duff, but Gerard Houllier was told that his £10m offer did not come close to activating the release clause.

With Duff and Bridge signing within hours of each other, Abramovich has now taken his summer spending spree to £36.5m in just 21 days, and Ranieri continues to deliver on his pledge to have a home-grown centre to his side. Bridge says, 'You need a certain number of British players if you are going to succeed in the Premiership and Chelsea now have more than they have had for quite a few years. You hear talk of the new owner coming in and drawing up lists, but the players Chelsea have brought in are clearly people that Claudio Ranieri has spotted.'

More good news. William Gallas signs a one-year extension to his contract, tying him to Stamford Bridge until 2007. He had three years remaining on his previous deal but further commits himself to the club he joined from Marseille two years ago. Gallas is not travelling with the rest of the Chelsea squad to the Asia Cup, because he played for France in the Confederations Cup. The spending spree did play a part in the decision, as he adds, 'Now I see that Chelsea want to win things, and that's why I signed a new deal with them.'

MONDAY, 21 JULY

Bates is in the departure lounge at Heathrow when he spots his old mates from Anfield, Gerard Houllier, chairman David Moores and chief executive Rick Parry. The Chelsea squad are heading to Kuala Lumpur for the inaugural Premiership Asia Cup, while the Liverpool party are on their way to their own Far East tour. Bates can't resist the opportunity to show off his unique brand of humour as he shouts across the lounge, 'Hello, boys, anyone want to come and play for Chelsea? We'll double your money!'

What the Liverpool group don't know is that Steven Gerrard and Michael Owen are on the list of potential signings! Bates thinks the joke is taken in good spirit, but later it is picked up by a newspaper and portrayed as if he is serious.

Bates tells me, 'It was an innocent remark made to some dear old friends; no malice intended and they took it the way it was intended. There was absolutely no nastiness in it at all. There is such a thing as camaraderie in the boardroom, you know, and David Moores took it in the spirit it was intended when he shouted back, "Fuck off!"'

Eyewitness Jamie Carragher finds the whole incident amusing. He observes, 'It was quite funny at the airport. But I thought it was interesting when Frank Lampard said a few lads were feeling a bit unsettled, as so many players are being linked with their positions. If you think you're going to be sold, it plays on your mind.'

Bates also proves he is no fan of Sven. 'Eriksson? I don't think any of us are over-enamoured with him, are we? At the last FA Council meeting, I stood up and suggested England caps are awarded only to players who appear in competitive internationals. They all applauded that and Geoff Thompson agreed the international committee should consider it. It cheapens the cap. And how can you have four bloody captains in one match? The armband has been tossed to the side of the pitch and it seems whoever is nearest gets to wear it. It's a shameful way to treat something that's part of our football heritage. Being captain of England should be the ultimate honour.'

The tone of Bates's comments proves highly embarrassing as clearly Eriksson is a friend of Abramovich's. Bates is asked for an explanation. He tells Abramovich's aides that he was livid the way his interview had been interpreted and reported. But coupled with the publicity surrounding his 'joke' with the Liverpool team at Heathrow, it causes a degree of disquiet within the Abramovich camp. Although it has been agreed that Bates will stay on until 2005, there are mutterings that his term of office might be shortened as a consequence.

Bates tries to defuse the situation with a call to Eriksson himself in Soho Square. Bates is an FA councillor and had been, at one time, on the FA executive board. He wants to extend a cordial invitation to Eriksson to dinner to explain how the headlines came about. The England coach is unavailable for such a social occasion but would see Bates, perhaps, at the FA instead. No meeting ever takes place!

Bates denies Chelsea are trying to coax Eriksson to the Bridge. 'It's not a fair assumption to make,' he says. 'People have put two and two together and come up with 85. Roman Abramovich is a friend of his and that's all there is to it. Sven is the England manager and we're hoping he's going to win the European Championship for us. He has known Mr Abramovich for a number of years so I suppose he's entitled to have tea with him. So they were pictured together, so what? All Claudio has to do is ignore it and go about his business as usual. And that's what I've told him. All these rumours that the players we have signed are Sven's players are just crap, they're utter rubbish. Claudio wanted Geremi last summer and he wanted Wayne Bridge – and Damien Duff too, for that matter. Agents will confirm that enquiries were made.'

Bridge and Duff jet out to Malaysia with the team. Bridge begs Southampton fans not to abuse him when he returns to St Mary's, 'It hurts to leave your hometown club, which you have supported since you were a boy; where you have played since you were 13 or 14. My dad, Mick, was a season-ticket holder at the Dell and he always came to watch me play for the club. But I sat down with him and my mum and we decided this was a big move. Many of my friends are Saints fans and they know why I have left. I didn't want to have to hand in a transfer request but that was the only way I could talk to Chelsea. I understand why I might get stick when I go back there but I hope the fans realise why I made this decision.'

Asked what had finally made up his mind to join, Duff responds, 'I suppose it was the gut feeling I had when I came down here. In the past week, I've flown down about three times. It just feels right. It's time to move on to a big new challenge for me. The easy thing would have been to have stayed at Blackburn where I was happy and played every week. I'm not guaranteed my place here, but it's a big challenge that I couldn't turn down.'

Duff was just ten minutes away from taking off on Blackburn's flight to the United States for a pre-season training camp when the call came through that a fee had been agreed with Chelsea. He took a further week finally to make up his mind after consulting friends, family and colleagues. Graeme Souness told him in the departure lounge at Manchester Airport that Chelsea had raised their offer to meet the buy-out clause. 'I'd heard snippets all week but I was getting on the plane when the gaffer said that Blackburn had accepted an offer and, with ten minutes to go, I'd better make my mind up!'

His rapid rise to become one of the most highly prized footballers of his generation has naturally meant that he's had to cope with an intense interest in his professional and private life. In the 2002 World Cup, he was mortified when his mother Mary revealed to the Irish nation that he played with a medal depicting the Catholic saint Padre Pio stitched inside his sock. Now installed in a luxury apartment in the Chelsea Harbour complex while he searches for a house, he still calls home to Dublin every day, talks regularly to his four brothers and sisters, and delights at the prospect of his 'ma' coming to London to do 'the shopping and the shows'.

He now drives a Mercedes sports coupé with a Celtic emblem hanging from the rear-view mirror. Having swapped a country cottage in the Ribble Valley for the frenzy and noise of the King's Road is a big change for him.

Duffer, as he's known throughout Ireland, is famous for his easy-going outlook on life. Brian Kerr, the Republic of Ireland manager, claims that he suffers from Adhesive Mattress Syndrome because he can sleep anywhere, any time, and generally looks as if he's just got out of bed.

Much time has been spent in bed recently recharging batteries drained by twice-daily training sessions. 'It's an important part of a footballer's life,' he says. 'You need to get your rest to do the business on the Saturday and train. Once the season starts, I'm just fascinated about keeping my energy levels high, so I'll probably do fuck-all! Coming to London, it's just a totally different world – it's at the opposite end of the scale, but I'm sure I'll get used to it. In Blackburn, it was a happy country life but coming down here it's just pure madness. But I won't let it bother me.'

The first four major signings are in place, but further transfer acquisitions are already being lined up as Ranieri now seeks his 'champions' – stars who have already proved themselves in the heat of battle at the highest level.

TUESDAY, 22 JULY

A move for Manchester United's Seba Veron is turning into a long drawn-out saga. He announces, 'It has never been my intention to leave Manchester United.

But I do not know what the club want to do.' Veron comes on as a second-half sub as the Reds beat Celtic 4–0 in Seattle. Ranieri, at first, suggests he knows nothing about a bid for the Argentina international, informing Italian reporters, 'We've not spoken to him [Veron]. I don't know what people are on about.'

It is a smokescreen. Central to Ranieri's plans is the signing of a combative central midfielder and, while Vieira and Gerrard would be anyone's primary targets, they are unavailable. Davids is a suitable holding midfielder having played in Juventus' back-to-back Serie A title campaigns, although, with only 12 months remaining on his contract, Juve are still holding out for a large fee. Chelsea's interest in the Dutch star does not tempt him into leaving Juventus, according to the player's agent Robert Geerlings, who tells Italian sports daily *Gazzetta dello Sport* that the Premiership side had attempted to sign Davids even before Abramovich had taken control.

A warning. During Freddy Shepherd's time as chairman, Newcastle United forked out nearly £200m on transfers and still don't have a single trophy to show for it. Shepherd says, 'Roman Abramovich may be the new kid on the block in English football, but he will quickly learn that money is no guarantee of success. We've been down that route and the evidence that big transfer fees don't necessarily bring results is shown by the spaces in our trophy cabinet.

'Our ambition was exactly the same as Abramovich's. We wanted the title and we wanted it quickly. Money was no object. Two seasons in a row we were runners-up in the Premiership. But we never quite got the big-name players to gel or got the right balance in the team. Abramovich clearly has the cash to bring in a host of world-class stars and it looks as if he is determined to make an immediate impact. But he could learn a lot from what happened at Newcastle. You should never spend money for the sake of spending it.'

Bates defends the club's new policy, 'We haven't spent that much. Up to now, we've bought four players for a total of £34m, which is only £4m more than Manchester United spent on Rio Ferdinand. Last season, Claudio Ranieri didn't spend a penny and we improved from sixth to fourth place in the Premiership. Because of players released at the end of last season, we're a bit thin in certain areas.'

Premier League chief executive Richard Scudamore has his own viewpoint. 'We live in such times of heightened awareness. Chelsea can't afford to go on doing this and there will be a point fairly soon when it will all settle down. I believe, though, that the uncertainty in the wake of Chelsea's activities has been good for us. As chief executive of the Premier League, I would like to have different clubs winning it every year. It's the nature of the game that everyone tries to steal a march on the opposition. If you look at the press clippings, there was once similar concern when Everton paid £300 for a player and the same thing happened when the "mercenaries" arrived from Scotland. The important thing is that clubs act responsibly and operate within their means. It's important Chelsea's actions do not prompt another hyper-inflationary period with other clubs overstretching themselves.'

WEDNESDAY, 23 JULY

Far from looking like a manager under pressure, Ranieri contemplates life as coach of the world's richest football club with equanimity. Striding off to lunch with John Terry at his side, Ranieri beams with relish at the possibilities that have opened up to him in his search for new players. 'I am the luckiest manager in the world ... Fucking hell, I have waited 20 years for this moment to arrive.'

Fresh from introducing Duff and Bridge to their first training session, he admits he still hasn't landed the 'big champion players the club needs', like Vieri, Crespo, Veron or Emerson. He says, 'There is pressure but I do not worry about losing my job. Everyone knows they will die sooner or later, but do you think every day, "I might die?" No, you live your life. A real problem is what I had 15 years ago, when I started my second season as manager at Campania Puteolana. I had only 10 or 11 players and no one for the bench. The bookmakers have closed the book on me being the first manager to get the sack. They should open it again because, if they do, they will make money.'

When asked which managers in Italy have had the most impact on his career, he replies, 'Capello, Sacchi, Trapattoni... and Eriksson... ha, ha, ha.'

Damien Duff recalls his first conversation with Ranieri, 'I didn't really understand a lot. He is just football mad. All he wants to do is talk about football. It is what he lives for.' Duff's new life with Chelsea is shaping up nicely. His five-year deal is worth a basic £70,000 a week, with signing-on extras in the region of £1.5m. Despite all the denials from Old Trafford, interest was declared behind the scenes through Roy Keane, who rang his fellow Irishman to ask him to consider joining United. He raised Duff's hopes, but the final word was Ferguson's. He rejected the price as too high. Pat Devlin's commission is reputed to be £2m, raising questions again about inflated fees to agents. More than £8m will eventually be paid to around a dozen agents as Chelsea's final transfer bill reaches £110m for ten new stars. As many as two or even three agents can be involved in any one deal, so the man credited with masterminding the majority of the deals, Zahavi, will collect far less than the £6m he is often reported as receiving.

THURSDAY, 24 JULY

Manchester United sound out Newcastle over midfielder Kieron Dyer, who is also on the Chelsea wanted list. Newcastle slap a £25m tag on Dyer's head, and that puts any move for Dyer from Chelsea on hold.

Ranieri says, 'We need players with good motivation so that we can continue to blend the team into one that can challenge Manchester United and Arsenal seriously at the top of the Premiership. But with the squad I have now, we will be very, very close to the bigger teams. It is important that the team continues to grow, and we continue to pick up the best players. While the team we had was good, we needed something more and the four new boys will surely be a big plus.'

Roma issue a statement that Brazilian midfielder Emerson is not for sale and that they are angry at what they describe as an illegal approach. Roma sporting director Franco Baldini says, 'It's true that we have received important offers for him, not only from Chelsea. But we will give everyone the same answer – this season Emerson won't move. But the thing that bothers us is when the player is contacted personally and not through his club. We are not going to ask for FIFA help, but this thing has to be stopped.'

Baldini claims that Chelsea offered personal terms of £21.34m over six years. An incensed Baldini insists, 'The situation is simple. Chelsea offered Roma €27m for Emerson and we told them that he is untouchable. At that point, Chelsea went straight to Emerson with an offer outside the market – a contract for six years and €30m. You can understand the turbulent frame of mind the player is now in.'

Emerson's agent, Gilmar Veloz, duly flies into London to discuss personal terms even though Roma insist they still have not given Chelsea permission to talk to him. Baldini remarks, 'It seems that Chelsea are continuing to go to the player directly despite our warnings. I understand Emerson's agent is in London right now, but nothing can happen without Roma's say-so. Even if Emerson says he wants to move, that does not mean we are going to let him.'

Chelsea then step up their interest in Makelele, who has fallen out with Real Madrid over his wages, a situation exacerbated by the arrival of Beckham. Negotiations to buy Real Mallorca's Cameroon striker Samuel Eto'o cease. The stumbling block with hard-up Mallorca is that half of any transfer fee must go to the player's former club, Real Madrid, under a sell-on clause. In any case, there are players ahead of Eto'o on the list of desired strikers.

Dutch outcast Winston Bogarde hasn't even been given a squad number. He doesn't seem all that bothered though. 'Not being given a number doesn't upset me. All I can do is carry on working as hard as I possibly can in training and see what happens. I won't give up.'

Duff takes the number 11 shirt, previously worn by Bolo Zenden, who realises he is well down the pecking order after being given the number 24 shirt. Johnson takes the number 2 shirt left vacant by Ferrer, Geremi takes on

Le Saux's number 14, while Bridge is 18 and Ambrosio 31, the shirt previously worn by Mark Bosnich.

Bates is excited by the new arrivals, particularly after Johnson's performance in Italy. 'He is an extremely talented young player with a tremendous attitude. He made a big impact.' Bates tempers his enthusiasm by advising fans against getting carried away. 'The expectations of fans are always impossible. I'm a fan myself. My expectations are wild but as a chairman they are more realistic. Every chairman wants to win everything – if they didn't, they'd be in the wrong job. But Chelsea has never expected to win silverware, so it is a bonus when we do.'

Bates is right behind Ranieri. 'To be a manager you have to be a fool or a strong man and we have 20 of them in the Premiership. Ranieri has a proven track record, both at Chelsea and previously in Europe, for being a shrewd judge of players.'

Bates insists Abramovich is in it for the long haul and no one is going to rip him off. 'How has Mr Abramovich made his £5.4bn? He's a shrewd businessman. People seem to forget all of that. It would cost him £200m to walk away. If he's worth £5.4bn then we are still talking about a significant amount of money. It would cost him five per cent of his wealth. Why would he have started something if he didn't want to see it through? The balance of power could be shifting; there is certainly a more level playing field now.

'I'm very happy, very happy indeed about what has happened to Chelsea. Chelsea is a success story, it was a success story before Mr Abramovich arrived, a great success story, and now he has fast-tracked it far further and it's just great. With no financial restraints, there is no limit to what Chelsea can achieve.'

Bates is too often shown in a bad light. 'Just the other week someone wrote that I cut a lonely figure on the end row. Well, I am in my usual seat, the one I have had for 20-odd years. I continue to host the directors' suite, the boardroom and the directors' box. Mr Abramovich comes along with all of his mates. He is not interested in the politics of football; he has put his money up to enjoy his day out and, believe me, he enjoys himself. But he sits up there in the box with his friends and he has a ball. He doesn't come down to the directors' box – he is not interested. He is like a very rich punter, there for the fun of it, and I am enjoying it too.

'I am chairman until 2005 which is also our centenary, then I become life-president, stepping back another stage. We won the title in 1955 and it would be great to win it 50 years later so it coincided with our centenary. But believe me, I won't have any problems if we win the Premiership this season as well. Two in a row? Yes, that would do me just fine. It seems to me that my enemies are stirring it up for me ... I'm going nowhere. I've got a job to do and I've started it and I'll see it through to the end. I'm not on my way out. No way.'

Miraculously, the deal for Veron is still on. Deportivo La Coruna's £12m-rated

Roy Makaay is mooted as a likely prospect. Ranieri wants new players as quickly as possible because he reckons he'll have problems bedding so many new stars into his team. 'I am used to not spending much money but now that has changed. I am an ambitious coach, I have ambitious players. In Italy, the pressure was crazy. I am used to working under pressure. I want to win things.'

Chelsea's opening tour game is against Malaysia, who are managed by former Chelsea player Alan Harris. Victory in the Asia Cup would be the perfect way to kick-start the challenge for major honours. Despite reports, John Terry denies there is any apprehension among the players. 'We've made four good signings so far and there's no problem as far as the lads are concerned. We will be playing a lot of games next season and, with players coming into the squad, it means the manager can rotate things. The atmosphere has been good.'

Ranieri throws down the gauntlet to Sir Alex Ferguson and Arsene Wenger by saying it is possible to cut the 20-point gap in the Premiership between their clubs. 'We will be going to win every competition – the Premiership, the FA Cup, the Champions League. But, for now, the preliminaries for the Champions League are very important and my team is not yet ready.'

Off the field, one of Abramovich's key aides must hold the record for the shortest term of office as a Chelsea director. Eugene Shvidler resigns after only three-and-a-half weeks in the job because of his heavy workload. An insider close to Citigroup, the bank which advised Abramovich on the Chelsea deal, explains that Shvidler had underestimated the time he would need to spend in the role. He will be replaced on the board by Bruce Buck, a partner at the law firm Skadden, Arps, Slate, Meagher & Flom, who acted for Abramovich during the takeover.

The Financial Services Authority is concerned about the owners of five offshore trusts that sold shares to the Russian. The issue is whether certain shareholders, hiding behind nominee accounts, were acting in concert or were connected in some other relevant way. If they were, then their identities should have been revealed under company law. The FSA enquiries do not affect Abramovich's takeover or the purchase of a 23.5 per cent stake owned by the estate of Matthew Harding and a 9.9 per cent stake from BSkyB. The simple fact is Abramovich has over 90 per cent of shares and can compulsorily request the rest. For his part, Bates issues a forthright statement condemning the FSA.

FRIDAY, 25 JULY

MALAYSIA 1, CHELSEA 4

Well, it is only Malaysia's fledgling national side that is on the end of a demolition but the architects of the win are Russian-bought. Ranieri watches three of his new boys – Duff, goal-scorer Johnson and Bridge – play an important role in a highly impressive and efficient victory. Also making his début is goalkeeper Ambrosio, in for Cudicini who, although suffering from a virus, is fit enough to start on the bench. Ranieri, often criticised for tinkering, has to make an enforced change after 25 minutes when German centre-back Robert Huth suffers a cut over his eye following a collision with Omar. Huth goes off to have stitches in the gash and is replaced by Johnson.

Johnson goes to his favoured position of right-back, with Melchiot switching to the centre of defence. Lampard opens Chelsea's account before Malaysia pull one back thanks to a horrendous blunder by Ambrosio, who lets a tame header slip through his hands. But Hasselbaink, Gudjohnsen and Johnson finish the locals off in an excellent last 20-minute spell. Duff makes his debut in the second half and runs the Malaysians ragged with several jinking runs, eventually setting up Gudjohnsen for a headed goal with a superb cross. Johnson's goal on only his second appearance also comes from a header, while Bridge lasts the full 90 minutes and looks solid.

'Glen, Damien and Wayne did very well for me... that is all of the new ones, isn't it?' Ranieri says through his interpreter, clearly losing track of how many he has actually bought and how many are on the way! The only new boy absent is Geremi, who has yet to resume training after an extended summer break. Terry is asked how it feels to be a fixture in the line-up, only to hear of so many illustrious new additions heading his way. 'Are we worried or excited? I can honestly say the players are fine about it,' says Terry. 'We are happy and the team spirit is still good. No one knows how far it will go. What is certain is that we're assembling a great squad.'

Among the crowd is Sir Bobby Robson, whose Newcastle team await the winners in the final. Ranieri observes, 'Newcastle will be a challenge for us on Sunday. At the moment, they are slightly better than us because we don't yet have Gallas or Desailly and Petit is injured. But this win makes for a good start to the season for us and is very encouraging.'

> **Team**
> Ambrosio, Melchiot, Huth (Johnson), Terry, Bridge, Gronkjaer (Kneissl), Keenan, Lampard (Nicolas), Zenden (Duff), C Cole (Hasselbaink), Forssell (Gudjohnsen)

Afterwards Ranieri is in the mood to crack jokes. 'Maybe I'll just have to buy another 22 players,' he quips in response to a question about whether his stars fancy playing Maccabi Tel Aviv in the Champions League after six players refused to travel to Israel two seasons ago. Ranieri has one eye on the

Champions League draw, which decides whether Chelsea will face either Maccabi Tel Aviv or MSK Zilina of Slovakia in a qualifying round. 'It is not important who we play but it is important that we win and get into the Champions League group stages.'

SATURDAY, 26 JULY

Ranieri is in daily contact with Abramovich and Trevor Birch as they search for new players.

Ranieri points out that it is no use assembling a galaxy of stars if they do not gel on the pitch. 'Only the pitch speaks,' he says, enigmatically. Players train in the hotel grounds at 6.00pm and are watched by 50 members of the Malaysia Chelsea Supporters Club.

SUNDAY, 27 JULY

The Asia Cup Final
CHELSEA 0, NEWCASTLE 0 (Chelsea win 5–4 on penalties)

The first Chelsea silverware since the Charity Shield in 2000, and Ranieri is caught on camera answering his mobile phone as the players gather to collect their first trophy under the Russian revolution. It's also their manager's first piece of silverware since he joined the club. Surely it wasn't Roman calling him? 'No,' smiles Ranieri, 'it was Trevor Birch congratulating us.'

Ranieri sees three of his new recruits dispose of Newcastle thanks to a penalty shoot-out. He says, 'I have received congratulations from the chairman and the chief executive, so maybe Abramovich will call later. This is just the fuel we need for the new season. We created chances, so we deserved to win, even if the scores ended level.'

Sir Bobby Robson describes the first half as like an old English cup tie, but in 90-degree heat Chelsea's heroes are centre-backs Huth and captain Terry, who scores the clinching penalty. Newcastle fall behind in the shoot-out, which the local crowd of 47,500 love, with Alan Shearer hitting the bar and Laurent Robert also missing the second kick. Shay Given hauls the Magpies back with two great saves from Duff and Hasselbaink. Robson, a victim of a famous penalty shoot-out when he served as the England boss, loses his cool with Jermaine Jenas after an atrocious spot-kick. With Newcastle trailing 5–4 in the shoot-out, the baby-faced midfielder strolls casually forward to deliver the most shocking chip. Robson makes no attempt to hide his disgust, waving his arms in anger and launching into a four-letter tirade from the sideline. Jenas simply covers his face in embarrassment, while Jonathan Woodgate tries to hide a snigger as his team-mate slinks off to face the wrath of his boss.

Gronkjaer is man of the match after winning an enthralling duel down his right wing with Olivier Bernard. 'Robert Huth was fantastic,' says Ranieri. 'I am very pleased with our performance. This sets a good pattern for us to follow. We have come through two very hard games in three days and played some fantastic football against a very strong Newcastle.'

> ## Team
>
> Cudicini, Johnson, Terry, Huth, Bridge, Gronkjaer (Forssell), Lampard, Nicolas (Keenan), Zenden (Duff), Hasselbaink, Gudjohnsen.

After helping Manchester United to a 3–1 win over Club America in the second game of their US tour, Seba Veron states his position. 'By no means do I plan to leave. I feel comfortable and happy with United. But if the club is planning to transfer me, that's another matter.'

Sir Alex indicates publicly Veron will stay and the Argentinian makes a special effort to impress Ferguson during United's tour. According to eyewitnesses, Sir Alex smiles and shakes his head in disbelief during one training session when Veron scores what the manager admits is one of the most amazing goals he has seen. Chesting the ball down 20 yards out, he crosses one leg behind the other and stabs the ball with incredible power into the top right-hand corner. His team-mates spontaneously applaud.

Privately, Ferguson has been disappointed with the return he has had from the Argentinian: just 11 goals in 82 appearances. Publicly, though, the manager often defends his big-money acquisition. Some United fans called for Veron, who has cost a total of £76.2m in five moves, to be sold earlier in the season. Yet Ferguson publicly insists at the start of their tour, 'You can't dismiss the class of the boy, the work rate, the desire to play. They are all great. Nothing has changed as far as I am concerned. There was an opportunity for Seba to go to another club but that has not happened. He will be an important squad player.'

Sir Alex insists Veron will stay as his side face Juventus at the Giants Stadium. Ferguson claims to know nothing of speculation suggesting a fee has been agreed with Chelsea. Instead, Ferguson suggests the player's agent is acting without authority and repeats his assertion that Veron will still be at the club when United begin the defence of their Premiership title.

'Seba is a terrific player and I want him to stay,' says Ferguson. 'I don't know anything about the speculation. Agents talk to a lot of people, they have a lot of power and sometimes they can think different things to the player. But Seba is a mature man. He is very experienced and he knows what he wants. If there was a situation arising, I'm sure he would talk to me. He hasn't done so and I'm quite happy about that. My impression was that he had settled down, everything had gone quiet and there was no problem. Seba is a marvellous player and he is contracted to us. It is going to be difficult for a deal to be done tomorrow. He will be playing for us.'

Not long after Ferguson has finished reiterating that the deal is over, Veron's agent, Fernando Hidalgo, is quoted as saying, 'The meeting with Chelsea on Wednesday is very important. Everything is OK at the moment but we will need to confirm what he discussed on Tuesday. If Seba is very happy with what Chelsea offer, then we will close the contract with Manchester United.'

MONDAY, 28 JULY

As the players enjoy a day off in Kuala Lumpur prior to a 10.00pm departure, Ranieri knows the arrival of new stars, no matter how many and how much they cost, will not be enough on its own to dethrone Manchester United, let alone Real Madrid. He says, 'When I first became head coach three years ago, my target was to win the Premier League, but first we had to reconstruct. Reconstruction has now gone well and we have some great players at Chelsea. Last season we didn't lose many games, but we had far too many draws. We must improve again this year and all the time look to our young players for the future. John Terry has shown the way but these players have achieved nothing yet for themselves and nothing for Chelsea, so together we must fight, fight, fight for that to happen.'

TUESDAY, 29 JULY

The team arrives in London at 5.30am; they have until Thursday afternoon off. Inevitable signs of discontent emerge virtually from the moment the new arrivals walk through the door. Gronkjaer is worried whether Geremi might play on the right rather than in the holding midfield role. Gronkjaer admits, 'It is unsettling because we read the newspapers as well. I know I have to perform consistently and I have been working hard. It is having an effect on the players. We are all just trying to concentrate on playing football. I am keeping my head down. It is going to be harder to get into the team but we cannot complain because it will be an advantage to Chelsea in the long run.'

Ranieri makes it clear he wants a 22- maybe 23-man squad, with at least two players for each position. Some player egos will be dented, but that's what happens at the really big clubs.

WEDNESDAY, 30 JULY

While he is enjoying the thrill of buying players, Abramovich is surprised at certain things that go with living in England. He says, 'If I feel we need to buy any particular player to get the results we want, I'll just spend more money. I didn't realise they'd write so much about me in the British newspapers. It's incredible. But I did know that, in England, football is a kind of religion so there was always going to be a lot of interest. Some people in Russia, who call themselves patriots, said I should have put money into Russian sport, not into a foreign team. The problem is that we Russians don't live in a free country. We're not used to people being allowed to spend their own money how they want to.'

But plans are still being made for that stadium in Moscow, for three local teams, funded by Abramovich. He would like to bring Chelsea over for a friendly.

He repeats that he is not demanding that Chelsea excel in his first season. 'I would love to think they will, but we have made many acquisitions, and so it is hard to say if it will be the most successful season in the history of the team. Even the best players don't immediately make a team. The internal structure of the team has been destroyed and time is needed for the players to play together and only then can you hope for a result.'

THURSDAY, 31 JULY

Duff is already impressed by the strength of the squad and expects further arrivals as he says, 'We looked strong in Asia and God knows who we will be bringing in over the next two weeks.'

The impending transfer of Veron reignites suspicions that the Argentinian has come highly recommended by Eriksson, who, of course, built his team around the player at Lazio. 'We have good midfield players like Emmanuel Petit and Frank Lampard, but they are only two,' Ranieri says. 'A big team needs three or four. We are working on it.'

In pursuit of Veron, Pini Zahavi makes the initial running with Sir Alex Ferguson, a close friend, before Trevor Birch keeps talks going with Peter Kenyon. Sir Alex watches Veron lead a 4–1 rout of Juventus in the States. Veron collects the man of the match honours in front of 79,005 delirious fans, capping a superb United performance with two outstanding assists which lead to goals for Paul Scholes and Ruud van Nistelrooy. Ferguson maintains his stance that the midfielder is going nowhere. 'I don't know what the hell is going on in England. People keep seeing him on this tour and people still keep saying he is going. Unless he is going to be whisked from right under my nose, they are wrong.'

Van Nistelrooy reveals how the dressing room has rallied round Veron in a bid to keep him out of Chelsea's clutches. He says, 'I am really glad for him because now he is staying. If you asked every player in the dressing room, none of us would be happy if he were to leave. We all want him to stay and I think he will. He sees this as a second chance.'

Van Nistelrooy may have underestimated the spending power at Stamford Bridge. Chelsea initially offer £13m, then raise it to £15m... United are holding out for £17.5m. But finally United agree in principle that Veron can leave. Kenyon admits that if United do sell they'll take a hefty hit on the money they paid out to Lazio two years ago. 'We write down players values over the length of their contract anyway, so it's not as though he is in the books at what we paid for him. There have been no other firm bids for Seba, although there was initially interest from Italy.'

Suddenly Fergie backtracks. 'We had an offer from Chelsea and have put it to the lad because the feeling we got was they had been talking to him. I put it to him to see if he wanted to go and he never gave me an answer.'

But, with another major player on the way to bolster his squad, Ranieri still advises caution. 'Alex Ferguson had seven years to win his first title and for me now it is important to build a team and a group. I want to create a spirit because you can have all the best players in the world but if you do not have a group you cannot win. I want to see if we can close the gap between us and Manchester United, Arsenal and Liverpool.'

August

PREDICTIONS FOR THE TITLE – AND COULD ROMAN BE

ABOUT TO SIGN BECKS?

Real Madrid's Ronaldo announces he is aware of Chelsea interest. 'An offer was made to me but it was not serious, because my friend knows only too well that there was no way I would leave Real Madrid at this moment. I'm a close friend of Mr Abramovich's business partner, so I've been hearing all about the big changes at Chelsea. It all sounds very interesting and I'm sure with Mr Abramovich's money the club will achieve a lot of success. The Premiership is certainly a possibility in the future. I'd be lying if I said I wouldn't be tempted to go on an English adventure at some point in my life.'

Abramovich is on the point of amassing even more money with the proposed merger of two of Russia's biggest oil groups, Yukos and Sibneft. Through his Swiss-based company Runicon, Sibneft is set to join forces with Yukos, multiplying Abramovich's wealth. In addition, he has just received £300m in oil dividends. He reaffirms his pledge to spend as much as it takes to make Chelsea successful; one day he might even bid for David Beckham. 'I have never met him, but if he ever considers the possibility of returning to England, if he doesn't make it in Spain... I like him.'

FRIDAY, 1 AUGUST

Ranieri unveils his first five signings of the new era – Duff, Geremi, Johnson, Bridge and Ambrosio – and vows to build a championship-winning side. He knows money alone will not guarantee success. 'The owner said you can buy the players but not the wins. But now we are building a good team – a team like Real Madrid, Milan, Manchester United.'

But who chose the new signings? Fed up with suggestions that the Abramovich dictated the biggest spending spree in the club's history and insulted by insinuations that it was Sven-Goran Eriksson who identified transfer targets, the Italian snaps momentarily, but tellingly, 'Maybe Eriksson.' Later, he dismisses the remark as a joke for the media.

Abramovich acquires one of the 15 super-executive boxes in the new Millennium West Stand. Bates originally put the best boxes up for sale for £1m a season on a minimum ten-year lease, but had difficulties in shifting them, even though Chelsea cater for a super-rich type of fan who might have been able to afford the £1m-a-season facility.

Franco Sensi, the Roma president, announces that he has rejected a Chelsea bid of £24.6m for Brazilian midfielder Emerson. 'Roman Abramovich offered me €40m and I said, "No." I told the player that I would never have sold him and I have assured him that we will extend his contract – he will get what he deserves.' Chelsea also try but fail to get midfielder Edgar Davids, Juventus's Dutch international.

SATURDAY, 2 AUGUST

CRYSTAL PALACE 1, CHELSEA 2

Chelsea's first pre-season friendly on English soil. So many people want to see it, the start is held up for 15 minutes. It is, however, worth waiting to see Geremi's stunning free-kick – à la Zola. His delightful 44th-minute effort proves there is life after the little Italian in the specialist free-kick department.

Mikael Forssell impresses on his return to Selhurst Park, after two loan spells at Crystal Palace, and Chelsea surge into a fourth-minute lead after he buries a low volley. A 37th-minute error by Bridge, when he passes straight to Andy Johnson, almost lets in Palace, but Cudicini's reflexes save them. The goalkeeper has no chance two minutes later when the defence is undone down the left from a quick Michael Hughes free-kick, and unmarked Dougie Freedman coolly lobs home. Chelsea regain the lead a minute before the break when Geremi, fouled by Hughes, takes instant revenge by curling home the 30-yard free-kick.

Forssell has started only six Premiership games in five years at the club, but Ranieri insists he will get more opportunities this season. Ranieri says, 'Mikael scored a fantastic goal and he will definitely get his chance to play for Chelsea this year. I wanted him to stay because I need a couple of players for every position. In front, I have good players with Jimmy, Eidur, Carlton, as well as Mikael, and I am happy with them.'

Then follows the inevitable question from journalists: what about Juan Sebastian Veron? Is he really on his way to Stamford Bridge? Ranieri laughs. 'I don't know anything – you like to stir.' But when asked again, Ranieri does an exaggerated Pinocchio-style motion with his hand on his nose, suggesting he knows a lot more than he's letting on.

Team

Ambrosio, Melchiot, Terry, Desailly (Huth), Bridge (Johnson), Gronkjaer (C Cole), Geremi, Lampard (Petit), Duff (Oliveira), Forssell (Gudjohnsen), Hasselbaink (Keenan).

SUNDAY, 3 AUGUST

Questions are asked when Juan Sebastian Veron is left on the bench for Manchester United's 3–1 win over Barcelona in Philadelphia. Sir Alex Ferguson says, 'You can't read anything into it.' But asked outright whether Veron will be part of the Red Devils' squad this season, he replies, 'I can't answer that.'

Chief executive Peter Kenyon confirms that United have received a bid but it is well below their valuation. Fergie's observation that, with the signings of Djemba-Djemba and Kleberson, he is a little 'overloaded' in central midfield reflects a belief that Veron's time as a United player could be over.

Agent Marc Roger lets it be known that Chelsea have offered Real £7m for midfielder Claude Makelele, who is keen to move on. 'Unless Madrid improve his salary, next Monday will be his last day at the club. David Beckham has just joined Real and he is being paid five times more [than Makelele]. An unhappy player is not a good player.' Makelele refuses to train with Real and is fined £100,000 and left out of a friendly at Valencia. 'Claude knows he cannot earn the same as the top stars, but he feels badly treated,' continues Roger. 'He would be a star for Chelsea but he will never be one at Madrid.'

Makelele, who has won 24 caps, is desperate to seal a move. The former Nantes player still has three years left on his contract at the Bernabeu after moving to Madrid from Celta Vigo in 2000. Yet Trevor Birch hints that the move has broken down. Birch says, 'I don't think there will be any movement with Makelele. We want to stay out of it.'

Marcel Desailly, the 34-year-old defender, had been expected to retire when his contract ran out at the end of the season. But he signs a new agreement until 2005. 'The new people running the club have shown that they are building for the long term. This means that I will be able to finish my career in Europe at a big club. I am captain and I think the new chairman wants me involved thoroughly.

'I believe we have recruited very cleverly. All the new signings are aged under 30. We look very well equipped to achieve a great season. It's really important that we progress in the Champions League and get to test ourselves against the big teams.'

A new training ground is being commissioned. Chelsea currently use Imperial College's sports ground at Harlington, near Heathrow Airport, and new signings have been shocked to see the facilities, compared to state-of-the-art bases such as Manchester United's at Carrington or Arsenal's at London Colney.

MONDAY, 4 AUGUST

Sir Alex Ferguson finally announces he is letting Seba Veron go to make way for younger legs in midfield. Veron's agent confirms that his client is ready to sign for Chelsea and play in central midfield. His father, Juan Ramon Veron, says, 'Ferguson didn't understand that Sebastian didn't want to play out wide on the wing. It's not his position. He moves a lot better in the middle, like he did in Italy. That's the position he'll play in at Chelsea and I know they'll get the best out of him.'

Sir Alex maintains that Chelsea must win the title or they will have wasted Abramovich's millions. He also tips a five-horse race for one of the most open championships in years. But he believes that, in the end, it will once again come down to a straight fight between a couple of clubs. 'Every year, we say there'll be four or five teams challenging for the title. But every season it comes down to two clubs – ourselves and Arsenal.'

Sven-Goran Eriksson is quizzed by the media about the infamous 'tea party' with Roman Abramovich. Clearly embarrassed, he asks the public to believe that he is just good friends with the Russian. Pressed on their furtive meeting, he replies, 'It was not the first time I've seen Abramovich ... I've seen him many times. It didn't embarrass me. Of course, we talked football, but if I meet Arsene or Ferguson, we talk about players. That is normal. What do you expect me to talk to Abramovich about? The weather? Or cards? I have been to David Dein's house many times, but I don't think I will be manager of Arsenal. It shouldn't be difficult to have friends in football without people assuming things.'

Has Abramovich asked him to be Chelsea manager in the future? 'No, no. You are invited to take a cup of tea in the house of a friend, and you are not going there to discuss making a contract with the club.' Has he spoken to Ranieri about the speculation? 'I talked to Ranieri.' Has he apologised to the Italian? 'I didn't say anything because there's nothing to say.'

Later a close associate of the Italian tells me, 'I spoke with Claudio and he told me that, yes, Eriksson had called, but it was not to reassure him about anything. He rang him before the opening game of the season to tell him he would be calling up John Terry, Joe Cole and Wayne Bridge, and to say that he would be at the game at Liverpool.' Asked later by a Sky TV reporter if he thinks that meeting was a mistake, Eriksson says, 'No', but then modifies his response to 'Maybe'.

The FA's new chief executive, Mark Palios, is only one week into his new post when the Eriksson–Abramovich summit first hits the headlines. At his initial press conference inside Soho Square, Palios suggests that he has contingency plans should Eriksson walk out. Palios says, 'Sven and I spoke at the time the photographs were published. He has agreed the timing was unfortunate. Of course, we will have a contingency in place with regard to Sven's eventual departure, but equally I would do that for all major business risks – from what happens if Soho Square burns down to the key employee walking out.'

Palios says he will open negotiations with Eriksson on a new contract – 'You always negotiate with key employees in case they get headhunted' – and stresses that, in his opinion, Eriksson is the best England coach of modern times.

Investing for the future, Chelsea join forces with Auckland club Football Kingz in a deal providing access to some of the best rising talent in Oceania. The Kingz, who play in Australia's National Soccer League, will now be used as a breeding ground for Chelsea's youngsters.

Chelsea opt not to go for Sporting Lisbon's Cristiano Ronaldo although he is one of agent Pini Zahavi's top picks. Zahavi says, 'He is world-class, can play on the right or left and, although he was one I really liked, he is only 18 and he was thought to be too young for the position.' Manchester United have been tracking the Portuguese Under-20 starlet for some time, but push the deal through at a cost of £12m when they become fearful of a bid from Barça.

TUESDAY, 5 AUGUST

WATFORD 1, CHELSEA 4

The Blues rip Watford apart as, behind the scenes, the spending continues unabated. Again the game is delayed by 15 minutes. Under Ken Bates, Chelsea originally agreed to travel to the cash-strapped club for a friendly on condition that they received 50 per cent of the gate money, so they are pleased with the attendance of 18,500 paying around £20 each... not that the new regime is actually in need of the money!

Johnson, Geremi, Bridge, and Duff all feature as Chelsea produce a very confident performance in their final pre-season friendly. Forssell, Hasselbaink, Duff and Neal Ardley (own goal) net for the Blues, with Heidar Helguson replying. Ranieri says, 'We were fresh tonight and the first half was fantastic. We passed and moved very fast and I like that kind of football. I saw Damien Duff grow and it's important that he and Jesper Gronkjaer played very well.'

Watford boss Ray Lewington agrees. 'People talk about the gap between Division One and the Premiership, but what about the gap between Division One and the top of the Premiership. It scared me after 20 minutes tonight. At that point, I thought the game was a slight mistake.'

Ranieri then adds that certain transfers may be imminent. 'Joe Cole is very, very near, but I don't know anything about Veron.'

> **Team**
>
> Ambrosio, Melchiot, Bridge, Terry (Keenan), Desailly (Huth), Gronkjaer (C Cole), Geremi, Lampard (Petit), Duff (Oliveira), Forssell, Hasselbaink (Keenan).

WEDNESDAY, 6 AUGUST

Joe Cole becomes the latest recruit from Chelsea's relegated east London rivals, West Ham. The Hammers decide to cash in on one of their most valuable assets rather than lose him for next to nothing when his contract expires at the end of the season.

Cole needs little persuasion that he is better off in the Premiership. Since giving Cole his international debut two years ago, Sven-Goran Eriksson has been faint in his praise of the player, even though he did take him to the World Cup finals in Japan and Korea. Now Cole has the chance to prove that he is more than just a bag of tricks and that he can transform matches on the big stage.

Cole's versatility will be needed as he tries to find a regular place at Chelsea where even established internationals such as Petit, Gronkjaer and Zenden must be wondering if they will even make it on to the substitutes' bench, while Mario Stanic must already be checking the dates for the Carling Cup, his only chance of getting a game. Cole insists, 'It was a difficult decision, but I feel now is the time to make a break from West Ham. It's going to be a challenge.'

Ironically, Cole used to go to Chelsea games as a youngster. 'I used to come to Chelsea and watch from the Shed. I used to love watching Dennis Wise and, before that, Kerry Dixon. Coming here and having the opportunity to play in the Champions League can only make me better, for Chelsea and for England.'

Ranieri has been tracking the 21-year-old for the past two seasons and Cole, who will wear the number 10 shirt, believes he knows why. 'I think I can bring a lot of quality to Chelsea. I was falling out of England contention last year, even though I felt it was one of my better seasons. It's down to me now. I've got the stage where I can play and show Sven-Goran Eriksson what I can do.'

Meanwhile, the FA levels misconduct charges against Cole and former team-mate Rufus Brevett after a brawl at Bolton in West Ham's crucial 1–0 defeat back in April 2003. The players are accused of damaging the tunnel canopy after a skirmish following the final whistle. Both were quizzed by police. No criminal charges followed after the matter was referred to the FA.

Cole is also accused of taking part in a mass confrontation that saw him square up to and apparently push Bolton defender Bernard Mendy, and he is alleged to have verbally abused the fourth official at the game. Each guilty verdict for misconduct normally brings a three-match ban, which could see Cole ruled out for up to nine games.

As part of the confidential internal discussions over the purchase of Cole, it had been suggested that he could be loaned out to Torpedo Moscow as a favour from Abramovich to his close friend and one-time banker Alexander Mamut. But Mamut's purchase of Torpedo has fallen through and the idea is quickly dropped which comes as a relief to Chelsea's latest acquisition.

Ken Bates and agent Pini Zahavi finally meet for the first time. Zahavi is at the Bridge helping to finalise the arrival of Juan Sebastian Veron and perhaps sort out the question of outstanding commission payments relating to the purchase of the club by Abramovich. The meeting takes place in Trevor Birch's office in the presence of Richard Creitzman. Bates walks into the office and over to Zahavi, shaking his hand. Zahavi remains seated. It is all a bit frosty. Bates tells me, 'We were introduced for the first time and I simply said, "Nice to meet you at long last."' Bates maintains he has not met Zahavi previously, he has not commissioned him in any way and that, if Trevor Birch has given him the impression that he could speak for all the shareholders, including himself, over possible payments, the chief executive was mistaken.

Bates has no intention of listening to Zahavi's case for commission. Zahavi has enlisted the aid of fellow agent Jonathan Barnett and entrepreneur Philip Green to contact Bates on his behalf. Bates offers the opportunity for a 'chat' but Zahavi is not inclined to talk, he just wants to be paid. Bates recommends Zahavi be paid commissions from certain transfers. Zahavi counters that Bates is offering something he has already had!

Barnett is similarly upset over the non-payment of any commission. 'How did Roman Abramovich come to buy Chelsea? Did he just turn up in a taxi one day? Of course not. Pini and I worked on the deal from the start and I am far from happy about the fact that no commission has been paid. Pini and Trevor no doubt had some arrangement while I had one with Pini. I am not prepared to discuss how much commission I had agreed with Pini but you could put it in seven figures.

'I have spoken to Ken Bates about this. I was shocked when he claimed he knew nothing about it. Ken insisted he knew nothing about it. Somebody surely afforded the introduction? It's all a mystery to me why no commission is being paid. Pini has behaved unbelievably well.'

Barnett still ends up moving two of his main clients to the Bridge – Glen Johnson and Wayne Bridge – but as he says, 'Yes, I will get my commission on two transfers, but from my clients, not from anyone else.'

Bates tells me, 'I got a call from Philip Green who said he wanted to act as the honest broker, but I told him there was nothing to broker, and that was it.' Indeed, it is true that Bates had not met Zahavi, who had dealt with Birch, but the issue remains a running sore.

THURSDAY, 7 AUGUST

It's definite. Juan Sebastian Veron is on his way. Alluding to initial doubts, his agent Fernando Hidalgo says, 'When decisions are made, everyone has to follow the consequences. Seba is proud to join Chelsea – but it was not his intention to leave the club [Manchester United]. The player will arrive in London at midday. He's going to take his medical.'

Manchester United make the announcement via the Stock Exchange, stating that £2.5m of the £15m fee is 'conditional on the performance of the Chelsea team over the next four seasons'.

One of the secret reasons for the hold-up was Ferguson's attempt to sign Glen Johnson, yet to make a competitive appearance for his new club, in part exchange. But in the end Sir Alex relents and sells Veron in a straight cash deal. Veron feels he has been forced out and vows to prove he is no Premiership misfit, believing the different culture under Ranieri will give him a second lease of life in English football. 'Ferguson trusted me when I first arrived. But later on, it seemed we didn't understand each other as well. There were times when I felt he preferred some of my team-mates. I think I'll understand Claudio Ranieri better because of the language. I can do a job in English football – and in London that will be reaffirmed.'

Celebrating the arrival of Veron, Ranieri enthuses, 'I think Veron is the best midfielder in the world and I'm very happy to have him at the club. When Veron comes to Chelsea, pure gold comes to Chelsea.'

Asked whether Veron and Joe Cole can play in the same side, Ranieri says, 'If you can speak football fluently, you can talk in every position and both Juan and Joe are fantastic with and without the ball. But Veron can play wherever he wants to play. He is the chief.'

Veron admits he had confronted Sir Alex about his future. 'Two months ago, a couple of clubs expressed an interest and he said I wasn't for sale. When I spoke recently with Ferguson, he said nothing, he just told me I was sold and that was it.

'The story was running and running and nobody in Manchester was denying it, so I asked Ferguson, "Do you want me in the squad?" He gave me a rather convoluted explanation about the tactics of his midfield. So eventually I just confronted him and said, "I'm not asking you if I will start every game, I am asking: do you want me in your squad?" Then he came out with the line about Chelsea's offer being very good, financially interesting, tempting. I realised it was all about money.'

Fergie doesn't take too kindly to any implication that he may have been less than straightforward in his dealings. 'Seba knew all along what was happening, so to say I was two-faced about it is a disgrace. I spoke to him a few days after we started pre-season training and explained that we had accepted a bid from Chelsea and I explained it was because of the midfield players we had. We shook hands and everything was fine. But the day before we left on tour, Chelsea changed their mind, said they couldn't pay £15m and wouldn't follow through with the offer. By then, Veron had taken all of his stuff from our Carrington training ground and his agent was talking to Chelsea. We had to phone him to tell him he was still a United player.'

It is all a far cry from the day when Fergie stormed out of a press conference on being asked if he thought Veron was struggling. 'People are always going on about fucking Veron. You tell me, what's wrong with Veron? He's a fucking great player. You are fucking idiots.'

Cole and Veron's arrivals take Abramovich's total outlay on players to £58.6m. Arsene Wenger jokes, 'Chelsea must buy a new team coach as well, then, to get everybody on.'

Wenger insists he is not envious. His captain Patrick Vieira has just ended months of speculation by signing a contract keeping him at Highbury until the summer of 2007. 'Either you try to make the best of what you have in your life or you always envy other people and are never happy. Ideally, I wish the club had more money. But, player-wise, I'm happy with what I have. Chelsea buy one player per day and we buy no player per month, so I can understand that we look a little bit poor or out of shape. Chelsea have won the lottery and we cannot compete financially, so we try to compete in a different way. What's important is what happens on the pitch and you will say that on the pitch we are good. To write us off just because we have not spent a hundred million pounds is too easy.'

Meanwhile Gianfranco Zola says he believes John Terry can help Chelsea win the league and hails Joe Cole as the player he would have signed as his own replacement, 'It's strange, but the most important player at the club could turn out to be the one player who cost no money at all. I watched John Terry for many years and I always thought he was going to be a special player, but he has surprised me because he has developed so quickly. Chelsea can be built around John, who is a strong character. He'll become a world-class player. He is the heartbeat of the side and will be there for many years. Arsenal had a leader in Tony Adams and I hope John does the same for Chelsea.

'Joe Cole is very similar to me. He'd have been the player I would have bought if I were Chelsea manager. He's a young boy with great talent. Going to Chelsea will help him make the final step. He has amazing skills and is beautiful to watch – like me.'

The deadline for registering new players for the Champions League qualifiers comes and goes, and Ranieri just misses out on a striker. Ranieri scotches speculation that Vieri is about to join, 'I think Christian will stay at Inter.' Samuel Eto'o, once valued at around £12m, is available for £6.9m because of financial problems at Real Mallorca. Tentative talks are held after Mallorca's friendly at Bolton, but interest fizzles out. Vieri would cost £25m, but Inter's sports director Marco Branca says, 'Vieri is not on the market. We have not received any official offers for Vieri. He will definitely stay at Inter Milan.' Asked if he feels he still needs to sign a top-class striker even if it is not Vieri, Ranieri rather tetchily replies, 'What I need I speak with Mr Abramovich about – not you.'

FRIDAY, 8 AUGUST

FA chief executive Mark Palios is asked if he has any concerns about the Abramovich takeover. He says, 'If you were to say that the Premiership would become the playground of ten Russian or other ethnic billionaires, then I might have a concern as it might distort the level playing field. But for one or two guys coming in and doing this, then I think it just adds to the competition and I'm pretty pleased to see it happening. My personal view is that it has provided a fillip to a pretty moribund transfer market.'

A straw poll of managers around the Premiership draws differing responses to the same question. Spurs coach Glenn Hoddle voices his worries. 'As far as Chelsea are concerned, the market is inflationary. I'm not sure the game can afford it.' Fulham's Chris Coleman is grateful that it might stop people expecting too much of him in his first full season in charge. 'Chelsea may take the pressure off me a bit. They have blown the transfer market wide open. They look like they are going to spend a lot of money and there will be a lot of pressure on them to succeed.' Jim Smith, the veteran managerial hand now

Harry Redknapp's assistant at promoted Portsmouth, is more forthright. 'It could be a disaster for football if the financial wheel turns again. It's scary. The timing, just when football was starting to follow more sensible housekeeping, is unfortunate.'

SATURDAY, 9 AUGUST

Kenny Dalglish steered Blackburn Rovers to the Premiership title in 1995 when the late Jack Walker bankrolled their bid, pouring £60m into his beloved club to achieve championship glory. Dalglish does not accept there are too many similarities between then and now, however. 'Chelsea are in a much stronger starting position than we were at Blackburn. They have a Champions League place and finished fourth last season. What is happening now can only make the next title race even more exciting. Apart from United, Arsenal and Chelsea, Liverpool and Newcastle will also look to make a push.'

Dalglish, the only boss apart from Ferguson and Wenger to have won the Premiership title, adds, 'Money alone won't win you the title – it's the players who will do that. I am sure Ranieri is comfortable with the situation. From his point of view, that is a great position to be in. He has already demonstrated he is one of the best-equipped coaches in the game. He is shrewd and knowledgeable and, when you look at who they have signed so far, you have to say they are all good investments.

'Now it's a question of everyone gelling and, until we see the outcome of that, you cannot predict just how quickly Chelsea will rise to the top. They were a good side last season and will certainly be an even better one this time. You have to take your hat off to Chelsea because they are creating so much excitement, not only for their own fans but increasing the competition and standards for the rest of the country.'

SUNDAY, 10 AUGUST

Even before the Abramovich takeover, Gianfranco Zola, Enrique de Lucas, Jody Morris, Albert Ferrer and Ed de Goey were already on their way out of Stamford Bridge, but talented young striker Leon Knight left voluntarily because he wanted regular first-team football. Other youngsters need regular games too, so Carlton Cole has gone on loan to Charlton and Mikael Forssell will later opt for Birmingham. Seasoned Dutch international Bolo Zenden disappears on loan to Middlesbrough, while Russian international Alexei Smertin will be loaned instantly to Portsmouth after being bought from Bordeaux.

Old hands Jimmy Floyd Hasselbaink and Manu Petit stay, despite rumours that they are on their way out. The loan of Cole, an England Under-21 striker who scored three in 13 Premiership appearances last season, raises the most eyebrows. Only months earlier Carlton Cole was being talked about as the future of the club. Before the Russian revolution, Ranieri said of Cole, 'He has a very long contract and a very big future at Chelsea. He's strong, quick, has two good feet and is a good header of the ball. In fact, I've never coached a young player like Carlton. He has everything he needs to explode.'

Now Ranieri explains, 'Carlton is a player I like, but how many games would he play this season if he was here? I would rather give Carlton the chance of playing every Saturday for Charlton, so that when he comes back here next summer he has improved.'

Knight, just 20, has been sold for £100,000 to Brighton. 'I want to get out of Chelsea because they've been holding me back,' he says. 'I have been at Chelsea since I was 13 and have started one game. It's a relief to know I will be in a place where they want me.'

Former striker Peter Osgood backs the big-buy policy to deliver major success, but reckons it won't happen this season. Osgood adds that he will be intrigued to see how the club keeps such a packed stable of egos happy, particularly in midfield.

MONDAY, 11 AUGUST

Romanian striker Adrian Mutu arrives on a five-year contract, to become the seventh signing of the season. Parma originally denied that he would leave but the deal is confirmed by coach Cesare Prandelli after the pre-season friendly against Southampton at St Mary's. He says, 'When the offer came in, we simply could not refuse it. Mutu was voted the best player in Italy last season. He scored a lot of goals, and has all the qualities to be a big success in the Premiership. He played wide left as a striker for us and showed great potential. He is not scared of anything and has a great personality. He is also very good at taking free-kicks.'

The £15.8m fee doubles Parma's original outlay on him after just one spectacular season in Serie A. Meanwhile, the police in Bucharest are investigating Mutu for allegedly assaulting his wife, Alexandra, a charge which, if proved, carries a six-month jail term. She later drops the charges, but is pressing ahead with divorce. Their 11-month-old son Mario has been placed in the custody of Alexandra. Mutu is trying to win custody of Mario so he can come and live with him in London.

Mutu is eagerly looking forward to his new-found celebrity status in London, 'I am not afraid of the beautiful women in England who, I hear, chase after footballers. I won't take the risk of losing my position as a player for the sake of a pretty woman.'

Across the country, agents are in raptures at the prospect of a steady flow of work from Stamford Bridge. So far Chelsea have accounted for £75m of the £172m spent on transfers among the Premiership clubs in the transfer window. And there is a knock-on effect for other clubs. The £7m paid for Wayne Bridge, for example, enables Southampton to bring in seven players. In fact, Chelsea's contribution so far comes to 44 per cent of the total spent by all 20 clubs and only £20m less than the other 19 combined, but there is still time to spend even more.

The awkward possibility of meeting Maccabi Tel Aviv in the qualifying round of the Champions League does not appeal at all; rather it revives painful memories. Chelsea crashed out in the second round of the UEFA Cup to Maccabi's neighbours, Hapoel Tel Aviv, two years ago, a defeat made more embarrassing by the refusal of six players to travel because of feared repercussions following the 9/11 terrorist attacks. Current players Desailly, Gallas, Petit and Gudjohnsen had all taken the decision to stay at home. Chelsea lost the away leg 2–0. Ranieri's team were then held 1–1 as Hapoel secured the best-ever result by any Israeli team in European club football.

Ranieri maintains he is not concerned which side he will have to face. 'It is important to be in the Champions League, the name of the opponent is not important.' Asked about facing an Israeli team and whether or not he is concerned that some of his players may refuse to travel, he jokes, 'That's why I buy 22 players.' Ranieri need not have worried. Slovakian champions MSK Zilina beat Maccabi Tel-Aviv 2–1 on aggregate. Chelsea are on their way to Eastern Europe.

TUESDAY, 12 AUGUST

Roman Abramovich explains his transfer policy: 'Initially, we wanted to get at least seven new players by 31 August but nothing is written in stone. It's fair to say that we could add at least one more quality player to the squad by the end of the month, but I will not say any more because every comment could result in an increase in prices.' Abramovich also makes a commitment to his coach. 'Ranieri will stay. He speaks simple English, so it's easy for us to converse.'

In turn Ranieri suggests Jimmy Floyd Hasselbaink could be staying too. Yet, even though Mutu is unavailable for the start of the campaign in Europe, Hasselbaink is left out of the team. Ranieri says, 'I have 26 champions. When I pick 11 and there are five on the bench, the other 10 will have to sit in the stand or at home. But we are aiming to build a strong squad here.'

Ranieri cannot afford any more European banana skins after three miserable and humiliating UEFA Cup campaigns. A good run in the Champions League is the minimum requirement and Ranieri selects £50m of new talent in the shape of Bridge, Veron, Duff and Geremi for the visit to Slovakia. Ranieri says, 'This is the first game of our season and it is important to do well. But I am sure the players will not be nervous. If they are nervous, I will shoot myself. For everybody at Chelsea, our life has changed.'

Ranieri's notorious tinkering with a much smaller squad was blamed for loss of form around Christmas 2002, but he remains adamant that he will continue to experiment this season. He is fascinated by tactical systems. Maybe it is significant that Zilina's premier tourist attraction is the Provazske Museum... dedicated to the history of tinkering! He says, 'I change my players because I am a "tinkerman". In my opinion, the modern game is all about changing things during the match. I will not play one team for Europe and one for the Premiership. There will be one team, one Chelsea, but I have a lot of players and they must be flexible. I gathered the list of players I wanted and now I'm happy.'

Strangely, there is little interest in the forthcoming game from most radio and TV outlets. The BBC eventually buys the rights for less than £50,000. Ranieri's pampered athletes are guaranteed an inhospitable experience in the uncomfortable, 12,000-capacity Pod Dubnom stadium. Veron earns more in a day than any of the Slovakians earns in a year. Although the side reached the quarter-finals of the European Cup-Winners' Cup in 1961, Chelsea's visit is the biggest event in the club's 95-year history.

Abramovich is still in Russia on business but he is given regular updates on progress aboard his yacht, *Le Grand Bleu*, which was bought from Microsoft founder Paul Allen for £50m and, at 355ft, is the fourth-largest in the world. He is perhaps fortunate to miss out on Chelsea's nine-hour trip to the most northerly outpost of Slovakia, which includes a final 180-mile coach trip from Budapest to Zilina. The Russian has fixed up to have the game beamed round the world via a live BBC satellite feed to the dining-room table of his luxury yacht in Alaska.

WEDNESDAY, 13 AUGUST

MSK ZILINA 0, CHELSEA 2

Ireland international Damien Duff earns BBC pundit Alan Hansen's praise after an exhilarating first half. A late own goal and a first-half strike by Eidur Gudjohnsen seal it. Cole comes off the bench to replace Duff and plays a part in the second goal on 75 minutes, releasing Gudjohnsen. Just as the Icelander is about to shoot, substitute Michal Drahno assists by curling the ball past his own keeper and into the corner.

Ranieri is delighted with a commanding display at full-back from Johnson, who also impresses watching England assistant coach Tord Grip. Chelsea take the lead in the 42nd minute with an impressive flowing move; Duff plays a one-two with Forssell before delivering a perfect low cross from the left that Gudjohnsen guides in at the far post.

From one corner of the ground, the Chelsea fans, all 260 of them, start their first celebrations of the campaign. Forssell makes his first Chelsea appearance in 14 months raising further doubts over the future of Hasselbaink.

Lampard is the only member of last season's midfield to start. 'I thought we had a good squad last year and, if we had not beaten Liverpool in the final game of the season to get into the Champions League, maybe none of this would have happened. I would like to think the likes of myself, John Terry and the others who were regulars last season are the heartbeat of the team and that we are going to be given the chance to help take the club forward.'

Veron starts on the right and demonstrates commitment and industry allied to his natural vision, but appears to relish more his spell in the middle. Lampard observes, 'Seba's got licence because he's used to playing on the left or through the centre. We want to get him on the ball and he can roam to find it. It's up to us to get him the ball because if we can do that he will pick the passes out, over the back four and in behind people. I know that, with him coming in, then maybe I will have to hold a bit more at times, but I would like to play the game I did last season.'

Johnson has been preferred to Mario Melchiot and grasps the opportunity with both hands as he allows Veron the freedom to wander by patrolling the right flank. Johnson says, 'It's hard to believe what's happened, but I have tried to take it all in my stride. Somebody told me Tord Grip was there. People say if I can break into this Chelsea team, I might have a chance for England, but I'm not paying any attention to that. It's good to be part of this.'

Team

Cudicini, Johnson, Bridge, Desailly, Terry, Veron, Geremi, Lampard, Duff (Cole), Forssell (Gronkjaer), Gudjohnsen.

FRIDAY, 15 AUGUST

It will be Chelsea's centenary in 2005. By then, it will be one of Europe's elite clubs. Abramovich arrives at the Bridge in the afternoon for a summit with key board members, Trevor Birch and Richard Creitzman.

First to arrive for the meeting is Ranieri, stopping only for a photograph with a young fan; then comes Pini Zahavi, looking tanned and as youthful as ever. Eventually, Abramovich arrives flanked by four minders; he is casually dressed in his trademark faded jeans, green, untucked Burberry polo shirt and open-toed sandals.

Abramovich and his advisers are analysing the most expensive experiment in the history of football – 46 days, £75m, nine new players. Speaking through an interpreter, he says, 'I can't wait for the season to start, I'm so excited. We have to build something special here at Chelsea.'

Eddie Barnett, Chelsea's box office manager, is rubbing his hands at the increase in income. 'The whole place is just electric with excitement. We've sold a record number of season tickets – worth more than £13m, which is a magnificent performance. I will be very disappointed now, with the quality of the team we have got, if we do not sell out for every home Premier League match.'

The season kicks off against Liverpool with 15 shopping days to go before the transfer deadline and Chelsea are still chasing at least two more players. There are discussions about Hernan Crespo, while the Makelele deal is still very much 'on'.

Parma receive the first instalment of the £15.8m fee for Mutu and, although he receives his work permit, he has not been granted his international clearance because of a public holiday in Italy today. Mutu flew into England on Thursday and trained with his new team-mates.

Starting out as a professional in 1996 with small Romanian side Arges Pitesti, Mutu's wages were just £75 a week, and rose to £6,000 a year when he joined Dinamo Bucharest in 1999. In his first season at Dinamo, he scored a goal a game, and he netted an impressive 17 goals in his final season in Serie A with Parma. Handed the number 7 shirt for Chelsea, he has already spent three weeks in summer training with Parma, playing in three matches, so he is fit. Ranieri says, 'Mutu will be the second striker. He is young and has scored many goals in Italy, which shows he is dangerous and he is clever and strong. I have said Jimmy is a shark and Carlton Cole a lion. Mutu is another predator – I have a zoo!'

Geremi is still struggling to find his bearings in the London area. He ends up on the outskirts of Oxford as he tries to find the Harlington training HQ. Geremi was travelling round the M25 after leaving his Chelsea hotel, but missed the turn-off for the M4 and took one for the M40 instead. Duff sympathises. 'I haven't a clue where I'm driving at the moment. London's streets can be a nightmare.'

As for the forthcoming game, Chelsea have won just once at Anfield since December 1935, and the big question is whether a new group of players who've been thrown together can become a team overnight. Ranieri observes, 'What we achieved last season was from unity. What everybody expects this season is the maximum. Mr Abramovich asks me, "What, Claudio, what do you want? What do you need?" I give him a long, long list, and one by one they come. It is like having a new Ferrari a day.

'No player is guaranteed a shirt. Look, I spoke to all my players and told them, "If everybody thinks they are first eleven, there is a problem. If you can think you are second eleven, we can bond very well." If you are not happy to fight for a place, don't come here. Intelligent players can create a good group feeling – and this group could win everything. But if your first opponents are your team-mates, you win nothing.'

Ranieri won't rotate one team domestically and one in Europe. 'No, no,' he says, 'There isn't a first or second Chelsea, there is one Chelsea.'

The last Anfield victory occurred in the season before the Premiership began and the goalscorers were Vinnie Jones and Dennis Wise... it will be some start, then, if the new Chelsea can win at Liverpool.

SUNDAY, 17 AUGUST

LIVERPOOL 1, CHELSEA 2

Abramovich's personal Boeing 737 touches down from Moscow at Liverpool's John Lennon Airport in Speke moments after 2.00pm, just as a posse of his friends and close associates arrives from the same destination on a Global Express business jet. A convoy of sleek silver Mercedes completes the journey to Anfield under heavy security.

The Abramovich party of 14 arrives with Roman in a smart suit but without a tie. He stops briefly at the entrance to Anfield to sign a few autographs. The Russian delegation breezes past a stunned-looking boardroom steward as Abramovich and his entourage take their seats a quarter of an hour before kick-off to soak up the atmosphere... suddenly Abramovich is wearing a tie, supplied because they are mandatory in the Anfield directors' box.

He is flanked by his wife Irina, and accompanied by the second-oldest of his five offspring, a ten-year-old boy named Arkady. The strict 'no children' rule has been waived. Irina is sporting a glittering £10,000 diamond-encrusted gold Chelsea pin, and so, too, is Arkady. They are presents from Bates who had them made the day after Abramovich bought the club – one for Roman and one for his wife.

As the atmosphere builds around Anfield, the England coach arrives. Sven-Goran Eriksson walks through the doors, bumping into a group of football reporters. One of them catches his eye and asks, 'Come to watch your team, then?' Seated beside Abramovich are business associates Eugene Shvidler and Richard Creitzman, with Suzannah and Ken Bates outside them.

The supposedly private, reclusive and unemotional Russian looks intoxicated by the whole occasion. His body language throughout signals unequivocally that he is enjoying himself, so much so that after the match he stays in the car park signing autographs for ten minutes.

Indeed, after kick-off, Abramovich becomes very animated, leaping up and down, exchanging high fives and yelling with delight at Veron's opener, burying his head in his hands and then politely clapping when Owen scores from the penalty spot at the second attempt, and cheering with sheer delight at Hasselbaink's winner.

The tinkerman starts with his wingers on the 'wrong' flanks, but quickly makes his customary tactical changes throughout the match, with the first bringing a goal after seconds as Gronkjaer switches wings and pulls the ball back for Veron to score.

Veron revels in the role as his team's anchor-man and playmaker in a five-man midfield that affords him the protection he was never given at Old Trafford. In just two games inside four days, he is looking like the player who tempted Fergie to splash out £28.1m two years ago. Almost everything Chelsea conjure up stems from Veron, like the cunning first-time pass which should have seen Gudjohnsen put the match beyond Liverpool before half-time. There certainly seems to be plenty of elation when he whacks home the opener as he arrives late to pounce on to Gronkjaer's cross. Veron proves what Phil Neville has been saying about his work rate. Veron is chasing back and harrying defenders or sliding in with well-timed tackles, or defending bravely by heading clear from corners.

Cole starts on the bench before replacing Duff. Johnson and Bridge are assured at the back, although Bridge's challenge for the Liverpool penalty is rash. The assistant referee gives Owen a second chance from the penalty spot after Cudicini strays off his line. Replays show that initially the linesman gets it wrong as Veron claims at the time and Chelsea should have had a throw-in; and it is harsh on Cudicini having the penalty retaken as he only moves minimally.

Lampard has a hand in both goals and his performance suggests a player determined to hang on to his place. Terry turns in an awesome display in front of Eriksson before joining up with Lampard for England duty. Ranieri insists Hasselbaink, who comes on as a substitute at half-time for Gudjohnsen, still has a future at Chelsea. The way the Dutchman celebrates, tearing his shirt off his back and twirling it over his head, suggests that he is making a statement of intent.

The final whistle brings smiles, punching of the air, back-slapping and congratulatory handshakes from Abramovich's entire entourage. It is the first time Liverpool have lost their opening game at home since 1962, before the Beatles' first single. Abramovich enthuses, 'It was worth all the money I've put into this club and I'm so very, very happy.' After the strains of 'You'll Never Walk Alone' die out, the away end is soon singing, 'There's only one Abramovich.'

> **Team**
>
> Cudicini, Johnson (Gallas), Terry, Desailly, Bridge, Gronkjaer, Geremi, Veron, Lampard, Duff (J Cole) Gudjohnsen (Hasselbaink).

MONDAY, 18 AUGUST

A player is signed for £4.2m, more than most Premiership clubs can currently afford for first-teamers, and is immediately loaned out to Portsmouth. Bordeaux's Russian midfielder Alexei Smertin will learn to adapt to life in the Premiership on the south coast. The 28-year-old midfielder was looking to return home to Torpedo Moscow until Abramovich's personal intervention. The big Italian clubs often sign players and then farm them out to gain experience and Chelsea are the first club in England to sign a player and loan him out before he kicks a ball for them!

It transpires Chelsea have made 'preliminary enquiries' about Swedish star Zlatan Ibrahimovic, 21, at Ajax, who indicate they are only willing to sell for £19m. Ajax defender Cristian Chivu is another target along with Real's full-back Michel Salgado, the 27-year-old Spaniard. Croatia striker Ivica Olic claims a deal has already been agreed for him immediately after completing a £6m transfer from Dinamo Zagreb to CSKA Moscow. Olic sets his sights on Chelsea. He says, 'I have every hope that Mr Abramovich will organise my transfer to Chelsea next year.'

Although linked with Lazio's midfielder, the Serb Dejan Stankovic, the number-one player still in their sights is Roma midfielder Emerson. Stankovic, incidentally, is reported to be an Eriksson recommendation.

Former MP David Mellor has savaged the decision to sign Veron, questioning its validity because of his links to football agent Pini Zahavi. Now, he admits he was wrong, 'As for Veron, I am a sinner come to repentance. I worried that he was spoiled but an early encounter with another sceptic changed his mind, and should have changed mine. Well, before Sunday's Premiership encounter my friend reported how fit and determined Veron was. Which was exactly how he looked, with end-to-end running and accurate passing, not to mention that goal. Already, Chelsea are building themselves around Veron and this could be a season to rival the one with Lazio three years ago where some of the most unforgiving fans in the world hailed him as a hero amongst heroes.'

Chelsea also ensure 'loan' stars farmed out for the season don't come back to haunt them. Forssell, Cole, Smertin and Zenden cannot play against Chelsea.

TUESDAY, 19 AUGUST

Ranieri still needs a proven goalscorer and a midfield dynamo. Inter's Hernan Crespo and Real's Claude Makelele could end up as the big two.

Crespo shares agent Fernando Hidalgo with Veron. Crespo, in July 2000, moved from Parma to Lazio for £35m, as the world's most expensive player. He has the speed, aerial ability and the nose for a goal to match Mutu. He scored more than 100 goals in Serie A, won the UEFA Cup with Parma in 1999 and has hit 19 goals in 36 matches for his country. Marco Branca, Inter's director of sport, insists, 'Crespo will remain at Inter; we are not willing to sell the player, he is an important player in our team.'

Despite the denials, talks are going on. In the 2000/01 season, Crespo finished top scorer in Serie A with 24 goals in 32 games for Eriksson's Lazio.

WEDNESDAY, 20 AUGUST

Ranieri speaks to Crespo to gauge whether he is prepared to move. When those talks are successful, haggling over the fee begins. Ranieri asks Veron to persuade him to move, while the pair are on international duty. Veron's influence proves vital. Veron says, 'The team is looking for Crespo, who is one of the greatest strikers in the world. It will be very hard, but not impossible.'

Mutu's international clearance finally arrives and he celebrates by scoring both goals in Romania's 2–0 win over Luxembourg. Gronkjaer puts Denmark ahead in their 1–1 draw with Finland, while Gudjohnsen takes just five minutes to find the target for Iceland in their 2–1 win over the Faroe Islands which takes them to the top of European Championship qualifying Group 5. Damien Duff turns out for Ireland in a friendly against Australia.

John Terry starts his first match for his country against Croatia, with Eriksson saying, 'Terry's improved as a player very much over the last year; he's much more mature and quicker than he was 18 months ago. He is a big, big talent and still very young. Hopefully, he's going to be in there for a long time now.'

Terry has plenty of familiar faces around him – Lampard, Bridge and Cole are all in the squad. He points out, 'If you think back a few years, Dennis Wise was the only Englishman playing for Chelsea but now there are quite a few of us. You have to give Claudio Ranieri credit for that. When he came in he said he wanted to get more English players and that's exactly what he's done.'

Terry leads his country against Croatia for the final ten minutes. As the only England player to stay on the pitch for the entire match, he is given the captain's armband. 'I'm going to have it framed. I was only captain because David Beckham had been substituted but I'm still very proud, especially as all my family were there. One day, I would love to be skipper on a full-time basis. But I know I'm a long way off and Becks is doing a fantastic job.'

Lampard hammers in a scorcher to finish off Croatia and could have had another. Eriksson adds, 'Frank Lampard is growing as a footballer. He is getting better and better, stronger and stronger and scored a marvellous goal.' Lampard, who came on as a first-half substitute for the injured Butt, caps another fine performance with his goal.

THURSDAY, 21 AUGUST

Inter Milan fax Abramovich's aides to call the Crespo deal off in the morning after the president is faced with a violent revolt from striker Christian Vieri and thousands of disgruntled fans. Massimo Moratti eventually sanctions the deal, even though Vieri threatens to walk out. Crespo tells the president his mind and heart are already with Chelsea. The fee is much less than Inter asked for (originally, £25m) but it is also much more than Chelsea offered to start with – £14m.

Over two dinner dates with Inter representatives in London, the price is thrashed out. Inter's sporting director Marco Branca and technical director Gabriele Oriali dine with Zahavi and Chelsea officials. Branca, speaking from the airport departure lounge, gives nothing away when he says, 'We will have to wait a couple of days to see if it's everything or nothing.'

But back in Milan, Moratti confirms the move. Ranieri, when asked if more players will arrive, says, 'Wait... but don't worry about it,' adding, 'I don't have a spending limit.'

As the day wears on, Crespo learns the deal is all but completed. He will earn £20m over a four-year contract. Ranieri compares Crespo to Van Nistelrooy and Henry and expects him to make a similar impact. Eriksson adds, 'You can expect goals from Crespo, always. He was top scorer in Italy and Argentina before that. He is a very gifted player and he is very clever in the box which, of course, is his great strength.'

'I am happy with these words,' smiles Crespo, whose own favourite players are Marco Van Basten and Gary Lineker. The £16.8m fee will take his personal total in the transfer market to more than £70m. Crespo has played in front of Veron since they were teenagers in Argentina. Crespo says, 'I always talk to Seba and he spoke very highly of Chelsea. That is why I am here. It is always easier for me when Seba is in the team. I have played most of my best football with him in Italy and for Argentina. Manchester United and Arsenal have dominated the Premiership for many years but we intend to break that up and make sure we challenge for the Premiership.

'Veron says that, with a bit of luck, we can turn English football upside down. Argentina wear light blue, Chelsea royal blue and next to me there will be Veron. If I shut my eyes, I'm going to think that I'm in Buenos Aires.'

FRIDAY, 22 AUGUST

Leicester City's Micky Adams knows the pressures a manager feels at the arrival of a big-spending owner. After securing promotion from Division Three at Fulham, the club was taken over by Mohamed Al-Fayed; Adams was sacked just ten games into the following season.

'When we lost games at Fulham, there were top people linked with the job on a daily basis. That will possibly happen to Claudio. It won't be a nice feeling for him. I don't know what relationship Claudio has got with the new owner. I had very little dialogue with Mr Fayed and you need a dialogue with a chairman, even if it's just to put his arm around you when you've lost a game.

'I can't imagine what the expectation is like for Claudio Ranieri; I can't know because I have never had any money to spend. I am not envious because I am here at Leicester City and I understand how my cloth has been cut so I get on with it.'

Mutu is looking forward to his debut against Leicester. 'Abramovich is a bit crazy as a president but I like such crazy people a lot. With that kind of guy in charge of our club, everything is possible. Abramovich has turned me into his number-one fan since he informed all the Chelsea players how crazy he is about our game. When he spoke to the squad last week, he told us he was once sitting in his house in Siberia, excited about a vital game from the Russian championship. Suddenly, his satellite connection failed and it became impossible for him either to see the game or get the system fixed in time. It was incredible what he did next. He took his personal jet and flew for nine hours.'

Ranieri says, 'Mutu can start. He is so clever, so cunning and stays hidden until it is necessary to apply the killer finish. No matter the size of our squad, I bought Mutu to play in the first team. The position of left-sided striker is made for him. He can ghost in from behind the main striker and, when he does, the goalkeeper will be a dead man. This is why I have dreamed of signing Mutu for such a very long time. He is really strong. I've never seen him crying when he gets hit. He's too hard for that. He always plays with his head up, which is why he reads the game perfectly and can smell out the goal. What he did at Parma last season was incredible. If Mutu brings even half that brilliance to Chelsea, he will have a great year.'

Previous Romanian imports, Florin Raducioiu and Ilie Dumitrescu, were failures. But Mutu has bags of confidence. 'I will succeed where other Romanians have failed because I am Adrian Mutu. If you doubt that, then wait until you see me on the pitch. Chelsea want to make a name for themselves and I want to be part of that.'

Ranieri says, 'If a striker can score 18 goals in Italy, he can score anywhere in the world and that is why Adrian will be very important for us. He is a different player to Gianfranco Zola but I hope the fans will take him to their hearts in the same way.'

SATURDAY, 23 AUGUST

CHELSEA 2, LEICESTER 1

Roman Abramovich is given a standing ovation with the latest and most expensive signing, Hernan Crespo, there to watch. In his programme notes, he pledges his spending to transform Chelsea into one of Europe's elite. Abramovich tours the perimeter of the pitch during the warm-up, shaking hands with fans and signing autographs. It is symbolic that so many turn up with a variety of T-shirts and flags with variations of the hammer and sickle (though the Communist-era flag was abolished with the collapse of the Soviet Union). His welcome is completed by a medley of songs, a Russian waltz and even 'Fiddler on the Roof' over the PA system as he takes his seat in his Millennium Box, with guests that include the President of Iceland and his wife, whom he'd flown to the game on his private jet after they had spent some time on an unofficial visit to Chukotka.

Abramovich can relax, tie-less, in the box directly over the halfway line in Chelsea's East Stand. Bates joins in the pre-match festivities. When the DJ airs a traditional Russian tune, 'Kalinka', Bates does a Cossack dance in the directors' box.

Touts are doing brisk business, charging £120 a seat. If the anticipation outside the ground is something, the scenes before kick-off are equally remarkable. No club can ever have devoted eight pages of its club programme to their summer signings, and introducing each to a thrilled audience takes a good 15 minutes. Mutu puts in a swashbuckling debut display, showing his full range of trickery and striking a thunderbolt from 20 yards to clinch victory just before half-time. He leaves to a standing ovation.

There are nervous moments, especially in a feisty second half when Geremi is dismissed with 23 minutes left. Leicester then have Alan Rogers and Riccardo Scimeca sent off in the closing stages. Chelsea enjoy some good fortune, through an own goal by Lilian Nalis, only for James Scowcroft to equalise when Muzzy Izzet's long-range free-kick floats into the area five minutes before half-time, and he outjumps Terry to power a header into the far corner.

The cameras zoom in on the directors' box. Abramovich manages only a shake of the head, a shrug of the shoulders, and a wry smile. Leicester fans are quick with a chorus of, 'Roman, what's the score?' When Mutu's free-kick flies straight into the wall and rebounds to him, he lets fly with a follow-up effort that rockets into the far corner on the stroke of half-time.

Four years ago, Leicester derailed Chelsea's title bid late in the season by hauling their way back from 2–0 down to draw 2–2. Not this time. Hasselbaink strikes the near post from a tight angle after racing past Ian Walker. Geremi is sent off with 23 minutes left for a two-footed tackle on Scimeca, a harsh decision from Rob Styles, especially as the Chelsea midfielder wins the ball. But he does go in studs-first and the official feels bound to act.

The task eases when Rogers is dismissed for kicking Gronkjaer on the ground after pushing him with six minutes left. Brian Deane still bursts straight through only to plant his header against the bar. But that is it for Leicester, who have Scimeca dismissed with two minutes left for his second bookable offence, a tackle from behind on Joe Cole, who then rattles the bar himself.

A montage of the magical Zola is played on the giant screens, but Chelsea have a new master of tricks and skills in Mutu. Micky Adams observes, 'That's what you pay £15.8m for – not that I would know!'

Ranieri is in no rush to put away Abramovich's chequebook. 'Is the spending over? Maybe. Perhaps there will be more. If I want others, I will speak with Mr Abramovich.' Ranieri struggles to hide the fact that Crespo will be next. 'I don't know what will happen there,' he says trying to keep a straight face, while making a gesture to suggest his nose is growing. 'Once I am told Crespo has signed, I will tell you.'

Team

Cudicini, Melchiot, Terry, Desailly, Bridge, Duff (Cole), Geremi, Lampard, Veron, Hasselbaink (Gudjohnsen), Mutu (Gronkjaer).

MONDAY, 25 AUGUST

Finnish striker Mikael Forssell is wanted by Borussia Moenchengladbach where he was on loan from January to May last season, as well as by Lazio. In the end, Forssell chooses Birmingham for an initial four months which is likely to be extended for the rest of the season. Birmingham manager Steve Bruce has beaten off 14 clubs to get the Finnish hitman and says, 'He is just our type – young, hungry and desperate for success. I've admired Mikael since Gianluca Vialli described him as Finland's Michael Owen. We are all trying to analyse what is happening at Chelsea. We told them that if they were ever going to let Forssell go they should tell us. If they want to get rid of Petit, Mutu, Hasselbaink or any of the others, I hope they will tell us first.'

With the acquisition of Crespo set to be completed, Chelsea's outlay is just shy of the £100m mark. Ranieri insists his squad will not become a cohesive unit for some time. 'I cannot say whether it will be ready tomorrow. I don't know when it will be ready. All I ask is that we play with concentration and a big heart – like we did against Leicester.'

He also accepts he is living in the shadow of Sven-Goran Eriksson, so often touted as his successor. 'There is a total feeling between Abramovich and myself. But it is obvious that feeling can only be kept or bought with victories. I wasn't born yesterday. I know how things go in football. I'm not worried. I realise I must live with this soap opera. There's nothing I can do if Eriksson comes out at every corner. I just try to do my best and then it will all come to account.'

How important it is to beat Zilina and qualify for the group stages of the Champions League is summed up by Chelsea skipper Marcel Desailly. 'We must just think about how it is going to be beautiful if we get into the proper Champions League, how beautiful it will be going and playing against Milan, Real Madrid, Inter, Juventus, and teams like that.'

TUESDAY, 26 AUGUST

CHELSEA 3, ZILINA 0 (Chelsea win 5–0 on aggregate)

Iceland's Prime Minister Olaf Gunnar Grimsson and his new wife Dorrit join Abramovich and his friends in the private box and eye-witnesses tell me just how much he enjoys himself. Abramovich introduces Crespo to the Prime Minister and his wife, who is the daughter of a famous London jeweller. Abramovich has one concern – the Bridge is far from full. The £35 ticket prices have deterred many supporters from coming to see an unglamorous opponent. Abramovich would have preferred the prices to have been £20 to encourage more support.

The pricing strategy for similar games will be reviewed. More than 19,000 empty seats, including the entire upper tier of the West Stand, show fans are more selective because of the cost. Admittedly, the tie is effectively over, Mutu is ineligible, Crespo has not officially signed, and the resting of star attractions like Veron and Duff has been widely publicised. The 23,408 gate is not a one-off. Crowds at Stamford Bridge fluctuate more than for their main rivals.

Crespo, dressed in all black, completes his move and is paraded at half-time. He receives the biggest cheer of the night. The announcer builds up his arrival before the start by suggesting, 'Stay in your seats,' because 'something very special' will be happening at half-time. Cue more Russian music. Crespo signs a four-year deal.

On the pitch, Ranieri makes five changes, but few of the incoming players seize their opportunity with any real conviction. Joe Cole again looks isolated on the left-hand side of midfield and Gudjohnsen, despite shedding several pounds, is not light on his feet. Johnson and Huth both score their first senior goals. Johnson only celebrated his 19th birthday on the previous Saturday, while Huth is also 19. Lampard's free-kick is only partially cleared and Johnson, lurking with intent just inside the box, is unchallenged as he steers a header inside the far post. Huth, a 64th-minute sub for Desailly, scores within three minutes of his arrival. The German rises powerfully to head in from fellow sub Petit's corner.

Hasselbaink, who had earlier been guilty of a horrendous miss from two yards, refuses to be denied in the 78th minute. He races on to Geremi's precise through ball and steers his angled shot beyond the reach of the advancing keeper. Not bad for a striker supposedly on his way out, just as Ranieri's decision to select him signals that he will not be leaving, as he is now cup-tied for European purposes. Chelsea claim their place among Europe's elite for only the second time in their history.

Several Chelsea players fancy themselves as free-kick experts, but there is a new kid on the block, the one they call 'The Wall'. Huth's awesome late free-kick captures Ranieri's imagination. Huth almost shatters the crossbar with a 30-yard pile-driver which flies back into play so quickly the match officials do not spot that the ball has already crossed the line. Ranieri says, 'He has more power in his free-kicks than anyone I have ever seen. Not even Roberto Carlos strikes them so well. We have a lot of big-name champions at the club but they all respect this young man because he almost breaks the goals with his shots in training.'

Huth is fantastic when he replaces Marcel Desailly. He scores one goal and should have another when that free-kick lands over the goal-line. Berlin-born Huth has now been at the club for nearly five years after being spotted by Chelsea's scouts playing in a youth tournament during Vialli's reign. The 6ft 3in defender only turned professional in February last year.

John Terry has no doubts about Huth's pedigree. 'Robert is going to become a Chelsea legend.'

Team

Cudicini, Johnson, Terry, Desailly (Huth), Babayaro, Gronkjaer (Stanic), Lampard (Petit), Geremi, Cole, Hasselbaink, Gudjohnsen.

THURSDAY, 28 AUGUST

Abramovich watches the draw for the Champions League via a satellite link on board his yacht, while Ken Bates and Trevor Birch represent Chelsea at the actual ceremony. Spokesman John Mann explains, 'Roman is a very private individual and would not have liked the attention his appearance at the draw would have undoubtedly caused. His style is to appoint people to work for him and then let them get on with the job.'

Chelsea are among the second seeds as Sven-Goran Eriksson tips Real Madrid to be champions for a record tenth time. 'I see a battle between Italian, Spanish and English teams. I see AC Milan, Juve and Inter, as well as Manchester United, as contenders. But for me the favourites are Real Madrid. They have the mentality and the strength to tackle the European games at their peak.'

Arsenal's David Dein attends the draw and concedes that the Russian revolution could change the face of English football. 'Roman Abramovich has parked his Russian tanks on our lawn and is firing £50 notes at us.'

Chelsea's summer spending has passed £100m, while their London rivals spent a mere £1.5m on goalkeeper Jens Lehmann. Former Inter Milan defensive legend Giacinto Facchetti, now vice-president of the San Siro side, says, 'In every time there is one president who comes into football and wants to make his club very strong and very important. Abramovich is the one now and he is trying to buy great players for his club to make them big. It's not the first time it has happened. We have had Berlusconi, Moratti and Cragnotti. Now we have Abramovich. You have to take Chelsea seriously. They are suddenly at the same level as Arsenal and Manchester United.'

Chelsea draw Lazio, Besiktas and Sparta Prague in Group G. Ken Bates says, 'It's a tough draw but we are confident of coming through. They [Lazio] are the only team that have won in Europe at Stamford Bridge, so we owe them one. I was hoping we were going to get Dynamo Kiev and Lokomotiv Moscow but, unfortunately, Arsenal got those. It would have been rather ironic given our new ownership. As for Veron and Crespo, they might feel they have a point to prove against Lazio. Will we win the European Cup? Who knows, but we have one chance in 32.'

Like Chelsea, Lazio finished fourth in their domestic league and had to win through the qualifying round. They beat Benfica 4–1 on aggregate. John Terry walked away with Veron's shirt after watching Chelsea hold the Italians to a 0–0 draw four years ago. 'I travelled with the squad and was really in awe of the whole experience. I'd always admired Veron greatly. I knew it was a long shot but I was determined to come away with a souvenir from the game, especially as Chelsea had done so well. Because I was wearing a Chelsea tracksuit, I managed to talk my way into the home dressing room. You can imagine I wasn't the most popular person in there. The Lazio players even started booing me and trying to get me thrown out. But I'd got so far, I wasn't leaving without a trophy and finally succeeded in getting Veron's shirt.'

Lazio got their revenge with a 2–1 victory at Stamford Bridge, the only team to beat Chelsea at home in the Champions League.

After the draw, Birch meets Real Madrid officials and Claude Makelele's agents. Makelele becomes Chelsea's tenth star signing. He says, 'Real do not want me to leave and I would not go if I considered it a backwards step for my career. But Chelsea are a very big club and it is flattering to know a club that wants to become the biggest in the world wants you to help out with that. I am still fiercely ambitious and I want to carry on winning things for many years yet.'

Despite the signing of Crespo, Ranieri wants Hasselbaink to stay. After renewed interest from Barcelona, Ranieri insists, 'Hasselbaink is not going anywhere. I want him here. I enjoy his football. He works hard, is focused and plays well when he is alone up front and alongside Adrian Mutu.'

Emmanuel Petit is attracting interest from Tottenham and Manchester City as clubs discover Makelele is on his way to the Bridge, but the 32-year-old Petit, with just one year left on his existing contract, remarks, 'I have the trust of my chairman and the coach at Chelsea. I have seen the rumours, but it is nothing. I won't be going to Manchester City. If other defensive midfielders arrive at Chelsea, I would be delighted. As it stands at the moment, we are starting the season with just two defensive midfielders.'

Glenn Hoddle is disappointed not to be able to bring Petit to Spurs for a bargain £1m. Hoddle says, 'It's a pity, but the plan doesn't seem to be going anywhere at the moment.' Hoddle adds that rumours of goalkeeper Neil Sullivan being offered in a part-exchange deal are wide of the mark, 'That's not something we are thinking of doing.' Sullivan does indeed move to the Bridge, but not as a makeweight in any Petit deal.

FRIDAY, 29 AUGUST

Makelele's agent Marc Roger insists his client is owed 15 per cent of the agreed fee, £2.1m. 'Real Madrid does not want to pay the percentage that every player has for every transfer. The player feels that he is being disrespected,' he says.

Real's sporting director Jorge Valdano insists the deal will be finalised when Real receive the necessary guarantees from Chelsea's bank. 'All is agreed. Some guarantees have to arrive by noon on Monday at the latest, but otherwise the contracts have been signed.'

Makelele finally becomes a Chelsea player after backing down on his financial demands and flies to London to undergo a medical. Makelele wages are trebled with a four-year, £70,000-a-week deal. He says, 'Some say I'm going to be the Roy Keane or the Patrick Vieira of Chelsea, but comparisons don't worry me. I've known Patrick for a long time and know how to get the better of him. I would also remind the Irishman that the Real team I was in defeated Manchester United in the Champions League. Chelsea have a more balanced team than Arsenal and United, especially in midfield.'

Privately, the powerbrokers at the Bridge concede they paid over the odds for Makelele, but as the player once trained as an accountant maybe he can be excused his belief that he came at a reasonable price. Add the £8m the 30-year-old pockets over the lifetime of his contract and it's clear that Makelele is not coming cheap. Yet the Congo-born player, who moved to France from Kinshasa aged four, is unlikely to grab too many headlines. Makelele did not score in 93 Spanish League appearances for Real and netted just one goal in 38 Champions League ties.

'That's it. No more. We've finished,' declares Birch, who only ties up the Makelele deal 30 minutes before the Spanish transfer deadline, much to the consternation of his former team-mates. Zinedine Zidane moans, 'Claude allowed me the freedom to play further forward where I can do more damage. It would have been ideal if we had kept him because now I will have to change the job I do for the team. Without Claude, we would be a much weaker side, unable to function in the way Real Madrid expect and want us to.'

Sullivan's transfer from Tottenham is finalised as Jurgen Macho has a serious knee injury, leaving Ambrosio the only other senior keeper apart from Cudicini.

SATURDAY, 30 AUGUST
CHELSEA 2, BLACKBURN 2

Abramovich again receives the appreciation of his adoring public as he takes his seat ten minutes before the start. But Blackburn spoil his welcome party with a deserved point, which puts an end to Chelsea's 100 per cent record. The strains of 'Kalinka' are just fading when Blackburn stun the crowd by taking the lead after 19 seconds. Chelsea kick off, Veron gives their third pass away, Matt

Jansen harasses Desailly, who keeps the ball from crossing the line, then slips to allow Jansen a free cross for Andy Cole to volley home from 12 yards into the left-hand corner.

The travelling fans can't resist the obvious taunt of 'What a waste of money'. Chelsea have not beaten Blackburn at home since 1988, but their bench reflects their new prosperity, with Crespo, Cole, Gallas and Petit. After a quarter of an hour, Ranieri switches Duff from the right to his preferred left flank with encouraging results. Mutu slides the ball in the net after 29 minutes but his celebrations are curtailed by a contentious offside decision. Mutu is not offside when he turns in Geremi's right-wing cross, but Hasselbaink had been earlier in the build-up. The timing of the flag suggests that the referee's assistant is penalising the final touch. Mutu strikes again in first-half stoppage time. Veron sweeps a ball forward to Hasselbaink, who lays it off to Lampard, and his through-pass sends Mutu racing through the middle, past the statuesque Lorenzo Amoruso. In rounding Brad Friedel, the Romanian seems to have taken the ball too far out to the right, but he scores from a testing angle.

No Makelele to parade at half-time, but at least there is the new keeper Sullivan, who manages to inspire only lukewarm applause. Ranieri makes a baffling substitution at half-time, sending on Petit in place of Duff. In the consequent reshuffle, Geremi finds himself switched to the left.

A ghastly gaffe by Cudicini presents Andy Cole with a second goal which puts Blackburn ahead again in the 58th minute. The busy David Thompson fastens on to possession again and crosses from the left, and Cudicini's ineffective flap at the ball leaves Cole to stab in his second from four yards. Again, Blackburn are unable to hold on to their lead. Within five minutes, Geremi's cross is handled at close-range by Lucas Neill and Hasselbaink makes short work of the penalty, dispatching it low inside Friedel's left-hand post in the 63rd minute to gain a hard-earned point.

Mutu gives way to Crespo, in his black and white boots, and Cole manages another brief cameo. 'In 20 years, we have not beaten them at home in the league,' muses Ranieri. 'Why is this? It is always difficult against our bogey team, Middlesbrough... sorry, Blackburn. Slowly, slowly, everybody played for the team, but we must learn to kill the opponent.' Cudicini is realistic. 'We've got a lot of work to do. You can see the team is not playing fluently. We've got great champions in the team but the manager needs time to work with them.'

Lampard is adamant Makelele will not be taking his place. 'I'm here to fight because I want to play week in, week out, and it doesn't bother me who the manager signs. I played 50 games last year and I want to do that again. I'm not planning to go back on the bench at this stage of my career.'

Geremi's impending three-match ban spares Ranieri any immediate decisions. Geremi starts in the middle, moves to the right-wing, the left-wing and then left-back. But it is Lampard's superb first-time pass which opens up Blackburn's defence for Mutu to score.

> **Team**
>
> Cudicini, Johnson, Terry, Desailly, Bridge (Cole), Veron, Lampard, Geremi, Duff (Petit), Mutu (Crespo), Hasselbaink.

SUNDAY, 31 AUGUST

Out-of-favour Dutch winger Bolo Zenden is linked with clubs as diverse as Charlton, Inter Milan, Ajax, Lazio, PSV Eindhoven and Hamburg. Zenden feels his style of play doesn't suit Ranieri, 'He has an Italian mentality; I have a Dutch one. He only plays not to lose and I always go on to the pitch looking for a victory. At PSV, Barcelona or in the Dutch national side I have been used to spending 20 per cent of my time defending and 80 per cent attacking. But with Chelsea, I spend 60 per cent of my time in my own half. Ranieri does not like attacking football, and he prefers to see his team wait in their own area and then break out on the counter instead of taking a game to teams.'

Zenden is anxious for first-team football to protect his international status ahead of the European Championship in Portugal. 'I have played 45 international games for Holland and I want to play a lot more. But I know I have to play every week for my club otherwise Dick Advocaat won't pick me. He only picks players who play on a regular basis.' Middlesbrough make a late move and they are in a position to ensure that his salary isn't significantly slashed in a beat-the-deadline loan deal.

Tony Banks, Labour MP for West Ham, raises objections over Abramovich's takeover. The former Sports Minister remains sceptical despite all the signings and a promising start. 'It is still quite difficult to come to terms with. It is like winning the lottery three weeks running… you can't quite believe it. The man clearly has the money, he is worth what he says he is, but you can't help wondering why this has happened to us in such a short space of time. Being one of life's great pessimists, I wonder what price we're going to have to pay. I suppose that comes from having been a Chelsea supporter for so long. I always work on the assumption that if something sounds too good to be true, it probably is.'

Banks calls for the takeover to be investigated by Sports Minister Richard Caborn. Spokesman John Mann responds, 'In Russian business, especially in the murky mid-1990s period, a lot of people went out looking for stuff. Sometimes it was politically motivated, sometimes commercially.' A leading City source refutes

Banks's suggestion that there should be an inquiry into whether or not Abramovich has the right credentials.

Mann says, 'Roman Abramovich, like Mr Banks, shares a passion for football. He is committed to Chelsea and, like Tony, wants the very best for the club. We have written to Mr Banks in order to introduce Mr Abramovich to him, and have offered further dialogue to assuage his concerns.'

Banks has been following Chelsea since he was a 10-year-old on the terraces, and has held a season ticket for 30 years. 'I was one of those lucky people who managed to see all of Chelsea's home matches in 1954/55 – I've still got all the programmes – and that was the last time, in fact the only time, we won the championship. Hopefully, I shall see them do it again before I die.'

Maybe that really will happen, thanks, perhaps, to Chelsea's new Russian godfather about whom Banks has so far been so sceptical.

September

ABRAMOVICH TAKES CONTROL AS THE FOOTBALL
SEASON GETS INTO FULL SWING

Abramovich likens himself to Moses. 'Do you remember Moses? He spent 40 years in the desert with his people to make them forget slavery.' The Russian has a pledge to make. 'I haven't thought about how much I am prepared to spend. I suppose that depends on how well we play and how determined we are to win; if I feel we need to buy any particular player to get the results we want I'll just spend more money.

'British football is a business venture and a very competitive one; the quality of the teams is pretty similar – there is not one big name overshadowing the others; that is why I liked British football. I guessed the papers would write stories but I didn't expect they would write so many and for so long. Football is almost a religion in Britain so I knew that such an event [the takeover of Chelsea] would produce a big bang.'

PREMIERSHIP TABLE – SEPTEMBER								
Pos Team	P	W	D	L	GF	GA	GD	PTS
1 Arsenal	4	4	0	0	10	2	8	12
2 Manchester United	4	3	0	1	7	2	5	9
3 Portsmouth	4	2	2	0	7	2	5	8
4 Manchester City	4	2	1	1	8	5	3	7
5 Chelsea	3	2	1	0	6	4	2	7
6 Birmingham City	3	2	1	0	2	0	2	7
7 Fulham	3	2	0	1	7	5	2	6
8 Southampton	4	1	3	0	3	2	1	6
9 Blackburn Rovers	4	1	2	1	11	8	3	5
10 Liverpool	4	1	2	1	4	2	2	5

In his home country, Abramovich's business interests continue to grow. Sibneft's plans to merge with bigger rival Yukos to become Russia's largest private oil producer – and the world's fourth-biggest – will give it a market capitalisation of $36bn. Eugene Shvidler says, 'By 2010, I see a company that differs little from BP or ExxonMobil.'

Yukos' core shareholders, led by Mikhail Khodorkovsky, will control 50 per cent of the group. Sibneft's core shareholders, led by Abramovich, will get 25 per cent. Meanwhile, Abramovich concludes deals to extend his Chelsea stake to 93 per cent, buying out the club's other major stakeholders, Ruth Harding and BskyB. He then takes Chelsea Village private. After seven years on the stock market, Chelsea delists from the AIM, and shares close at 35.5p, a 35 per cent discount on the 1996 flotation price of 55p.

Abramovich has offered all shareholders who sell to him a 'limited edition commemorative share certificate' which includes facsimile signatures of the players and coaching staff, as well as returning existing certificates once the deal is completed. This is to entice the final 12,000 small shareholders into selling up.

MONDAY, 1 SEPTEMBER

Claude Makelele's move brings Abramovich's spending to a colossal £111.25m on ten star recruits in 62 days – £1.79m a day. World football, let alone the English game, has never seen anything like it. His transfer fee is the world's second-highest ever for an over 30, after the £19m Roma paid Fiorentina for Argentinian striker Gabriel Batistuta. Ranieri calls the French midfielder the world's greatest playmaker.

Says Makelele, 'A player like me is not often appreciated and yet I know I have an important role to play, particularly in the modern, high-tempo game. We "water carriers" are the new number 10 of the team. We are the ones dictating the flow and bossing the play. I don't stand out like a Marcel Desailly or a Zinedine Zidane and that forces me to impress in other ways. Some players get a kick out of scoring; I get a kick out of winning a tackle and getting the team moving forward again.'

Makelele stands at 5ft 7in, weighing in at just over ten stone, though his footballing stature is considerably greater. He was known as Three Legs at the Bernabeu, a nickname which carries more than a hint of innuendo, though the official line is that it refers to his awesome ability to get around the pitch. Makelele featured in UEFA's Team of the Year in 2002 and 2003 and last season was named the Champions League's best player. Overvalued, most definitely, but a key signing as Arsene Wenger observes:

'Makelele's signing shows Chelsea are now on a different planet. Real Madrid didn't want to sell but Chelsea can buy when they want and that makes them a world force. None of us can compete financially with Chelsea.'

As part of his new lifestyle, Roman Abramovich is taking polo lessons, according to the specialist polo press. His mansion in West Sussex, which has its own stables, used to belong to the Australian polo enthusiast and media mogul Kerry Packer.

It is also rumoured the Russian will expand his investments into Formula One after he attends the European Grand Prix at the Nürburgring as a guest of Bernie Ecclestone, the Formula One commercial rights holder. Ecclestone dismisses the idea. 'Roman will not be a team-owner in Formula One in 2004, or the foreseeable future. He likes football too much. We speak all the time. He is a nice guy and full of enthusiasm for what he is doing, but the truth is he has decided Formula One is not for him. I've become a Chelsea supporter, though.'

TUESDAY, 2 SEPTEMBER

Richard Creitzman, an adviser to Abramovich, reflects on the whirlwind transfers. 'I speak to Trevor [Birch] a lot and Roman fairly regularly, and there are a couple of other people involved on the Russian side and they have access to Claudio. And Roman can call up Claudio if he wants to. He's got his mobile number.

'The players we have bought will play for the club for three, four, five years, and I think they will be very successful, and their value will not necessarily fall away. What we have bought is the entity of Chelsea Village. There are bars, restaurants, a hotel. It is a fantastic venue outside of the football. So if you say are we looking to sell it, we are not, but I think it was a good investment.

'It is difficult to make money in football. I don't think he [Abramovich] is going to go out of this making billions of dollars because that is not realistic, but I think he wants success. But if they are not successful, then he understands; he runs a hockey club in Russia. He knows what sport is all about. It is an emotional thing. He wants to win but it doesn't mean he will chuck his toys out of the pram if Chelsea don't [make it]. For him, Chelsea's another challenge and that's what he's all about – pushing himself. He has not said to me, "I'm doing this for two years or for ten years," it was just, "I want to buy a football club." And he has done it. A man who does what he says.'

Is Abramovich intent on making Chelsea the world's biggest club? 'He doesn't have an ego like that ...' Creitzman insists. 'Roman will be at games and has discussed the players we've brought in with Claudio, because his knowledge of football isn't small. He will run Chelsea like he runs all his other businesses – setting his managers targets and letting them manage. Claudio knows what he has to do and he wants success as much as Roman does. In oil and aluminium, his managers have certain targets to meet and they get rewarded for those targets. There is regular contact between Claudio and Roman, and Claudio wants success as much as Roman does.

'They've discussed players and we have to get the green light from Roman for players we have signed. We'd say, "Duff is going to cost £17m. Yes or no?" He said yes on that deal but he's said no on a number of occasions because he felt the price was too high.'

There are plans to increase revenues, such as rebuilding the Shed End stand to increase the capacity by 10,000 seats. Creitzman says, 'Stamford Bridge is one of the best grounds in Europe. But it's not the biggest at the moment. If we can increase the capacity then we will. The problem is the access out to the Fulham Road. There is a rail track down one side of the ground, houses on the other side and housing at the back. So while other grounds have exits and access all around, we don't, we only have the Fulham Road. At the moment, there is just the main entrance, a side entrance and a little alleyway and, if something happens, you have got to get 40,000 people out, just like that. That's the problem. But if we can find extra points, we will probably do it.'

Chelsea make an average of £42 per seat, bringing in £1.76m per game. There would be an extra £15m a season from an additional 10,000 seats. 'Manchester United have more seats but I know we make more money per seat than they do,' adds Creitzman. 'The add-ons such as catering were part of the reason we chose Chelsea and why we would be eager to expand the capacity if it's possible.'

WEDNESDAY, 3 SEPTEMBER

MP Tony Banks insists that the pros and cons of foreign investment in football clubs need further consideration. 'When I was in Government, I said that no football club should be taken over until the football authorities had satisfied themselves about the bona fides of the proposed new structure.

'If the FA are not satisfied, they should be able to say to the board, "You will not have a licence to operate a football club." Clubs are part of people's lives, whether they are Chelsea or Cheltenham. I've invested 50 years of my life in Chelsea FC and I'm concerned about what happens. I just hope he's true to his word, that we win the Premiership and become the greatest team in the world. If so, I'll kiss his boots.'

Ex-MP and *Evening Standard* columnist David Mellor has mellowed in his objections. 'Having met him and his entourage, they are very pleasant people with nothing untoward about them. The way he conducts himself around the club is impressive; he is modest and unassuming and very pleasant. It is a smart move putting a Londoner, Richard Creitzman, on the board, and he is working well with Trevor Birch and Ken Bates.

'Let's face it, it is incredibly exciting these days ... they have bought sensibly with a clear strategy of recruiting half home-based players and half from abroad. One Saturday over dinner, Trevor [Birch] told me it was wonderful to be part of it and that within five years there was a genuine chance of winning not just the Premiership but the Champions League. He also said that you cannot be taken seriously unless you buy one of the world's top five strikers and they've done that.'

THURSDAY, 4 SEPTEMBER

The transfer window closes, but there is one more surprise signing. Pini Zahavi is behind yet another amazing coup with the appointment of Peter Kenyon as Chelsea's new chief executive – in other words a member of Manchester United's board has been recruited very much in the same style as signing a star player.

Abramovich's brief was to find the best man and Zahavi turned to someone who three times in his three-year tenure as Ferguson's immediate boss had signed cheques that broke the British transfer record. Just 24 hours after the Abramovich takeover, Kenyon was deep in conversation with Zahavi in Les Ambassadeurs, the upmarket Park Lane casino-restaurant. That was not unusual, as Zahavi and Kenyon had completed many transfers together and were attempting to secure the Brazilian Ronaldinho's services from Paris Saint Germain for Manchester United.

The Manchester United chief executive made a quick exit when spotted by a couple of city journalists he knew. Normally, he wouldn't be so jumpy. But the seeds of Kenyon's appointment had been sown. Les Ambassadeurs, ironically, was the venue for the first meeting between Zahavi, Jonathan Barnett and Trevor Birch when the discussion had turned to the need for a new investor. To fulfil Abramovich's long-term strategy to develop Chelsea into a worldwide brand, Zahavi told him there was no one better than 'my friend Peter'. Kenyon called an unscheduled meeting in London with Sir Roy Gardner, chairman of United's plc, to tell him he was resigning.

At about the same time, two of Abramovich's right-hand men, Eugene Tenenbaum and Bruce Buck, tell Trevor Birch they still want him to stay even though they are hiring Kenyon. United's directors, as well as Sir Alex Ferguson, are unaware of Kenyon's proposed move; Ken Bates is also kept in the dark. 'Within football circles, it was more unexpected than any of the Russian billionaire's dressing-room signings,' observes *The Times*.

Birch has performed an efficient job supervising the purchases of players for Abramovich, but his expertise is taking care of companies in financial difficulties. His departure is cushioned by a £2.9m pay-off, a generous gesture by Abramovich – the severance in Birch's contract was £2.25m.

Kenyon had been a United employee for six years and a fan since the 1968 European Cup final, taken there as a 13-year-old. He trained as an accountant after attending the local grammar school and gained a reputation for turning around troubled companies. In 1986, he joined Umbro International, the loss-making sports retailer, and helped to sell it to an American group before joining United in 1997, where he became football's highest-paid administrator. He joined as deputy chief executive at Old Trafford before succeeding Martin Edwards as chief executive three years later. Since then, Kenyon secured Nike as United's sponsor, bringing in £303m over 13 years and was instrumental in numerous other deals with the likes of Vodafone, netting the club more than £100m a year. He also brokered a groundbreaking agreement with the New York Yankees. Kenyon turned the club into the world's biggest football brand, with an estimated 53 million fans worldwide.

Kenyon recognised the need to expand Old Trafford, which now has 15,000 more seats than the next largest stadium in the country, bringing in £1.5m per match. He earned £625,000 in 2002, including bonuses, and he more than doubled his salary by joining Abramovich. When Ferguson was intent on retiring, Kenyon offered the job to Sven-Goran Eriksson. His move heightens speculation that the England coach will follow him to Chelsea. Kenyon orchestrated United's £28.1m purchase of Veron and the £30m move for Rio Ferdinand. Zahavi was instrumental in both transactions.

At Chelsea, Kenyon is hired on a three-year, £1.5m-a-year (plus bonuses and incentives package) worth £7.5m plus, to include a one-off, £2m 'golden hello', more than most 'signing-on' fees agreed by the world's top footballers. A £500,000 payment is promised to compensate Kenyon for giving up agreed benefits at United, including highly lucrative share options worth £222,262, plus £150,000 bonuses for the profits made his old club.

FRIDAY, 5 SEPTEMBER

Alan Hansen puts his view on the appointment. 'Peter Kenyon's move was an unbelievable statement by Chelsea, a real coup over their rivals Manchester United. But it is only the start of what will be a very long battle to catch up with the Premiership champions.'

The question of Ken Bates's future as chairman arises again, but he says defiantly, 'There have been no discussions to the contrary.' Yet it is obvious that Bates and Peter Kenyon could have a tough working relationship. Kenyon is a leading light at the G14, the collective of Europe's biggest clubs. One alternative to Kenyon was Arsenal's David Dein. Soundings were taken through the usual intermediaries but Dein tells me it was a non-starter. How intriguing it would have been if Dein had turned up at the Bridge to be 'welcomed' by his old foe Ken Bates.

SATURDAY, 6 SEPTEMBER

Birch seems undecided about accepting a lesser role at Chelsea. He meets up with his close friend, FA chief executive Mark Palios, at Old Trafford for the England international and several players phone him to say they are 'gutted' for him, notably John Terry. Damien Duff's agent also calls, as Birch was instrumental in convincing him of London's qualities.

SUNDAY, 7 SEPTEMBER

Kenyon begins 'gardening leave' while lawyers sort out when he can join the club. Kenyon's appointee Paul Smith moves in as temporary chief executive. Former chief executive Colin Hutchinson says that Keynon 'is a very good businessman. If you look globally at their financial situation – compared to Real, who have assembled a superb squad but also piled up a load of debt – they are on a sound footing. And he will be a big loss to United. It is a shock out of the blue, considering the rivalry down the years between the two clubs. Chelsea, in recent times, has got its soul back. There has been a feeling among supporters over the last couple of years that perhaps the priority was not football.'

MONDAY, 8 SEPTEMBER

Sir Alex Ferguson's inference that he rejected an approach from Chelsea immediately after Abramovich's takeover is leaked after the announcement of Kenyon's defection. Is it the opening shot in his new round of contract negotiations? It raises further doubts over the future of Claudio Ranieri. Ferguson was not actually made an offer, although he was made aware that he would be a top target if Ranieri was not successful. An official source tells me that neither Ferguson nor Eriksson have actually been formally offered the job.

Ferguson issues a denial. 'It would take something catastrophic for me to leave this club. My whole life is Manchester United. You get woven into the fabric of the place.'

Ranieri says that he has a good relationship with the new owner. 'The understanding between us was immediate. He had read up on me and I have judged him on his behaviour – and he has been all fire and no smoke! I want us to be one of the best teams in the world but everyone wants to crucify me. I am a strong man and I'm used to fighting with all my passion and I like winning. When I was linked with the manager's job at Barcelona I didn't say anything. I don't speak about who wants me if I'm happy at Chelsea. I like working with my players and we will succeed. My boss also wants to win. I will be building a team for a year and then handing it over to Ferguson, Eriksson or Graeme Souness.'

He takes one last swipe at his Old Trafford rival. 'Ferguson had to wait seven years before winning his first trophy with United. Slowly, slowly we will start to win things.'

But the Manchester United boss excels at mind games. Says Sir Alex, 'What we've seen so far is a clear indication of how committed they are to turning Chelsea around. It's a declaration of intent, to show they mean business. I'm sure they'll be interested in some of our players – but we are quite good at holding on to them when we want to.'

TUESDAY, 9 SEPTEMBER

Monaco manager and ex-Chelsea midfielder Didier Deschamps emphasises the global interest Chelsea are attracting. 'Everybody is talking about Chelsea and the players at Real Madrid are no different. Everyone is talking about the ambition of this club.

'Chelsea are now a very strong team with a lot of experience; they have a great chance to qualify for the quarter-finals of the Champions League and, if they get to the last eight, they will be capable of making it all the way to the final. It's incredible. I look at the names now – Desailly, Veron, Crespo, Hasselbaink and now Makelele – phew!'

WEDNESDAY, 10 SEPTEMBER

Patrick Vieira is also impressed by Chelsea's capture of Makelele. 'If he settles in well, then they are a team capable of winning the title. They have signed several top-notch players like Juan Sebastian Veron, Hernan Crespo and Claude Makelele and they look like one of the big sides in Europe. But so far, it's just on paper.

'They will have a big problem keeping everyone happy. They have got great players with strong characters, and they will want to play all the time. But the Premiership won't just be about Manchester United, Arsenal and Chelsea. Liverpool and Newcastle will have a say as well, despite the poor starts they have made. Teams also need to go to places like Leicester and win – those are the sorts of games where titles are won and lost.

'I am not worried by Manchester United and Chelsea making all those signings. Our club's bosses have instead opted for stability in giving contract extensions to Titi [Henry], Robert and myself. We have got some good people at the club – just look at our bench with Dennis Bergkamp and Kanu.'

Thierry Henry adds, 'Chelsea are contenders, but I couldn't care less about the recruitment they made. It's not my problem.'

THURSDAY, 11 SEPTEMBER

Ranieri says Abramovich has never doubted his judgement. 'Last June, if a genie had come out of a bottle and told me what would happen at Chelsea in the next few months, I would not have believed him. At the time, I was mainly concerned with finding a way to keep Gianfranco Zola at Stamford Bridge and worrying about how to strengthen the squad for the Champions League with little money available. The last thing I imagined is that someone like Mr Abramovich would materialise out of thin air. I believe he has fallen in love with football and now he wants to know everything about it.'

FRIDAY, 12 SEPTEMBER

The Sun extend their light-hearted £1,000 competition for readers to guess the manager's next team. Ranieri is in a similar mood when he says he doesn't know what his side will be to face Tottenham… and that he will have to ask Sir Alex Ferguson!

Frank Lampard is phlegmatic about the rotation system. 'You've got to look at the bigger picture. If we're successful, we'll play sixty or seventy games, which would be asking a lot of anyone, so you have to knuckle down and work hard and hope you play a big part in Chelsea's success. It's not like any other club.

'You can't think you are a regular going to play all the time, or that you're out of the team and not going to play. The important thing is that people who aren't playing don't sulk because that's really going to be detrimental to the team. Though sometimes you'll get the hump.'

Spurs fans have in the past been the target for anti-Semitic abuse at Chelsea. Now, Chelsea have a Jewish owner. Abramovich's spokesman, John Mann, hopes this will usher in a new era of tolerance. 'I think Chelsea fans are smart enough to understand that anti-Semitism of any kind won't be tolerated no matter who the owner is. It supersedes Roman Abramovich; it is a matter of taste and tolerance.'

Ken Bates, who has worked hard to rid the club of its reputation as a focus for neo-Nazi activists, believes Spurs fans are contributing to the problem. At a UEFA anti-racism conference in March 2002, Bates said, 'It is hard to criticise Chelsea fans for calling Tottenham supporters something that they call themselves.'

Claude Makelele waltzes into Stamford Bridge 15 minutes late for a 3.00pm press call. Ranieri says, 'I have a fantastic watch and every good watch needs a good battery – Claude is the battery for my watch. He will play just in front of the defence and is one of the best in that position. He was one of the top names on the list of players that I wanted to buy. It is also very important to have that link between the left flank, right flank and the middle of the field.'

Makelele will sit out tomorrow's clash with Tottenham.

SATURDAY, 13 SEPTEMBER

CHELSEA 4, TOTTENHAM 2

The revolution is proceeding at such a pace that not even the match-day magazine can keep up. Page ten features a picture of the now ousted Trevor Birch signing Makelele!

Abramovich is afforded another standing ovation by adoring fans before kick-off. Eriksson is again in attendance as Chelsea maintain their unbeaten start. Ranieri begins with only Duff and Mutu of the summer signings, while Makelele and Cole are on the bench. Ranieri is gratified by the sight of Abramovich standing and applauding Mutu, whose two goals take his total to four in his first three games. Hasselbaink contributes the fourth in added time. In between, Lampard, who needs a good performance in front of Eriksson, heads the equaliser.

'It is a spectacular game,' Mutu says afterwards through an interpreter. 'I love it. The atmosphere is fantastic. Very different to Italy. It has been so far, so good. I just hope it can continue. But it is impossible not to play well when you have so many good players around you.'

Spurs are the better side for 40 minutes, leading through Frederic Kanoute, who adds a second with five minutes remaining, but Chelsea deserve the points. Gronkjaer's left-footed cross from the right is headed in at the far post by Lampard and then a delightful, disguised pass from Duff, in behind the Spurs defence, enables Mutu to beat Kasey Keller with a low shot, past the keeper's right hand. Petit, given his first start, takes his chance well and is solidly influential until he gives way to Makelele midway through the second half.

The second half belongs to Chelsea with Duff impressive throughout. Mutu fastens on to a through-pass from substitute Cole and shoots in, right to left.

The same pair combine again five minutes later, when Cole's shot is spilled Keller and Mutu, unaccountably, prods wide of an open goal. It looks like it could be a costly miss when Kanoute scores his second, after 86 minutes. Instead, it is Chelsea who have the last word: Cole and Babayaro combine to set up Hasselbaink six yards out.

Ranieri is pleased with the points, but 'not too happy' with the performance. 'Conceding two goals is not so good,' he says, adding that his team are developing a habit of only starting to play after falling behind.

Mutu limps in at the interval with a bruised ankle. 'I want to continue,' he insists. 'I seem to have picked up a few cuts and bruises but this is just the price you pay for success. Unfortunately, my physique is not exactly made for this tough kind of football.'

Mutu, Duff and eventually Cole are the most skilful artists on view and they are also among the hardest-working. Seeing Mutu putting his ankles in among opposing studs helps the team bond. 'Every time he's come in after a game he has a gash on his body somewhere,' says Cole. 'He has a great attitude and it doesn't bother him.'

Chelsea are steadily developing into a cohesive unit. Ranieri already feels like he has won something. 'I am still here after two months this season, and that is a big trophy for me.'

Team

Cudicini, Babayaro, Desailly, Terry, Melchiot, Gronkjaer (Gallas), Petit (Makelele), Lampard, Duff (Cole), Hasselbaink, Mutu.

SUNDAY, 14 SEPTEMBER

Chelsea are Premiership favourites with the bookmakers! Former Arsenal striker Alan Smith believes Mutu 'will prove to be an absolute sensation'. He predicts, 'By the end of this season he will be up there with the best, alongside Thierry Henry and Ruud van Nistelrooy in the Premiership stratosphere of strikers.' Chelsea's best signing? 'He's got to have a chance – as do Chelsea if they carry on like this.'

MONDAY, 15 SEPTEMBER

Abramovich wants success in the Champions League. 'There are ten or twelve teams who can win the Champions League, and we are one of them.'

Ranieri observes, 'Chelsea are born again, but we now have to become an established team. I remember Valencia got to the final twice in a row, but when you have Real Madrid, Bayern Munich and the Italians, one of them is going to get to arrive at the final. We must work to be a team like those clubs. No matter what competition we're playing in, everyone will want to kill Chelsea. I always have problems, I'm always under pressure, but I like it. The first to put pressure on me is me, because I want the best. My focus is to build a foundation, but if I win something it will be fantastic.'

Flying off for Chelsea's Champions League encounter with Sparta Prague, Makelele, Petit, Gallas and Ambrosio are moved on by a Mrs Mop at Gatwick Airport. They are seated at a table reserved for McDonald's customers in the South Terminal but have not bought anything as they wait for their flight. Petit sheepishly leads the way out, explaining the problem to Makelele who is clearly amused. Meanwhile, Ranieri attempts to take the pressure off his players when he says, 'I have big champions but Sparta are the better team. We just want to compete with them.'

Hernan Crespo trains with his team-mates for just the third time, in the 20,000-capacity Sparta Stadium. It is Makelele's second training session. Will Ranieri play them both? 'It's a risk, isn't it?' he smiles. 'Maybe in one or two years Chelsea will be among the favourites, but at the moment we are simply a curiosity in Europe.'

TUESDAY, 16 SEPTEMBER
SPARTA PRAGUE 0, CHELSEA 1

Sven-Goran Eriksson is pictured at the Bridge while Ranieri is away in Prague! This time he's not there for another meeting with Abramovich, who is also in Prague. The England coach and those not in the squad, such as Mario Stanic, are playing their part in launching a good cause. Ali Abbas, the Iraqi orphan who made the front pages when he was rescued from bombing during the second Gulf War of 2003, meets Eriksson at Stamford Bridge to support a charity event aimed at promoting peace.

Ranieri's starting XI includes seven summer signings, as a cohesive passing game misfires on a cool autumn evening. Sparta's game plan is clearly designed to frustrate and deny time and space, strategies usually employed by the visiting team.

Realising the game isn't going to plan, Ranieri makes radical changes at half-time, abandoning the diamond formation to revert to a conventional 4-4-2. 'I wanted to give Sparta very little space and try to play them on the counter-attack. In the first half, Sparta closed all the space in front of their penalty area with eight players,' explains Ranieri. 'I thought that we'd have more success in the second half with two wide players who could open the door for us. I am such a lucky man to have so many fantastic players. It means I can change my system at any time. We don't have a first XI at Chelsea any more. All the players are in my first team. I would have settled for 0–0 but Gallas sums up the philosophy of this team because they want to win every game. Just before we scored, Gallas lost possession near our goal and I had to shout at him to stay back.'

Ranieri pushes the disappointing Geremi out to the right flank and introduces Duff on the left, but it is the arrival of Lampard in the heart of the midfield that suddenly sparks their passing game into life. Lampard has started all the previous matches and is disappointed to find himself on the bench when Ranieri unveils his side. Terry, Cole, Gronkjaer and Babayaro do not make it either. It won't have improved the England trio's mood to know that assistant coach Tord Grip has been sent to keep an eye on them. But Lampard comes on for the second half, replacing Petit, with Duff coming in for the injured Mutu. It is not a convincing display but the half-time changes improve it and an 85th-minute Gallas goal is enough to give them a winning start to the campaign.

Ranieri is happy with an away win which sets his team up nicely. Of concern is the display of Crespo, who squanders a succession of opportunities on his first start. Veron twice sends his pal clear with only keeper Jaromir Blazek to beat and on both occasions Crespo shoots wide. Another opening provided by the industrious Johnson is chipped half-heartedly at Blazek before Ranieri runs out of patience and replaces Crespo with Hasselbaink.

Makelele makes an impressive debut. 'Too many people who should know have said what an important player Claude is,' says Lampard, 'and he certainly showed glimpses of that. He sweeps up in front of the back four, wins tackles and is clever on the ball without trying anything too drastic. He will be good for someone like me because, when I go forward, he will be the insurance.'

> **Team**
>
> Cudicini, Johnson, Gallas, Desailly, Bridge, Geremi, Makelele, Veron, Petit (Lampard), Crespo (Hasselbaink), Mutu (Duff).

THURSDAY, 18 SEPTEMBER

England international Owen Hargreaves reveals that Chelsea tried to sign him but Bayern Munich rejected the approach. Hargreaves was a possible replacement had the Makelele deal fallen through. He says, 'Bayern told me it wasn't possible. I was quite happy about that because I want to play in this team and they really need me here, but it's good to know that there's a market for me.'

Paul Smith signs up to act as chief executive until the arrival of Peter Kenyon.

Smith observes, 'It's a terrific time to be here. I've been involved in football for about 20 years now, working for FIFA on the World Cup, with UEFA in the European Championship and, more recently, advising some of the European clubs on how to maximise their commercial interests.'

Ken Bates attends a charity dinner at the Galleria for the Matthews Harland Trust, raising £100,000. One of the items auctioned is a night out with Bates!

FRIDAY, 19 SEPTEMBER

'This year Ranieri the psychologist may have more work to do than Ranieri the coach,' says the manager. 'I speak to all of the players and try to be a father to them, to ensure the team functions perfectly as a unit.

'Modern football is a business which looks for profits and nobody is secure here, especially me. Since Roman Abramovich arrived, Chelsea have been under the magnifying glass and the first person to be examined is the coach. As long as things continue to go well, I'm not bothered what people say.

'In any match I can only line up 11 players and the majority of them understand it. The ones who don't should think about switching clubs, because I'm not going to change the formula.'

Desperately short of form, Crespo is suffering from a form of football schizophrenia and is in urgent need of therapy. 'It's true that the club has seen only my useless twin brother so far because my shooting in front of goal all depends on split-second timing and I can't pretend that I've got it right yet. That is why I missed those big, big chances in Prague – but that won't be the norm with me. I promise that when the talented twin of Hernan Crespo comes back – and that will be soon – that I'll score as many goals here as I did with Lazio and Inter.'

On the plus side, Crespo cannot believe the absence of stress and aggression in England. He was used to rioting fans ripping up the training ground at Lazio when they were unhappy with the team, or being pelted with fruit and cans when things went awry at San Siro. 'Claudio Ranieri told me that this was the time to start enjoying my football like I did when I was a 10-year-old boy in the streets of the town in Argentina where I grew up. That was music to my ears because, in Italy, football is regarded as a precise science when nothing should go wrong and footballers must play like machines. Here in England it is still a beautiful game. You live your life on and off the pitch as if football was still a sport, not a duty.'

Next team up is bottom club Wolves searching for their first Premiership win. Ranieri expects a tough game from a defensively-minded side. Geremi is suspended and Mutu rests an ankle injury. Terry, Lampard, Hasselbaink and Gudjohnsen return to the starting line-up. Ranieri's ability to focus his men on the relatively low-key trips will decide whether or not they can be genuine title-contenders. 'If we don't understand how risky this sort of game is for us, we cannot improve. For us these are the matches with more difficulties. We must increase our mentality, our focus, our motivation, this is true. I think we are ready to play against Wolves, I feel this but I want to see it.'

SATURDAY, 20 SEPTEMBER

WOLVES 0, CHELSEA 5

Abramovich is in his regular smart suit with open collar when his wife Irina is overheard outside the Wolves boardroom explaining in English that they do not realise that the club has a strict collar-and-tie policy. The group waits outside the directors' lounge while staff go to find Sir Jack Hayward, who promptly takes his own tie off and invites his Chelsea counterpart in.

Beforehand, the Russian's adviser, Richard Creitzman, makes a rare TV appearance to discuss Ranieri's position. 'We have had no discussions with any other manager here at Chelsea. We are very pleased with the performance he has put in so far, as we are with all the players.'

Abramovich will have to fork out more than £7m if he wants to sack Ranieri, who had a lucrative compensation clause inserted in the new contract handed him by Ken Bates the previous year – and the FA would want a pay-off too if Eriksson was poached.

Chelsea's romp against the bottom club helps. Mutu, Veron and Desailly all have knocks and are left out but, when asked what is wrong with another absentee, Wayne Bridge, Ranieri replies, 'Nothing. At Chelsea we now have 22 champions.'

Crespo takes 80 seconds to score with his first touch to open his account in style. He grabs a second with an equally impressive finish. This is the real Crespo and a tonic for Pini Zahavi who placed a bet with a Chelsea insider immediately after Crespo fluffed his lines in front of goal in midweek that the Argentine would score 25 goals. Crespo comes on in the 65th minute to underline with ruthlessness the colossal gulf in class between the teams, delivering his first Premiership goal with his first touch after being set up by Duff. One minute from time, he rounds off a highly impressive performance by blasting home from Lampard to grab the fifth goal necessary for his side to go temporarily to the top of the league.

But from the 17th minute, when Lampard strikes a superb opener, the result has never been in doubt. Lampard fires home from the edge of the box after a fine set-up by Hasselbaink. He does his future chances no harm when he becomes the club's top scorer with his fifth goal of the season. Duff's third continues to show the amazing strength in depth of a team changed in no fewer than seven places by Ranieri.

The manager plays down going top so early. 'Being top means nothing, not now. Maybe it helps everyone to work better and stay there. We are building.' Meanwhile Wolves' skipper Paul Ince says, 'I'm very disappointed. I don't give a monkey's that Chelsea have spent so much money –we shouldn't be losing 5–0 at home to them.'

Team

Cudicini, Johnson (Huth), Terry, Gallas, Babayaro, Gronkjaer (Cole), Makelele, Lampard, Duff, Hasselbaink (Crespo), Gudjohnsen.

SUNDAY, 21 SEPTEMBER

After all the rumours, Glenn Hoddle is finally sacked at Spurs. Goalkeeper Neil Sullivan has little sympathy for his old boss. 'I am not surprised. He was on borrowed time.'

Trevor Birch has been keeping a low profile but turns up as a speaker at the Euromoney Seminars football finance conference. He says, 'It remains to be seen whether the publicity generated by Mr Abramovich leads to other incredibly rich people moving into the game. You certainly can't rely on it as an economic model ... It's fundamentally flawed because any significant revenue enhancement goes in player salaries. I remain to be convinced about the concept of global brands.'

Embarrassingly, Birch's identity badge still refers to him as Chelsea's chief executive. He declines to answer questions about his departure from the club. But he does say that, despite Abramovich's fortune, Chelsea could suffer a financial slump if salaries are not controlled and the owners lose interest.

MONDAY, 22 SEPTEMBER

England captain David Beckham joins the persistent debate over Eriksson's future but is non-committal. 'I am sure it annoys him more than it annoys me but we will have to wait and see what happens.'

Eriksson himself says, 'Maybe one day I would go back to club football. First, I would like to finish the job I have because I am extremely proud. We have a big game against Turkey and, hopefully, we will do well in Euro 2004. Then, one day, back to club football – but where I don't know. Football is not like other work. You can't ask for work. There must be an offer.'

Ranieri has a mandate from the board to fulfil everyone's aspirations. He dare not fail, though. As he admits, 'It would be a dream to win the Champions League this season and it is not impossible for us to do it. All of my players are really motivated because they know there is a big chance to do big things in the Premiership and Europe. But first we have to build the team. We are like a baby; first we will start to walk on our hands and knees, then we will walk like a little boy, then afterwards like a man and then, finally, we will be running.

'I know last season we started very well; in December we were second in the table behind Arsenal, but I was playing always with the same team. And at the end of the season we were very tired. Now I can give some rest to everybody and at the end of the season everyone is fresh. I explained everything and they are happy, they understand it's a new reality; Chelsea is a new team. We want to compete in every match, FA Cup, league, for us everything is three points. That is what's important.'

TUESDAY, 23 SEPTEMBER

The first few weeks have been tricky for Crespo. 'The language, culture, food, training methods and playing style are all very different to Argentina and Italy, so it is going to take me a while to adapt to my new surroundings. Seba [Veron] has been helping me a lot and we speak every day, which is a great support. We sometimes recall how Osvaldo Ardiles and Ricardo Villa came to London to sign for Spurs, and we discuss how much we would love to become legends like them.

'Serie A gives you the best possible grounding, because you have to be strong to survive there. I wouldn't say that life in the Premiership is in any way easy, but it is a lot more approachable, both on and off the field. Not only are training sessions never interrupted by angry and sometimes violent fans, but Sunday afternoons can be spent walking through parks or visiting museums without being harassed. The lifestyle here is totally different.'

Crespo is looking forward to playing against his former club Lazio. 'The chance of playing in the Olympic Stadium is going to help me do well. I can't wait to go back, although I am even happier for my wife, because she's originally from Rome and is keen to do some shopping there again.'

Crespo says he will not be indulging in any retail therapy himself. 'There is no need, because I have only just swapped my football boots. I used to wear white ones in Italy, but felt that I needed a change to mark my arrival in England properly, so that's why I put on a grey pair at Wolves. I think it has done the trick.'

WEDNESDAY, 24 SEPTEMBER

Adrian Mutu is acclaimed the best of the new signings so far by team-mate Mario Melchiot. 'All of the players Chelsea have signed this season are very good footballers, but for me Adrian has had the most special start. He looks such a clever player. Adrian is only young but on the pitch he acts like a man. He isn't scared of anything and he fights hard too.'

Mutu has adapted fast to the English game, with four goals in as many Premiership matches. 'Playing in Italy was a great experience. You come away knowing you are a better player than when you arrived. I never came here with a game plan about how I'd adapt – I just went out and played the only way I knew how. And I think my game suits English football.

'You know it's going to be tough when you look at the size of players you are up against. I'm not the best-built lad and maybe I'm just paying the price for being brave when I shouldn't. But if that's the price you pay for success then I'm OK with that.'

The club take 19-year-old Brazilian centre-half Gustavo De Araujo on a four-month loan, and he scores for the reserves in a 2–0 win over Nottingham Forest. Chelsea also hijack a double deal for top Nigerian starlets Jon Mikel and Promise Isaac after Manchester United fly the pair in to sign for them. But, after a couple of days at their Carrington HQ, the African kids head off for Chelsea instead. The Nigerian prospects were watched in the World Youth Championships in Finland. The only snag is where to put Mikel and Isaac for the next couple of years while they wait for work-permit qualification. They have their eyes on a 'partner' arrangement in Belgium. Chelsea are also in competition with United for American whizzkid Freddy Adu.

THURSDAY, 25 SEPTEMBER

Abramovich is set to extend his sporting empire by buying a Canadian ice hockey club. He is reported to be in negotiations with senior figures at National Hockey League side Vancouver Canucks.

UEFA chief executive Gerhard Aigner warns that buying too many stars will stifle home-grown youngsters. 'We can now have a world select team and nobody can do anything about it. Somebody can buy a team and suddenly they can be a candidate to win the Champions League. I don't think football should be about that. We must have a rule where the clubs have to field players they have educated themselves, which allows clubs who are working well with youngsters to compete.'

Bayern Munich chief executive Uli Hoeness voices his fears too. 'A club must live with its own sources of money. I am watching the developments at Chelsea with a degree of concern. We will need to observe this new mode of financing carefully. After all, we are talking about a club that is quoted on the Stock Exchange [Chelsea have in fact been delisted].'

In Madrid, Raul insists he is not interested in Chelski's cash. He says, 'I am never going to leave Real Madrid because of money. I am in the team and enjoying myself.' Can it be that Chelsea are becoming as 'unpopular' as Manchester United? Damien Duff explains, 'I get the impression people want us to slip up. We're the men with all the money, and if you have loads of money, people want you to do bad. That's the way it is in life. We have to be strong and stick together, I suppose. Chelsea have been up there for some time, top three, top four, but they haven't had that extra bit of quality to get into the top two. Maybe it's just a feeling we have, but the manager is always saying it, too: "They all want to beat you because you're the big shots, the fancy boys from London."

'I'm just a big kid at heart. When we signed Veron and Crespo, I'm like "Whooaa!" To me, it's just a big buzz. I can't let it overawe me. That's what I did for the first couple of years in the Irish team – took me two years to get going. Learnt from that, and I've felt at home here.'

The £70,000 Duff earns a week is much better than the £30,000 he got at Blackburn. 'I get paid on the last Thursday of every month, from there my mam looks after it. If I need anything, I just go and take it out of the machine on the wall. That's how it works. I don't go around flashing the cash, that's not me. I came here for ridiculous money, I get paid ridiculous money. It's the job I'm in, it's not my fault. I didn't ask for the game to be like this. I play because I love the game. That, and the fact that it's the only thing I'm good at. You turn the money over to your mam and I don't ask her what she does with it. I like to think she has a good head on her. I mean, she is my ma.'

FRIDAY, 26 SEPTEMBER

On the Jewish New Year, a list of the top 20 most influential Jewish people is published by the *Jewish Chronicle*. It includes Abramovich as well as Nigella Lawson and the country's best-connected lifestyle guru, controversial Carole Caplin. It cannot find room for such luminaries as Philip Roth, Henry Kissinger, Steven Spielberg and Eli Wiesel, the Nobel Peace Prize winner.

Ranieri is shocked at the FA charge sheet after the mayhem at Manchester United's clash with Arsenal at Old Trafford, where all hell breaks loose as the game reaches its climax. 'I always, always tell my players the referee is always, always right.' Chelsea have had just six players sent off in the Premiership since Ranieri took charge three years ago.

For tomorrow's game against Aston Villa, Chelsea welcome back Mutu, Veron and Desailly from injury. Ranieri has a full-strength squad for the first time so some of his big names will not even make the bench. 'I can choose from all my players. This week has been fantastic; every second of every session was amazing because of the sheer talent on view, their strong mentality. And they want to improve. All my players have showed me how much they want to play.'

Villa haven't won away from home in the league. Ranieri is also keen to find out how his team react when the going gets tough. 'When a team wins they are all singing. I want to see how they react when we lose. I hope that doesn't happen for a thousand years. We conceded a goal against Leicester and our reaction was very strong. After we did the same against Tottenham, it was the same response.'

SATURDAY, 27 SEPTEMBER

CHELSEA 1, ASTON VILLA 0

Hasselbaink's sixth goal puts Chelsea a point behind the leaders with a game in hand. When Villa manager David O'Leary was at Leeds United, the Dutchman deserted him to seek his fortune overseas four seasons ago. Now he is the match-winner.

O'Leary says he might have known it would be Hasselbaink who would wreck his plans. 'We got £12m for him in one big bundle when he left Leeds. Jimmy was always a great scorer. I didn't sell him because he wasn't getting goals.' Ranieri says, 'Jimmy is one of the best strikers. In every league he plays in he scores a lot of goals.'

Hasselbaink himself says, 'There was a lot of talk about me going, but I never had any doubts that I wanted to stay. I am very happy here because Chelsea are winning and I am fitter than ever.'

Eriksson is again at the Bridge. 'We don't need Eriksson,' chant the fans yet again and follow it with a pro-Ranieri rhyme. The Italian even gets the chairman's dreaded vote of confidence in Ken Bates's programme notes.

Ranieri make sfive changes; he has now used 23 players in six Premiership matches. With a tough Champions League clash coming up, Crespo, Terry, Babayaro, Gronkjaer, Makelele and Gudjohnsen are all rested. Lampard remains an ever-present in the Premiership, a distinction he shares only with Cudicini. Johnson stays in and is again outstanding. After buying him, Chelsea thought about loaning him back to West Ham for the season. That plan, though, was scuppered when the manager saw him in training.

Hasselbaink confounds all those who thought he was a spent force. Veron's one telling contribution comes in the build-up with a tackle that sees the ball fly to Mutu. The Romanian's pass to Lampard is instant, the shot crisp and Hasselbaink mops up Thomas Sorensen's spillage. Cole replaces the disappointing Veron as Lampard continues to be the most consistent midfielder. The only time the fans cheer Veron is when Ranieri puts him out of his misery and subs him. In six games, Veron has been tried on the left of midfield, in the middle and now wide on the right. If Mutu's radar had been more finely tuned, this would have been over before half-time. Twice he is through, racing on to perfect passes from Lampard and Petit but the chances are squandered.

O'Leary says, 'I mean no disrespect to Chelsea, but they were the luckiest team today. Great credit to the lads but the bottom line is we got nothing out of the game.' When it is put to him that O'Leary thinks his team very lucky, Ranieri is in agreement. 'Yes, it's true. They deserved a draw.'

Team

Cudicini, Johnson, Gallas, Desailly, Bridge, Veron (Cole), Lampard, Petit (Makelele), Duff, Mutu (Gronkjaer), Hasselbaink.

SUNDAY, 28 SEPTEMBER

Former World Footballer of the Year Rivaldo issues a 'come and get me' plea to Chelsea. 'At Chelsea it would be very easy for me to fit in quickly because there are already so many stars.' The Chelsea players pin a cheeky message to the dressing room door, reading, 'Sorry, we're full.' They need not have worried. Rivaldo's representatives had made contact but there was no interest.

MONDAY, 29 SEPTEMBER

Rivaldo repeats his message that Chelsea is the club he wants to join. 'Chelsea is interested in me, I know that, although I've been told not to say anything more about a transfer at the moment.' Richard Creitzman comments, 'We seem to get linked with every big-name player who wants to move. We will always be interested in signing good players, but not just because one of them asks.'

Manchester City and Middlesbrough both want £5m-rated Eidur Gudjohnsen. But he is desperate to stay and Ranieri wants to keep him. Dutchman Winston Bogarde is relegated once more to training with the reserves and the youth team. 'I haven't been training with the first-team group in recent weeks, which has been frustrating. There are several experienced first-team players at Chelsea that aren't involved at the moment but I am the only one that is with the kids. I am still a Chelsea player and there have been no talks between myself and the club to change that.'

TUESDAY, 30 SEPTEMBER

Ranieri describes himself as Michelangelo, carving impressive footballing figures from promising blocks of marble. 'I feel like Michelangelo. If the marble is good, then fantastic, then I can improve the player. Lampard is a fantastic player. He was always a potential champion, but I had to chip away at the marble and improve him so that all the little things would work and make him an even better player. Now you see what I was doing. It has been a fantastic experience for Frank and the other young players like him.'

Lampard says, 'For two years he has kept on at me about defensive duties and I appreciate that and I am a lot more aware of them than I was as a West Ham player. It makes your whole game stronger. Something Claudio said, which I didn't realise at first but now I believe is true, is that if you go forward a few less times during a game into the opposition area it is more of a surprise to them. If you can show the quality when you get into those areas, that is what makes the best players dangerous. The best in the world, someone like Michael Ballack, show real quality when they arrive and that is something I have tried to add to my game.'

There are now 16 different nationalities in the squad. Ranieri, who still uses an interpreter to help him during press conferences, admits he deliberately tries to confuse the opposition. 'When I'm on the bench I try to speak another language to my players so the other manager can't understand my orders. But that won't help me against Besiktas because I know their coach Mircea Lucescu very well and he speaks all my languages.

'Lucescu likes his teams to go forward with purpose. He's a clever manager who knows tactics very well. For Besiktas, it is very important not to lose, but with their personality and their experience they will try to win. I believe however, they will defend and try to counter-attack us. They will know that, following their defeat by Lazio, another defeat would probably finish their Champions League hopes.'

2003

October

DEFEAT IN THE CHAMPIONS LEAGUE –
THE FIRST LOSS IN TEN GAMES

Real Madrid's Ronaldo is keeping an eye on events at Stamford Bridge. 'I am following Chelsea's progress. I hope things work out for them because if the investment they have had goes well then other people will want to put money into the game. I don't think of them as a threat to us yet. They still have to find their level, but they will be in the same position as Real Madrid at some point.'

Acting chief executive Paul Smith gives an insight into the level of interest in team affairs taken by Abramovich. 'Roman has full confidence in Claudio. He is getting more and more interested in the mechanics of the team and he has briefings from Claudio on the tactics. He does not interfere. He is just interested.'

Smith insists that reports which continue to link Sven-Goran Eriksson with the job at Stamford Bridge are unfounded. 'At the moment from Chelsea's perspective, Claudio is certainly the number one man and he has the full

Pos	Team	P	W	D	L	GF	GA	GD	PTS
1	Arsenal	7	5	2	0	14	5	9	17
2	Chelsea	6	5	1	0	16	6	10	16
3	Manchester United	7	5	1	1	13	3	10	16
4	Birmingham City	6	4	2	0	8	2	6	14
5	Manchester City	7	3	3	1	14	8	6	12
6	Southampton	7	3	3	1	8	4	4	12
7	Fulham	6	3	2	1	13	9	4	11
8	Liverpool	7	3	2	2	11	7	4	11
9	Portsmouth	7	2	3	2	9	7	2	9
10	Everton	7	2	2	3	12	11	1	8

PREMIERSHIP TABLE – OCTOBER

confidence of everybody at the club. There is no internal pressure for Claudio to produce that [the Premiership title] this season. But there is a general expectation that Chelsea will win the Premiership in the foreseeable future.'

As for when Peter Kenyon will end his gardening leave and take his place as chief executive, he says, 'It's something we have got to work out with United. But the likelihood is that he will join us after the transfer window closes in January. He should certainly have a good lawn by then!'

Oleg Deripaska, the joint owner with Abramovich of aluminium company Rusal, arrives by private jet in Farnborough on the morning of the Champions League match against Besiktas. He has come to set the seal on a deal to buy half of Abramovich's stake in Rusal for around £1.38bn in cash, leaving Deripaska with 75 per cent of the second-largest aluminium producer in the world.

Ahead of going to Stamford Bridge, Deripaska sits in London's Savoy Hotel and spells out his grand ambition – to be Russia's Rockefeller. Deripaska, a boyish 35-year-old, exchanges the traditional Russian businessman's end-of-deal poem with Abramovich, which roughly translates as, 'more pies and doughnuts, less black eyes and bruises'.

'Three years ago Roman bought his stake [in Rusal] from Transworld for $540m,' an aide says. 'Now it's worth upwards of $2bn.'

WEDNESDAY, 1 OCTOBER

CHELSEA 0, BESIKTAS 2

Up until now Ranieri has tinkered with the team rather than the system but now he changes both. He opts for a back three in the first half and Besiktas take full advantage to go two goals up. Ranieri reverts to a back four at the interval and brings off Crespo and Mutu when he needs goals!

Two first-half goals from Sergen Yalcin seal Chelsea's fate. The worst thing is that Chelsea crash to defeat against a side which has striker Ilhan Mansiz bizarrely sent off five minutes after half-time for two time-wasting incidents.

Around 8,000 fans stay away on a drizzly evening and will be glad to have missed a harsh lesson in Champions League football. Besiktas, who lost 2–0 at home to Lazio in their opening group match, soak up some early pressure before opening the scoring after 24 minutes when Chelsea slumber at a free-kick and a cross from the left ends with Yalcin poking the ball home off Terry. Five minutes later, Oscar Cordoba thunders a long kick downfield, Desailly slips and Cudicini flaps while Yalcin can't believe his luck as he slips the ball into an empty net.

Chelsea are given a helping hand by Mansiz, who is booked in the first half for kicking the ball away and then, unbelievably, does exactly the same thing five minutes into the second half, to be given his marching orders. Chelsea's best chance after that is a Veron header which flashes wide of an upright, but their hopes of recovery are not helped by an injury to Gallas, which reduces him to the role of passenger.

Ranieri replaces the injured Babayaro with Bridge and makes two other substitutions at half-time, with Duff and Hasselbaink replacing Crespo and Mutu. Ranieri wants to widen out the game and there are more crosses from both flanks in the second half but no goals.

At the end of the game, Abramovich comes into the dressing room to console the team. Ranieri refuses to accept his tinkering is to blame for defeat. 'It is easy to second-guess after the match but I did what I thought was right. We made mistakes and in the Champions League if you make mistakes, you concede a goal 99 per cent of the time. My players tried everything to get a draw, but we faced an organised team who closed down all space in the second half. It was difficult to create chances and whenever we shot we had a wall in front of us.' The only plus is that Lazio are held 2–2 by Sparta Prague. Ranieri says, 'I still feel good and I still feel confident. The group is wide open.'

Besiktas coach Mircea Lucescu suggests Chelsea are less of a unified team than they were last season. 'Their new players are not integrated yet and it showed,' he says.

> **Team**
>
> Cudicini, Babayaro (Bridge), Makelele, Desailly, Mutu (Duff), Lampard, Gallas, Geremi, Veron, Crespo (Hasselbaink), Terry.

THURSDAY, 2 OCTOBER

Criticism is predictable, focusing on Chelsea's rotation system and the selection of 23 players so far compared to 19 at Manchester United. There are suggestions Ranieri changed the formation to accommodate Veron. Ranieri is under pressure to give the new signings their opportunity. Hence his promise that Joe Cole will soon be given his first start. Last Friday Chelsea TV asked viewers to name the team they thought Ranieri would select for the following day's game against Aston Villa. Nobody got it right. Nobody really knows who is playing until Ranieri convenes a team meeting two hours before kick-off.

FRIDAY, 3 OCTOBER

Abramovich has bought one of London's most sumptuous properties, spending £28m on an imposing six-storey classical house in Eaton Square, part of the estate of the Duke of Westminster. His new neighbours will include Charles Saatchi and his wife Nigella Lawson, Jimmy Choo shoe empire chief Tamara Mellon, Leonora Countess of Lichfield, and Princess Alexandra's brother-in-law James Ogilvy.

Abramovich is advising a 74-year-old pensioner to seek the advice of a solicitor because he is stubbornly refusing to sell the 100 shares he owns in Chelsea Village. Abramovich is offering Alex Malcolm £35 for his shares and is entitled to do so because, having acquired the vast majority of Chelsea shares, he can now use Section 429 of the Companies Act 1985 to force any reluctant shareholders to sell at a price he names.

'I paid £120 for them,' says Mr Malcolm. 'I hear that Mr Abramovich made £500m in just one deal. Now he's forcing me to sell my shares for 35 quid! It's like daylight robbery. And, after all the money he's spent on players, it's very insulting.' Mr Malcolm has been fighting to keep his shares since a letter arrived at his home in August from Richard Creitzman, explaining that he had six weeks to go to court to stop Abramovich seizing his stake.

'I'm not giving in but I simply cannot afford to go to court,' Mr Malcolm says. 'I was at Stamford Bridge long before Mr Abramovich was born. I was at Chelsea just after the War, when the first Russians arrived. I was in a crowd of more than 100,000 for the game against Moscow Dynamo. I'm prepared to do only one deal with Mr Abramovich, which will guarantee that I can stay part of Chelsea for the rest of my life. I will compromise if he offers two season tickets for life. And I mean, for life. Somehow, though, I suspect the price might be too high even for Mr Abramovich.'

SATURDAY, 4 OCTOBER

Ranieri is confident that whatever team he selects for the next league match, the players will demonstrate their characters. 'I am sure that we will show a good reaction at Middlesbrough. We did not play that badly in the first half against Besiktas and had chances to go in front. This was only our first defeat after 10 matches.'

Marcel Desailly reckons the fans had better get used to rotation. 'The best XI for Ranieri is the best that he sees in training during the week. Even if you have a good game during the weekend, he will not put you in the side if he feels there is another player who can do better next time. There will never ever be a best XI for the manager this season. Collectively, we are not at the level of Manchester United or Arsenal. Not yet.'

Adrian Mutu pledges to lift his shirt the next time he scores to reveal the message 'Who cares about Romania?', echoing UEFA's 'We care about football' slogan. 'Mutu will wear the shirt in the next few games and will reveal the message every time he scores,' says Costin Stucan, editor of *Gazeta Sporturilor* in Romania, founder of the 'Who cares' campaign. The campaign is in response to what *Gazeta* see as the 'marginalisation of Romanian national teams in terms of refereeing' after a series of decisions apparently went against them in Euro 2004 qualifying. The Romanian team will wear the T-shirt when they play Japan in a friendly in Bucharest tomorrow week. FIFA and UEFA have banned such messages, but the FA takes a 'sensible' line. If the match officials fail to caution Mutu, then the FA will certainly charge him and warn him that if he continues to defy the rules he will face a ban.

Mutu has made an immediate impact with four goals in as many league appearances. Dubbed 'the Brilliance' since his early days at Dinamo Bucharest, the Chelsea boys named him Puff Daddy after one of Mutu's musical heroes. Separation from his son, Mario, continues to be great pain. 'I miss him so much but now that I've been to see him I'm ready for the game against Middlesbrough. It was only for a few hours but I gave him a little Chelsea kit so he can think of me while I'm playing. I have asked my boy's nanny to dress him in the kit I gave him when I play. I know he will be with me whenever I play for Chelsea. We will be together out there on the pitch.'

Zenden can't play for Middlesbrough against Chelsea following a stipulation at the time the loan deal was agreed. Manager Steve McClaren warns, 'They won't be happy about defeat against Besiktas; there will be anger and they will be desperate to put things right. There could be a backlash.'

SUNDAY, 5 OCTOBER

MIDDLESBROUGH 1, CHELSEA 2

Crespo's winner two minutes from time leaves Chelsea a point behind Arsenal with a game in hand. In a mostly one-sided first half, Duff creates Chelsea's opening goal after Lampard has seized the ball from George Boateng with a brutally effective challenge. The ball is threaded through to Gudjohnsen, who has the time, space and confidence to beat Mark Schwarzer. Until Szilard Nemeth drives home an equaliser precisely 19 seconds after the restart, it seems Chelsea are in command with Duff and Gronkjaer given a free hand on either flank. Boro have not won so much as a corner, let alone forced Cudicini into a save. But they are transformed by Gaizka Mendieta. His run absorbs the attentions of three defenders, and a beautifully measured pass finds Nemeth, who scores the equaliser.

Ranieri has made seven changes to the team and reverts to a back four. Makelele and Lampard form a central midfield that is rock-like – with Makelele making vital interceptions and Lampard a series of foraging runs. Huth starts his first game and his inexperience becomes increasingly apparent. The cannonball free-kicks cannot mask his defensive failings and he is to blame for Nemeth's equaliser. Bridge is regularly bamboozled by Mendieta in the second half, while Johnson also shows defensive weaknesses.

Crespo, part of £45m worth of talent on Ranieri's bench, has been, according to his manager, operating at '60 per cent capacity', unused to the rhythm of the English game. Mutu and Cole play the final 12 minutes, Crespo comes on for Hasselbaink at half-time and misses one glaring opportunity, driving the ball squarely into Schwarzer's face when through on goal. But two minutes from time, after Duff crosses to the far post, he manages to convert from a far tighter angle. At the end, Gudjohnsen is first from the dug-out area to congratulate Crespo. Gudjohnsen has been substituted 12 minutes from time despite opening the scoring. If he feels aggrieved, he isn't showing it as he hugs the Argentinian.

Afterwards Ranieri is cautious. 'The table says we are a point behind them but we are not close to Arsenal or Manchester United in reality. We are working to close the gap but we still need time. We are not used to coping when something strange happens. When Middlesbrough had us under pressure, we had to be calm and close down spaces. When Arsenal played Liverpool in the last five minutes, they kept possession. We wanted to score a third goal and almost let Middlesbrough back in. We have a good fighting spirit but we must improve our patience and our tactics. Arsenal or United know how to slow the tempo down; they have a maturity which we don't yet have. My players never thought it was too easy out there but we suffered a lot after conceding that goal.'

Middlesbrough manager McClaren says, 'The result was a travesty of justice. I don't think you'll see any team dominate Chelsea as we did in the second half. I couldn't see Chelsea scoring again after we equalised. Yet that's what happens when you play against a top-quality team. You only have to look at their bench. They have players there who can come on and turn a game.'

Team

Cudicini, Johnson, Terry, Huth, Bridge, Gronkjaer (Cole), Lampard, Makelele, Duff, Gudjohnsen (Mutu), Hasselbaink (Crespo).

MONDAY, 6 OCTOBER

Mario Melchiot is working out at home to revive his first-team chances, frustrated at the elevation of newcomer Glen Johnson. The Dutchman explains, 'There is no way I'm giving up on a first-team place and I'll battle as hard as possible to get it back again. I'm actually doing extra training in my spare time, so that when my chance comes I grab it. I'm fired up to show I'm ready to do a job for Chelsea when they need me. For those people who are asking why I'm not playing at the moment, I'm afraid you will have to ask the coach because I don't have an answer.'

Veron is also on an intensive fitness programme. He takes advantage of a free international week to regain the physical condition he was in when he inspired Lazio to the Italian title in 2000. Veron blames Manchester United's pre-season for the dismal start to his Chelsea career. He says, 'I talked to the manager and I explained to him that the best thing I can do was to stop playing in the first team so that I could train and get back to my best physical condition. Remember I did not make pre-season training with Chelsea and now I want to put myself right so that I can play regularly. Ranieri told me he understood and we came to an agreement. There are no problems between us. I believe I will play next Tuesday against Birmingham. I do not know if I will be in my best condition, but I will perform much better.'

Steve Bruce insists Birmingham are keen to sign Mikael Forssell permanently next summer providing they retain their Premiership status. But Forssell remains determined to make an impression at Chelsea. 'I have just signed a four-year contract with Chelsea and I want to show at Stamford Bridge what I'm capable of.'

TUESDAY, 7 OCTOBER

Houllier is concerned that training sessions for England are being used as opportunities to recruit players for Chelsea. He phoned Eriksson during the summer, alarmed that stories had circulated linking Gerrard with a transfer to Stamford Bridge. When asked if he is nervous about releasing his players to join the England squad for the Euro 2004 qualifier with Turkey, Houllier responds, 'Stevie wants to stay here.'

Ranieri insists he has a good relationship with Eriksson. 'I am very good friends with Sven and we laughed together when the story appeared. There is no problem between us. Sven calls me up to talk about my players – Joe Cole, John Terry, Frank Lampard and Wayne Bridge – as any England manager would. I have known him from when he was in Italy and we have a lot of respect for each other.'

Ranieri believes Sir Alex Ferguson may have tried to cash in on his situation. 'Maybe it was true that he was offered my job but I don't know when this happened. It could have been any time in the past. The point is he spoke out at the time he was renegotiating his contract.'

WEDNESDAY, 8 OCTOBER

Emmanuel Petit blasts Arsenal's behaviour in the match against Manchester United which has led to six players being charged by the FA. Arsenal and

Chelsea go head-to-head at Highbury in 11 days time and Petit is sure to face a hostile reception after his outspoken attack.

Petit declares, 'What happened in Arsenal's game at United was uncalled for. We have a squad of great quality. Since the start of the season we have won eight times, drawn once and lost once. All that is still missing is for us to all be on the same wavelength. We need some leaders to assert themselves. It is difficult when you put so many stars together in a team. But everything is going well for us so far. The manager rotates up to six or seven players every game – he tries to keep everyone happy and we all want to play our games. I have played in five matches out of nine and I am happy with that. I am not worried about the competition, it gives our squad a boost. When you've got as big a fortune as Roman Abramovich, you could end up squandering it all. He is a charming, calm and discreet individual, who exudes great self-control and tries to keep his enthusiasm in check. But once he's in the stands, he'll let himself go. He is a passionate guy and he's taking his first steps in the football world.'

Jimmy Floyd Hasselbaink is assaulted in Mayfair club Funky Buddha at 3.15am after refusing to sign an autograph. But Hasselbaink has changed his ways on the field. 'I knew that this year was going to be important for me because I want to go to the European Championship. Last year was a really difficult year for me. [This year] I came back from a really nasty injury and then I had a really good pre-season. Even in my holidays I was training for myself and I think I have benefited from that point. If my football is better from that I don't know, but I definitely feel better inside and that helps.'

Hasselbaink turned down a lucrative offer to end his playing career in Abu Dhabi. After being left out for the first game and a half, he came on at Liverpool and scored the winner. His celebration was a clear release of emotion. 'Everybody was speculating that I was going and I had to go. I wanted to fight for my place. Now that there's been a lot of signings, it makes it a little more exciting for me. I was just really happy that I scored and that it went in and that we won. We got the three points and our start was really good. That was the most important thing.'

THURSDAY, 9 OCTOBER

Ranieri has never won a championship in his managerial career and George Graham believes he won't break his duck this season. Graham, who guided Arsenal to two titles, believes Ranieri makes too many changes. 'Claudio has been with big clubs on the continent and won the Spanish Cup with Valencia and the Italian Cup with Fiorentina. But he has not won a championship. Claudio is making an awful number of changes, but he is also changing the system of play and I don't think that adheres to consistency. You don't get the continuity you need to win championships. You have to have a core of the team and your best players playing in every game.'

Club doctor Neil Frazer hopes that William Gallas will be in the reckoning against Birmingham. 'We were quite worried about him obviously when he came off the pitch in the Besiktas game. He had an MRI scan and an X-ray, which were not terribly helpful in telling us whether he'd got a very small crack or not. He had another investigation, a bone scan, on Monday, and that showed essentially that he hasn't got a crack. He's got quite nasty bruising to the outside of his fibula bone, and we're hoping that with treatment that's going to get better quite rapidly, and that he'll be in the picture for Birmingham.'

Gallas was not happy to stay on the pitch against Besiktas. 'I did what I was told without thinking but it was stupid. I don't know if Ranieri took a calculated risk but I could have really made the injury a lot worse.'

Meanwhile Carlton Cole is back for treatment on his hip injury; he has not played for Charlton since August.

FRIDAY, 10 OCTOBER

Eriksson stonewalls at the press conference before the England–Turkey game in Istanbul and leaves it to his agent to deny reports of an imminent move to Chelsea. His business manager Athole Still insists that he has had no discussions with Abramovich. The FA makes a valiant attempt to steer talk towards football matters after a week of turmoil over Rio Ferdinand's missed drugs test.

Eriksson says, 'If you take the position I had one week ago, nothing has changed between then and today. I think we shouldn't talk about that the day before we play Turkey. I never said I should go. Should I always tell you the same thing? Nothing has changed.'

Vincenzo Morabito, who brokered the deal to take Ranieri to Chelsea, believes Abramovich must make a public statement. Morabito says, 'A club like Chelsea has a duty to protect its manager and its players. All these rumours can be killed by one show of support. And that needs to come from Mr Abramovich. He needs to say, "Claudio Ranieri is our manager. We have complete faith in him. He knows his targets and we support him in his pursuit of those targets." Sven should have ended this whole thing out of respect for a colleague.'

As the England Under-21s lose 1–0 in Turkey, Glen Johnson is sent off five minutes from time after being booked twice in quick succession. Coach David Platt says,

'Glen is a winner. He is a Premiership player with Chelsea and will be playing in some very big games. I have spoken to him and he needs to learn to channel his desire to win. He wasn't malicious, he was just looking for something extra in his game.'

SATURDAY, 11 OCTOBER

After the goalless draw in Istanbul which takes England through to Euro 2004, Eriksson finally gives an assurance that he will still be in charge for the finals. Eriksson says, 'Nothing has changed and you must believe me.' Probed again, however, he replies, 'As the situation is today, then yes.' When pressed even further on the subject, he finally responds with a simple 'Yes'.

SUNDAY, 12 OCTOBER

John Terry enters the managerial debate. 'Sven is doing a great job with England and Claudio is fantastic at Chelsea. I would like it to continue that way for the foreseeable future. I have a lot to learn regarding England but I was happy with my game. All that I can do now is to keep playing well for Chelsea. Rio is a good defender and will be back before long. It was good to play alongside Sol Campbell. It's the second time I've played with him for England and it was brilliant. I'm obviously very proud to be in the [European] Championship next year, it is a big thing, it was obviously one of my biggest games.'

The focus has been on Ferdinand and Terry admits, 'I was a little bit annoyed, but at the same time I knew that I was going to be playing and was looking forward to the game. I knew all along Rio wasn't going to come and it was going to be my big chance. It was a big test for me, a chance for me to go out there and prove to a few people that I deserve a chance for England and I think I played well. It gives Mr Eriksson a difficult decision but I know deep down who is first choice and when I come in I've got to take the chance and maybe give him a little bit of food for thought next time.'

MONDAY, 13 OCTOBER

A point at St Andrews will mean Chelsea leap-frog Arsenal in the table. Marcel Desailly says, 'If we win at Birmingham that would be great because if we go to Arsenal as Premiership leaders that will give us a psychological advantage.'

Cudicini jokes, 'It's been a rubbish start to the season, really, 11 games, and 9 wins! We could have done better definitely! No, I think it's been a great start to the season definitely, apart from the game against Besiktas. Otherwise, we've been fantastic.'

Ranieri keeps Terry in the side to face Birmingham three days after his heroics in Istanbul and decides to pair him with Gallas, as Desailly hasn't fully recovered. Neither played for France as coach Jacques Santini decided to rest them. Mutu scored his seventh goal in six internationals for Romania against Japan on Saturday.

Birmingham manager Steve Bruce says, 'It is a huge test for us because Claudio Ranieri has built up a squad which is quite staggering. Chelsea gave us one of our biggest hidings at Stamford Bridge last season but we have come on.'

TUESDAY, 14 OCTOBER

BIRMINGHAM CITY 0, CHELSEA 0

Abramovich congratulates his players in the dressing room on leading the pack. Wayne Bridge says, 'He told us how proud he was that we were top of the Premiership. The lads are grateful for his support. If we are in this position and everyone is still telling us it takes time for players to gel, then the future is looking good for us.'

Chelsea last led the Premiership under Gianluca Vialli back in January 1999, eventually finishing third. This point takes them above Arsenal on goal difference and sets up a Highbury humdinger between the two unbeaten London giants. Ranieri insists, 'Being top now is not important, it's too soon to talk about that. Yes, I'm pleased. But what matters is being top next May. What happens in training is more important than looking at the table. We just have to keep working and improving our performances. I was pleased with the performance against Birmingham. It was very difficult for us as they played very deep. It's important to play well against Arsenal and put in another good performance.'

Ranieri mixes up his team again under the eagle eye of Eriksson. He leaves Duff on the bench, so Cudicini and Lampard are the only ever-presents in his starting line-up in the league. Joe Cole replaces the Irishman for his first Premiership start after seven successive appearances as a substitute. Playing behind the front two, Cole takes his chance well and produces a fine array of passes before he is replaced by Duff with 25 minutes left. In another example of Ranieri's tactical perversity, Duff is instructed to take Cole's place in central midfield, but he finds himself sliding towards his preferred position on the left flank. Duff's introduction at least manages to spring Lampard into life and Birmingham are hanging on by the end. 'He played very well,' Ranieri says of Cole. 'Joe knows he is my key to open the door. We aren't used to playing with one player behind the strikers, but I will try it again.'

On the debit side, Desailly's sore back is still giving him problems, while

Gallas, who was named on the teamsheet, aggravates an ankle injury in the warm-up. Huth, a stand-in for Gallas, is looking as shaky as he had in the previous game and Terry earns a booking when he upends Stan Lazaridis. Chelsea have their first-half moments. Crespo heads wide from Hasselbaink's corner and also forces a fine near-post save by Maik Taylor. On the hour, the increasingly influential Lampard finds Hasselbaink, who brushes aside Kenny Cunningham but sees his angled drive divert behind off the underside of Taylor's legs. Lampard has a 25-yard shot deflected wide and Bridge causes havoc on the right side of Birmingham's defence.

After his first full 90 minutes of Premiership action, Crespo observes, 'It was a difficult game for me, but it was good that I played the whole match. There was not a lot of space. Birmingham played with a lot of men in defence and that made it difficult. I hope it's not always like that in England.'

The satisfaction of returning to the top is dimmed by the feeling that two points have been dropped. Terry says, 'We were the better team and I can't remember them having a shot in the second half, so it's disappointing. We played our football in the second half.'

Birmingham are fourth in the Premiership – their highest position in the top flight since 1956 – after keeping a sixth clean sheet in eight games. 'We've got to be pleased with the draw,' Bruce says. 'We were delighted with the effort against a top-class team and in the first half it was possibly as good as we've played in my time here. What has happened there over the summer is mind-blowing. We are all intrigued by Chelsea and they will certainly be up there next May with the array of talent they have.'

> **Team**
> Cudicini, Johnson, Terry, Huth, Bridge, Makelele, Lampard, Cole (Duff), Geremi, Crespo, Hasselbaink (Gudjohnsen).

WEDNESDAY, 15 OCTOBER

Cole hopes his display at Birmingham will kick-start his season. 'I'm desperate to play against Arsenal and if I get the nod I'll be right up for it. I had to come off with cramp and it was difficult finding space, but I thought I did a good job. I will get fitter and stronger the more games I play.'

Adrian Mutu comes up with his personal mission statement. 'I want to make history but if I don't win things I'll be just another football player. I'm on the right track but the trophies are yet to come. Chelsea can have all the best players in the world but need to get the results. Since I arrived at Chelsea I do not know what it's like to lose a league game, so we're not doing too badly.

Above: Roman Abramovich returns the fans' applause.

Top: Moving the goalposts at Chelsea. From left: Duff, Gallas, Gudjohnsen and Terry in training.

Bottom: Spot the superstar in tights – from left, Terry, Parker, Cole and Lampard train together.

Top: Mutu and Crespo train with the Tinkerman.

Bottom: Jimmy Floyd Hasselbaink (middle) was the top scorer who couldn't be guaranteed a place in the team!

Top: A rare picture indeed – Peter Kenyon, on the day he begins work at Chelsea, with Ken Bates.

Bottom left: Marcel Desailly, the ageing world superstar.

Bottom right: Adrian Mutu celebrates with Frank Lampard, but his early form disappeared without trace.

Top: Jesper Gronkjaer's goal against Liverpool ensured Chelsea's qualification for the Champions League.

Bottom: Roman Abramovich inherited Eidur Gudjohnsen, one star with the talent to be part of the new Chelsea.

Top: Joe Cole – still to prove he is more than a showman without a finish.

Bottom: Scott Parker, left, was the sole January signing. But where is he supposed to play?

Mikael Forssell is a goal-scoring success – on loan to Birmingham.

Carlo Cudicini is one of Roman Abramovich's favourites, but will he be a first choice for Jose Mourinho?

'I have a very sincere relationship with the football – she always goes to the places I want her to go. She's the only one that loves me unconditionally, without any ulterior motive. As a child I took my ball to bed with me and she's my one true love. She's honest and has never betrayed me.

'My parents had gone to a party and specifically told me not to go to football training, but I had to take my chance. I sneaked out and never looked back. I had it rough and tough as a child but enjoyed it all the same. In those days our only enjoyment was playing in neighbourhood games against kids from different blocks of flats. We had to play with cheap plastic balls that were very bouncy and no one could afford a leather one. I stole some money from my grandfather to buy a leather football and when my father found out, I got a beating.

'He caught me sleeping with the football and asked where I'd got the money from. I remember that first ball very well – it was green and white – and I used to bathe it after every game. It was very expensive and no one else had one so I had to look after it. It was my first trophy. My father was always on at me to study and I had to solve 30 problems every day before I was allowed to go out and play. My girlfriend was at the other end of the phone telling me the answers so I could finish quickly. I was pretty good, actually, and scored 91 per cent in my final exams. Studying law keeps my brain going but I may never use the qualification as I want to be a manager when I finish playing.'

Mutu's divorce is finally settled out of court, with the couple's son continuing to live with his mother in Milan.

THURSDAY, 16 OCTOBER

The front page of the *Sun* suggests Abramovich will sanction a £35m bid to sign Everton prodigy Wayne Rooney. Ian Monk, a spokesman for ProActive Sports Management who look after Rooney's affairs, says, 'As far as Wayne's agents and ProActive are concerned it's complete speculation. Wayne is happy at Everton; he's under contract for the next three years. There is absolutely no basis to this.'

Goodison deputy chairman Bill Kenwright raps back, 'David Moyes and I have always said any club would have to pay a king's ransom for a player like Rooney. He is part of the fabric here. A talent like Wayne's comes along once in a lifetime. We are only concerned at his progress in the blue shirt of Everton. He's a blue – and wants to remain a blue.'

Ian McDonald, chairman of Everton's Independent Supporters Club, says, 'If Rooney was sold, the board would have to leave in a taxi with him because they would not be welcome any more.'

Paul Smith completes the series of denials. 'We've not spoken to Everton about any of their players and it's not a question of negotiating. It's too far from the window to get on with the job of compiling our target list. No one is included and no one is excluded, as it's far too premature.'

But Ranieri stokes up the story by saying, 'Wayne is a fantastic player who can do everything. He has skill and power with the ball at his feet. He is unmarkable. It is difficult to compare Rooney with any other player. For me, he is a very big champion. When he runs he is like a panther, just so strong. He is worth the entrance money alone.'

Moyes is angry about Smith's quotes and rings Chelsea to demand a retraction or face official action for an illegal approach. Worried Chelsea back off and within hours of Moyes's call they clarify their position and put on their website a watered-down version. 'Like all people in football we think he is a big talent but he is not a Chelsea target. We are only at a preliminary stage of identifying potential targets for the January window – if there are any. Recent headlines do not represent the club's transfer policy.'

Moyes has also got to the bottom of reports that Rooney's agent Paul Stretford met Ranieri to discuss the deal. It turns out that Stretford was out in a Cheshire restaurant on the night in question, but with Claudio Reyna – the Manchester City player who is also one of his clients!

FRIDAY, 17 OCTOBER

Chelsea's unbeaten start is recognised with awards for Claudio Ranieri and Frank Lampard, respectively the Barclaycard Manager and Player of the Month for September. Ranieri compares himself to Christopher Columbus on the day he picks up the Best Performing Manager award for the first quarter of this season from watchmakers Tissot, along with the Barclaycard Manager of the Month. 'If the Tinkerman doesn't change all the time maybe we'll get better – I'm only joking. I have been changing teams around since I was manager in Italy. It's like Christopher Columbus; he set out to discover India and discovered America. He could have stayed at home.

'You have to rotate the squad with so many games in a season. You have to be aware when players are tired and when they are not playing their best. But I don't need to motivate any of my stars.'

The next league game against Arsenal is vital. 'This is a good test to compare ourselves with them. We want to get to the same level but we are not there yet. I think a lot of people will be behind us because we have made the Premiership more exciting. People have been used to seeing one, two or three horses in the race. Well, maybe we can now be included in the Grand National and have a race with Arsenal, Manchester United and Liverpool. We want to be the third horse for this bigger race of course; we start well but I always say I want to see my horses at the end, not at the beginning.'

Chelsea have not won in the league at Highbury in 13 years. 'We have played very good matches against Arsenal. Sometimes we dominate them, but they score on the counter-attack. I have spoken a lot of times to my players about that. For us, it's important to concentrate for 95 minutes.'

Arsene Wenger says, 'Chelsea are now the main force in English football, the most powerful side in the league. They are on a different planet to us from a financial point of view. We are fourth in terms of numbers available but that doesn't mean the Premiership will finish that way. My players want to fight for the championship. They know that Chelsea have the potential to be there as well. Over the years we've not lost a championship game against them. We've always found a way to be on top of them. I hope we can continue that.'

John Bumstead was the last man to score a winning goal in the league at Highbury for Chelsea. Now a cabbie, he says, 'It wouldn't be a surprise if Chelsea won at Highbury and then went on to win the Premiership.'

SATURDAY, 18 OCTOBER

ARSENAL 2, CHELSEA 1

Three teams lead the table on the same day: Chelsea in the morning, Manchester United after beating Leeds at lunchtime and then Arsenal by 5.00pm. The blunder of the season by Cudicini presents Arsenal with the final word. The Italian trudges off the field head-down after his gaffe. Abramovich is straight into the dressing room. Ranieri says, 'Mr Abramovich is a very kind person. He went into our dressing room after the match to comfort the players. That was very kind.'

Cudicini's howler comes 16 minutes from time, soon after he has made a miraculous save to keep out Thierry Henry's close-range shot on the turn. Then Kanu hits the post with a header from the corner. But when Robert Pires crosses low from the right Cudicini lets the ball slip through his hands and it hits Henry and bounces into the net. Henry admits, 'I didn't see the ball coming. Like everyone else, I thought he had the ball in his hands. Cudicini played unbelievably well and it was unfortunate for him. We should remember what he did just before that. I don't know how the hell he saved my shot. He arrived from nowhere. It's a bit harsh on him. Things like that happen. But without that mistake, who knows, we might not have won.'

Ranieri says, 'Arsenal deserved it. We defended too deep and they took their chance. Carlo made a mistake. But I said to him, "Don't worry, you have saved lots of chances for Chelsea. Today you were unlucky."'

Maybe Chelsea's is not such a big squad as Ranieri is forced to field the less-than-formidable central defensive pairing of Melchiot and Huth. Johnson's first intervention hands Arsenal the lead. The full-back's deliberate handball just outside the penalty area is picked up by Durkin. Edu's free-kick strikes the trailing leg of Parlour which catches out Cudicini.

But Chelsea come back. Although Geremi's pass to Crespo is lovingly weighted, the Argentine still has plenty to do. He takes one step inside and unleashes a goal of the season candidate from 25 yards that bends at least three foot at tremendous pace and flies past Jens Lehmann. Crespo has just come back on the pitch from behind the goal-line after doing up his laces and goalkeeper Lehmann argues with referee Paul Durkin, who consults a linesman before deciding the goal should stand. The ref says afterwards, 'I didn't know he had gone off, but he wasn't breaking any law.'

With Makelele enjoying his best game – save for a yellow-card lunge at Ray Parlour – Chelsea are imposing a fair degree of control. Wenger calls a halt to Parlour's labours, the stand-in skipper and Sylvain Wiltord making way for Dennis Bergkamp and Kanu. Ranieri responds by rattling off his own changes, Gronkjaer, Cole and, eventually, Hasselbaink joining the fray. Duff is surprisingly deployed in 'the hole', behind the strikers. Mutu is condemned to a frustrating afternoon and inevitably comes off. The Arsenal changes count. Kanu starts the move that leads to Henry bringing a sensational save out of Cudicini and the Nigerian also thunders a header against a post.

Bergkamp's quick free-kick leads to the winner but the irony of Henry's finish after Cudicini's cock-up is that the Frenchman has barely ventured into the box. Wenger admits, 'In the end, we were lucky because Cudicini – who is normally very reliable – made that mistake. But overall, I thought we could find an extra something. In the second half we had far more drive. I think they would've been happy with a draw but we were not happy to draw. The game was won with an error but we had two good chances before that. We keep showing consistency and mental resources every time we have to. We always find something to win the game.'

Ranieri's conclusion is that his team still have to gel, while Arsenal have grown up together. 'When Pires receives the ball, Ashley Cole knows what to do. That's true. Arsenal's left flank is better than their right because Cole, Pires, Wiltord and Henry use that area more than the other side. Why? Because they have been used to playing alongside each other for a long time. When Duff gets it, Mutu and Crespo don't.' Mixing his metaphors with characteristic wit, he adds, 'I will work hard to get Chelsea alongside Arsenal and United, because I want my horse in the Grand Prix!'

Wenger says, 'The table shows it will be very tight at the end of the season.

Chelsea maybe need a little more time, but their huge squad will be an advantage to them in March and April.'

Ranieri believes team spirit will enable Chelsea to recover. 'One thing I am not worried about is our ability to bounce back. What is lacking at times is cohesion, the tactical unity which we had last season, before all the new arrivals. And that will take some time.'

> **Team**
>
> Cudicini, Johnson, Melchiot, Huth, Bridge, Geremi (Hasselbaink), Makelele, Duff (Cole), Lampard, Mutu (Gronkjaer), Crespo.

SUNDAY, 19 OCTOBER

Pavel Nedved, one of the world's top goalscoring midfielders, is a Chelsea target. He says, 'I can confirm Chelsea's interest and Abramovich's offer of €40m, but I am very happy with Juventus and I have no need to say you'll never know, as I want to end my career with Juve.'

At the club, there is some internal disquiet about Makelele wanting a rest and becoming increasingly outspoken and critical on a wide range of subjects. Talking about his opponents in England, Makelele says, 'They are sometimes on the brink of breaking your leg. There is no safe place. The players have got to be protected. I have had four or five real batterings since I have been here. It's a matter of being the first to hurt someone to avoid being hurt yourself. I knew about the physical commitment but, frankly, I didn't expect there to be such a difference.'

Real Madrid's Roberto Carlos dismisses speculation he might join Chelsea. 'It could be that there is something, but I want to continue at Real Madrid, enjoying myself as I have up to now. They say I have had a meeting with Abramovich? But I don't speak Russian.' The left-back's current contract runs until June 2005 with a buy-out clause of £60m. He could be set to sign a new contract which would see him play out the final years of his career in Madrid.

Real are equally dismissive of attempts to buy defender Michel Salgado. Director of football Jorge Valdano says, 'Chelsea don't seem to have any respect for the laws of football. We've had a massive row over Makelele and, if it is true they have made Salgado an offer without our permission, we will report them to FIFA.'

Chelsea come to the conclusion that there are some clever agents negotiating bumper new contracts for their clients on the back of 'leaking' information that world-class stars are on their way to the Bridge. A Chelsea insider tells me, 'Every player in the world would love to come to Chelsea. They are all welcome, but it seems to me it's all about improving their contracts by saying they are on the way.'

MONDAY, 20 OCTOBER

Mutu says, 'Abramovich asked Ranieri to come up with a list of the players he would most like to come to Chelsea. I was on that list because, as I found out later, Ranieri thought I was the player who had improved most in Europe in the past season. All of those who were on the list have come to Chelsea, apart from Totti, Nesta and Vieri. The boss's list was a little like those that fans draw up – their dream team.

'We have only just got together, whereas Manchester United and Arsenal have played together for years. But I have a feeling that our passing and attacking ability will always bring goals, whereas their style of teamwork does not always produce results. It also looks to me as though Manchester have fewer players this season and they will be stretched to cover Premiership and Champions League games.'

Mutu has been taking a keen interest in the result of the referendum in Romania on whether the country should join the European Union. He has agreed to be the face of the pro-Europe campaign on billboards all over Bucharest. He also features in a promotional video. The broadcast was filmed by a Romanian television crew on a playing field in Harlington, after Chelsea refused to allow filming at their own training ground.

Makelele announces he is surprised at the all-out attacking philosophy that characterises most of the Premiership's top teams. He explains, 'European teams know how to take their time. They are always trying to outmanoeuvre their opponents.'

He also confesses, 'Most people have realised – and I am not denying it – that coming to Chelsea was a financial decision. If Real Madrid had given me half of what I am getting at Chelsea, I'd have stayed with them.'

Looking forward to the Lazio game, Hernan Crespo says, 'Of course it is a special match for me. After the game I will have a problem as I've had so many phone calls from people asking for my shirt. But I'll just be thinking about three points. We can't afford another slip-up in Europe. Lazio have many good players such as Claudio Lopez, Jaap Stam, Demetrio Albertini. However, for me, Mihajlovic is the man we really have to watch. His free-kicks and corners are the best and he has the ability to win the game with just one kick, as he did at Chelsea before.'

Crespo, who made 11 Champions League appearances for Lazio scoring twice, believes the fans can play their full part. 'We first have to be very careful because Lazio are very good at the counter-attacking game. But we are at home and we have to put on a show for our fans. We have to let the Lazio players know that they're playing away from home.'

Crespo, who has scored twice in his last three games, admits language problems have made things difficult so far but says through his interpreter, 'I am beginning to enjoy my football in England. It is a very dynamic game here while, in Italy, it was more technical. The best thing I have found so far are the pitches. In Italy there are some very bad examples.'

The fans have taken to him but he is keen to apologise to them for his lukewarm response to their chants. 'It is a worry for me. I have heard the fans shout my name but I haven't been sure whether or not to salute them or not. The reason? I haven't understood what they have said. I hope it was nice but I wanted to be sure.'

When asked how serious a Lazio win would be, Crespo, for once, needs no interpreter. 'We will not lose,' he says in slow but lucid English. 'No, no, we will *not* lose.'

TUESDAY, 21 OCTOBER

Makers of the reality TV show *I'm a Celebrity – Get me Out of Here!* invite Roman Abramovich to the Australian outback for their show! Unsurprisingly, the offer is rejected. He does make a surprise visit to Arsenal's London Colney training ground, to examine their state-of-the-art training facilities with a view to making improvements at his own club. Chelsea have spent £15m purchasing land to develop a training complex in Cobham, Surrey, but have yet to receive planning permission. Acting chief executive Paul Smith has been on excellent terms with Arsenal vice-chairman David Dein for many years. Relations between the clubs have changed dramatically as Dein and Ken Bates could not stand each other.

Veron is reluctant to repeat the reasons behind his departure from Manchester United. 'It's not something that's been eating me up. I'm not bothered [about being called "a disgrace"]. I know what happened, and so does he. My conscience is clear. All I can do is give my best to the club I am at, and right up until the last minute that's what I did for United. At no point did I go to the manager and say, "Look, I want to leave." There's a saying in Argentina: "When they pat you on the back and are all nice to you, that's the time to leave."'

He laughs off a story from Old Trafford that he was so worried about his fleet of expensive cars getting damaged while being transported to London that he spent a week personally driving each of the £600,000 collection (which includes two Ferraris and a US Army Hummer H2 truck that does one mile to the gallon) between the cities. A friend claims to have heard this from a United player. 'Who was it? I'll cut his hand off,' grins Veron. He is warming to Ranieri. 'He's more like an Argentine style of manager. Fortunately, I can understand what he's saying. I don't have to listen to Scottish any more. That was a joke, by the way.'

Abramovich has been making visits to morning training sessions and to the players' lounge in an attempt to get to know his squad personally. Veron observes, 'He's an everyday kind of guy. He's just got an ordinary manner, and dresses in an ordinary way, sometimes in jeans and trainers.'

Ranieri sits next to Veron for his pre-Champions League media conference and says to his controversial signing, 'The sharks have gathered.' He declines to respond to a report that Abramovich has guaranteed his job until May. When Ranieri signed Veron, he claimed he had captured the best midfield player on the planet. 'He still is,' he declares. The esteem in which Veron was held by Lazio contrasts with the broad scepticism in England. 'I didn't get the kind of continuity in my game for United that I had in Italy,' Veron says. He is excited to be facing Lazio. 'It's going to be an extra stimulus and a very special match for me.'

Lazio fear Veron's ability to link up with Crespo. Ranieri hopes Veron, Crespo, Cudicini and Mutu will make good use of their Serie A experience. Ranieri is still sensitive about his rotation system. 'I am the Tinkerman. You write what you want and I will continue my way. It doesn't change anything.'

It is ironic that in the three years since Lazio last came to Stamford Bridge – and won – their roles have been reversed. Then, Lazio were the big spenders of Serie A with Eriksson given an open cheque book. Lazio's finances are now in tatters.

WEDNESDAY, 22 OCTOBER

CHELSEA 2, LAZIO 1

Ranieri hails the bulldog spirit that inspires Chelsea to leapfrog Lazio to the top of Group G. Victories over Italian clubs are rare; wins squeezed from a deficit are unheard of. Goal hero Frank Lampard and fellow Englishman John Terry prove they are up for a battle and Mutu's 65th-minute winner tops off the night, sending the arena into delirium.

The visiting fans chant Veron's name. Ranieri cannot resist his urge to alter and begins the contest with a diamond formation. Chelsea are the better side in the first half, but after his team are a goal down at half-time, Ranieri abandons his experiment for the staightforward 4-4-2. The midfield of Duff, Veron, Makelele and Lampard seem to know what they are doing after the confusion that has gone before. Chelsea have some width, with Duff particularly dangerous, and in the 57th minute they make a deserved breakthrough. Gudjohnsen, surprisingly preferred to Hasselbaink in the starting line-up after Crespo fails a fitness test, sets up Lampard with a perfect pass. Lampard combines precision and power to steer the ball into the top right-hand corner.

Then Ranieri surpasses himself with his tinkering in the 64th minute, replacing Veron with Gronkjaer. Within a minute Gronkjaer repays his manager's faith. His first touch, an excellent cross, finds Mutu who pounces on the rebound to fire in with his right foot after his first effort, with his left foot, is blocked. The Chelsea fans take great delight in singing 'Are you watching, Arsenal?' after the Gunners' defeat at Dynamo Kiev the night before.

John Terry praises Cudicini. 'Carlo is still a fantastic keeper. His shot-stopping, his agility, his quickness off his line and his kicking are all first class. I wouldn't swap him for any other keeper. He is the best in the league.'

Team

Cudicini, Johnson, Gallas, Terry, Bridge, Lampard, Makelele, Veron (Gronkjaer), Duff (Geremi), Gudjohnsen, Mutu (Cole).

THURSDAY, 23 OCTOBER

Incoming chief executive Peter Kenyon is still negotiating his pay-off from Manchester United – their accounts show Kenyon's cash entitlement was £710,000 last year – while the media claim that Jimmy Floyd Hasselbaink is on a list of players earmarked to move out when the transfer window opens in January along with Mario Melchiot and Celestine Babayaro.

Among other rumours, Sebastian Frey, the 30-year-old Parma keeper, is too expensive for Arsene Wenger's budget but perhaps not for Chelsea. Brazilian midfielder Emerson remains a target but he says, 'Chelsea? I choose Roma. Nothing has changed.' Zinedine Zidane, however, says he wouldn't be tempted to join Chelsea. 'If Abramovich called me, I would certainly talk to him, out of respect for the man, but I would tell him that I do not want to move and that I am happy at Madrid.' Meanwhile, Nilmar, an exciting 19-year-old Brazilian forward, is on trial at the club.

FRIDAY, 24 OCTOBER

Ranieri takes his players for a fitting for specially-tailored club suits. The new wardrobe is an exclusively-designed cotton and lambskin car coat with matching driving gloves, navy lightweight wool, two-button bespoke suit with the Chelsea crest embroidered on the Chelsea blue lining, two bespoke shirts made by a master shirt-maker, sapphire cufflinks, personalised buttons, a striped club tie subtly embroidered with the CFC crest, embroidered name tags, and specially commissioned Jermyn Street shoes. Whether or not they turn out to be the best club, they will be the best dressed.

Mutu turns up for the fitting in baggy jeans. 'When I said I bought a gypsy, I wasn't joking,' laughs Ranieri. Hasselbaink is sporting his £7,000 diamond stud earrings. As ever, goalkeeper Carlo Cudicini looks immaculate but casual. 'I'm Italian, I like clothes – what you wear and how it fits is very important. I don't wear mad things like my team-mates.' Ranieri explains the significance of the event. 'It's not about glamour and photos, it's about team spirit and unity. When you see us in these suits you will see Chelsea, London's team.'

Chelsea fans have started having sweeps on who will be in Ranieri's line-ups. In 14 matches, he has played the same striking formation for only two successive games (when Hasselbaink and Mutu started the home Premiership matches against Blackburn and then Spurs). Of Hasselbaink's eight starts, only one has been in the Champions League, at home to MSK Zilina. The other seven matches he has started have been in the Premiership. Mutu has started all three matches in the Champions League.

Although Mutu is called Puff Daddy at the Bridge because of his love of R&B music, his favourite artist is 50 Cent.'

Mutu loves fashion, jewellery and cars, and has a passion for law, mathematics, poetry, acting, and history. 'I guess I am the ultimate split personality! I love football, first and foremost, but if I wasn't in this job I would be more than happy doing all the others.' Mutu is studying for the final year of his law degree. 'I like to keep my mind stimulated, and there can be no better exercise than law. It is difficult with the football taking up so much of my time, but I hope to graduate next summer from my university in Romania.'

Credit for his development goes to his parents, Rodica and Spiridon, both computer-programmers. Evenings in the Mutu household were usually spent trying to work out complicated mathematical puzzles around the table. He speaks quietly and thoughtfully. 'This is the way Adrian is,' Ranieri, says. 'And he plays like this, too. You never hear him shouting or complaining. He just gets on with things. That's why when Mr Abramovich asked me to draw up a list of the players I wanted, I put Mutu right at the top. Adrian is a natural poacher. When he sniffs an opening, he takes it. Right foot, left foot – it does not matter to him.'

'Adrian is not a top, top striker,' Ranieri says. 'Not yet, because he is still young and has a lot to learn. But he has all the attributes to become one of the best ever.'

SATURDAY, 25 OCTOBER

CHELSEA 1, MAN CITY 0

Abramovich has just turned 37 and is in urgent need of cheering up after masked and armed special forces surround a private jet on a Siberian runway before dawn and arrest its occupant, Russia's richest man and Abramovich's friend and business ally, Mikhail Khodorkovsky, in the latest and most dramatic move in the

Kremlin's crackdown on political opponents. Khodorkovsky is escorted from his plane and reportedly beaten before being taken to Moscow for interrogation. He is later charged with forgery and fraud amounting to more than a billion dollars.

City fans goad Ranieri with a recital of Joe Dolce's pseudo-Italian classic 'Shaddap You Face'. ('Whatssa matta you, eh? Why you looka so sad?') An animated Ranieri is bellowing almost non-stop from the touchline. Ranieri's tinkering sees four changes yet he retains the essential thread from that success against Lazio – from Cudicini, Terry and Gallas through Lampard in midfield to Mutu up front. Terry again proves a tower of strength although he has his hands full against Nicolas Anelka and Robbie Fowler.

Opposition managers have given up trying to guess Ranieri's line-up as Keegan jokes, 'I just put up Cudicini's name on the board and then concentrated on us.' Even the mascot for the day is called Joseph Tinker! Chelsea think they have broken the deadlock in the 28th minute when Gronkjaer's cross is headed home by Lampard. The celebrations are cut short by a linesman's flag. Five minutes later, Cole releases Mutu with a terrific pass down the left. Mutu immediately zeroes in on goal, and skips beyond David Sommeil before drilling over a low cross. David Seaman tries to cut it out but succeeds only in pushing it to Hasselbaink, who sees the ball bounce off him and into the net for his seventh goal of the season. Keegan refuses to criticise his 40-year-old keeper.

Later Melchiot is caught in possession by Michael Tarnat, who whips in a perfect cross for Fowler to bring a superb save from Cudicini, who pushes it onto the post. City achieve sufficient attacking pressure in the second half for Ranieri to bring on an extra defender, Huth, and change shape. Ranieri explains, 'Yes because they put Wanchope on and he is a very tall man, very good in the air, so with Robert I balanced my defensive line.' Mutu is man of the match.

Ranieri comments, 'Manchester City had a good chance, but Cudicini is Cudicini, and he saved a great chance for them.' At the final whistle, the faithful acclaim the seventh Premiership victory. But the volume of applause is nothing compared to the noise when the result from Old Trafford is announced. United have lost 3–1 to Fulham.

Team

Cudicini, Bridge, Gallas, Melchiot, Terry, Cole (Duff), Gronkjaer (Geremi), Lampard, Makelele, Hasselbaink (Huth), Mutu.

SUNDAY, 26 OCTOBER

Ranieri makes an honest appraisal of Joe Cole at a private dinner. Ranieri's

English is definitely improving as he entertains at a fund-raising evening at non-league Wingate & Finchley FC, Rymans League North. The Gentleman's Dinner is followed by a question session and he performs without an interpreter. Ranieri doesn't dodge a question about Cole and why he cannot get into his team. Ranieri responds, 'He is a good player, with the potential to become a fantastic player. But at the moment he's "good". But for the moment he is not good enough to become a permanent fixture in the team. I played him from the start on Saturday and he will be playing in the next match against Notts Crownty.'

'You mean Notts County!' someone shouts.

'Yes, I knew it was something like that,' he responds.

MONDAY, 27 OCTOBER

Jimmy Floyd Hasselbaink is seething after Dick Advocaat ignores him for the Holland team to face Moldova despite Ruud van Nistelrooy's absence. Meanwhile Alexei Smertin is regaining fitness and happy to be at Pompey. Smertin is amused by the suspicions aroused by his loan deal. 'People have been watching too many old movies about spies and stuff! There is nothing dodgy about my move to England. I am here because I, and Chelsea, want me to be here.

'It is good for Chelsea because they have so many new players trying to find their feet, and it is good for me because it allows me the time to adapt to the country and the style of football. I think that after a year with Portsmouth I will be ready for the challenges at Chelsea. Very few Russians have ever played, let alone succeeded, in England, so it is sensible not to rush. There is no question that Roman helped me, but he did not just buy me to get me out of France at all costs. Claudio Ranieri also liked me as a player and was part of the negotiations that brought me here.'

Aston Villa manager David O'Leary steps up his interest in Mikael Forssell ahead of the transfer window reopening, but Birmingham City have a gentleman's agreement with Chelsea which gives them first option to keep Forssell until next summer. Leeds appoint Trevor Birch as their chief executive, although he is also wanted by Aston Villa. Manchester United are considering whether to report Chelsea to the Premier League for recruiting his successor Peter Kenyon. The clubs appear to be close to an agreement that Kenyon can start in February but United's attitude hardens. They insist Kenyon serves the full 12 months of his notice period.

TUESDAY, 28 OCTOBER

Ranieri is not confident Veron can play two games in three days. But he is back against Notts County, the struggling Second Division side. Says Ranieri, 'We will show Notts County every respect and I will pick a team to win the match.'

With a weekend Premiership match at Everton followed by a Champions League trip to Lazio, the manager will be rotating again. The Carling Cup is bottom of the priorities but Ranieri will countenance no easing up. 'Everything is a priority. I want us to play football in every competition. That is my philosophy and I want my players to believe in that. I was loud from the touchline against Manchester City, just like Pavarotti, because I wanted to stimulate my players. I thought they needed my support against a very good City team. We did not play as well as we did against Lazio but it is not easy to recharge your batteries in such a short time.'

Notts County urge Abramovich to donate Chelsea's portion of the gate receipts. Members of the Notts County Supporters Trust write to the Chelsea owner, requesting that their hosts double the 45 per cent take of the ticket receipts due to the visiting club. County expect to recoup between £150,000 and £200,000 from their share of the receipts. If that could be doubled with the help of a public relations masterpiece from Abramovich, their future will be more secure.

County, the world's oldest professional club, dating back to 1862, face a 9 December deadline, by which time they must prove to the Football League that they have been taken out of receivership and are a going concern again. Chelsea donate a full set of tops because County's players have been told not to swap shirts as they can't afford to buy a new set from their kit suppliers.

Instead, Chelsea hand them a complete signed set of shirts to be auctioned to raise funds. County's irreplaceable black-and-white tops are washed by the long-suffering wives and girlfriends of the club's 16 senior pros. Interestingly, Veron's weekly wage would be enough to finance County's playing staff for six weeks.

While Ranieri ponders how many changes to make, his Notts County counterpart, Billy Dearden, has no such distractions. 'Rotation?' he asks sardonically. 'I haven't got a squad to rotate, although, if you like, we can pick the groundsman and a couple of ball boys to sit on the bench. The players, though, will be determined to give it their best shot and not be humiliated.'

WEDNESDAY, 29 OCTOBER

CHELSEA 4, NOTTS COUNTY 2

County take away a £300,000 share of gate receipts thanks to a bumper crowd of 35,997, but little else. Duff, Gudjohnsen, Johnson and top scorer Hasselbaink are all in the starting line-up as County put up a good fight. 'It's just like watching Juve' is the County fans' response as the club that provided Juventus with their first black-and-white shirts start by outplaying the richest squad in English football.

The Blues, however, take the lead through Hasselbaink on 15 minutes as he swerves a 30-yarder into the top corner after being teed up by Duff, but Tony Barras stuns Stamford Bridge with a 28th-minute leveller. Gudjohnsen restores the lead, heading home Johnson's deft cross eight minutes before half-time. He extends the lead 25 minutes from time when he spears home a penalty after Gronkjaer has been brought down by the keeper. Mark Stallard keeps County believing when he worries Ambrosio out of a routine catch, then slots home. Cole, soon after coming on, fires in a sizzling, right-foot drive after Steve Mildenhall has pulled out a brilliant stop to deny Stanic.

Then Ranieri substitutes himself for the post-match conference as Gudjohnsen steps into the spotlight. Gudjohnsen's second goal of the night, a penalty, is also his 50th goal. 'We were at home against a Second Division side and on a hiding to nothing. But they gave us a good game and we just have to take the positives out of the game because we have got many important games coming up.'

County manager Dearden says, 'To come and score two goals at Chelsea was better than a lot of Premiership sides, who will not get a goal here. The Chelsea supporters have seen that we are not a bad little team. Everybody thought we were coming here tonight just to make the numbers up.'

The favourites for the competition now travel to the Madejski Stadium to face Reading for their next assignment and few would bet against them progressing to the fifth round.

> **Team**
> Ambrosio, Johnson, Melchiot, Huth, Babayaro, Gronkjaer (Cole), Geremi, Veron, Duff, Hasselbaink, Gudjohnsen.

THURSDAY, 30 OCTOBER

Emmanuel Petit undergoes a knee op in Strasbourg in the hands of French professor Jean-Henri Jaeger, the specialist who treated him for a groin injury earlier in the year. Treatment failed to cure the problem that began when he was hurt in the win over Villa towards the end of September.

FRIDAY, 31 OCTOBER

Wayne Rooney inevitably takes centre stage as Chelsea prepare to face Everton less than three weeks after a tabloid newspaper led its front page with a story linking 'Roonski' with a £35m move to Stamford Bridge. His agent Paul

Stretford's company, ProActive Sports, has financial issues and sources suggest the only way Stretford can make any serious cash from him is through a major transfer deal.

Everton manager David Moyes does not believe that Chelsea's re-emergence as a genuine title challenger makes them a certainty to win against his team. 'You go into games like this with no one really expecting you to do that well. We should always be hard to beat, especially at home. It is tight between the three sides at the top. I'd like to think Everton could add their name to that list.' But Everton have won only once in their past eight Premiership games.

Joe Cole pledges to stay and fight for his place after West Ham offer him an escape route. New West Ham boss Alan Pardew admits he would like to take him back to Upton Park on loan until the end of the season.

November

INTO THE KNOCK-OUT STAGES OF THE CHAMPIONS LEAGUE

A bramovich rockets to the top of the *Sunday Times* pay list as Britain's highest earner at £564m a year. Abramovich subsequently sells a 50 per cent stake in Russian Aluminium for £1.8bn to raise his personal fortune to £8.2bn. The deal makes Abramovich the world's richest man under 40.

Abramovich pledges his commitment to Chelsea for maybe the next or 50 years. 'I said from day one I wanted to enjoy myself and that's what I've been doing. I like the English lifestyle. The English are used to mixing with people of different nationalities. Anyone could feel comfortable in England.'

Abramovich has taken to a new sport for the winter: skiing. He explores the possibility of buying the best properties in a swish Alpine resort for more than £150m, setting his sights on Courchevel 1850, so called because it is pitched at 1,850 metres in the French Alps. It is traditionally a winter retreat for royals such

Pos	Team	P	W	D	L	GF	GA	GD	PTS
	PREMIERSHIP TABLE – NOVEMBER								
1	Arsenal	10	7	3	0	19	8	11	24
2	Chelsea	10	7	2	1	20	9	11	23
3	Manchester United	10	7	1	2	18	6	12	22
4	Birmingham City	10	5	4	1	9	5	4	19
5	Fulham	10	5	3	2	20	13	7	18
6	Southampton	10	4	4	2	10	5	5	16
7	Manchester City	10	4	3	3	20	12	8	15
8	Newcastle United	10	4	3	3	15	12	3	15
9	Charlton Athletic	10	4	3	3	14	13	1	15
10	Liverpool	10	4	2	4	15	11	4	14

as Prince Michael of Kent and King Juan Carlos of Spain but is fast becoming a playground for nouveau riche Russians too.

Oleg Tarovinski, who started a Chelsea Supporters' Club in Moscow, thinks Abramovich will improve Russia's image in Britain. 'It's good that he bought a foreign club. It's very good PR for Russia. And very good for the Russian people. English people see Russia as just a big, cold country with bears. Mr Abramovich is changing all that.'

On a more parochial note, Everton director Paul Gregg tells his club's AGM, 'Chelsea have been really fortunate, but it's ruined the Premier League. What it's created for the other Premier League clubs is a massive hill to climb. It would be lovely just to write a cheque but we're not in a position to do that.' Chelsea are 8–1 with William Hill to win the Champions League. Manchester United are 5–1, Real Madrid 100–30, Arsenal and Celtic 66–1 and Rangers 80–1.

SATURDAY, 1 NOVEMBER

EVERTON 0, CHELSEA 1

'Chim Chiminey, Chim Chiminey, Chim Chim Cheroo, who needs Wayne Rooney when we've got Mutu?' The message in the fans' ditty is re-emphasised when Mutu heads the winner after 49 minutes, his sixth goal of the season. Everton manager David Moyes claims the goal should have been ruled out. 'It looked to me as if he definitely got his arm on to the ball before it hit his head. I've seen it again on the video.'

Moyes is left to rue a host of squandered opportunities, but adds, 'Chelsea have the players to be right up there with Arsenal and Manchester United. We got very close for long spells but the money they've spent made the difference in the end. We made more chances against Chelsea than we have made against far lesser teams. In many ways it was a top-notch performance. Chelsea are now deservedly in the top three in the country.'

Rooney is off-form, and Moyes is tetchy when asked if he should be rested. Everton miss a chance to take the lead in the opening minute when Tomasz Radzinski races clear after Terry misses a tackle, but he shoots wide. Rooney, ready to celebrate his 18th birthday later in the day, lets fly from 35 yards but Cudicini has it covered. The home side appeal for a penalty in the 19th minute when Terry and David Weir tangle in the box, but referee Jeff Winter is not impressed.

Alex Nyarko lets fly in the 22nd minute but hits the bar. Chelsea escape again when Cudicini almost drops another clanger. Terry rolls the ball back to the keeper, who tries to give it straight back to the defender. However, his pass goes to the unmarked Rooney, who tries to lob the ball home – but it flies over. Lampard goes sprawling in the box but again Winter ignores the penalty claim, while in first-half injury-time a superb run by Cole takes him half the length of the pitch before he too is toppled in the box. Again, Winter refuses to point to the spot.

Everton almost catch Chelsea napping at the start of the second half, when Radzinski has his final effort, a smart shot on the turn pushed away by Cudicini. Three minutes later, Geremi crosses from the right, Hasselbaink misses it at the near post but Mutu dives in among the bodies to plant a header into the back of the net. Ranieri admits, 'It was very competitive and both teams could have won. They had three good chances and it wasn't easy for us. In the second half we played much better. We were able to calm the pace down while they wanted to increase the tempo. We were waiting for them in the first half rather than going to them. I asked Geremi to get tighter and close people down after that. We improved in midfield and Cole was fantastic. That was his best game for us.'

Team

Cudicini, Bridge, Terry, Gallas, Melchiot, Cole (Gudjohnsen), Makelele, Lampard, Geremi, Hasselbaink, Mutu (Duff).

SUNDAY, 2 NOVEMBER

Abramovich watches the team's light training session, mostly warming down. Off the pitch, Argentinian defender Roberto Ayala is linked with a move from Valencia. Former Valencia coach Ranieri is well aware of Ayala's abilities but keeps his own counsel on new signings. 'I was asked about signing Michel Salgado from Madrid and I have other things in my mind. It's not possible in November. We're doing well but must improve more. I've been pleased because our start has been good but I am not satisfied. We have a lot of match-winners and goalscorers but we have to kill the match when we have the chance.'

There are strange goings-on in Madrid. First it is announced on Spanish radio that Salgado will sign for Chelsea with president Florentino Perez quoted as telling the player, 'If I were your father, I'd advise you to go.' It seems Chelsea virtually have the Salgado deal sewn up until Real announce that he has agreed a new five-year deal with them.

John Terry urges Ranieri to resist the temptation to bring in more players. 'I don't think we need any more defenders,' he says. But French keeper Sebastien Frey from Parma is on the club's list. Chelsea are also interested in a £5.4m move for Brazilian wonderkid striker Nilmar, who was on trial with the club in October. The club are also interested in the next generation of stars, tracking Derby's left-winger Lee Holmes, who isn't 17 until April when he can sign his first professional contract.

Chelsea are concerned that they do not have enough academy players challenging for the first team. Freddy Adu, Ghana-born, America-based and already an Under-17 international, signs a new contract that ties him to Major League Soccer for six years. Chelsea will be happy to loan him back to a club in the US to speed up his progress if they can pull off a deal and beat Manchester United to his signature.

Ken Bates contradicts Abramovich and his advisers when he publicly states there are doubts whether ground expansion is possible at Stamford Bridge. 'We would have to knock down the hotel, all the restaurants and the apartments. It would take three years to complete, if it was practical. The other problem is our safety certificate depends on how many people we can evacuate in an emergency and we are only 300 below our limit. I don't know how the other 10,000 will get out.'

MONDAY, 3 NOVEMBER

Roman Abramovich sets off for Italy aboard his new £72m, 378ft yacht, *Pelorus*, so luxurious it even has its own submarine, and of course all the extras any security-conscious oil baron could wish for: bullet-proof glass, a missile-detection system and quarters for the security guards. The five-level vessel has a crew of 40, boasts a restaurant, casino, dance floor, luxury bedrooms, bars, a state-of-the-art gym and sauna and on deck there is a helicopter landing pad and a massive sun deck with whirlpool. Abramovich already has one giant yacht, *Le Grand Bleu*, which has a huge aquarium and a glass bottom through which to observe the sea bed.

Chelsea are second in the Premiership and top of their Champions League group, but, on his way to his hometown of Rome for the game against Lazio, Ranieri is not yet satisfied. 'This team could improve and must improve. I'm pleased because our start is good but we could get better. Now is the time to improve.' He calls on his players to be 'more clinical'. Eight of their 10 wins have come by a single goal.

Ranieri continues, 'The next month is very important but every match is important. Lazio are playing good football. They're very direct and have more confidence than they did in the first game. When you're playing an Italian team the players understand how difficult it will be. We're going to a great stadium, a real theatre with a great atmosphere. My players want to show this is a stage for them to play on. Lazio are a good team, a very hungry team, and they are confident. But we are ready for them. Mancini has put together a team that plays good football. I'm sure it'll be an interesting match.'

Ranieri's wife, Rosanna, still lives in Rome and will get the rare opportunity to see her husband at work. Rosanna owns two shops selling classic furniture from the 1950s and 1960s, both aptly named Retro.

A denim-clad Abramovich observes training from the touchline, arms folded. Ranieri remarks, 'For Mr Abramovich, every result is important, but he does not put me under any pressure.' How could he? Chelsea have lost only twice in 17 matches in all competitions.

Serbian international Sinisa Mihajlovic predicts Lazio will come out on top because Premiership clubs find it difficult to get results when they travel abroad. 'I don't just think we are going to win, I am convinced we are going to win. The thing with English teams is that they have a big problem when they are not playing at home. They always play well in front of their own fans, but they can be very poor when they go away to another country.'

TUESDAY, 4 NOVEMBER

LAZIO 0, CHELSEA 4

This is one of the best results of all time by an English club on Italian soil, a devastating performance that stuns the rest of Europe and confirms Ranieri's team are genuine Champions League contenders. Afterwards Ranieri is asked whether this has been the best display of his reign. 'I don't know. Of course, I'm very pleased tonight, because Rome is my city and [so it counts] a little more, but it's OK. I always look forward and I hope at the next match it will be better.'

Around 5,000 Chelsea fans witness a famous victory destined to become Stamford Bridge legend. But for Crespo missing a number of chances, Chelsea would have surpassed their record 5–0 Champions League victory against Galatasaray in 1999. Chelsea fans are understandably ecstatic, bellowing out chorus after chorus of 'Are you watching Arsenal?' and 'Are you Tottenham in disguise?'

They celebrate along with Gianfranco Zola, who has made the trip from Cagliari to see the game. Zola milks the applause of the travelling fans and his former team-mates. Frank Lampard says, 'We had been performing as well as we can do, but tonight I think it all clicked. Some teams were always going to feel it, and tonight it was Lazio.'

Goals from Crespo, Gudjohnsen, Duff and Lampard leave the Blues three points clear at the top of Group G and needing only a draw from their remaining two games to make it through to the knock-out stages. The only blemish is Glen Johnson, shown a second yellow card for kicking the ball away having conceded a free-kick.

Veron also shows why Ranieri insists he is the world's best midfield player. This is his first game back at the Olympic Stadium since his move to Manchester United. But he does not instantly help his cause with the Blues fans after wrapping a Lazio scarf around his shoulders when treated to a standing ovation before the match.

Yet Veron is man of the match, and it is his ferocious 15th-minute free-kick which opens the floodgates and signals the beginning of a nightmare night for former Ipswich keeper Matteo Sereni, making his Champions League debut in place of the injured Angelo Peruzzi. The keeper gets both hands to Veron's drive yet punches rather than catches, pushing the shot into the chin of the incoming Crespo, who literally does not know what hits him as the ball crashes back into the empty net.

A miraculous double save by Cudicini, first from Dejan Stankovic and then from Bernardo Corradi's follow-up, ensures the Blues keep their nerve as Lazio totally lose theirs when they are reduced to 10 in the 53rd minute. The odious Sinisa Mihajlovic has already got away with kicking Mutu in the shin and spitting in his face. The offence is missed by the referee but captured by TV cameras to alert UEFA. It is only a momentary reprieve. Booked for tripping Duff, Mihajlovic then leaves Russian referee Valentin Ivanov little option but to reach for his red card when he repeats the offence three minutes later. He troops off down the tunnel to get an overcoat and then sits on the medical vehicle used for injured players. The fourth official tells him to shift and, after doing as he is told, he chucks a water-bottle in the direction of the Chelsea bench.

Gudjohnsen makes the game safe when he lashes in after Lampard's shot is saved. It gets even better when Duff dances through the Lazio defence to add the third, and Lampard smacks home another rebound to complete the rout.

Ranieri says, 'I wanted my team to play with heart and soul and that is what happened here. I am very pleased with that performance. We were calm early on when Lazio started strongly and showed that winning mentality. It was also a very fierce match, sometimes dirty but Chelsea stood up to everything Lazio did. I'm very pleased with my players because they never joined the battle. They stayed calm and continued to play fantastic football.'

Team

Cudicini, Johnson, Gallas, Terry, Bridge, Veron (Cole), Makelele, Lampard, Duff, Mutu (Gronkjaer), Crespo (Gudjohnsen).

WEDNESDAY, 5 NOVEMBER

Sergeant Mark Skipper, one of the Army's top bomb experts, announces he is quitting his £30,000-a-year post to be part of the security unit for Abramovich and his family. The Royal Engineer will get a £170,000-a-year pay rise.

Lazio's Mihajlovic faces a disciplinary investigation by UEFA. 'I'm not interested in whether he's punished or not,' Adrian Mutu says. 'Certain things should be left on the pitch. I won't hold a grudge against him. These things happen on the pitch and football is a man's game. He brought shame upon himself and Lazio. The good thing is that we won. It was tough for me to restrain myself after he spat at me. But I just told him to have a little look at the scoreboard. That felt pretty good. Then, when he was being sent off later in the game, I told him to get off the pitch more quickly, as maybe he had something more personal to do under the shower and we didn't want to delay him!'

The confrontation is the culmination of a four-year running feud between the two stars. Mutu reveals, 'It was not the first time he has treated me like this. Whenever we faced each other in Serie A, it was always a war on the pitch with him. He elbowed me in the face when Chelsea played Lazio in London and the rivalry even spilled over into our national teams: Mihajlovic was just the same when Romania played Yugoslavia a couple of years back. He got me sent off in that match, but I have grown up since then. So when he got his red card I told him the wheel had turned full circle.'

Former Blues defender Ron 'Chopper' Harris is disgusted. He fumes, 'Spitting is the lowest of the low. They should make an example of Mihajlovic and ban him for a year. Whatever has gone on beforehand, gobbing is inexcusable. Mutu has done well not to give him a right-hander because, if someone gobs in your face, you're entitled to lamp them.'

THURSDAY, 6 NOVEMBER

David Beckham and his superstar Real Madrid team-mates sit up and take notice of the margin of victory in Rome. Beckham says, 'I'm sure the result the other night surprised all of Europe because of the way they went to Lazio, which is a hard place to go to. To perform like that in Italy and get a result like they did, you have to congratulate them for that. They are going to be a good team in the future. But as far as the threat to other teams in Europe and in the Premiership, we will have to see at the end of the season.'

Ranieri says one man was the key to victory. 'Everything starts from Veron. When he plays like that, you will see the real Chelsea. Veron can change the face of the match because he has very good vision. I know him very well and I believe he can improve again. It's important for everybody to understand his movement. He has a long range on the pitch and it's important that his team-mates understand him and he understands them. Veron did what we needed, with long or cross-field balls to Adrian Mutu, Damien Duff and Hernan Crespo, while Claude Makelele and Frank Lampard linked with him.

'The team showed the bit more I was asking for. This was the first time we've seen what I've been working at. My players are linking better every day. We are improving and we are building the foundations and that's important. Lazio was a leap forward but we have to show the same intelligence against Newcastle United.'

FRIDAY, 7 NOVEMBER

Mihajlovic is suspended for eight matches, the second-longest sentence of its kind. Luckily, UEFA will not investigate the set-to in the tunnel involving Makelele and Fernando Couto as the referee's report makes no mention of it.

Ken Bates hails Ranieri as the perfect gentleman. 'He is calm under pressure, that's the important thing, and the team are very disciplined, and that comes from leadership from the top. When was the last time you heard him slag off an opponent or another manager? He leads from the top and that's why we don't have any disciplinary problems at Chelsea. Whenever Chelsea win, he is always generous to the team we have beaten. When we lose, he gives full praise to the winner. He sets the right example.'

Strangely, Ranieri must give Bates a free holiday as part of his £30,000-a-week contract. He is legally bound to open up his Tuscan villa to Bates and his new wife Suzannah every summer. Bates adds, 'We like him, his wife, and family. How I found him is a trade secret. We took him round to our terrace and showed him our one olive tree which is on our 10th floor penthouse terrace. Claudio remarked, "I have 500 olive trees, you must come and stay with us," so I said OK and put it in the contract.' Bates recalls how Ranieri laughed and said, 'Mr Chairman, you are a bandit.'

Eidur Gudjohnsen praises his dad Arnor, a winger with Anderlecht during their heyday in the 1980s, for convincing him to stay and contest a place at Chelsea. 'I saw my name was being thrown around in the papers and I was being linked with other clubs. But I called my dad at the start of the season and we had a long chat. He told me it is a matter of rising to the challenge. He said you couldn't find a top team in Europe now that hasn't got three or four top strikers in the squad. He said if I play to my best I'll have nothing to worry about.' Gudjohnsen's dad, now 42, had his crucial penalty saved by Tony Parks to hand victory to Tottenham in the 1984 UEFA Cup final.

Meanwhile Ranieri is planning to add to his blue-chip squad when the transfer window opens in January. 'I am looking and maybe I think that this or that player will improve the squad.'

At Highbury, Arsenal come from behind to beat Spurs 2–1 in the north London derby to stretch their lead to four points. Chairman Peter Hill-Wood insists, 'We can't provide Arsene Wenger with £100m – but when we get to the new stadium he will have plenty to spend. I'm not envious of Chelsea and the position they are in, not at all. I'd rather be where we are than where they are. Arsenal are more stable. I think the long-term future is more solid at Arsenal. And why should we be concerned? Arsene will cope – we're top of the league, aren't we?'

SATURDAY, 8 NOVEMBER

Ranieri is beginning to thrive on the nickname 'Tinkerman'. He says, 'Tinkerman? The press, or was it Colin Hutchinson, called me that – it's true because I like to change.' He also plays down the pressure he is under. 'When you start to be a manager you know that the pressure is a lot. I'm a lucky man because I love my job. For me it is not my job, it is my life. My philosophy is the same as before. I want to win, I want to win, I want to win.'

Ranieri has changed the formation this season. Chelsea have usually been playing with a diamond-shaped midfield; last year it was a straight 4-4-2 with two wingers. 'Last season we did not buy any players. This season we buy 10 or 11 players and change everything. Now we are working to build a good team. I know that Roman Abramovich wants to put Chelsea at a high level like Milan or Real Madrid. I said to Mr Abramovich that Real Madrid are one of the best teams in the world and they have a great player and everything goes around him, and this man is Claude Makelele. I would like to buy him.

'For me Real Madrid was Claude Makelele. With him in the team Zidane played well, Figo played well – everyone played well. Now in England everybody is slowly understanding that maybe you don't notice him, but he is everywhere. He always stays in the middle and is such an intelligent player who can link with the attacking players and has good balance in his play. He is one of the greatest players in the world.'

So Chelsea bought him. Ranieri reveals the club's owner has been supportive in other ways. 'He is a good man and always comes into the dressing room after a match. Always he is smiling. After losing against Arsenal he was fantastic. I had said to him that it is important when we lose that he stays with us. When we lost against Besiktas and against Arsenal he was the first in the dressing room and we all appreciated that.'

But Ranieri wants the spending to stop for just a while. 'I have 25 players now, please! What do you want... do you want my blood? No, no, no more players. Slowly we are looking a team and the next match against Newcastle will be another brick in the wall of building the team. I am very curious to see our performance against Newcastle. After winning 4–0 [at Lazio] and with everyone talking about Chelsea, I want to make sure my players still have their feet on the floor. The next performance will tell me a lot about the make-up of my players.'

SUNDAY, 9 NOVEMBER

CHELSEA 5, NEWCASTLE 0

Formula One tycoon Bernie Ecclestone is a guest of Abramovich and the two are captured in friendly pose by the TV cameras prior to kick-off. There are rumours that Ecclestone is in talks to sell the most expensive home in Britain to Abramovich. The house in west London, which comprises two former embassies knocked together to create a giant mansion, is being discreetly marketed for £85m, a world record for a private residence.

On the pitch, goals from Johnson, Crespo, Lampard, Gudjohnsen and a sizzler from man of the match Duff complete the rout. Ranieri remains cautious. 'My players are young. They don't understand what a long season it is. I want them to have this kind of spirit, I like it. But the manager must keep the right balance. I believe we will win the title when I touch the trophy – and not before. Last season we were close to Arsenal and Manchester United. Then on Christmas Day they went away and said goodbye. My players are young and can dream but I am a concrete man and must work hard. I dream sometimes but when I wake up I start to work. The dream ends when the match starts.'

Again the midfield diamond sparkles, so it is only a matter of time before the opener arrives and, when it does, it is from an unlikely source on 24 minutes. The move that leads to Johnson's strike glows with intricate passing on the edge of the box involving Lampard, Mutu and Crespo and leads to a panic clearance to the lurking Bridge on the left flank. Bridge looks up and delivers with pace and precision, with Johnson, unmarked at the far post, bringing the ball down before rifling his first Premiership goal into the roof of the net.

A three-minute spell brings two more goals and a 43rd-minute red card for Newcastle defender Andy O'Brien, finishing the contest before the interval. Six minutes before the break, the second comes as Johnson's searching centre falls to the feet of Duff and, when he fires goalwards, Crespo is in the perfect place to stab home. Within a minute Mutu catches O'Brien in possession and heads for the box. The initial shirt-tug is outside the box, although Mutu's legs are taken from under him as well, and when assistant Phil Norman signals penalty to referee Paul Durkin, the dismissal is automatic.

Lampard's spot-kick is close to Shay Given's dive, but sheer force takes it past the keeper. Sir Bobby Robson slams Durkin. 'We might have had a chance, and then that happens. I had a word with Mr Durkin at half-time and I told him that

I thought the boy overran it, the linesman ended up giving it and it killed the game. You don't expect to win here with 10 men.'

Thirteen minutes from time Duff latches on to Given's poor clearance for a sumptuous bottom-corner finish with that glorious left foot. A 19-pass move for the fifth sums up Chelsea's domination. Olivier Bernard allows Gudjohnsen to wander in from the right and feed Bridge, but then also to walk into the box unchallenged to meet the left-back's measured ball with a simple header from eight yards. Robson says, 'I don't know where my centre-halves were, they must have been sat next to me!'

Chelsea goals are raining in from all sides. Five different players have scored against Newcastle; four different individuals did the trick against Lazio. Each of the four main forwards has scored at least half a dozen times. Crespo, Gudjohnsen and Mutu have six, Hasselbaink eight. Sven-Goran Eriksson says, 'Claudio Ranieri is doing a great job. The result they got at Lazio in the Champions League was fantastic. The top of the Premiership is very open and it depends on which team keeps most injury-free to the end of the season.' The bookies can now barely separate the three title favourites quoting Manchester United at 13–8, and Arsenal and Chelsea at 7–4.

Team

Cudicini, Johnson (Huth), Gallas, Terry, Bridge, Veron, Lampard, Makelele, Duff, Crespo (Gudjohnsen), Mutu (Cole).

MONDAY, 10 NOVEMBER

Glen Johnson is awaiting his first England call-up and Wayne Bridge says, 'Glen definitely deserves a chance and Gary Neville now has a contender for his place. It'd be great to see us playing in the same England team.'

Chelsea are delighted when it becomes official even though it means a bonus payment for West Ham if he plays for his country at senior level. Johnson says, 'Mr Ranieri told me straight after the game about England. He said, "Congratulations, Sven has picked you. Enjoy it." It was just minutes after the whistle went. Everyone was there waiting to shake my hand – all the players. They said, "Congratulations, and hopefully you will be there for years."'

Marcel Desailly quickly endorses that viewpoint. 'Glen Johnson has great quality for the future. He is still making small mistakes but you can feel he's going to be one of the best right-backs in the world. This is the type of game to give him a lot of confidence.'

On the debit side, Johnson has had two red cards already this season – one for England Under-21s and the other at Lazio. Bridge says, 'I saw only one of the yellow cards against Turkey and I thought it was a bit harsh. He's young so he's still learning. He's big enough and man enough not to do it again. He's down to earth and works hard and has got his head screwed on.'

Ranieri says, 'I hoped Glen would be in the England squad. Glen is a good man and he's doing well. He has a very bright future. His skill is fantastic. Physically he can run for two matches and never stands still. When I chose him I remembered when he played against us – he was fantastic. I also looked at videos of him and was very impressed.' Johnson joins up with an England party that also features Terry, Lampard and Cole.

TUESDAY, 11 NOVEMBER

Ranieri sometimes conducts 13-a-side training sessions! Eidur Gudjohnsen says, 'There are a lot of great players here now; one day we had about 26 in training so we had to play 13-a-side. There was no one you could ask to sit it out.'

The club's Harlington training ground is so crowded that training bibs have become prized possessions. As Duff says, 'We have a squad of 24 or 25 players, so we could field two different teams every Saturday. Even with the Republic of Ireland team, when bibs are handed out in training you know what the starting line-up will be by the colour. Here if they hand out 11 bibs, there really is no clue as to what the team will be because both sides are so strong. What this means is you can't just go to training and mess about. Other places you might get away with a dip in form, but not here.

'I get the feeling you could score a hat-trick one week, and not get in the side the next. Everyone knows we have to win the Premiership this year after all the money we've spent. I really don't think we can afford to wait two or three years to win the championship after the quality that has been brought in. There's no point lying; we're all looking to win the league this year.'

Gudjohnsen reveals the high aspirations of the new owner. 'He spoke about his vision for Chelsea and made it clear he wanted to take the club to the top. He said, "I want to make your life as easy as possible. I want you to concentrate on performing. I'll make sure everything is provided for you." And I have to say, the man was very impressive.'

Hernan Crespo denies that his Italian team-mates were surprised by his decision to join Chelsea. 'On the contrary, many of them wanted to come and join me as well! In a way, it surprised me that I swapped Inter for Chelsea, but I can help them become great. At other clubs, the history is already written, but at Chelsea, a lot more remains to be written and we, the players, can do that now. It's scary learning a new language, but I'm confident I can do it because when I went to Italy at 21 I didn't even know how to say, "Hello" in Italian and now I'm married to an Italian lady.' Crespo is also asked whether it is true he once wanted to be a bin man? 'Where did they get that from? Oh, no, no, no,' he says.

Carlton Cole makes a long-awaited comeback for Charlton lasting 78 minutes in the reserves at The Valley – against Chelsea. Who else?

WEDNESDAY, 12 NOVEMBER

Sven-Goran Eriksson fears Chelsea and Manchester United's Champions League campaigns could wreck his Euro 2004 preparations as key players will join up with the England squad without a break.

Eriksson will gather his players on 23 May, one week after the end of the Premiership campaign but just 24 hours after the FA Cup Final. And with Manchester United and Chelsea both set to go through to the knock-out stages of the Champions League as group-winners, Eriksson is concerned at the prospect of sustained runs by both clubs. The final is on 26 May and Eriksson fears an all-Premiership affair. Eriksson has not hidden his annoyance at the Premiership's refusal to end the season on 8 May.

THURSDAY, 13 NOVEMBER

Sir Alex Ferguson congratulates Chelsea on their success so far. 'The long term looks good for Chelsea, and they haven't done much wrong since the start of the season. You keep looking for them to hit some kind of blip, but they haven't yet. What has surprised me is that they've hit the ground running. The great start they've had has allowed them to get rid of all the questions like who's a good buy and who's a bad buy, and how they're going to keep happy all the players they've bought. But Chelsea are winning and that settles everyone at the club. Having such a good start has taken away a lot of the pressures.

'Looking at the way the league has shaped up, you'd have to say it now looks as though it's between ourselves, Arsenal and Chelsea. Liverpool and Newcastle will improve over the season because they're big clubs with huge resources, but I have to say it looks like the winner will come from one of the top three. I have been surprised at how quickly Chelsea have gelled as a team, because I think many people, including myself, thought that might take time. Claudio Ranieri's doing a fantastic job, because it can't be easy with so many new players coming in.

'They've bought an interesting choice of players, young players to build a team for many seasons. That represents a clear statement of intent for the future. Glen Johnson, Damien Duff, Wayne Bridge, they're all young. And the players already there, the likes of William Gallas, John Terry and Eidur Gudjohnsen, all young too. Bringing down the age of the squad is something we've tried to do here with the young players we bought in the summer.'

The countdown to the confrontation between the two sides has clearly started early, as Fergie concludes, 'That'll be some game. It will be a big test for both sides. And it's St Andrew's day of course, so I can't let my country down.'

FRIDAY, 14 NOVEMBER

In Liverpool, it seems Gerard Houllier had set himself a five-year target for winning the Premiership but he is now concerned about the Abramovich factor. 'I talked about winning the league in five years and I think we can still do that. I said that in 1999 and I still believe that, but there is the Chelsea factor to consider. We can win the league so long as another Roman Abramovich doesn't come along at another rival club.

'Sir Alex Ferguson and Arsene Wenger are as concerned as I am about things like that. The arrival of Abramovich has changed everything in English soccer, and not necessarily for the better. Manchester United and Arsenal know, as much as we do, that it is impossible to compete against the sort of money Chelsea are spending. If there are more clubs like that, then it makes life very difficult.'

Yet, Houllier himself has spent in excess of £110m since he arrived at Anfield! He goes on, 'If you get a couple of people like Abramovich, then it will be all about buying success, and nothing else. And that will cause problems to the entire game. Sides like Manchester United and Liverpool have spent money, but not on that scale. And they have always combined it with a policy of developing from within. What would be damaging is if it becomes just a contest about who can spend the most money in winning the championship – and that could happen if more people like Roman Abramovich come along.'

Meanwhile Marcel Desailly says, 'Five–nil against a title rival like Newcastle following a 4–0 Champions League win in Rome has sent out a massive psychological message to our rivals. I know previously they were all thinking, "Chelsea have decent players but they still can't play well enough together." We have forced a total reassessment. Now they know we can handle pressure but, most importantly, can also fight to the death to win crucial matches.

'Suddenly I can see other players and managers understand that this is a Chelsea side which is going places – and going there fast. After the win in Rome we needed to come back to England and show everyone we were still focused and belonged at the top. We did it and it will have a huge effect. Morale is absolutely sky-high and our psychological strength is simply formidable. We know we have the quality to make the difference in any game we play.'

Manchester United insist they are not seeking an Abramovich. New chief executive David Gill says at the AGM, 'We don't need a sugar daddy.' Gill tells the meeting that, yes indeed, the club had tried to sign Duff before Chelsea did. 'We were interested in Damien Duff and assessed the value of the player. We knew his personal terms and were in discussions with his agent and discussed that with the manager. The assessment of the manager and the executives was that Damien wasn't worth that money. It became apparent he was using us as a stalking horse.'

SATURDAY, 15 NOVEMBER

Eriksson suggests Joe Cole could play as a second striker for England despite a goal ratio of one in 13 at club level. Cole says, 'I might have a reputation for just coming off the bench but reputations can change.' John Terry chuckles when he begins singing Cole's praises... only to realise his mate is in the room. Terry says, 'Joe would do brilliantly playing off the front two.' Cole yells, 'Thanks, Tel.' Terry laughs, 'Sorry, change that – he's shit.'

But Terry adds, 'Seriously, Joe has so much talent you can play him anywhere. If you said he was in goal then he would go out and do it. For Chelsea this season, he's made five or six goals when he's come on. He's the best player we've got at opening up defences and the manager knows that.'

Terry's first-team place looked under threat at the beginning of the season but not any more. He says, 'I was worried I wouldn't be playing. But I worked hard, I've had some games for England and things couldn't be going better now. If I'm playing well for Chelsea I will be picked by Mr Eriksson. And it will be my fault if I'm not doing it.'

Terry has come through after the dark days of a court case which could have finished his career. 'I owe a lot to Gianfranco Zola who helped me through that. He used to take me out to play golf and I would open up to him. He made me realise I had to concentrate on my football and I've grown up a lot in the last two years. I'm going out doing the right things with friends and family. Claudio Ranieri has been great for me as well. He's a great character and I will never forget what he's done for me.'

SUNDAY, 16 NOVEMBER

Glen Johnson comes on in the first half for the injured Gary Neville, while Joe Cole plays all but the last 15 minutes of England's 3–2 defeat by Denmark and scores his second international goal. Cole is one of six Chelsea players on the Old Trafford pitch at one stage, with Lampard, Terry, Bridge and Johnson for England and Gronkjaer in the Denmark team. The average age of the five who play for England is 22 – with Lampard the oldest at 25 – and already they have 50 caps between them. Ironically, the five have started only one game together for Chelsea – against Birmingham City.

Republic of Ireland manager Brian Kerr stresses that his players have not been affected by an armed raid on the team's hotel, the Portmarnock Golf and Country Club, on the outskirts of Dublin shortly after 6.30pm. Masked robbers burst into the foyer and escape with an estimated £600 in cash, firing one gunshot into the ceiling as they do so. Members of the Irish squad – preparing for Tuesday night's friendly with Canada at Lansdowne Road – have vacated the area only minutes earlier for a meal downstairs, and the incident does Duff no harm since he scores a magnificent goal in the 2–0 win.

MONDAY, 17 NOVEMBER

'I welcome criticism from people like Mr Eriksson, especially when people have the experience that he's got,' Joe Cole says at the launch of his personal website. 'Criticism and experience are the only way you learn. I've been on a high since Sunday. There's nothing better than scoring for England and to do it in front of 65,000 fans at Old Trafford was wicked. I did not score enough goals in the past but I will put that right this year. I was not getting forward as much last year. Scholes plays in the same position as I do but there's no reason why we can't play in the same team. I don't consider myself a bit-part player. I want to make myself a regular for Chelsea and England, and I don't see why I can't do that.'

Eriksson hints that Cole is unlikely to start for England in the friendlies against Portugal and Sweden in February and March, news which leaves Cole visibly stunned. 'I didn't know Mr Eriksson had said that, but three months is a long way down the line, so we'll have to wait and see.'

An investigation into insider trading at the company that owned Chelsea before the takeover by Abramovich is dropped by the City watchdog. But there will still be a second inquiry into the "nature and status of certain shareholdings" in Chelsea Village plc in the days before the bid.

TUESDAY, 18 NOVEMBER

Marcel Desailly is to return to France when his contract runs out. He says he was forced to start almost from scratch when he moved to England because of the difference in style. 'It's a more violent, a faster game. I came from Milan, where the game was more intellectual, more orderly, almost quiet.'

Desailly says his compatriots could take some lessons from English crowds about respect for players. 'I love their coolness and their civic sense. At three I'm on the pitch and they cheer me and, three hours later, I'm in a museum and they leave me alone. That's great.' He also praises English fans for 'realising that the players give it their all' but adds Italian football will always remain closer to his heart. 'Even today, between a big game in Italy or in the Premier League, my choice is easy.'

There is some suggestion he might quit at the end of the season. 'I am beginning to tire of everything. Training does not please me every day. There are mornings when I don't want to go. I stubbornly maintain to my wife that I won't go and get shot down in flames for the umpteenth time by a manager who is on my tracks every day. As with all jobs, there is a weariness beginning to show through. Physical limits can push you into retirement, but it's the mind that goes first. It is a daily battle against this feeling. Sometimes I ask myself what I am still looking for in football with all the things I have won.

'I am one of the lucky ones who can still play at the top level at 35, but things are not easy every day for me. My recovery time is longer than before. All the craziness that surrounds football tires me when I long for a certain form of peace. If this season goes well, if my body and mind follow, I'll continue. If I have to stop, I'll do so without any bother.'

He also stokes up the clash with Manchester United. 'The danger is judging England by London. Manchester is good for playing a match in, that's all. I could not imagine myself playing anywhere except the capital.'

A spokesman at Manchester Visitors' Centre replies, 'The only thing Manchester lacks is a beach. If it was good enough for Eric Cantona, I'm sure it's good enough for Desailly.'

WEDNESDAY, 19 NOVEMBER

Abramovich hires an executive box at the Millennium Stadium as Russia beat Wales 1–0 to qualify for Euro 2004, with Alexei Smertin outstanding in midfield.

Ex-manager Ian McNeill, now 71, and chief scout at the Bridge, who discovered Hasselbaink for Leeds and advised Ken Bates to sign Cristiano Ronaldo for £2m when he was just 16, says of the Portuguese starlet, "Manchester United had to pay £12m but Alex Ferguson has got a great player. That is the type of player I have to target so Roman doesn't have to dig into his bank account too often.

There has never been an owner in the game like him and there are nothing but good vibes about the guy.'

THURSDAY, 20 NOVEMBER

Chelsea refuse to take up their ticket allocation for the visit to Besiktas because of inadequate Turkish security measures. English and Turkish fans have clashed repeatedly over the past few years: two Leeds supporters were killed before the club's UEFA Cup semi-final against Galatasaray in Istanbul three years ago. The FA refused their allocation of tickets for England's European Championship qualifier in Turkey last month, though a small number of fans defied the travel ban and entered the stadium. In the end though, the tie is certain to be switched from Istanbul to a neutral venue following terrorist atrocities.

Acting chief executive Paul Smith says, 'We put in our request to move the game to a neutral territory and have not heard back from UEFA. We made our position clear that in the interests of safety and security we feel the match should be moved.'

Birmingham City reach agreement to keep Mikael Forssell until the end of the season. Manager Steve Bruce says, 'We've shaken hands on it. There is no danger of him going anywhere else in the transfer window and we are delighted he will be with us until the end of the season. Obviously, if Chelsea suffer a spate of injuries up front then things may change but that is the same with any loan deal. Barring any unforeseen circumstances, Mikael is with us until May. In the summer if there's a deal to be done, and Chelsea are willing to sell Mikael, then great.'

Celestine Babayaro is expected to be missing for six weeks during the African Nations' Cup but he says, 'Of course in January Chelsea are going to have massive games again and it could be a bad time for me. But whatever happens, I'm ready to battle for my place in the team.

'Roman Abramovich is a cool guy, a young man who loves football. He is at all our games, both home and away, and afterwards, he comes to see us in the dressing room. His involvement with the club has been great – and it can only get better.'

FRIDAY, 21 NOVEMBER

Less than four years ago the Blues made soccer history at Southampton when Gianluca Vialli fielded a Chelsea team without a single British player. Now, it is packed with English players. Ranieri says, 'It was a very proud occasion for me to see five Chelsea players in the England team against Denmark. That was a very important moment for the club – and also for English football.'

Frank Lampard is setting a trend with a marvellous unbroken Premiership run. He says, 'A lot of people like to have a dig at Chelsea, and think we're a flash bunch with all the foreigners we have at the club, but the brilliant spirit this season hasn't surprised me. After all, we have a good core of young English lads here and, whatever you say about us, we do add that bit of steel to the side. You need only look at someone like John Terry to see what I mean. He doesn't shout like some captains but he always leads by example out on the pitch. Credit to the foreign lads – they've shown a real desire to fight. People have been waiting for Chelsea to slip up but I think we've proved that we're here to stay.'

Ranieri has kept the same team for the past two matches but is expected to make changes for the Premiership match with Southampton, with an eye on the Champions League game against Sparta Prague. He is not underestimating the team from the south coast though. 'It is always difficult for us against Gordon Strachan's team because they fight from start to finish.'

Saints have failed to score in five of their last six Premiership games, but Chelsea have a poor record against Strachan's men in recent seasons. However, the admiration Gordon Strachan seems to have for Ranieri knows no bounds. 'I'm such a big fan maybe I should have a picture of him on my bedroom wall. He is an example to all of us how a manager should behave in adversity and under pressure. He has stood head and shoulders above everyone else this season with the way he conducts himself. He has blown away everyone who has tried to criticise him.

'He is great and his team is very good. They are good enough to win the title, and about six weeks ago I told my son that if he fancied a wee gamble then put money on them to win the European Cup. In recent seasons it has been all about United and Arsenal. Now there are three genuine challengers. Yes, money can buy the title, but it also takes a great manager and that's what Chelsea have. I'm not envious; I'm more excited about what has been happening at Stamford Bridge.'

SATURDAY, 22 NOVEMBER

SOUTHAMPTON 0, CHELSEA 1

Ranieri watches the final of the Rugby World Cup at a hotel in Southampton. 'It was fantastic, a fantastic final and a fantastic spirit. Both the teams... Boum! Boum! I like that spirit. Amazing! I am speechless! Fantastic!'

Before the game at St Mary's, Chelsea trail Arsenal by a point, with United a further point behind. Ranieri makes four changes: Gudjohnsen partners Hasselbaink up front, while Cole is given a start in midfield, and Melchiot comes in at right-back. Melchiot, named as one of a group of Dutch players spotted out on the town after their 1–0 defeat in Scotland last weekend, strikes just after half-time as Chelsea secure their seventh straight Premiership victory. Melchiot begins the move, finding Lampard unmarked in midfield, who slips a precision pass to Hasselbaink, whose first time lay-off cuts the home defence to ribbons. Melchiot, having continued his run down the right flank, latches onto the pass, and cuts in on the angle before beating Antti Niemi with a low drive into the corner. Melchiot's first goal for 18 months is enough.

Kevin Phillips should earn Saints a point when presented with a golden chance four minutes from time, but, unmarked, he heads just wide from Fabrice Fernandes' cross. Ranieri says he 'suffered a lot' near the end as Southampton put great pressure on his team in the heavy rain.

The 32,149 crowd is a record for Southampton. Ranieri's verdict? 'The first half was very bland, but the second half was a good match. We scored a goal and made another two great chances to finish the match, but when you don't score it's difficult and we were fortunate they missed chances. We showed good character.'

Despite his earlier pleas for clemency, Wayne Bridge is a target for home supporters with his every touch. Ranieri singles out Makelele as his man of the match. 'In the first half we played with a diamond and Makelele was in front of our centre-backs, then I changed it to 4-4-2 and he was with Frank Lampard in midfield. Makelele is not a big star, but he's my battery. He's Chelsea's battery.' His contribution can be gauged by a fourth consecutive clean sheet.

Graeme Le Saux proves he has not lost his sense of humour. 'There were a couple of times I wanted to shout at Jimmy Floyd Hasselbaink, thinking he was a team-mate, rather than an opponent – so I just shouted at him anyway.'

Team

Cudicini, Melchiot, Terry, Gallas, Bridge, Makelele, Lampard, Cole, (Gronkjaer), Duff (Stanic), Gudjohnsen, Hasselbaink (Mutu).

SUNDAY, 23 NOVEMBER

Manchester United's best start in 10 years still leaves them only third. Ryan Giggs observes, 'Panathinaikos are up next, but we all know the Chelsea game's a big one. The way the Premiership is, with Arsenal, Chelsea and ourselves not dropping any points, we have to keep winning. Chelsea are riding high and playing really well, and they appear to have gelled very quickly as a unit. Stamford Bridge is a difficult place to go at the best of times and we know we'll need to be at our best if we're to beat them.'

John Terry says, 'The Manchester United game will be a massive challenge and it's a chance for us to prove ourselves. We've already played Arsenal and a lot of people are saying that those two will be our big rivals. We're confident that we're as good as them and, if we keep on winning, we can put them under pressure. We lost at Highbury so it's important to prove we can beat one of the big two. It's vital and beating United would give us a big psychological boost. Since we lost to Arsenal we've won seven games in a row and proved we can bounce back. We're going to get into United in the first 20 minutes, take the game to them and see what happens.'

Ranieri is looking for signs Chelsea are ready to challenge for the championship. 'It's very important for the whole league to not always have the same two teams at the top and now there are three. We are the little boy who wants to achieve this and we are ready to fight with them for the title. I'm happy that we are close to two great teams but it's only November. I'd like to be in the same position in April.'

MONDAY, 24 NOVEMBER

Having scored for Argentina in both World Cup qualifiers against Bolivia and Colombia, Hernan Crespo is in form. Meanwhile Joe Cole is focusing on the forthcoming match with Sparta Prague. 'It's a massive game for us. Sparta gave us a good match over there when we only just won 1–0, and they have some really good players like Karel Poborsky. It's at our own ground so we're expected to win, but as we've seen recently it's not always the big teams with the big players who win. We have to make sure that we don't let anything go wrong.'

Babayaro resolves his differences with the Nigerian FA and now says, 'Nothing will stop me from playing for my country.' Robert Huth joins reserve striker Sebastian Kneissl in the Germany squad for the World Under-20 Championships in the United Arab Emirates. Marcel Desailly makes his long-awaited comeback. Sinisa Mihajlovic begins his eight-match ban by missing Lazio's Champions League match against Besiktas. 'I apologise to my team-mates, to the coach and the club for being sent off against Chelsea, which clearly influenced the final result. Children should not use my behaviour that night as an example. But I want to clarify that if I had such a reaction it was due to the fact that I was provoked in an undignified way. That is why, just as it had occurred with Vieira, I have not apologised to Mutu. Whether it is good or bad, this is my character. But I'm disappointed that TV proof has only punished me when there were images showing what I'd gone through.'

TUESDAY, 25 NOVEMBER

Ranieri challenges his team to have the same spirit and discipline as England's triumphant World Cup-winning rugby side in the two vital home matches Chelsea have to play within five days.

So, what's Claudio really like? Some of his players try to explain. Joe Cole says, 'Claudio is an Italian Kevin Keegan, always smiling and making jokes. He's an enigmatic character. I like his honesty. He will always tell me what he thinks. He has no trouble getting his point across and is definitely the man to lead Chelsea to a lot of success over the coming years.'

Eidur Gudjohnsen weighs in with his own observation. 'This season we can see excitement in Claudio. Now he has the chance to take on the best clubs in the world and he's really happy about it. This is what he has always wanted. For Claudio what has happened with the money from Roman Abramovich must be like a genie coming out of a lamp, because it's given him the chance to build his dream squad.'

Behind the smiling exterior lurks a training-ground demon. Damien Duff reveals, 'He's a very tough manager to work with. He makes it really intense for us every single day in training, and there is absolutely no let-up. There are so many players breathing down your neck here, you can never take it easy.'

UEFA's emergency committee in Brussels decides the Besiktas game will be taken out of Istanbul and played in a neutral country. But looking forward to the next game, Ranieri reminds everybody that it will be no formality. 'Sparta can go through to the next round only if they beat us. They play better away from Prague, so they are very dangerous.'

WEDNESDAY, 26 NOVEMBER

CHELSEA 0, SPARTA PRAGUE 0

The score is enough to secure passage into the knock-out stages, but if Crespo's first-half effort had been allowed, Ranieri's men would have confirmed top spot in the group. 'Crespo's goal was good,' pronounces Ranieri. 'I do not understand why the linesman did not give a goal. It was not offside. A point was OK, but now it is important to get another against Besiktas to win the group. It is important to avoid the big teams in the draw.'

Duff's teasing centre begs for Crespo to finish, and while his header beats the keeper, it rebounds off the bar. Mutu is first to the loose ball and Crespo stabs home, but the flag is up. Nine minutes from the end, substitute Geremi's deep free-kick from the left finds Terry popping up to head along the goal-line. Gallas hurls himself at the ball, but he fails to make contact a foot from the line.

Cole, hoping to make a point to Sven-Goran Eriksson's assistant Tord Grip, tries hard to impress. He makes the starting line-up for only the sixth time in 21 matches and plays well, only to be substituted in the second half, straight after carelessly conceding possession. Clearly angry, he hurls a water bottle to the ground as he takes his seat in the dug-out. 'That was just frustration after giving the ball away a couple of times. I wasn't angry with the manager's decision, it was just that I wanted to do so well, and it wasn't nice to leave the pitch on a negative,' he says. Ranieri comments, 'Joe was great. Joe is full of skills. He can make something special, and I was pleased with his performance.'

The last game in the group will be played at the AufSchalke Arena in Gelsenkirchen which will also host the Champions League final. Chelsea need a point to top their group, and Lampard believes that is vital. 'Winning the group will give us confidence and put us in a stronger position for the next round. We need a draw against Besiktas but we will go to win the game. We've got the means to do that. We're always a threat away from home.'

Diego Forlan's 85th-minute strike against Panathinaikos confirms Manchester United's passage to the knock-out stages but Sir Alex Ferguson admits he had one eye on the Chelsea clash. 'Irrespective of the result tonight, everything would still have hinged on whether we beat Stuttgart in our last game,' says Ferguson. 'If we win, we will win the section so I wasn't prepared to risk anyone with an injury tonight.' He rests several first-team players. With group-winners likely to include Real Madrid, holders AC Milan and Juventus, Ranieri and Fergie are desperate to avoid Europe's leading lights until later in the competition.

Team

Cudicini, Melchiot, Terry, Gallas, Bridge, Duff, Makelele, Lampard, Cole (Geremi), Crespo (Gudjohnsen), Mutu.

THURSDAY, 27 NOVEMBER

Abramovich's planned merger of oil companies Sibneft and Yukos stalls. Yukos share prices plunge ten per cent and Sibneft shares by six per cent. About 75 percent of Yukos shareholders vote against the tie-up, in which Abramovich is seeking to liquidate many of his Russian-based assets. The share price falls wipe millions of dollars from the value of Abramovich's holdings but it is only temporary.

He makes a surprise visit to the training ground ahead of one of the biggest games of the season against Manchester United. Joe Cole may be pie-and-mash at heart, but it's fruit-salad days at Harlington. 'They go in for a lot of Italian grub here, and I don't like the sauces. I've learnt not to say anything to the chef, otherwise he gets the right hump.'

Cole has started consecutive matches for the first time, and is naturally anxious to make it three in a row. 'It's a case of having to make yourself indispensable to the boss, otherwise you won't be a starter. Once you do get in, you have to ensure that he can't leave you out. It's no good just having a good game, you have to be outstanding to keep your place. The main difference since I moved is that at West Ham I had to do everything. In my first few games for Chelsea, I was still thinking like that, and coming deep. The gaffer kept telling me to stay forward and not track runners as much. He wanted me to get on the ball. At West Ham, I was trying to do everybody's job, whereas at Chelsea they want to free me up.' Cole describes the clash with United as the 'acid test'. 'They are the champions, and if we want to win the league, then they are the team to beat.'

If John Terry had followed his initial instincts he could have been a Manchester United player. A massive United fan, Terry was regularly ferried to Manchester for training by club scout Malcolm Fidgeon. Alongside him in the back seat was David Beckham – four years older – and United thought highly of then midfielder Terry. 'When I had the chance to go up there it was a dream come true. I was about 14 and Malcolm used to drive me and David up for training.

'United made an effort to sign me and that was a great experience. They were playing at West Ham one day and invited me and my family to have the pre-match meal with them at the Swallow Hotel. I was sitting at the same table as Paul Ince and Eric Cantona, who were my idols. I had my photograph taken with them. They gave me beans on toast but I was too scared to eat it. But when I came here I loved it so much that I decided to sign for the club. Chelsea looked after me and my family, giving me boots and training kit to play in. They might seem silly things but they made all the difference to me.'

Frank Lampard believes the Blues have been given a huge helping hand by Sir Alex, by allowing Veron to move. 'Seba really is a world-class performer. Maybe he wasn't appreciated at United because he doesn't run around making tackles all the time. But his quality is unbelievable and he'll be a big factor in how far we go in the title race and Europe.'

FRIDAY, 28 NOVEMBER

In the press conference before the United game, Ranieri concedes he will be sacked by Roman Abramovich if he doesn't finish a winner. 'It's not difficult. When you have a good relation with the owner, where is the problem? In my work, if you win, you continue. And if you don't win, you're out. I must build something special this year. If I don't, I'm out. And if Sven-Goran Eriksson arrives or somebody else, it's all the same for me. Now you tell me what's easier: to win with champions on your team or to win without them? I want to win. The pressure is my pressure. I want the best.'

The agent of Bayern Munich midfielder Michael Ballack claims Chelsea are ready to bid for the German international. The player's representative Michael Becker claims his client may be about to quit the Bundesliga for England.

SATURDAY, 29 NOVEMBER

Abramovich invites 250 of his pals from Moscow for the United game. Acting chief executive Paul Smith tells me, 'We could have sold this game twice over, demand has been formidable. Normally Roman brings over between five and twenty of his associates depending on the game, but for this one it was more than 200 but not as many as the 400 quoted in the papers.'

Tickets are going for £400 on the black market. The top three are on course for the first, second and fourth best records in a top-flight campaign since 1892. Mutu observes, 'I never missed a Manchester United match, especially if Cantona was playing. Cantona was my idol. No one was like him; no one was more important to me. I liked everything about him – his personality, his game, his variety – he was simply magnificent. I think, as far as grit and passion go, I have very similar characteristics.'

Mutu has already grasped much of the English language, even its nuances. What of the cuisine? 'Only Italian restaurants for me, English food is indigestible.'

SUNDAY, 30 NOVEMBER
CHELSEA 1, MANCHESTER UNITED 0

England draw France, Switzerland and Croatia in the European Championship as Sven-Goran Eriksson withstands a predictable bombardment of questions regarding his contract before Chelsea's big match.

Inside the Pavilhao Atlantico, a futuristic convention centre perched on Lisbon's sea front, he is grilled about a newspaper report declaring that he has agreed a four-year contract with Chelsea worth £18m. 'How much?' Eriksson splutters when asked about the story. 'Jesus, I think I should sign at once. No, I have never heard about that.'

The FA aims to flush out the Swede's intentions by offering him more money to ensure he will stay the full distance to 2008. He is irritated. 'The only thing that annoyed me was that it should never have come out, that it should have stayed in private, but that's football. I have always said that I miss being at a club, but in every job you have advantages and disadvantages and this job is huge, bigger than I thought, with so much prestige. Sometimes it is easy, sometimes very difficult, but a bigger job is difficult to have. Brazil? I don't know, it's on the same level, maybe.'

Paul Smith makes it clear there is 'no substance' to the renewed media frenzy of speculation about Ranieri's future. 'At the moment Claudio is focusing on the team. He doesn't bother with these kinds of stories. I am not aware of anything, and if it was to materialise then I would be aware of it.'

Asked whether the club are 100 per cent happy with Ranieri, he replies, 'Absolutely. It's clear he's been very successful so far this season. The attitude within the club is that there is complete commitment to Claudio and we are very responsive to anything he requires. I've not had to give him any reassurances.'

The showdown starts with a moving reception for Rugby World Cup-winners and Chelsea fans Clive Woodward and Lawrence Dallaglio. It ends with a standing ovation for Ranieri and his Chelsea heroes. After hearing that the owner has just bought a £72m yacht, Ranieri reckons he is himself due a lucrative bonus. 'If he wants to give me a yacht, I will say, "Thank you." That would be great. But we only want to be favourites to win the league after we have played Manchester United for a second time in May.

'We are very pleased with a great result against the champions. The first half was very good, we moved the ball well and we created a lot of scoring chances. In the second half, they put us under pressure from wide positions and I changed the system, bringing on Damien Duff and Jesper Gronkjaer on the flanks. But we suffered a lot simply because Manchester United is Manchester United. This result will give us good confidence. We are not thinking of the title – for us it is important to continue to build and improve. When I compare today's performance to the level Manchester United and Arsenal are at, I would say we played well and showed good character but we must keep possession of the ball better.'

Arsenal's failure to beat Fulham earlier in the day means victory for either team carries them to the top of the table. With so much at stake, it is inevitable that the sides should opt for caution. Duff looks a certain starter but the unpredictable coach selects Cole instead at the top of his diamond formation, with Geremi and Lampard the wide midfield players. Lampard and Makelele run the show against United. Lampard thumps home the match-winning spot-kick despite Mutu being the designated penalty-taker. Ranieri explains, 'Our penalty-taking order is Jimmy Floyd Hasselbaink, Mutu, then Frank – but every time Frank grabs the ball I say, "Yes, very clever."'

United have more possession as the game goes on but Ranieri brings on Gronkjaer and Duff to combat United's tactical changes. Cole makes the crucial breakthrough, racing on to Crespo's 28th-minute through-ball to burst United's defensive line. Roy Keane's last-ditch lunge is always going to be too late to reach the ball and his challenge sends Cole down in the area. Keane and his team-mates inevitably argue fiercely with referee Alan Wiley. Yet contact is made and TV replays prove Wiley right. Tim Howard's stalling tactics are to no avail as Lampard coolly converts his sixth goal. Such is Chelsea's superiority it is not until the 73rd minute that Ruud van Nistelrooy mounts his only serious effort on goal.

Ranieri even claims Sir Alex Ferguson has taken over his mantle as Tinkerman. He makes only one alteration from the starting line-up while Fergie rings the changes. Chelsea's most significant domestic win under Abramovich is more emphatic than the scoreline suggests, and all without Veron, Desailly, Johnson, Petit, Gudjohnsen and, for most of this match, Hasselbaink. At the end, Ferguson storms off, mumbling about the inadequacies of referee Wiley and the injustice of the penalty award. Chelsea have not conceded a goal in almost eight hours of Premiership football.

'Have you ever seen Chelsea win the league?' chant the visiting supporters. But Ferguson concedes, 'It was a great result for them but it's too early to say what it means, only 14 games into the season. It's when you are top in April that you start to feel the pressure.'

'We've made a big statement here,' John Terry says after marshalling the defence to its sixth successive clean sheet. 'There's a long way to go but psychologically this was brilliant for us. It's another clean sheet and the defensive lads are well happy, but we put 11 together a few years back so there's still a way to go for our record.'

At the final whistle Ranieri quietly takes off his spectacles, tucks them in his pocket, raises his eyebrows and his face instantly gives him away: Ranieri is a happy man, and can, temporarily, forget about Eriksson. The Morecambe and Wise standard 'Bring Me Sunshine' is playing over the PA system as the players celebrate, while Manchester United's stars make their morose exit.

The bookmakers install Chelsea as 5–4 favourites for the title.

Team

Cudicini, Melchiot, Terry, Gallas, Bridge, Geremi, Makelele, Lampard, Cole (Duff), Crespo (Gronkjaer), Mutu (Hasselbaink).

December

Air Alex Ferguson warns Chelsea to wait before dreaming of the championship. 'It's not a bad thing them being top. But the questions are not asked now but in March and April. People keep falling into this trap.'

Chelsea's acting chief executive Paul Smith tells me there is only a 'slim' chance of a January signing as the very best stars are still in Champions League teams. Smith reiterates the official position on Ranieri. 'There's no interest in Eriksson and we've not even had one conversation about him. It's just the same old story. How can you criticise Claudio? We are top of the league and through to the last 16 of the Champions League. Everyone at the club is very happy with the work he's been doing and we want him in charge at the start of next season. We've given him the players he wants and the freedom to develop the team. That's all a coach can ask for.'

Pos	Team	P	W	D	L	GF	GA	GD	PTS
	PREMIERSHIP TABLE – DECEMBER								
1	Chelsea	14	11	2	1	28	9	19	35
2	Arsenal	14	10	4	0	28	10	18	34
3	Manchester United	14	10	1	3	25	9	16	31
4	Fulham	14	6	4	4	24	18	6	22
5	Charlton Athletic	14	6	4	4	20	17	3	22
6	Liverpool	14	6	3	5	21	15	6	21
7	Newcastle United	14	5	5	4	20	19	1	20
8	Birmingham City	14	5	5	4	12	14	-2	20
9	Manchester City	14	5	3	6	22	19	3	18
10	Middlesbrough	14	5	3	6	12	15	-3	18

Abramovich backs the annual dinner given for the Chelsea Pitch Owners – a separate group set up by Ken Bates to protect the playing surface by ensuring it could never be developed, no matter what happened to the rest of the Chelsea Village. Abramovich had politely declined to sponsor the dinner in its entirety, but has now taken two tables at £7,000 each.

Among Abramovich's guests at the Manchester United match was Boris Becker, but more interesting was the appearance in the directors' box of Inter Milan president Massimo Moratti. On the agenda is Chelsea's entry to the top table of European club football, the lobby group G14. Set up some years ago, G14 has swelled to 18 members, and now Chelsea are sure to be put forward as club number 19. Inter have been strong allies of Chelsea since the lavish summit dinner between Abramovich and Moratti when talks opened on buying one of the Serie A club's strikers.

MONDAY, 1 DECEMBER

Referee Alan Wiley receives backing from Keith Hackett, the acting manager of the 21 Premiership referees, for the contentious penalty decision against Manchester United. Former World Cup ref Clive Thomas tells Sir Alex Ferguson to learn the rules if he does not think it was a spot-kick. Fergie retorts, 'Clive Thomas has always got something to say. Roy definitely got the ball.' But Joe Cole declares, 'It was a penalty. Roy made contact with me. If he had thought it wasn't a penalty, he would have given me a mouthful. He said nothing. I felt definite contact and went down. The replays showed it was a penalty.'

Ferguson takes the opportunity to have a dig at Chelsea for trying to buy success and failing to put faith in younger players. Yet Fergie himself has spent £114m since September 2000, when Ranieri took charge! Fergie refuses to panic about United's current position. 'I'm actually quite pleased Chelsea are top at this moment. It's good for the game. People were getting fed up with Manchester United and Arsenal winning everything all the time. You cannot deny any club the opportunity to progress and Chelsea clearly have the resources to do that. But Manchester United are in a different position to Chelsea, a unique position, if you like. We put great store in producing our own players and our transfer policy is always worked out with that in mind. When things heat up between February and April, that is when Manchester United historically do well.'

Claude Makelele joins United and Arsenal stars in Barcelona to film an advert for Nike. Bayer Leverkusen defender Lucio announces he would rather play for Juventus than Chelsea; Real Madrid's Roberto Carlos declines to move to the Bridge; meanwhile, Ranieri rejects the chance to take a third Brazilian, Rivaldo, because he doesn't want to disrupt the 'camaraderie' he has created in his already large squad, despite the fact the superstar is willing to take a pay cut to come to Chelsea. Inter's sporting director Marco Branca announces that he is unwilling to sell his club's prize asset. 'Vieri is not under discussion. Chelsea have offered €12m (£8.3m) for him? Vieri is not on the market.' But that, of course, was an offer Chelsea made prior to the deal for Crespo.

TUESDAY, 2 DECEMBER

Joe Cole is banned for two matches and fined £15,000 by the FA for an incident which occurred when he was still a West Ham player at the end of a game at Bolton in April. Cole will miss the game at Charlton on Boxing Day and the home match against Portsmouth. Ken Bates immediately attacks the 'total incompetence' of the FA in taking 227 days to punish Cole. The FA claims the delay was because of Cole's club and international commitments and because it had to wait until the end of a Greater Manchester Police investigation. Bates is not impressed. 'I can't comment on the severity of the punishment because I don't know the crime. What I will say is that those responsible for keeping him waiting seven months should be suspended for three months and have their wages withdrawn. Either that or they should be sacked.'

Sven-Goran Eriksson adds weight to Bates's argument. 'Look at Joe Cole. He's just been banned for something that happened last April. He was a West Ham player but now Chelsea are being punished. In Italy punishments are dealt with swiftly. If a player gets a red card, he is sentenced on the Tuesday. If he requests a personal hearing, it's dealt with in Milan on the Thursday.'

Gianfranco Zola says his only regret from his time at Stamford Bridge was leaving without ever winning the title. 'I don't think Mr Abramovich is interested in coming second to anyone, be they Arsenal or Manchester United or whoever. He is not spending this money to help the tax man in England. He is spending it to win, and every Chelsea fan should welcome it with open arms. Claudio Ranieri has done a good job since joining Chelsea but I don't think he will get too long to win the league. Maybe two or three years but not any more, because football owners have very little patience.

'Everyone kept telling me about how Chelsea had only won the title once, in 1955, and that had to end. We came very close but we still did not win it. I will be dancing for joy if they do it this season. The championship has been a two-horse race in recent years and now it is definitely three. I would love it if Chelsea were at the front at the final post.'

Back on the subject of the Carling Cup and the forthcoming tie with Reading, Frank Lampard insists he wants to win the first available silverware. 'Straight after the United game, the manager was telling us to focus on Reading. We haven't conceded a goal for six matches and want to keep that run going.'

WEDNESDAY, 3 DECEMBER

READING 0, CHELSEA 1

After Jimmy Floyd Hasselbaink's 58th-minute winner finally beats Royals keeper Marcus Hahnemann, Ranieri jokes, 'Their keeper was so good that afterwards I grabbed Roman Abramovich and said, "Look, look, shall we buy him?" In the first half alone he must have saved four or five great shots.' Hahnemann takes it in good spirit. 'Buy me? I suppose Chelsea is not a long drive from Reading. It was easy to get up for a game like this, to run out to a full house with not an empty seat. I knew I was going to be busy as soon as the draw came out.'

Fielding six changes, Chelsea still boast 11 full internationals worth £76m. By contrast, Reading's side is worth £2.3m. On a night so cold even the second-half streaker keeps his pants on, the keeper makes five superb saves from Crespo. A free signing from Fulham, Hahnemann also denies Lampard, Gronkjaer, Cole and Babayaro. Makelele comes on for Cole at half-time to allow Lampard to go on his marauding runs.

Finally, Andy Hughes and Nicky Forster collide, gifting Lampard possession. He sweeps the ball to Crespo, who feeds Hasselbaink to drill home. Hasselbaink's strike is the 17th Chelsea attempt on goal!

Reading have two chances. Bas Savage scares debut keeper Neil Sullivan with an 18th-minute header which hits the post, and they are unlucky not to get a penalty when the same player is bundled over by Babayaro seven minutes later. Reading manager Steve Coppell says, 'I was half hoping they would field their reserves. But then you look at their line-up and realise what a great experience it is to be playing against players like that, a squad that cost many, many millions to accumulate.'

Ranieri is happy to put plenty of his big guns out. 'I will always field my strongest team in this competition. We want to take every competition seriously. I want to make sure that I always have a strong solution for every match. Sometimes you can win by a lot of goals. Sometimes no. But 1–0 is OK.' Team: Sullivan, Johnson, Desailly, Terry, Babayaro, Lampard, Cole (Makelele), Geremi, Gronkjaer (Stanic), Hasselbaink (Mutu), Crespo.

THURSDAY, 4 DECEMBER

Manchester United's Paul Scholes says he would not join Chelsea even if they offered to double his salary. 'That doesn't interest me at all. I would never join Chelsea: they are the enemy now.'

Neil Sullivan is hoping to dislodge Cudicini having got his first start against Reading. 'Being the number one is what it is all about but I know it will be difficult to knock Carlo out of the team. It has been a completely new experience for me since I first arrived here. Everything is geared up to winning the championship. There is a totally different mentality.'

A Channel 5 documentary about Abramovich boasts that it 'looks at the man who has changed the landscape of English football by the sheer weight of his wallet'. But Mario Melchiot reveals how Abramovich makes the players feel at ease behind the scenes. 'Everyone is on their toes now. He comes in the dressing room he speaks to the guys; he tries to say, you know, as much as he can. If you want to talk directly, then you probably speak to one of his right hands and they will translate to him. He's quite generous. He's quite open to speak to anybody. So many are on their toes now because you have to succeed, you understand. You have to be on top of your game all of the time.'

'Suddenly we are the richest club in the world,' says Chelsea fan and former Sports Minister Tony Banks, changing his tune from before. 'It's like all our Christmases have come at once.'

There's also a bizarre interview with the comical agent Eric Hall, who not only claims to know Abramovich, but also reckons he was the first person the Russian confided in about wanting to buy a football club. Hall says, 'I was coming out of a night club with Terry Venables, and Roman came down with his friend Pini Zahavi, and that's where I first met him. I found him a very charming man. Only upset me that I asked him to sing on the karaoke and he wouldn't. I wanted him to do that Irving Berlin song 'Russian Lullaby'. And he said, "Eric, do me a favour, nice Jewish boy," so he wouldn't sing.

'People say you can't buy success. But you can buy success, that's a fact, if you know how to spend the money. I heard that he was richer than God – he's got about £4 more than God has – so I said, "Right then, Roman, do me a favour give me a few quid. Phone me up and we'll do a deal."'

FRIDAY, 5 DECEMBER

Ranieri has 'unfinished business' at Elland Road from last season. In an attempt to keep his squad fresh, Ranieri made six changes against Southampton on Boxing Day but the team could only draw 0–0. His response was to make seven changes at Leeds just a couple of days later and, following a 2–0 defeat, admitted to a 'costly mistake' as an 11-match unbeaten run and their title quest ended. Ranieri says, 'I want to win at Leeds. Last season, we went there at Christmas time and lost 2–0. It was a painful result because we were second in the league. But every defeat is hard to digest.'

Leeds United chief executive Trevor Birch is facing his old club, one that now has millions to spend, while he's at a club that is bust. He recalls the Abramovich takeover. 'Suddenly, we went from fighting fires to all the riches in the world. It was fantasy football, the most exhilarating time of my life in the game. The previous season, because of the financial restrictions, I negotiated one free transfer, Enrique de Lucas. Suddenly, in the space of two months, I was involved in signing players worth £120m.

'It was a unique situation. Roman Abramovich was looking for a football club and there were two third parties involved, including a bank. He did have talks with Tottenham also but it didn't progress – they didn't read the signals. As far as we were concerned, our dreams had been answered. Before that time, it was a football juggling act at the club. Claudio Ranieri had done a fantastic job to keep it all together and our objective was to smooth things with our creditors and give us the time to reschedule the debt. At the same time we knew that, with the club having qualified for the Champions League, we had to do everything in our power to keep the squad together. Suddenly all the rules changed and I had the possibility of negotiating the transfers of any player in the world.'

Birch made a commitment to move his family down to Kingston although, such was the frantic pace of movement at the club, he had precious little spare time to spend with them during August. Then, even more suddenly than Abramovich's arrival, Birch's world fell apart as the club hired Peter Kenyon from Manchester United. He adds, 'It wasn't easy knowing that I wouldn't be part of that excitement any more. It's not something on which I want to elaborate and I have absolutely no hard feelings. When you make the kind of investment that Roman has, that gives you the absolute right to make any decisions you need to. It was felt the club needed Peter Kenyon and I respect that. Those are the rules and you obey them.' Birch can at least console himself with a more than generous compensation package.

With the Leeds game looming, John Terry recalls being understudy to centre-back Michael Duberry at Chelsea. 'He really looked after me. I also had to clean Wisey's boots and, at Christmas, Michael and him would come up and give you £100, though some other players weren't so generous. When the draw was made at the start of the season for whose boots you cleaned, you always hoped for Wisey or Doobs.'

Leeds are rock bottom, financially and in the league table, but Terry adds, 'That will count for nothing on the pitch. Leeds still have some real quality players. It is incredible how times have changed so quickly. We are very lucky to have Mr Abramovich, who seems very committed. On Wednesday, he flew in from Russia just to see us play at Reading in the Carling Cup. After we won, he was in the dressing room practising his English, saying "Well done" and "Congratulations" to everyone. His actions tell me he is not just a five-minute wonder.'

SATURDAY, 6 DECEMBER

LEEDS UNITED 1, CHELSEA 1

Damien Duff preserves Chelsea's nine-game unbeaten run and keeps the team on top with a goal just after the hour, cancelling out Jermaine Pennant's opener. It is the first goal Chelsea have conceded in more than 12 hours. Ranieri admits, 'This was a difficult match and I always knew it was going to be after seeing how wonderful Leeds were at Charlton last week. We started well and dominated but they got the goal which gave them a lot of confidence. We had some good chances and Robinson made some fantastic saves. It was a wonderful atmosphere, too.

'Of course, we want three points out of every match but we were pleased to see the Arsenal result because we are still top of the league. I was disappointed to concede a goal at last, but you would expect that because I am an Italian manager!'

Highbury cast-off Pennant says, 'It's the best goal I've ever scored.' It all happens after Alan Smith wins a header against Cole and from then on it is all about Pennant. He nicks the ball off Makelele and, after accelerating away from Terry's sliding tackle just outside the box, he eases past Gallas and sends a left-footed shot past Cudicini.

Ranieri throws on Crespo after the break in place of Cole to link up with former Leeds striker Hasselbaink and Mutu. Hasselbaink has to overcome the mandatory chants of 'There's only one greedy bastard' on his return to Elland Road. But he crosses from the right and, when Mutu's effort is palmed into the path of Duff, the Ireland winger makes no mistake to put Chelsea level. Afterwards Lampard confesses, 'It's two points lost. We're in that frame of mind at the moment where we want to keep on winning games week in, week out. We got beaten here last year, and our first half was similar this time. The difference is we battled back into this one after going a goal down, and we couldn't do that last time we were here. Desire, determination, character, call it what you will. But, yeah, it's something we've added to our game.'

With this point, Leeds lift off the foot of the table. A delighted Eddie Gray says, 'If you'd have offered me a point before the game I'd have taken it, but it's a measure of how well we played that I'm a little disappointed.'

Team

Cudicini, Melchiot, Terry, Gallas, Bridge, Makelele, Lampard, Cole (Crespo), Duff, Hasselbaink (Gronkjaer), Mutu.

SUNDAY, 7 DECEMBER

Chelsea are instant favourites for the FA Cup at 7–2 after being drawn away at Watford. For Watford it is a financial lifeline. A full house at Vicarage Road plus a £265,000 Sky TV pay-out is a huge boost to the struggling First Division club who recently announced a loss of £10.3m. Manager Ray Lewington describes the tie as 'a fantastic prospect'. Lewington, whose family are all Chelsea fans, is instantly inundated with requests for tickets. He says, 'We will have to improve on pre-season, when we lost 4–1 to Chelsea and it could have been a few more.'

Lampard's desire for pay parity inspires speculation about a new £80,000-a-week, five-year contract. Lampard initially signed a £40,000-a-week deal when he moved from West Ham in 2001. But the contract has built-in clauses which increase his weekly salary by £5,000 for every year of his contract, so he is now getting £50,000.

MONDAY, 8 DECEMBER

Ahead of Chelsea's Champions League match with Besiktas, Ranieri is inspired by watching the England rugby team's World Cup victory parade through central London on TV. 'Yes, I watched it, they showed a fighting spirit. That is what I like in a team. That is what I want from Chelsea.'

If he gets enough fighting spirit from his team, Ranieri can end his season back in the AufSchalke Arena in the Champions League final on 26 May. 'I believe in these players and we've come a long way as a club this season. We've played well in all the matches and shown good character. I hope our large squad will come into their own in the next few months. I can't say we've got the best squad in the competition yet. But there is a difference between having the best players and having the best squad. If we were playing tennis, one player against another, it would be different. But football is a team game. When I compare Chelsea with other teams I always say we don't have a pedigree. I haven't finished my job of building the team yet.'

Ranieri anticipates Besiktas will produce rather more adventure than they showed at the Bridge, when Sergen Yalcin was gifted two goals on the counter. Besiktas, second in the group, also need points to prevent either Sparta Prague or Lazio overtaking them and Ranieri believes that should make for a good game. 'Besiktas must attack because they need the points. Maybe that will be better for us because at Stamford Bridge they defended very deeply and played on the counter-attack. Our philosophy is to win and we won't change that.'

Almost 10 per cent of Gelsenkirchen's 288,000 population are of Turkish origin and, combined with the large numbers of Turks from nearby Dortmund and Düsseldorf, the 54,000 tickets have sold out in a matter of days. Only 980 Chelsea fans have been able to summon up enough enthusiasm and euros to make the trip.

TUESDAY, 9 DECEMBER

BESIKTAS 0, CHELSEA 2

For much of the second half Ranieri is forced to sit under an umbrella to protect him from missiles thrown from the crowd but he refuses to condemn the Turks. 'It was a difficult match played in an unbelievable atmosphere and my players were excellent. It was 300 Chelsea fans against 50,000 and, at the end of the game, I was pleased to hear that it was only our supporters who were still singing. That's what mattered to me most. I was interested to see just how my young players would react to such a strong atmosphere and they came through very well.'

The players themselves are pelted with coins, bottles, cigarette-lighters, flares, batteries, mobile phones, oranges and even sour milk. A knife is reported by TV cameramen and referee Anders Frisk delays the start of the second half by eight minutes after Cudicini's goalmouth is covered in hundreds of toilet rolls. Lampard observes, 'The noise before the game was fantastic and really got us up for it but it was soured when things were thrown on like that. Even in the warm-up before the game there were bundles of coins being thrown at us. It was very disappointing.'

Astonishingly, Besiktas coach Mircea Lucescu sees nothing wrong! Instead he accuses Terry and Desailly of elbowing Ilhan Mansiz. 'There was nothing to worry about, just a few pieces of paper thrown. Elbows are far more dangerous. What the fans did wasn't important.'

When the game gets going, Makelele, Lampard and Geremi run the show in the middle, with Hasselbaink and Gronkjaer always looking dangerous on the counter-attack. In the 77th minute Geremi picks out substitute Duff and his perfect through-ball leaves Hasselbaink racing free to demonstrate his predatory powers. Predictably, the goal is greeted by a hail of missiles. Five minutes from time, Hasselbaink turns provider to set up Bridge, who shows nerves of steel to claim his first goal for Chelsea. At last, Ranieri is hailed as a tactical genius after making five changes and reverting to a back three, with Gronkjaer played out of position up front.

The players warm down on the pitch after the game and get the next day off. Terry explains, 'Straight after the game the lads were all happy and the manager came in and was focusing straight on Bolton. That sums Claudio up. He was telling us they are a good side and there is no point us coming here and winning 2–0 and then going back to Stamford Bridge and losing – we have got to bounce back. We were given the day off so that we could go home and catch up on a few hours sleep and it was worth doing because we just needed to shake out our legs and get it out of our system.'

It is a system that has produced dividends all season. Chelsea have won all five of their league games immediately after Europe and are now unbeaten in their last 12 matches.

> **Team**
>
> Cudicini, Johnson, Gallas, Terry, Desailly, Babayaro (Bridge), Lampard, Makelele, Geremi, Gronkjaer (Duff), Hasselbaink.

The win confirms Chelsea as group winners, meaning they will avoid being drawn against Real Madrid, AC Milan and Juventus much to the delight of Ranieri. 'Winning like that is a big step. We wanted to win the group and we have. I hope we're in the same condition when the knock-out comes.'

WEDNESDAY, 10 DECEMBER

The squad are stuck for three hours on a plane on a runway at Düsseldorf airport waiting for fog to clear. Ranieri misses a Sky TV appearance in the studio with Graeme Souness and Alan Shearer because he has lost his voice shouting so much the night before.

Abramovich watches Arsenal top their group by beating Lokomotiv Moscow at Highbury, but without the correct pass he is not allowed access to the dressing room area to speak with the team. There is even more confusion over whether he has made a bid for Thierry Henry. A couple of days later, David Dein seems to think he did. 'Roman Abramovich came to Highbury and presented us with a formal offer for him. But we told him the same as we will say to Real Madrid, Chelsea or any other club if they are planning to present an offer to us – "Read my lips: Thierry Henry is not for sale at any price." Thierry is under contract until 2007 and is very happy here. We will not sell our best players and make the opposition stronger.'

Yes, Chelsea would happily pay £50m for Henry. But Chelsea did NOT actually offer £50m or ask Arsenal to name their price when Abramovich went visiting Highbury. My Chelsea insider tells me, 'Roman went to Highbury as a private individual taking a couple of his Russian mates to watch Lokomotiv for obvious reason, and he does enjoy watching Arsenal. But he didn't talk to anybody at the club; he didn't make an offer, either formal, informal, written or verbal. Who knows how all this happened? There are a number of agents out there trying to set up deals and it would be no surprise that one thought he would be clever and try to persuade Arsenal to name their price on Henry knowing how interested we had been from the summer when Roman took over. But Henry is no longer on our radar. We discovered in the summer it was not realistic. We know that the Arsenal board would be run out of town if they sold Henry.'

Meanwhile Abramovich is busy spending £29m for a luxury penthouse and the apartment on the floor below. The four-bedroom apartment will be finished with limestone slabs and American walnut boards in the reception room, and granite on the bathroom floor. Abramovich has been overseeing the renovation of a former college in Kensington and, when told work is ahead of schedule, he puts £5,000 behind the bar of a local pub for the 360 workers on site to have a party. One of the carpenters says, 'His penthouse will be amazing when it is finished in August next year.'

Abramovich faces demands of £1.7bn in compensation from Mikhail Khodorkovsky for allegedly scuppering Russia's biggest corporate merger – between the oil companies Yukos and Sibneft. Under the terms of the merger, each side was to pay the other a £570m penalty if it backed out 'without cause'.

THURSDAY, 11 DECEMBER

Ranieri opts out of the Champions League draw in Nyon, Switzerland as he puts his team through their paces in training. The battle for the Premiership occupies all his thoughts. 'I am curious to know the name [of Chelsea's next opponents], but after that I will forget. I told my players to focus on the Premiership. I'm not thinking about the draw. Real Madrid and Manchester United can say they will win it, but not Chelsea. They are used to playing at that level but for us everything is new. Every match is a good step forward but we're not there yet. My baby has started to walk but is not yet able to run. She is a baby girl of one-year-and-a-half. I hope we'll be running quickly but I don't know.'

As for Ranieri's constantly changing tactics. 'I am the Tinkerman and will never change my mind. If you prepare your team in different ways your opponent will never get to know you very well. I've always changed my systems as a manager and don't understand why people are so curious.

'When you have money of course you can buy the best players, but money alone cannot make them link together and make everyone work for one idea, but the manager can only be good if he has good players. Without good players what can you do? It is like a chef. With good ingredients you can cook anything, a fantastic dinner. I hope I can become the Gordon Ramsay of football. At the moment, Sir Alex is Gordon. I have only one Michelin star and he has three.'

Pavel Nedved's agent claims Sven-Goran Eriksson was involved in attempts to bring the player to Chelsea. The Czech international seriously considered an offer and, according to his agent Zdenek Nehoda, Eriksson strongly recommended the midfielder to Abramovich. Reports in Italy suggest Chelsea are willing to pay up to £25m. Chris Coleman wants Emmanuel Petit to join Fulham, but with Veron injured and Geremi due to leave on African Nations' Cup duty, Chelsea need him. Roma's Emerson is still keen on a move. Cash-strapped Parma want a Leeds-style fire sale of stars with striker Adriano on Chelsea's wanted list. The 21-year-old Brazilian is regarded as one of the hottest prospects in world football. Meanwhile Roberto Ayala signs a new deal with Valencia insisting he is not interested in playing in the Premiership. 'I must be the Argentine footballer most wanted by English teams in history. Over the past five years, they have talked about Leeds, Manchester United, Arsenal, Liverpool and now Chelsea.'

Meanwhile, UEFA charges Besiktas with improper conduct on the part of their fans. Ken Bates wants them banned. Referring to Sinisa Mihajlovic, who was banned for spitting at Adrian Mutu, he says, 'If they can fine one man for spitting within 48 hours and ban him for eight matches, then what should they be doing to a club who don't seem to be able to control their fans? Besiktas should be banned from European competition for a year. It annoys me that there seems to be one rule for the British clubs and one for the rest.'

FRIDAY, 12 DECEMBER

The bookmakers favour one of the Premiership sides to win the Champions League. In the last 16 Chelsea draw VfB Stuttgart, who finished behind United in group E, in probably the toughest fixture of the three. Sir Alex's 100th match in the tournament will be against FC Porto, the UEFA Cup holders, and Arsenal are presented with Celta Vigo.

As seeded clubs, all three play their away legs first. Stuttgart lead the Bundesliga, and have beaten Manchester United, Rangers and Panathinaikos in their own stadium. This tie is a repeat of the 1998 Cup-Winners' Cup final, which Chelsea won 1–0 through a Zola goal. Stuttgart have never won in England. Stuttgart president Erwin Staudt says it is payback time. 'We have long had a bone to pick after losing five years ago. Now the time has come to make tables turn.'

Right now, Chelsea are about to face Bolton in the sort of match that always used to be a potential stumbling block. Chelsea have so far won all their games in the immediate aftermath of Champions League action by the odd goal. Ranieri insists he is not developing a Serie A mentality. 'I want an English result every time – 2–0. In Italy we say 1–0 is an Italian result and 2–0 is an English result. Sometimes you only score once but I would never say one is enough and defend it. Once you score one you must focus and try to score a second, then try to score a third.'

SATURDAY, 13 DECEMBER

CHELSEA 1, BOLTON 2

John Terry's own goal ends Chelsea's unbeaten home Premiership record. As Terry walks off, disconsolate, Sam Allardyce's side celebrate coming from a goal down to pull off a remarkable victory.

Earlier it all looks very different. Manchester United's lunchtime derby success leaves Ranieri's men needing three points to return to the top, and the Blues look in the mood. Duff picks out Crespo in the middle, and he celebrates as his shot deflects into the net off Simon Charlton. But Crespo's joy is doused by a raised flag; the strike is ruled out for handball. It looks only a matter of time before Chelsea make the breakthrough and, in the 22nd minute, they do. Gronkjaer sees his cross deflected for a corner. Duff sweeps it over, Terry meets it with a thumping header and Crespo applies the final touch, stooping to nod in from a couple of yards.

A minute later, Bolton have the ball in the net, but it is rightly ruled out. Replays show Kevin Nolan going in dangerously on Cudicini and ripping the ball out of the keeper's grasp. Chelsea continue to attack, and their approach play is a joy. However, the finish is elusive and they are made to pay for those wasted openings when Bolton draw level six minutes before the break. Youri Djorkaeff curls in a right-side free-kick, harshly given, and Bruno N'Gotty's towering header beats Cudicini for the first home goal conceded in the Premiership since September.

The equaliser undermines confidence and the home side's fluency and flair evaporate. Allardyce throws on Stelios Giannakopoulos for Nolan in a bid to make sure of at least a point, while Ranieri withdraws Gronkjaer and sends on Hasselbaink. He also calls Cole and Geremi into action with 12 minutes left. Allardyce then makes his intentions more than clear, using up time by sending on Henrik Pedersen in the dying minutes, but the Dane's arrival does much more than that. With the seconds ticking away, he bursts down the left, skips past Johnson and drives in a low shot that deflects off Terry into the net. Allardyce admits, 'Bruno's equaliser changed the game, and we nullified a very good team on their own ground. I'd have settled for a draw – but I'm delighted with a fantastic win. Of course there is no better time to score than in the 90th minute.'

When a Finnish journalist inquires politely whether Forssell would have taken the chances better than Crespo, Ranieri replies, 'Maybe, also Peter Osgood!' In their last nine Premiership games, Chelsea have scored more than one on just a solitary occasion. Allardyce identifies Chelsea's weakness, 'They've been winning but four of their last six in the league were 1–0. That means they've been very good defensively but not fluent scorers. Some of the football they produced against us in the first half was out of this world. I can never sit back and enjoy matches when my team are playing, but there was a part of me that was in awe of some of Chelsea's football.'

But one point from their last two league matches, and troublesome injuries to Veron and Petit force Ranieri to admit he is finding it difficult to rest tired players. 'Some players are jaded and need a little rest. Frank needs more rest but it is difficult to play without him.' Chelsea will shortly be back in action again with their Carling Cup quarter-final at Aston Villa. Ranieri says, 'You see, I change four or five players in every competition but there are one or two I must play right now. United and Arsenal don't make mistakes. When you compare Chelsea with them I always say no – because they are a team and we are still learning. Maybe now you will listen to me.'

> **Team**
>
> Cudicini, Johnson, Desailly, Terry, Bridge, Gronkjaer (Hasselbaink), Lampard (Geremi), Makelele, Duff, Crespo (Cole), Mutu.

SUNDAY, 14 DECEMBER

Thierry Henry pledges his future to Arsenal. 'As long as people are happy with me at Arsenal I would like to stay there. Hopefully one day we will win the European Cup. That is the plan.'

Acting chief executive Paul Smith says, 'In the summer there was talk of Chelsea moving for Thierry, but Arsenal made it clear he was too central to their plans. I can see why.' Ranieri adds, 'Thierry's a very good player but Arsenal will not sell him. I do not know whether Chelsea made a bid. I am not Mr Abramovich.'

Smith explains how rumours got out of hand. 'David Dein called me to apologise and sent his apologies to Roman. The journalist put two and two together and got five. Roman was at the game as a spectator and there's nothing in it whatsoever.' Dein says, 'Mr Abramovich didn't table a bid and we didn't refuse it. There was a face-to-face meeting and a formal inquiry, but we told Chelsea that Thierry was not for sale at any price, £50m or £150m – that's not the point. It makes no difference what the figure is. He's not for sale. But I would stress that Chelsea's conduct was entirely proper.'

MONDAY, 15 DECEMBER

Scotland Yard confirms that burglars have broken into offices at Stamford Bridge, taking a number of laptop computers. It is not known if the computers held any sensitive information.

Joe Cole is available, after all, for the games against Charlton and Portsmouth after the club decide to appeal against his two-match ban. Cole admits using abusive language but denies it was aimed at the fourth official. He will make a personal appearance before an FA disciplinary panel in the New Year where he will be represented by leading QC Jim Sturman.

Sam Allardyce reassures Chelsea about their title aspirations. 'Some people seem to have decided, on the basis of one match, that getting beaten by "little old Bolton" shows why Chelsea aren't good enough to win the Premiership yet. I disagree. I hadn't seen an awful lot of them before Saturday, but despite the result, I left Stamford Bridge even more convinced that they have the makings of a championship-winning team. The amount of quality they have in their squad is absolutely frightening.'

TUESDAY, 16 DECEMBER

Paul Smith confides that the transfer budget has no set limit. But the main thrust of new transfer activity will be next summer. Roberto Ayala, it turns out, was ruled out for Chelsea because he was ineligible for the Champions League having already played in the UEFA Cup. Smith says, 'If Pele was on the market today for £100m then we'd maybe go for him, but we won't pay £30m for Joe Nobody.

'If Ruud van Nistelrooy was priced at £60m and we considered it a good investment, then we would probably pay that. It's not about the fee but about getting good value. We want the right quality and the right value. We do care about the money and it's a misconception that we don't. There's not a finite budget but we want to get good value. Roman is a businessman and is determined not to get ripped off. We won't pay the tourist price.

'We're looking to strengthen the midfield as Frank Lampard and Claude Makelele are looking a bit tired. If Petit and Veron were fit there wouldn't be a problem and we need to know when they'll be back.'

Abramovich has transformed Fantasy Football into a reality show at the Bridge, so when the name of Ronaldo pops up as a potential transfer target, no one laughs. Wayne Rooney is now a long way from being ready. Michael

Owen's preference is to go abroad. But Juventus's David Trezeguet is a possibility and has professed himself interested. 'It's always a pleasure to know clubs like Chelsea, with their ambitious owner, are interested in you. For the moment I cannot say anything more as there has been no direct contact.'

However, like Real's Michel Salgado, the suspicion is that he is using any link with a move to England as leverage for a bumper new deal to stay in Italy. Roma's Walter Samuel has all the right ingredients for a new centre-half. Meanwhile Makelele has been finding it difficult to settle and says there is 'no comparison' between Chelsea's squad and the glittering array of talent he left behind at the Bernabeu, 'I've had a huge number of problems adapting to the place itself and the weather – it's been really difficult. Most players need two, three, maybe six months to settle down. But in terms of playing I had to be up and running right from the very first day.

'I've been surprised by the commitment of the players and the high tempo of the game for 85 of the 90 minutes. In terms of commitment and aggression, the Premiership is very strong. There are certain tackles that in other leagues the referee would blow for, but here they let play go on.

'Here there are some extremely good players who will go on to become big names, but you can't really compare the two. Real have some Golden Boot winners, very talented players. But Chelsea are starting to show they can play attractive football and stand up and be counted. Let's say I wouldn't have left Real for just any club.'

Winston Bogarde continues to pick up his £40,000 a week despite not playing a league game since December 2000. Not surprisingly, he says, 'I often have the feeling that I am stuck in a tunnel, that I'm wearing a straitjacket. I can't move, can't turn over, can't even look back. So I walk on, on to the light, to the end of the career, to freedom.' Meanwhile Geremi could miss up to a month participating in the African Nations' Cup. Geremi expects to join up 10 days before the tournament in Tunisia and could miss up to five Premiership matches as well as the FA Cup fourth round.

Ranieri challenges his players to show a defiant reaction in their Carling Cup quarter-final against Aston Villa. 'It's another day and now I want to see our reaction after the bad defeat we had against Bolton. It's an important competition for us and also for Aston Villa. David O'Leary said at the start of the season that he could not win the league, so everything was about the two cups. We know that and we are ready to fight.'

WEDNESDAY, 17 DECEMBER

ASTON VILLA 2, CHELSEA 1

Villa book their place in the semi-finals with goals from Juan Pablo Angel and Gavin McCann, and Ranieri questions his team's desire. Ranieri may have again tinkered with his formation, but he blames his players. 'I do not think there was anything wrong with the system we played, that was not why we lost. Aston Villa played better than us and Juan Pablo Angel was magnificent, especially his goal. But Aston Villa had more heart for it, they wanted to win the game more than us. At half-time I had to tell them that the warm-up was over. We didn't get into the game until the second half. Everything was wrong.'

The action is absorbing though. Angel scores a stunning opening goal and sets up McCann's winner. Gallas helps Angel by missing an attempted header but by the time the striker collects the ball he is still 40 yards from goal. He first takes the ball away from Gallas, who is trying to recover from his mistake, and evades Terry before unleashing a thunderous drive from 25 yards that flies past Sullivan.

Ranieri replaces Makelele at half-time, bringing on Lampard. There is renewed vigour. Ten minutes later, Gronkjaer is sent on for Duff and Crespo for Johnson. Ranieri's side come back on 67 minutes with Cole deserving his equaliser. He starts off the move by releasing Crespo on the left, then sprints to collect the return in the six-yard box and clips it through Thomas Sorensen's grasp.

At that point Chelsea look likely winners, but Angel unleashes another long-range shot, forcing Sullivan to push the ball away, and the advancing McCann makes no mistake with the keeper stranded. If it had not been for Sorensen, who brilliantly keeps out Terry's close-range header in the dying seconds, the tie would have been heading for extra-time.

If Chelsea finish the season as league champions and fulfil their dream in Europe, this night will be considered an irrelevance. But Chelsea have lost two successive games for the first time since March, and have created few goal-scoring opportunities against very ordinary teams, part of a longer-term trend with only eight goals in the last eight matches. The strikers are all off-form: Crespo is frustrated with one goal in his last six, Hasselbaink has one in his last four, while Mutu has gone nine games without a goal. A superb defensive record has masked that weakness, but the fact remains that, when Chelsea concede, they struggle to win.

Team

Sullivan, Johnson (Crespo), Terry, Gallas, Babayaro, Melchiot, Geremi, Cole, Makelele (Lampard), Duff (Gronkjaer), Hasselbaink.

THURSDAY, 18 DECEMBER

A low-key Christmas party is held at the training ground with Abramovich and his wife Irina joining players and staff. Ranieri says, 'Mr Abramovich didn't say anything to me in particular. He is a very nice person. He showed his support and that is everything. He knows and understands teams cannot always win and they go through good and bad spells. At a time when the club are having a bad moment, he wanted to show he was close to them. I know some will say there are no excuses for us not doing well because of the quality and quantity of players here.

'But I don't want there to be excuses either from myself or my players. I don't believe in that way of thinking. I said at the beginning of the season that it was important to put down foundations this season and build on them. If we exceeded that, then so much the better. But I never promised the supporters anything. The team has already exceeded my expectations. I didn't think we would be in this position, second in the Premiership and with a good chance in the Champions League, by now. I expected it to take a long time to gel. It's not easy linking 11 players who have not worked together before. I hope it's not a crisis. We've had the good times against Manchester United, Lazio and Besiktas. They were good steps but now we have another difficult exam and this is the time when we discover how good the team is.'

Fickle fans begin calling for the head of Ranieri, demanding he be replaced by Sven-Goran Eriksson. Supporters bombard radio station TalkSport. They criticise the controversial back three and slam the rotation policy. One supporter rings a radio phone-in to threaten to return his season-ticket. Ranieri responds, 'Our fans are not impatient. Maybe some fans want to win always but that is not possible. I've always said that this season is about building a foundation. We will see at Fulham whether the team wakes up.'

FRIDAY, 19 DECEMBER

The players take a trip to the kids' ward at the Chelsea and Westminster Hospital and organise a whip-round to buy presents for the children. Everyone turns up at the hospital on Fulham Road and the Chelsea squad spend over two hours talking to the kids.

With Manchester United and Arsenal showing no signs of faltering, Chelsea cannot afford to drop more points against Fulham. Ranieri comments, 'Until two weeks ago, everything was fantastic and good. Everything we did was right but now when we want to pass through the midfield, through the defender, we're finding it very difficult. It's a bad moment but we're strong inside and feel good. It's very important that we recover for the derby.'

Skipper Desailly urges his team-mates to avoid their usual Christmas dip in form. 'Last year as we approached Christmas, we were second in the Premiership and hoping for many things, like this year. Last Christmas was not a good period for us. Now we must continue to work and not dream. We have achieved nothing yet. I'm happy with the atmosphere in the squad and we have to keep that even if things do go a bit wrong.'

SATURDAY, 20 DECEMBER

FULHAM 0, CHELSEA 1

Not the prettiest of games for watching celebrities including Rod Stewart, Sven-Goran Eriksson and girlfriend Nancy Dell'Olio, plus mega-wealthy club owners Mohamed Al Fayed and Abramovich, but it ends the recent blip. The win seals Chelsea's best-ever start in the top-flight of English football. The total of 39 points after 17 games eclipses their previous best during the 1964/65 season when, under the three-points-for-a-win rule, they would have had 35 points at the same stage. This is also the closest Chelsea have come to leading after 17 matches, as they were in second place 39 years ago.

Ranieri makes seven changes, back to the 11 who lined up for the surprise home defeat to Bolton. Once again Eriksson is watching. Chelsea very nearly find themselves a goal behind after just 80 seconds, needing a fine save from Cudicini to divert Louis Saha's header round the post. Duff forces Edwin van der Sar into a full-length save with a 20-yard shot. In the process he is sent tumbling by a Sean Davis challenge that sees the winger stretchered off with a dislocated shoulder. A lack of sharpness lets Crespo down, and on 13 minutes he allows a golden chance to pass by when, with just Van der Sar to beat, he pokes a tame effort wide. But he breaks the deadlock after 62 minutes when he meets Bridge's cross with a powerful header that goes in off the post.

With Arsenal held to a 1–1 draw at Bolton, Chelsea are all smiles again. Fulham haven't beaten Chelsea in 13 meetings now since April 1977. But for man of the match Van der Sar, they would have suffered a lot more. Crespo's eighth goal for the club ends talk of a crisis, and victory moves Chelsea back level on points with Arsenal.

As Eriksson leaves Loftus Road he smiles, winks and gives the thumbs-up sign when asked about John Terry's form. Ranieri later confirms that Duff's shoulder injury will keep him out for some time. 'I hope he will be back in a fortnight or maybe three weeks. My 84-year-old mother Renata will probably be onto me, she is a big fan of his. When I don't put Damien in the squad my mother calls me to ask, "Is it true? Why? Why?" Now she will kill me and I'm scared of my mother – it is true!'

Team

Cudicini, Johnson, Desailly, Terry, Bridge, Gronkjaer, Makelele, Lampard, Duff (Cole, Geremi), Crespo (Gallas), Mutu.

SUNDAY, 21 DECEMBER

Manchester United's Gary Neville says, 'Normally you don't think about the championship until January or February. This time is the earliest we've ever been in the position of going into games thinking, "We can't afford to lose." The title race is usually like one of those 5,000m races where you trot round, jostling for position, then strike with 1,000m to go, but this season the sprint feels like it's started already. There's an emphasis on getting three points in every game. Between ourselves, Arsenal and Chelsea, the bar has definitely been raised this season.

'If you ask who United's main challenger for the league is, I can't look beyond Arsenal. Chelsea, while they've got players who've won titles in other countries, have only got one – Juan Veron – who's won it in this country. When March or April comes, the pressure starts to get to you a little bit. I'm not trying to play mind games with Chelsea, I'm just saying they've got all that to look forward to.

'Ourselves and Arsenal have something they lack, but Chelsea have certain things we lack. If we get an injury to Ruud van Nistelrooy, it could be a massive problem for us. It's the same with Arsenal and Thierry Henry. Chelsea have an immense squad, players to cover in every position.'

Manchester United's 2–1 win at White Hart Lane takes them back to the top of the table by a point. But Rio Ferdinand will miss the rest of the season unless he succeeds in his appeal against an eight-month ban for missing a drugs test. Eriksson is searching for a new partner for Sol Campbell, and Ranieri insists the beneficiary of the United player's suspension should be the man starring at the heart of Chelsea's defence, John Terry, who was as commanding as ever in the west London derby success at Fulham.

Ranieri says, 'John deserves to play for England even without what happened to Ferdinand. He's good in the air, good with his feet and understands when he must stop opponents. John's improved a lot and is one of the best centre-backs in England. He gets strength from playing with Marcel Desailly, who is our rock. Now he is getting experience in the Champions League – and that's important for him, Chelsea and England.'

MONDAY, 22 DECEMBER

Pavel Nedved insists he would never move anywhere just for the financial rewards. He says, 'Of course there was a time when I'd have been flattered by interest from Premiership clubs, but that time passed a long time ago. The trouble is, no matter how many times I say I'm not interested in Chelsea, the speculation still continues.'

Nedved was poised to join Manchester United two seasons ago but then the price soared above £20m. Ranieri says, 'While not being Raul, Zidane or Ronaldo, he is a great player. They illuminate the scene; he completes the scene. He is the image of the will to dedicate oneself to results at all costs. Any coach would want him in their side.'

TUESDAY, 23 DECEMBER

Marcel Desailly lends his backing to the off-form Crespo. 'All Hernan needs is a bit of confidence. It has not been easy for him as he is an Argentinian just arrived from Italy. He is happy to be here but he has missed plenty of goals during the season and also in training. When you lose the confidence, you miss many things.

'But now with the goal against Fulham, it will give him a bit more confidence and, hopefully, he will score rather than put it wide. Hernan is a great player and there is nothing more I can say about how much quality he has.'

Adrian Mutu is voted Romania's player of the year. Damien Duff goes for a scan on his dislocated shoulder to determine the extent of the muscle damage. Chelsea doctor Neil Frazer put Duff's shoulder back into place in the dressing room at Loftus Road, and then went with him to hospital where he was X-rayed. It turns out there is no bone damage but until he is scanned the club will not know whether he will be out for just two weeks or up to six.

At the club's training ground it is apparent that Duff's shoulder is causing him some discomfort when he uses his left arm to shake hands with Veron. For the Boxing Day game at the Valley, Ranieri has Hasselbaink available again after a one-match suspension. Gudjohnsen, Veron and Petit are all still carrying injuries. Lampard laughs off suggestions from within the camp that he is tired because of too much football. 'I feel fine. If I cannot handle 50 games a season now I never will.'

WEDNESDAY, 24 DECEMBER

Ranieri recommends more English lessons for his foreign recruits. 'It is very important for me that they make an effort to learn about each other on the pitch, but, of course, it's also true about the language. Now when I speak my English, my little English, everybody understands and that is important for the team.' He jokes, 'If I am their teacher they will not learn very well!'

Arsene Wenger says, 'Chelsea have always spent more than Arsenal and had classy teams with Zola, Wise, Poyet, Leboeuf, Desailly, Petrescu and Gullit. They've always been big investors but now they're super big investors and have taken things to a new level. Duff and Mutu have made big impacts but Lampard has been magnificent this season and he's not a new signing. Mutu, though, has perhaps had the biggest impact. He was unknown in England and yet has made a very good impression.'

THURSDAY, 25 DECEMBER

Sir Alex Ferguson is waiting for another big transfer raid by Chelsea. 'I don't think we can eliminate that from our thoughts,' he says. 'But I think the three-horse race is terrific for us. I'm enjoying this thoroughly and I only wish it were five teams up there, not three.'

Alan Curbishley thinks Ranieri will not tinker with his team for the upcoming game against Charlton. 'I don't believe Claudio will rotate against us. The big teams rarely do because they know how difficult we make it. It should be an interesting skirmish between Lampard and Parker. They're both strong in the tackle. The two are slightly different players but it is possible they could be after the same England shirt. Who knows what will happen by the time we get to May, but Scott is good enough to go.'

Ranieri delivers his Christmas message to his players. 'The season starts here. It's not important being at the top now – it's important in May. Charlton were our bogey team for two years before last season, so it will be difficult.'

FRIDAY, 26 DECEMBER

CHARLTON 4, CHELSEA 2

Manchester United and Arsenal forge ahead with comfortable victories over Everton and Wolves respectively. A second defeat in three league games therefore comes as a heavy blow. 'This time last season, Sir Alex Ferguson told his players they could only afford a maximum of five defeats if they are going to win the league,' Ranieri says. 'I have just told my players the same thing after the match. We want to stay in this race but we have to learn very quickly from what happened today. I don't think I have ever seen my team defend as badly as they did. But I'd rather concede four bad goals in one go than in four separate games.'

Charlton deserve their victory in front of their highest crowd for 11 years – 26,768. Chelsea kick off and a poor pass from Mutu and equally poor control from Gronkjaer concede possession immediately. Charlton break, earn a corner, get a second one, and score after just 42 seconds. Terry fails to clear a swinging corner from the right by Paolo di Canio, and Hermann Hreidarsson rises to head the ball powerfully past Cudicini. Mutu's free-kick on the left swirls into the penalty area where it is met by a glancing header from Terry eight minutes later. The goal brings a trademark grin to the face of Abramovich.

But, in the 34th minute, Cole loses possession to Scott Parker on the halfway line, and the ball reaches Jonatan Johansson surging up the left. Johansson's teasing left-foot cross takes a deflection and loops up for Matt Holland to beat Desailly in the air. Ranieri sends on Gudjohnsen for the disappointing Gronkjaer at half-time, but Chelsea are again stung by a lightning Charlton raid. The half is only two minutes old when Di Canio weaves his magic down the left flank, twisting and turning past Terry before supplying a pinpoint cross which Johansson turns in at the far post. In the 53rd minute Jason Euell latches on to a defensive lapse from Bridge to slide the ball past Cudicini for a 4–1 lead. Chelsea get one back when Gudjohnsen collects a loose ball in the penalty area and fires home.

Ranieri says, 'We left them too many chances to score a goal. They scored four goals but they could have scored more. They started very, very well. They scored immediately, it was not easy. It was a strange match for us. We tried to do our best today but it was wrong and now we must think about Portsmouth.'

Curbishley is glad that the prospect of Parker leaving Charlton to join Chelsea seems to be collapsing. 'That deal was set up before Roman Abramovich arrived and Chelsea didn't have two pennies to rub together, so I don't know how they were going to finance it. I was told this week I've spent £18m in my 12 years at Charlton, which is just about what Chelsea paid for Damien Duff in the summer. So yes, it is nice to beat a team like Chelsea.'

> **Team**
>
> Cudicini, Johnson, Terry, Desailly, Bridge, Gronkjaer (Gudjohnsen), Lampard (Geremi), Makelele, Cole (Gallas), Hasselbaink, Mutu.

SATURDAY, 27 DECEMBER

Sir Alex Ferguson is after a new striker but he says, 'Apart from maybe Chelsea, nobody is paying big money. Even Chelsea's impact on the transfer market hasn't spread. Clubs have always tried to get the most out of clubs like Chelsea and ourselves, who are the only ones who seem to have money, and you can understand that. But these days the transfer market is different and we won't be held to ransom. I read somewhere that Chelsea were thinking of making a bid for Ayala but he'd cost £20m, which is huge money.'

Ferguson and his stars have been coping with pressure for years, and that's why there was no panic when they were written off after losing at Chelsea. 'If we lose a game like we did at Chelsea, people start writing our obituary, but they have been doing that for years. Chelsea have to face that. There's no doubt that Chelsea have carried bits of luck. We have analysed some of their games and they have been lucky.'

After beating Tottenham 2–0 at Fratton Park, Harry Redknapp is hoping Pompey will give Ranieri's men a fright. 'Chelsea have had a couple of defeats. So we've got to go to Stamford Bridge thinking we're going to get something and make it difficult for them.'

SUNDAY, 28 DECEMBER

CHELSEA 3, PORTSMOUTH 0

Spanish newspaper *Marca* carries a report that Abramovich has faxed a contract offer to Spain's international coach Inaki Saez and will sack Ranieri today! Ranieri says, 'Maybe they want me to go back to Spain. I like life in London, I'm working well here and I will continue at Chelsea. This sort of story is part of my life. I'm used to it. I enjoy this sort of pressure. Back home in Italy, they tell me that every time Chelsea win they say that Abramovich is victorious or Gudjohnsen scored. When we lose, they say Ranieri fails. I am still here and intend to stay. I'd prefer to have this pressure on me than on my players. December has been a bad month for us and I am sure that the New Year will be better.'

The story turns out to be the Spanish equivalent of an April Fool's Day prank on their Feast of the Innocent day! The Sunday papers also perpetuate suggestions that Sven-Goran Eriksson and Steve McClaren will re-create their former England partnership at Stamford Bridge.

Once more Ranieri prepares for a vital game with speculation about his job making huge headlines. It clearly doesn't put him off his tinkering; he makes five changes. Desailly and Johnson are out in favour of Gallas and Melchiot, Cole and Hasselbaink are ditched in favour of Gudjohnsen and Geremi, Sullivan comes back in for Cudicini.

Harry Redknapp's pre-match assertion that Chelsea are non-runners in the title race backfires. The 3,000 Pompey fans goad former Southampton player Wayne Bridge into retaliatory action with his first league goal. Just to complete Redknapp's misery, his nephew, Frank Lampard, collects a brilliant second.

But Lampard is unlucky when a stunning 30-yard shot on the turn smacks against the post shortly before the break. Sullivan, making his Premiership debut for Chelsea as stand-in for the injured Cudicini, is back in action two minutes after the restart to save from Steve Stone. With 65 minutes gone, Bridge surges on to Geremi's hopeful long punt, chesting the ball beyond sub Sebastian Schemmel with his first touch and thrashing a low shot into the far corner with his second.

Eight minutes later Geremi's pass down the line is taken on the chest by Mutu, who swivels before rolling the ball into the path of Lampard, who detonates an unstoppable right-foot shot on the run. Chelsea finish the day with a swagger thanks to Geremi's 82nd-minute wonder strike. Gronkjaer's cross is only headed clear to the edge of the area, where Geremi unleashes a stunning right-foot volley for his first goal.

> **Team**
>
> Sullivan, Melchiot, Gallas, Terry, Bridge, Gronkjaer, Lampard, Makelele, Geremi, Gudjohnsen, Mutu.

MONDAY, 29 DECEMBER

Veron is still some way off a comeback. Ranieri says, 'He has started training but will need another 20 days.' Duff opts for strengthening exercises rather than surgery. 'Another couple of weeks and he could be ready,' says the coach.

After dropping eight points out of 12 but beating Portsmouth, Chelsea stay within four points of leaders Manchester United. Gudjohnsen explains the feeling within the camp. 'It's not been a great month for us but we can go into the New Year on a high. We're right up there and it's good to be in the position we're in. It was disappointing we had that blip around Christmas but we're still right up there and have a great platform going into the second half of the season. If we're going to win the league, we'll have to be strong mentally and now it is all about finding the right team spirit and being prepared to work for each other. There are plenty of winners in our dressing room and there is no doubt that we have the quality to go all the way.'

Every paper has a different Chelsea story to do with the transfer window: Jermain Defoe, Luis Figo, Rio Ferdinand, Wayne Rooney, David Trezeguet, Roberto Ayala, Roberto Carlos, Rivaldo, Christian Vieri...

With Duff injured, Real Betis wing wizard, Joaquin, is targeted, but the Spanish club are about as co-operative as Arsenal when Chelsea inquired about Henry. Real Madrid's Ronaldo continues to fuel speculation he wants a move to the Bridge. 'I still have this thing in me about wanting to play in England. The Premiership offers a wonderful style of football. I believe the English league has more flair than those in Italy or Spain.'

TUESDAY, 30 DECEMBER

Carlo Cudicini observes, 'Mr Abramovich showed what an intelligent person he is in the summer because he realised he had to ask the manager what kind of players he needed. It can happen that, if you want to win everything, you don't listen to anybody. Instead, he moved very smartly. Mr Abramovich is smart because he didn't start by completely changing everything. He just changed the right things first and slowly, every now and then, he's changing something else.

'At the end of last season we thought some players would leave and were not expecting a lot of buying. Then Mr Abramovich took over. He moved smartly in the market, the atmosphere became electric and it's been amazing. Now we hope 2004 will be an even better year.'

WEDNESDAY, 31 DECEMBER

Hernan Crespo might be eight goals behind Alan Shearer in the scoring charts, but as he sees it, 'Being the top scorer is not the main thing but it can be an objective. Why not? It would certainly be satisfying after finishing top scorer in Argentina and Italy. If you look at the scorers' table today, I'm giving everyone an advantage. I've only played in 10 of the 19 matches, not all from the start, and scored seven goals.

'The most important thing is to win a trophy, not for me to top the goalscorers' chart. When we get to March we'll see what I dedicated myself to: the scorers' table, the championship or the Champions League.'

Marcel Desailly responds to claims he can no longer cope with the demands of captaining France and Chelsea. Ranieri suggested Desailly was not able to play two games inside 48 hours after leaving him out of the Portsmouth game. Desailly says, 'Two days after our defeat against Charlton the coach decided to rotate his squad and to rest me, and suddenly everyone created a controversy, in England as well as in France, when there is none.

'What people have to understand is that since the season started, the coach has decided to practise a turnover policy which concerns every single player. Chelsea is the only club in Europe where there is such a regular turnover. With John Terry, William Gallas, or Marcel Desailly, Ranieri knows that he has quality in his team so why wouldn't he rotate it? The objective for us is to remain hot on the heels of our main rivals Arsenal and Manchester United until the end of the season.'

Desailly laughs off links to a return to Marseille. 'Things have to be clear, I am Chelsea's captain, my family and I want to stay in London. I am playing for one of Europe's greatest clubs and I am determined to help it win titles.'

January

CHELSEA GO INTO THE NEW YEAR WITH HIGH HOPES, BUT HAVE THEY GOT WHAT IT TAKES TO BE GENUINE CONTENDERS FOR HONOURS?

Johan Cruyff says he would love to see Chelsea upset Arsenal and Manchester United in England, and Real Madrid, Juventus and AC Milan in Europe. He insists, 'Chelsea are superseding everything they have done before and it looks to me like they have the power, hunger and motivation to make history. The question is: can they possibly buy a championship team? But I know the answer depends not on the star names who everyone is so fixated by. The key to Chelsea winning something huge rests with their English players.'

Chelsea start the New Year four points adrift of the top. Ranieri says, 'I don't see not winning the title as a disappointment. The thing is not to turn it into an obsession. This year is still about the foundations. Winning a trophy, whatever trophy, will be a major psychological boost.'

Pos	Team	P	W	D	L	GF	GA	GD	PTS
	PREMIERSHIP TABLE – JANUARY								
1	Manchester United	19	15	1	3	38	13	+25	46
2	Arsenal	19	13	6	0	35	12	+23	45
3	Chelsea	19	13	3	3	36	16	+20	42
4	Charlton Athletic	19	8	6	5	27	22	+5	30
5	Fulham	19	8	4	7	30	26	+4	28
6	Liverpool	18	7	5	6	28	21	+7	26
7	Newcastle United	19	6	8	5	26	22	+4	26
8	Southampton	19	7	5	7	18	15	+3	26
9	Birmingham City	18	7	5	6	16	20	-4	26
10	Aston Villa	19	6	6	7	19	23	-4	24

THURSDAY, 1 JANUARY

John Terry makes a bold assertion. 'We can win the Premiership this year. All the players believe it and want it very badly. When Abramovich first arrived, no one quite knew what was going to happen or how big the club would become. But now we are competing on level terms with United and Arsenal. Now we are equals.'

Ranieri continues to advocate a midwinter break. 'I would like to see a New Year break; it is better to give the players two weeks to rest and recover from injuries.' Such matters are not helped by the 'bog of a pitch' on which Chelsea must take on Watford. But the FA Cup remains a top priority for Ranieri. 'I want to win the FA Cup as badly as I want to win the league title and the Champions League. I put that over to the players as well and I know how keen they are to play in the FA Cup and win it. When you come up against a team like Watford from a lower division with nothing to lose, it is so dangerous. I will make sure my team treat the game as if they were facing a team at the top of the Premiership.'

FRIDAY, 2 JANUARY

Watford manager Ray Lewington, who began his playing career at Chelsea, admits that the Vicarage Road pitch is currently one of the worst in the Nationwide League. Lewington, whose family are Chelsea fans, is realistic about his team's task. 'If it was most other Premiership clubs we were playing, I would think we might have a chance, but against Chelsea it will be very difficult.'

Watford's promising goalkeeper Lenny Pidgeley is actually on loan to the club from Chelsea. The 19-year-old says, 'Having trained with all the players, you get to know the way they take their chances at close hand. Eidur Gudjohnsen might come in and flick the ball with the outside of his foot, but Jimmy Floyd Hasselbaink you know he's going to hit the ball so hard. The trouble is I know just how hard Jimmy can hit his thunderbolts and I know how much they can hurt you when you get in the way of them!'

Pidgeley sat on the Chelsea bench for three months at the end of last season without making a debut, and signed a new two-year contract. 'I was very happy to sign and actually agreed the contract about two weeks before Roman Abramovich arrived at the club. Maybe I should have held out for another few weeks and then I could have asked for an extra £5,000 a week!'

Ranieri has high hopes for the keeper. 'I'm hoping he will play well. For him it is a good experience – I want him to have this and to keep improving. Young players need to play. I don't think a good young player should spend more than a year or two in the reserves. After that, if he can't become a regular in the first team, he should move.

'Selfishly I would have enjoyed having Carlton Cole and Mikael Forssell around, because it would have given me two more top-level strikers. But keeping them here would also have meant them losing a year of their careers and that would not have been fair to them. More importantly it would have been the wrong decision for Chelsea. The two of them need to gain experience and continue to grow because they can be part of the future of this club. I'm not surprised that Forssell is doing well at Birmingham City, he is pre-destined to become a superstar.'

SATURDAY, 3 JANUARY

WATFORD 2, CHELSEA 2

Laurence Marks, award-winning comedy writer and a big Arsenal fan, finds himself around the table with Roman Abramovich and David Mellor for the pre-match meal at Vicarage Road. 'Nice man,' muses Laurence of Abramovich, 'he speaks the same amount of English as Ranieri did when he first arrived in England.'

But it is an uncomfortable match for Abramovich to watch, with his team vulnerable every time the ball is pumped long into the Chelsea penalty area. The major talking point is the opening strike by Watford which fails to cross the line. But there is no Russian linesman, as there was in England's 1966 World Cup win, to help out Chelsea's Russian owner. Icelander Heidar Helguson has time and space to connect with the ball, though he is as surprised as anyone when referee Alan Wiley gives the goal, accepting the word of linesman Dave Bryan that the ball has gone in.

Desailly clears a 27th-minute shot off the line from Paolo Vernazza which would have given Watford a two-goal lead, but the Frenchman still fails to command the back-line. Ranieri, with an eye on the forthcoming Liverpool game, says, 'I left out John Terry and Wayne Bridge today and I would have liked to have given some rest to Frank Lampard and Claude Makelele. Terry – we missed him. We never dealt with the high ball.'

Then, two goals in two minutes bring a capacity house to fever pitch. First another Icelander, Eidur Gudjohnsen, rolls in a 33rd-minute penalty after Pidgeley knocks over Gronkjaer on the chase for a sumptuous Lampard ball. But Watford are ahead again almost immediately when Gudjohnsen makes a compete hash of a free-kick, allowing Marcus Gayle to knock the ball over for Gavin Mahon to score easily with Sullivan all over the place. Four minutes before the break, Lampard equalises with a deflected 18-yarder. And although Watford should have a 60th-minute penalty for Gallas's challenge on Mahon the match ends level.

Lewington promises more of the same in the replay. 'We looked at the tapes of Chelsea's previous games, saw that they conceded goals from corners and set-pieces and we worked in training on exploiting that. It didn't surprise me that Helguson did so well against Desailly because he's as good as anyone in the air. Maybe Chelsea will bring Terry back for the replay but Heidar will give anyone a run for their money.'

Ranieri concludes, 'At the moment, I am happy. The replay won't be easy either. The word "easy" doesn't exist in football. You need hard work, and we will have to work harder than today.'

> **Team**
>
> Sullivan, Johnson, Gallas, Desailly, Babayaro, Gronkjaer, Lampard, Makelele, Geremi, Gudjohnsen, Mutu.

SUNDAY, 4 JANUARY

Lewington springs to the defence of Ranieri over more speculation about Eriksson succeeding him at Stamford Bridge. Lewington says, 'No other manager has had to put up with this kind of pressure. OK, he has spent a lot more money than anyone else, but he was starting from a much lower base. He has spent the money wisely and Chelsea have a chance of honours on three fronts. I have no axe to grind but, for me, he's doing a fine job and should be left alone to complete it.'

Romania captain Cristian Chivu, centre-back with Roma, is linked with the Premiership. Chivu says, 'I would love to play with my friend Adrian [Mutu] in the same team. I am surprised to see such big interest in me and it is an honour to be a target for two great clubs like Manchester United and Chelsea. But it is true that Roma have financial problems and we have not been paid for some time.'

Ron 'Chopper' Harris is worried by Marcel Desailly's loss of form. 'Desailly has been shocking lately and I think the defence needs strengthening. Everyone saw with John Terry not playing what a mess they were in and I think Chivu fits the bill. There's been a lot of money spent – but I think Chelsea could do with some reinforcements.'

Chelsea have offered £6m for Czech international keeper Petr Cech at French club Rennes. The 21-year-old's agent Pavel Zika confirms that he is negotiating a deal. Cech, rated the best young keeper in the world, has in the past been linked with moves to Arsenal, Barcelona, Real Madrid, and Inter Milan. Wenger was desperate to sign him but couldn't get a work permit. Now the youngster has played sufficient international games. After Neil Sullivan's recent displays, the club want to push the deal through immediately. But the French club decide to keep hold of him until the end of the season.

Barcelona demand a ludicrously high £25m for defender Carles Puyol. Ajax defender Hatem Trabelsi, nominated for the African Player of the Year award, is also a candidate. The Tunisian will be considered in the summer when Mario Melchiot's four-year contract expires and there is the possibility of a swap deal taking Melchiot back to his former club Ajax.

Chelsea move to sign Brazilian defender Eduardo Alcides in order to add him to the deal with Ajax to lure Trabelsi. Alcides is an Under-17 World Cup winner with Brazil and is valued by his selling club Vitoria at £2.6m, despite the fact that the full-back is only 18. Alcides settles financial terms and agrees to go out on loan to Ajax. He is scheduled to return to Chelsea once he has played long enough in Holland to gain EU status or he qualifies for a work permit in England through having made sufficient appearances for the full national side.

Winston Bogarde would welcome a loan move to another Premiership team, but no club expresses an interest. 'I know I am the biggest outcast in England, but I can assure you that I always do the very best I can. Whatever Chelsea want me to do, I do it without any problem. I give my all every single day and I know that I cannot do any more than that.'

Bogarde is suffering the indignity of training with the youth team. 'I read that I am commuting from my home in Holland but I live in London. Full stop. For everybody who wants to know the truth, I am honouring my contract to the letter. I never miss training and I give my all every day.'

It is now more than 14 months since his last first-team appearance, a 2–1 Worthington Cup win over Gillingham, during which time he has been paid £2,440,000, starting four games and earning £1,820,000 for every full appearance.

MONDAY, 5 JANUARY

Eddie Jordan sidesteps speculation that Abramovich is interested in buying his Formula One team. A Jordan spokeswoman confirms only that the two met last year at a Grand Prix and a soccer match.

Ranieri believes video replays should be used when it is easy to stop play and consider the evidence. 'I make mistakes, as do players, referees and linesmen. But sooner or later, all stadia, especially in the Premier League, must have a camera to say whether it's a goal or not. It's not because of what happened to us [at Watford], just for football in general. It would be very interesting for the fans, like in tennis.'

Conference side Scarborough could face a home clash with Chelsea if both sides win replays against Southend and Watford respectively. Despite coming out of the hat first, the cash-strapped Seadogs are already considering giving up home advantage by switching the fourth-round tie to Stamford Bridge for a

£500,000 pay-day. But chairman Malcolm Reynolds wants the game at the 6,250-capacity McCain Stadium. As he argues, 'Our fans have been magnificent and it would be a slap in the face for them if we moved the tie.'

TUESDAY, 6 JANUARY

Chelsea prepare to face Liverpool in a vital Premiership match that they are expected to win. But it is not as important as their last Premiership meeting at Stamford Bridge, on the final day of last season.

With Chelsea in serious financial trouble, a place in the lucrative Champions League was not so much an ambition as a necessity, as then chief executive Trevor Birch made clear in his speech to the players before kick-off. 'Trevor told everyone that this was not only an important match for the club and the supporters but for the players too,' says Ranieri. Chelsea won a monumental match 2–1 and, as Ranieri adds, 'This was the start of our new story, the Roman Abramovich story. All the year we had been near the top – second, third, fourth or fifth – and we wanted to achieve something. We had got there without spending anything and the players had arrived at that final game having fought very, very hard. This was the biggest match of my time at Chelsea.'

On the European front, Ranieri is worried that Stuttgart will benefit from their mid-season break. 'I definitely believe we are at a disadvantage to a club such as Stuttgart, who we meet in the next round of the Champions League next month. Like other leagues in Europe, they are enjoying a rest right now. Soon they will be back, have a little pre-season and then begin to play again. By the time they play us they will be back in their rhythm while, all the time, we have been playing every three days. That is why I want two players to every position. It is impossible for one player to sustain the same high level right through.'

Ranieri declares himself satisfied with striker Adrian Mutu, even though he has not scored for two months. 'Early in the season he was scoring but I was not happy with him. Now he passes the ball well and makes chances for himself and others. I have had a chat about it and I told him to stay calm. And it does not worry Mr Abramovich. We had a meeting recently and the subject of Mutu came up. He told me he is satisfied with him.'

WEDNESDAY, 7 JANUARY

CHELSEA 0, LIVERPOOL 1

Ahead of the night's big game against Liverpool, Ronaldo flies into London on a private jet, accompanied by Makelele's agent, Marc Roger. Abramovich is informed that he will be coming to the game and is looking forward to meeting him. But the Russian's aides feel it is wise to inform Real. Madrid's president Florentino Perez is not amused. Real order their player not to take his seat. Instead Ronaldo meets Makelele for dinner. It is interpreted that he wants to check out the set-up in case Abramovich decides he wants him. It also fuels speculation that Chelsea will attempt to capture him.

Howls of derision echo round Stamford Bridge for the first time. As the final whistle sounds, Ranieri embraces Houllier with a broad smile before disappearing back down the tunnel. It is some time before he is seen again. Following lengthy talks with Abramovich, Ranieri laughs off renewed speculation surrounding his future. But he looks drawn.

In fact, Abramovich spends 40 minutes talking to players and management in the dressing room and it takes Ranieri 90 minutes to emerge for his post-match press conference. Ranieri says 'Well done' to his players and claims that 'they had played to their maximum'. But Chelsea fans are distinctly underwhelmed and the presence of Eriksson reminds Abramovich of his future options. Ironically, the England coach was seen popping into Ranieri's office before kick-off.

On the pitch, Chelsea's cause is hampered as Crespo limps off after 12 minutes and is out for several weeks with a calf injury. Liverpool's first Premiership win at Stamford Bridge is sealed by a first-half goal from Bruno Cheyrou, which leaves Chelsea seven points behind Manchester United, who win at Bolton as Arsenal draw at Goodison Park. Apart from a late Mutu header that hits the bar and a first-half Gudjohnsen volley that goes just wide, Jerzy Dudek – and then, after he damages a groin muscle, his replacement Patrice Luzi Bernardi – hardly has a shot to save.

Mutu becomes more and more frustrated and is involved, late on, in a fracas with El-Hadji Diouf which results in the Liverpool man being unjustly sent off. Afterwards a surprisingly relaxed Ranieri emerges to declare, 'Don't worry everybody, I'm still here! You will still be seeing me for a long time. Mr Abramovich is not happy but he is patient. You will see me tomorrow.' Three defeats in five Premiership games, and two wins in their last seven in all competitions, make for depressing stats.

Houllier says, 'Chelsea are a great technical team but they are going through a bad patch. We came here with a plan and made them look ordinary. Chelsea can still win the league but it has been a very good night for Manchester United and now Claudio must keep calm and cool.'

Ranieri is convinced his players have to show greater mental strength. 'At the moment everything is going against us. In the last three or four games we had an offside goal against us at Charlton, a goal that wasn't over the line at Watford and then we didn't get a penalty we should have in the last minute against Liverpool.

But what I want to see against Leicester is our reaction. I'm sure we will react very well. We have the character to do that.'

> **Team**
>
> Cudicini, Johnson, Gallas, Terry, Bridge, Makelele, Lampard, Cole (Gronkjaer), Geremi, Crespo (Gudjohnsen), Mutu.

THURSDAY, 8 JANUARY

Abramovich cancels his return to Russia and goes to the club's training ground to watch training before holding another meeting with Ranieri. He orders the coach to spend whatever it takes to win the title.

John Terry reveals how stunned the dressing room was after the Liverpool defeat. 'It's a bad run. Liverpool did just what we were doing ourselves a few weeks ago, winning a game when not playing particularly well. They had one shot on target all night but they got the job done. That hurt. Everyone was silent in the dressing room afterwards. Normally there is chit-chat and banter. But this particular night, the lads were in their own little worlds. But we cannot afford to dwell on these things. It will just sap us as we prepare for a difficult match at Leicester and a tricky cup tie at home to Watford.'

Chelsea give Rennes a deadline to accept their offer for Petr Cech. The clubs have failed to reach agreement after talking late into the night in Paris and will speak again after Rennes' match against Toulouse. Cech is desperate to complete the move.

FRIDAY, 9 JANUARY

Ranieri explains his latest discussions with the owner. 'Roman Abramovich does not expect me to win the title or the Champions League – he does not expect anything. This season is about building a strong team and it takes time. He has not been happy in the last month. But that's normal. Our fans are not happy, I'm not happy, the players are not happy. Chelsea had 38 points last season and now we have 42. We are making progress.'

But Chelsea have slipped seven points adrift of Manchester United. John Terry says, 'Chelsea are not out of the title race by any means. It is not an exaggeration to say we face the biggest week at the club since Mr Abramovich took over. Leicester and Watford have become two massive, massive games for us.'

Leicester manager Micky Adams promises a battle. 'We respect Chelsea and they have some world-class players. But we won't be overawed. I'll guarantee Chelsea will not enjoy playing us, whatever the outcome.'

SATURDAY, 10 JANUARY

Suddenly Roma manager Fabio Capello is being linked with Ranieri's job – that's if Eriksson does not take it. Capello says, 'I know nothing apart from what I read in the papers, but I must admit that Chelsea's interest makes me very happy.'

Ranieri will either stay with silverware or walk off with a fortune in compensation if Chelsea win nothing. He says, 'In terms of pressure, I have the worst job in football but I can still smile. I don't worry about it. Every manager has pressure but some cope better than others. You have to remember that, every time I prepare for a match, I'm told another manager wants my job. But I started my career managing an amateur team and I worked hard to get to where I am today. This is why I have the experience to cope with bad situations. When there is pressure, I'm happy. In fact, I want the pressure. It gets the best out of me. This is my character and I have no problem when things get tough.

'The players know what I can be like. I'm a different type of manager to Sir Alex. I'm relaxed and don't show my temper to the public. But you must remember the Claudio Ranieri you see here today is very different in the dressing room. I get very intense and the players soon know if I'm not very happy.'

Ranieri needs midfield reinforcement with fears over Veron's back problem, Petit still injured, and now Geremi off to the African Nations' Cup. Brought up to speak French, Geremi's command of English is impressive, arriving in London via Paraguay (Porteño FC), Turkey (Genclerbirligi), Spain (Real Madrid) and Middlesbrough. 'I like London – it's an improvement on Madrid,' he says. 'I'm here for five years and intend to enjoy every moment.

'Players have to be egotists and like to play every week, but with the squad we have, you have to accept that there are other good players in your position who all want to play. My job is to be fit and ready when the manager wants me, and then to play well to make sure he carries on wanting me. I'm going away for up to a month, depending on how well we do, and it does worry me that I'm going to lose my place at Chelsea.'

Abramovich has been a regular feature in the dressing room. Gudjohnsen reveals, 'He doesn't really speak to the players. He's more there to feel the atmosphere. He just wants to be part of it. It shows that he cares about what he is doing and where the club is going. It gives us the feeling he wants to see what we are like when we lose and what we're like when we win. He wants to see how we react as human beings as well as players. I suppose that's the way all the players perceive it. I certainly do. But he has paid a lot of money to take over at Chelsea and also a lot of money on bringing in players. So he has every right to know what is going on in the dressing room.'

Robert Pires writes off Chelsea as title rivals. 'Their defeat at home against Liverpool means we practically have one less rival now. I'm a bit surprised after all the money they have spent, but it goes to show that being able to buy lots of players doesn't bring automatic success.'

SUNDAY, 11 JANUARY

LEICESTER 0, CHELSEA 4

This is the most convincing performance since the win over Manchester United six weeks ago. Ranieri makes six changes, dispensing with the diamond formation in favour of a flat midfield, and such tweaking works. He turns to two strikers from the pre-Abramovich era in Hasselbaink and Gudjohnsen, a pairing that yielded 52 goals two seasons ago, raising the question of why they haven't been paired more often. Joe Cole enjoys possibly his best game on the left of midfield.

Hasselbaink marks his return with his 11th and 12th goals of the season, opening the scoring in the 12th minute with a delicate back-flick following a great run by Cole, before doubling the advantage with a free-kick on the stroke of half-time. Hasselbaink is fouled 25 yards out by Billy McKinlay. He takes the free-kick himself and it smashes in off the head of Nikos Dabizas, leaving Ian Walker with no chance. His 98th league goal ends a Premiership goalscoring drought stretching back to 25 October.

Leicester stage a late rally – Cudicini tips a Callum Davidson drive over the bar and Terry clears James Scowcroft's header off the line. Mutu scores his first goal in 14 games, triggering wild celebrations, though nothing compared to the acrobatics with which Babayaro marks his first in over a year. Mutu, a late replacement for Gudjohnsen, collects the ball from Babayaro, sprints past two defenders and curls a wonderful shot around Walker from the edge of the area.

Afterwards Ranieri comes into the press conference beaming happily, but he does not try to deny the last few weeks have been difficult. 'When everything is going wrong,' Ranieri says, 'it is right that I should take the responsibility. The new squad is like a child. If he makes a mistake and you put him under pressure because of it, he cannot grow properly. I don't mind if everyone is against me, if they pick on me, because I am an old man. A squad is like a family, and it is good to see the family when something is wrong because a good family sticks together in times of trouble. I thought we played well – but then I thought we played well against Liverpool last week when we lost.'

Leicester manager Micky Adams admits he has some sympathy. 'I was manager of Fulham when Mr Fayed took over and there were people being linked with my job on a daily basis. It does wear you down in the end.'

> **Team**
>
> Cudicini, Melchiot, Desailly, Terry, Babayaro, Gronkjaer (Geremi), Lampard, Makelele, Cole (Gallas), Hasselbaink, Gudjohnsen (Mutu).

MONDAY, 12 JANUARY

Richmond Magistrates Court confirms that a 35-year-old builder has been charged with aggravated burglary for breaking into a house in the upmarket neighbourhood of Barnes. It belongs to Juan Sebastian Veron. Residents reported a burglar had climbed through the bedroom window at the £2m home previously owned by Marcel Desailly and threatened the occupants, demanding jewellery. Veron handed over jewellery worth £60,000.

The robber snatched Veron's trademark diamond ear studs, together with Rolex watches, diamond rings and necklaces. A CID source says, 'They were put through a terrifying ordeal.' The man threatened Veron's girlfriend's mother with the blade and went from room to room rounding up the eight occupants. All eight captives were finally locked in a bedroom and the intruder fled. As he drove off in a Ford Transit, he skidded on the wet road and crashed into railings 200 yards away. Police were alerted by a passer-by and discovered the driver slumped over the dashboard. Veron is now protected round the clock by private security guards.

Michael Owen is linked with a move to Chelsea by a Sunday paper. However Chelsea sources tell me that Owen is not on their wish list anymore. Nor are the club chasing Bayern Munich's right-back Willy Sagnol, another announcement from the media rumour mill. David Beckham suggests Real Madrid have no need to fear Abramovich's financial muscle. 'I don't think there is any panic. He has got a lot of money and he has bought a lot of great players, but Real can pull any player.'

But can Chelsea 'pull' Charlton's Scott Parker, who is targeted as the solution to their midfield crisis? In pre-Roman times, a deal was agreed by Ken Bates for £6m. Now Charlton have doubled their valuation. However, Parker wants the move to enhance his chances of breaking into the England squad for the European Championship. But Charlton chief executive Peter Varney says, 'Scott Parker is not for sale and we do not welcome this enquiry. We sincerely hope that Chelsea will accept our decision in this matter.' Parker starred when

Charlton demolished Chelsea at The Valley on Boxing Day. That made up Ranieri's mind that Parker should be his prime target during the January window. The player, at first, insists he is happy to stay at Charlton.

John Terry reveals how a pep talk from Abramovich inspired the rout at Leicester. Abramovich spent 40 minutes talking to the players individually following the home defeat to Liverpool, but had much less to say after the impressive performance at The Walkers Stadium.

TUESDAY, 13 JANUARY

Ranieri is not upset at Charlton rejecting his approach for Parker. 'I am very happy with the players I have. I have 21 outfield players and then goalkeepers as well. I am not considering anything and the only thing I am thinking about is the Watford game.'

Veron faces surgery on his back. He has been joined in the treatment room by Crespo. Ranieri says, 'Crespo could be out for a month or six weeks. Duff and Petit will be back soon but Veron will be out a little longer. He may need an operation.'

Ranieri is still loving life at high-pressure Chelsea. 'I love my job and I am always happy when I am doing my job. I've said before that my players are like my sons and that's true. I love all my players.' But he has stern words as the team prepare to take on Watford again. 'We didn't play well at Watford and now I want to see us play like we did against Leicester.'

The FA blocks Conference side Scarborough from moving a potential clash against Chelsea to Stamford Bridge. Scarborough are already assured a big pay-day after Sky agree to screen the fourth-round game live. But they were hoping to double that with the extra gate receipts from playing the tie at Stamford Bridge.

WEDNESDAY, 14 JANUARY

CHELSEA 4, WATFORD 0

A swap deal with Inter Milan involving Christian Vieri and Adrian Mutu is mooted when directors Marco Branca and Gabriele Oriali meet Abramovich at Stamford Bridge, but the Russian rejects the deal out of hand. Fulham's Louis Saha is offered to Chelsea but the French striker is desperate to move to Old Trafford.

Abramovich unveils his latest big-name signing – Peter Kenyon. Kenyon watches alongside Abramovich as he prepares to take over as chief executive.

Watford gave Chelsea a fright in the first meeting. The tormentor that day, Heidar Helguson, is missing with a thigh injury. Any hopes of an upset quickly diminish in the seventh minute when referee Alan Wiley infuriates Watford by allowing Mutu's opener, and TV replays show that his decision is spot on. Lampard's 20-yard shot is parried by keeper Pidgeley, Neal Ardley tries to clear but inadvertently gives the ball to Mutu who looks offside. Watford are incensed that the referee overrules his linesman. But because Ardley has played the ball last the goal stands.

Watford nearly grab a 31st-minute equaliser when Jamie Hand's shot shakes the woodwork. But minutes later Hasselbaink hits a second to give them breathing space with a strike that has quality written all over it. Gallas's sublime 40-yard pass over the top finds Hasselbaink and he brings the ball down with his left foot before hitting a superb right-foot shot into the bottom corner. Mutu soon adds a third to kill off the First Division side and Gudjohnsen strikes late on to ensure all Chelsea's main strikers have made a point. Hasselbaink's strike, his third goal in two games, clocks up 13 goals for the season. Mutu makes it three goals in two games after a barren streak.

Duff comes on for the final 11 minutes and has a hand in the final goal. Quite what Chelsea will make of Scarborough in the next round, no one knows. Ranieri says, 'I have never been there but I might even like the place; it has a good beach although not at this time of year. It's a bit chilly, maybe my English players like John Terry and Frank Lampard like that kind of weather but not me.'

Watford manager Ray Lewington has two pieces of advice for Chelsea's next FA Cup opponents. 'One is to hijack the Chelsea coach on the way up, and the other is to sneak two, preferably three, extra players onto the pitch!'

Team

Cudicini, Melchiot, Terry, Gallas (Huth), Babayaro, Gronkjaer, Lampard, Makelele, Cole, Mutu (Duff), Hasselbaink (Gudjohnsen).

THURSDAY, 15 JANUARY

Sven-Goran Eriksson insists he has had no approach from Chelsea but he would take any such offer seriously. Ranieri responds, 'What is the change? He is right. He must open the door – it's normal.' Ranieri jokes, 'Maybe we could job swap. I said a long time ago that I would like to manage a national team – Italy, England – a big team. It would maybe be better, but I like to manage Chelsea Football Club.'

Scott Parker is axed from Charlton's trip to Everton because he has been unsettled by Chelsea's bid. Alan Curbishley asks him to stay away from the club's New Eltham training ground for two days as Parker is 'disappointed' at the decision not to allow him to leave. Curbishley claims even £15m is not enough to let Parker go.

Chelsea test the market with enquiries for Czech wonderboy Tomas Rosicky of Borussia Dortmund. The 22-year-old was bought for £11m a couple of years ago and can play just behind the strikers or wide on the right.

Anticipating the next round of the FA Cup, Scarborough kit-man Brian Hodgson looks around the cramped and Spartan away dressing room and admits, 'I just don't know what those boys will make of all this. We've only one little fluorescent light working in this dressing room and there will be a minimal amount of heating in here on the day. The good news is that there is lots of water for the showers the Chelsea players are going to use. The bad news is it will all be freezing cold. It's going to be a real culture shock for them.'

It is 15 years since Scarborough pulled off their last headline-making giant-killing – and Chelsea were the victims in the second round of the Littlewoods Cup.

FRIDAY, 16 JANUARY

Ranieri can see signs of improvement. 'When we are in difficulties, I want to see how the team has grown up. I have seen it in the last month, players link better together, and that's what I wanted. Look at Adrian Mutu. He was playing very well without scoring a goal. Now he has scored three in two games.'

Damien Duff is back; Ranieri's mum is happy again. Renata, 84, lives with her 86-year-old husband Mario on the second floor of a 12-storey apartment block in Rome. Ranieri says, 'I'm very happy to have him back. When he goes with the ball one on one against an opponent, he is devastating. He is an intelligent, smart player. And when I call my mother, she will say, "Well done, son," for bringing him back.

'She is always asking me about what players we are going to buy too. She reads all the newspapers and watches the TV and she believes what they say. She doesn't believe her son. She is like a shark, just like the journalists.'

Duff has turned to judo to strengthen his shoulder. He says, 'I've been practising my rolls and falling on it. It's been hard work but I'm glad to be back.'

Duff took a risk avoiding surgery. Veron gambled on advice that he could avoid it, but is now heading back to Argentina for surgery. He damaged a disc on a previous trip home two months earlier on international duty. Chelsea discovered the Argentina team doctors told him he had a problem two days before the match, but the player took painkillers so he could appear as a second-half substitute.

SATURDAY, 17 JANUARY

Abramovich has thick pile carpet and heated seats installed in his luxury 24-seater box, but the heat is still on Ranieri. Abramovich says diplomatically, 'I am realistic enough not to expect overnight success. I accept it takes time to bring a team together, no matter how much you spend. I have no real expectations. I don't expect us to win anything in our first season. There is pressure on anyone in any job to be successful. A football manager is no different. What football manager isn't under pressure? I have expectations, but they are realistic. Of course I would love Chelsea to win something sooner rather than later but I have faith in my manager and he will be given time to succeed.'

Hasselbaink should soon become only the second foreigner to reach 100 goals in the Premiership, Dwight Yorke being the first. Ranieri says, 'Jimmy is a great striker. Maybe if he played in every game he could challenge Henry or Van Nistelrooy – but I am the Tinkerman and I will continue to change.' Hasselbaink's future remains in doubt; he was not even on the bench against Liverpool, but he started the next two games and responded with three goals.

In the run-up to the Birmingham game, it emerges that Steve Bruce 'bunged' Ranieri a crate of red wine to sign Forssell. A laughing Bruce confesses, 'It's true I sent Claudio a crate of red wine for letting us have Mikael for the season. That was his "bung". But I'm not sure whether he was sufficiently impressed by the vintage because we paid £12.99 a bottle from Oddbins! Considering all that's been going on around him, some of which really disgusts me, he's handled himself magnificently. He never grumbles and did a smashing job, even before Roman Abramovich came along.'

As part of the loan agreement, Forssell is not able to play in this game. He will watch the match on television in Finland after being allowed to take a short break. Forssell says, 'Do I know where I am going at the end of the season? I honestly do not know. The official thing is that I am going back to Chelsea at the end of the season. That's it. That was the original deal. There is a lot of speculation about things, but I am quite calm. If Chelsea said, "You are not in our plans," then I can say something, but nothing has been said. That's why I came to Birmingham; I could have stayed and fought for my place but I know I will play here in the Premiership. I know Ranieri likes me as a player but I understand his situation. If you buy someone for £18m, he has to play.'

The future is even less clear for Eidur Gudjohnsen who is wanted by Bordeaux as well as Newcastle manager Sir Bobby Robson who views him as one of the candidates to succeed Alan Shearer who is retiring after next season.

SUNDAY, 18 JANUARY

CHELSEA 0, BIRMINGHAM 0

Abramovich's discomfort is hugely visible. Not even the newly installed carpet and heated seats cheer him up as his team are frozen out. The draw leaves

Chelsea six points behind Arsenal, who win at Villa after United's shock defeat at Wolves 24 hours earlier. Sven-Goran Eriksson is seated just behind Ken Bates in a prominent position in the directors' box. No doubt the new seating 'order' is down to Peter Kenyon, now visibly involved if not fully in charge yet.

Remembering the frustration of October's goalless draw at St Andrews, Ranieri goes back to basics and sends out a side based on last season's squad. Only four of his summer signings make the starting XI, yet still the changes have little effect. What Birmingham lack in attacking quality, they more than make up for in commitment and attitude. Ranieri withdraws Gronkjaer at half-time. Unfortunately Duff is not much more effective. Cole deserves a goal midway through the first half, cutting inside Olivier Tebily to curl a precise right-footer against the far post. But Cole's frustration is all too apparent when he launches into an ugly lunge on Jeff Kenna and is instantly surrounded by six angry players before being rescued by the yellow card of referee Jeff Winter. Cole has yet to complete a full 90 minutes in the Premiership for Chelsea – a run maintained when he is replaced by Mutu half an hour from the end.

There are a number of near misses. Gudjohnsen works a neat one-two with Mutu on the edge of the box in the closing minutes but slashes wide under pressure from Darren Purse. Hasselbaink is denied only by the trailing foot of the keeper as Chelsea launch a desperate late surge. Tebily's heroic goal-line clearance to keep out Gallas's 48th-minute chip and a low Lampard drive, which needs a sharp, full-stretch save from Maik Taylor, are also close calls. Chelsea perhaps deserve a second-half penalty when Makelele goes down under Tebily's challenge. But Birmingham should score two minutes after the break. Makelele is slow to react to a loose ball in the box and Robbie Savage lashes wastefully wide.

Mutu and Purse clash just before the end, and the feud erupts as both head towards the tunnel. Mutu is moaning, gesturing and has to be dragged away by team-mates after an incident in which Purse catches him in the face. Purse says, 'I got him with an elbow by accident and then he wanted some "afters" in the tunnel. But the two goalkeepers and a few players came between us so it was over really before anything happened.' Purse later goes to the Chelsea dressing room to see a friend, and Mutu greets him with what witnesses claim is a volley of expletives. Mutu's team-mates are forced to intervene, dragging him back into the dressing room to cool off.

Afterwards Steve Bruce says, 'It's easy to see why we haven't been outside the top 10 all season. I am very proud.' Ranieri says, 'I prefer to see the glass half full rather than half empty and I'm always positive. My players did everything, but their keeper Maik Taylor was man of the match. It was very frustrating today. But Birmingham are one of the best teams in the Premiership at pressing the opposition.'

The scoreboard operator informs the fans at the end of the match they can watch the whole 90 minutes all over again on Chelsea TV tonight. No thanks!

> **Team**
>
> Cudicini, Johnson (Melchiot), Desailly, Gallas, Bridge, Cole (Mutu), Lampard, Makelele, Gronkjaer (Duff), Gudjohnsen, Hasselbaink.

MONDAY, 19 JANUARY

Brazil's leading newspaper *O Globo* reports how Ronaldo has told Real that Chelsea have offered him a fortune to sign and that he wants to join Abramovich's revolution. Under the headline 'Hello, Adios', the article states that Ronaldo is going to be playing in England next season.

Brondby coach, former Arsenal midfielder John Jensen, watches Sebastien Kneissl, the German striker, in the reserves' 1–0 defeat by Southampton with a view to a loan deal. Meanwhile, the Bridge pitch is being dug up and a new one will be laid in time for the next home game. The new turf should mean that a reprise of last season's row with Charlton, who described the pitch as a 'beach', should be avoided. Ranieri is concerned about the pitch. 'It is not good at this moment and it is not helping my players play the way we want them to.'

Ranieri's football-mad mother Renata says, 'Every time Chelsea are on television I make sure Mario and I are sitting down to watch the game together. I like to see what Claudio has been up to and who he has picked for the team. Claudio's a good son but sometimes he doesn't listen to his mama, and so I have to tell him off especially when Duff doesn't play. He should always be in the squad if he is fit.'

Renata is in no doubt who the fans should thank for the team's brand of play. 'It's all down to Claudio. He is very popular there and he always tells me how much he enjoys living in London.' She also likes to keep up with how rivals Arsenal and Manchester United are doing, 'You can't get luckier than Arsenal. Don't referees know their decisions make or break championships?' Chelsea face Scarborough in the FA Cup. She says, 'I shall speak to him about the team selection later this week.'

TUESDAY, 20 JANUARY

Marcel Desailly intends to see out his career at Stamford Bridge. 'Give me one reason why I should leave Chelsea today? They are one of the best clubs in the world, a club who are in the process of building superb foundations. Whatever happens my career will be finished when my contract runs out in 18 months.

'At 35, I am not the player I was at AC Milan when I ran about everywhere. I could make it up and down the pitch 10 times in those days. Now it is six times. I have less endurance but more experience. I compensate for my lack of physical power with positioning and through experience I have acquired over the years.'

WEDNESDAY, 21 JANUARY

Goalkeeper Petr Cech signs a five-year deal, but will stay with Rennes until June. Cech has just established himself as the Czech number one. Carlo Cudicini is reported in a newspaper as wanting to move in the summer 'following repeated pleas from his wife Carola, who has been unable to settle in England'. The Italian goalkeeper reacts with bewilderment. 'It's total madness. I'm here and I intend to stay as long as possible. As for my wife, sadly we separated four months ago and she's now back in Rome! I have never, ever thought to leave Chelsea. I have a contract here until 2008, so if possible I would like to stay here until 2008.

'I'm really happy here. I love the club and I love the fans. I want to stay here and try to get some trophies. I really love my team-mates as well. If you read the newspapers, they said that I've got kids! And as far as I know I haven't! I have got a dog, yes, and he's really happy to stay here in London. I don't want Chelsea fans to think that I am trying to move on and make more money now that I have made a name for myself at Chelsea. The club have been good to me the whole time I have been here and I want to pay them back for the faith they showed me.'

He recalls the reaction after his Arsenal howler when he stepped out on to the pitch against Lazio. 'They gave me a wonderful reception and it was very emotional for me. Everyone makes mistakes. We are human beings not robots. Fortunately, the fans, the manager, my team-mates, everyone at Chelsea, understands that. It made me stronger and it helped me so much because I recovered well.'

As for Cech, he warns, 'We will both challenge for the place and the manager will decide. I don't have any problem with Chelsea signing another goalkeeper. We need to have competition for places and greater strength in depth. All I can do is play my best and hope the manager picks me.'

Charlton reject a fresh £7.5m plus add-ons bid for Scott Parker. Alan Curbishley reiterates that the player will not be sold without his blessing. The row intensifies as Parker states his belief that he was given a verbal undertaking in the summer, when he signed a new five-year contract, and again at Christmas, that he could leave if a big club came in for him, and the undertaking referred specifically to approaches from Arsenal, Manchester United or Chelsea.

Charlton insist no discussion was held about the size of the bid that could trigger any release and deny there is a formal get-out clause in the player's new contract. Chairman Martin Simons insists there will be no caving-in like Fulham did over Louis Saha's £12m move to Manchester United. 'We are fourth in the league, they are third. In the last few weeks we have been catching them up. So it hurts when a club with their buying power has the ability to see the club beneath them and say, "Oh, let's spend a few million and take their best player." Well I say, "Get lost, Abramovich," and I think I speak for the rest of football. Somebody has to make a stand. We don't want Chelsea's money.' Sorry, but didn't Charlton accept the £6m sale of Parker to Chelsea pre-Abramovich with payments spread over five years?

PSV chairman Harry van Raay confirms Chelsea have also joined the race to sign winger Arjen Robben, attempting to steal the 19-year-old Dutchman from under the noses of Manchester United, who have already given Robben a tour of their facilities. Robben has three years left on his contract with PSV. His father and agent has already declared that his son will sign for the Red Devils or stay at PSV. Robben's transfer to Old Trafford is expected to be completed in the summer but Chelsea's interest sparks a bidding war. Chelsea are linked with another left-back – Lille's £7m-rated Eric Abidal, dubbed 'the new Lilian Thuram', with AC Milan and Inter also keen. This highlights the need for new full-backs since Ranieri has concerns about both Glen Johnson and Mario Melchiot who is in his final season.

THURSDAY, 22 JANUARY

Scarborough has been hit by heavy rain over the last four days but the club are doing everything they can to combat the bad weather. A £12,500 pitch cover is installed and the club are confident the game will go ahead. Striker Mark Quayle jokes that Chelsea's millionaires won't be able to fit into their tiny dressing-rooms. 'They are in for a shock when they see our place. Our changing-rooms probably won't be big enough for them to fit in with their wallets, let alone all that gear.'

Scarborough are on £4,000 a man to dump Chelsea out of the FA Cup. They are normally paid around £350 a week. But with so much interest in the tie, the players' pool is worth around £12,000 even if they lose. Sponsors McCain's provide caviar and chips to fans and bring in singer Frances Ruffelle, star of the West End musical *Chicago*, to sing the national anthem and 'Abide With Me' before the game.

One of Scarborough's most outrageous stunts is their plan for a goal celebration. Their players will line up, pull down their shorts, bend over and proudly display letters making up the name of new weekly men's magazine *Zoo*

Weekly on their backsides to the viewing millions. *Zoo Weekly* promoted its first issue with the help of leading football agent Eric Hall. Needless to say the stunt is blocked by the FA!

Meanwhile, the extent of the financial disaster facing Chelsea in the dying days of the Bates regime is revealed in the latest set of accounts filed by Chelsea Village, disclosing losses of more than £26.5m in the year to the end of June 2003, the third-biggest loss ever recorded by a British football club, exceeded only by Leeds United and Fulham. The accounts, filed at Companies House, reveal that the club's core football activities made a loss of £10.1m, while the travel agency and 'leisure services' business were also in the red. There is also a huge and unexplained increase in 'central costs' from £1.4m to £5.1m. The club ended the year with debts of £79.2m, including £74.1m from the Euro Bond. The playing squad is valued in the balance sheet at £87.1m.

The report says that £117m has since been spent on new players, slightly more than the reported figure of £111m. Abramovich is planning more changes. Among them, is a scheme to increase the Bridge's capacity. The expansion of the Matthew Harding stand will threaten the luxury health club, another of Ken Bates' pet projects. Bates responds, 'It is Roman Abramovich's toy shop now and it is up to him what he does with the toys.'

FRIDAY, 23 JANUARY

Abramovich's aides are in talks about a landing pad for his helicopter in Scarborough. They need not have bothered. Abramovich will be on a cruise. A Chelsea spokesperson says, 'This is only the second match Mr Abramovich has missed and he is doing all he can to organise some kind of direct TV feed to his yacht.'

Chelsea are to donate £25,000 plus signed shirts to boost Scarborough's cash-raising events which means, among other things, that Abramovich will effectively be financing their Centre of Excellence for six months. Meanwhile, the *Sun* dispatches an Abramovich look-alike to the town to pose for pictures.

Ranieri calls a players' meeting to ensure his expensive squad do not take the tie for granted. Makelele admits Chelsea will be a laughing stock if they lose. Ex-Chelsea centre-forward Kerry Dixon was in the team that lost 3–2 to Scarborough in 1989. He warns, 'Memories to that day are far from pleasant ones. We went up there sitting second behind Liverpool in Division One and I still don't know how we lost. It was just a feeling of complete embarrassment afterwards. Chelsea have the chance to put the record straight, but they have to put the work in. I will be shocked if lightning strikes twice, but I never thought we would lose either.'

Scott Parker, who first shot to fame as the kid playing keepy-uppy on a McDonald's TV ad, is finally in discussions with Chelsea over his personal terms.

SATURDAY, 24 JANUARY

SCARBOROUGH 0, CHELSEA 1

John Terry, superb in defence, is the difference between Chelsea and the team 104 places down the league ladder. He even heads the 10th-minute winner after Melchiot flicks on a Hasselbaink cross. Scarborough striker Mark Quayle says, 'Terry was awesome. It was a pleasure to play against him. Every time we shot at goal, the ball seemed to hit his arm or leg.'

The Premiership stars waste a succession of chances. Yet, two crucial moments – Colin Cryan's point-blank miss and a penalty appeal against Gallas which is turned down – cost the non-leaguers another £500,000 pay-day.

It takes Scarborough 80 minutes to force Cudicini to make a save. In the 81st minute Gallas rises to meet a spinning up-and-under and TV replays show he handles. But referee Barry Knight decides it is ball to hand and, crucially, not the other way round. Cryan's moment of destiny comes a minute earlier when Chris Senior flicks on a long ball, but the Irishman directs his header straight at Cudicini. Lampard's second-minute sizzler against a post, a vicious Hasselbaink corner cleared off the line in the ninth minute and a string of heroic saves from Leigh Walker are evidence of Chelsea's determination.

Perhaps it is just as well that Abramovich is not here. His look-alike Jeremy Corenbloom accepts the caviar on offer in the directors' box and the crowd taunt the Londoners with 'Premiership, you're having a laugh'. Terry concedes, 'We should really have beaten a team like Scarborough more comfortably. After we scored, we didn't seem to play. We had a lot of good chances but we didn't finish them off and it was the same against Birmingham. We've been struggling to score lately and against better teams we'll get punished if we don't score more. That's something we need to sort out.'

> **Team**
>
> Cudicini, Melchiot, Gallas, Terry, Bridge, Cole, Lampard, Nicolas (Oliveira), Gronkjaer (Petit), Gudjohnsen, Hasselbaink.

SUNDAY, 25 JANUARY

At the end of the game, Scarborough goalkeeper Walker was given a shirt signed by Carlo Cudicini. Unfortunately, his mum has washed it! Walker explains, 'My mum threw the shirt in the washing-machine when I got home on Saturday night, because it was caked in mud. So Carlo's autograph has been washed out of his jersey – which is a real sickener. I'll just have to get in touch with him and ask if he will send me up another one of his signed jerseys.' At least he wins a five-day jaunt to France's Cote d'Azur as his reward for conceding just one goal.

Emmanuel Petit, who made his comeback as a substitute, says he wants to end his career at Stamford Bridge. The club has yet to begin talks about a possible extension to a contract that expires at the end of the season. Winston Bogarde is offered the chance to resurrect his career at PSV Eindhoven, while Ajax defender Hatem Trabelsi says that Arsenal and Italian clubs are in the hunt for him along with Chelsea.

MONDAY, 26 JANUARY

On a sunshine break at La Manga, the players hear they have been drawn against FA Cup holders Arsenal in the next round. Chelsea have not beaten Arsenal in the FA Cup since 1947. Mario Melchiot reacts positively, 'None of us wants to lose at Highbury again. Most of us know what it's like to suffer defeat there, but that isn't necessarily a bad thing because we will all have a lot of determination in our bellies. We'll go there and give it our best shot. It's a chance to knock out one of our biggest rivals for the FA Cup and it would be nice to spring a surprise. We are not disappointed with the draw and, as always, we'll look forward to facing them.'

Arsenal, unbeaten in 16 FA Cup ties, want to become the first club since Blackburn in the 1880s to lift the trophy three years in row. The tie is switched to a Sunday lunchtime kick-off on police advice. The BBC, who get first pick of televised matches, normally broadcast their prime FA Cup tie on Saturday evenings and last year's quarter-final between the teams was a 5.15pm kick-off. But there was crowd trouble after that game and police insist the match cannot be played in the evening.

TUESDAY, 27 JANUARY

More goals, more often – that is the target if Chelsea are to make up the six-point gap on Arsenal. With four successive clean sheets, they are edging back to the consistency in defence they had in November. John Terry argues, 'We've not been playing so well lately and the results have shown that. But we're still not a million miles away from the two teams in front of us. Sooner or later, they will slip up.'

Meanwhile, Joe Cole starts an immediate ban after failing to overturn a two-match suspension.

WEDNESDAY, 28 JANUARY

The sunshine break at La Manga turns stormy as Terry hobbles home early for scans to determine the extent of damage to his right leg. He is on crutches after a training ground accident with Huth, who was also crocked in the clash and forced to leave the Blues' training camp. Terry says, 'I am suspended for the following weekend against Charlton and that could mean losing out on two games at the very least. Me and Robert Huth mistimed a tackle and kicked each other and we have both got the same problem on the ankle. We both stayed down for about five minutes.'

Arsenal's audacious £16m deal for Jose Antonio Reyes catches the Blues off guard. When Chelsea discover that Arsenal have moved in, Seville tell them a deal has been done with the Gunners. Wenger had stated publicly that his club couldn't compete financially in the transfer market, so no one believed that the Gunners would give Wenger such a transfer budget when so much money was being invested in their new ground at Ashburton Grove. Yet, Reyes becomes the club's record signing, providing a huge boost to their title challenge after close rivals Manchester United strengthen their squad with the £12.8m capture of Louis Saha.

Peter Kenyon is finally cleared to take up his post as Chelsea's chief executive on 1 February, once the transfer window closes.

THURSDAY, 29 JANUARY

Chelsea train again before returning to London to complete their preparations for the game against Blackburn at Ewood Park. Ranieri indicates there is still significant rebuilding to be done, suggesting a hectic period of comings and goings next summer. 'Roman Abramovich is very ambitious and he wants to put his club at the same level as Real Madrid.' Ranieri is remarkably candid as he admits that eight of his players are still not good enough. 'What I have asked him is to take us to a squad of 22 excellent players. At the moment we have 14 or so but I want to be able to count on two players of the highest level for every position in the team.'

Scott Parker is now training on his own in the afternoon after his Charlton team-mates have gone home. He practises in an empty gym as his rift with manager Alan Curbishley continues. A statement on the official Charlton website reads, 'As it has become abundantly clear that Scott Parker wishes to leave Charlton, and following a further bid from Chelsea, Charlton now confirm that they are in negotiations with Chelsea with a view to completing the transfer of the England international midfielder.'

Chelsea are determined to force through Parker's move in time to meet UEFA's 11.00am Monday deadline for the registration of players for the knock-out stage of the Champions League. But he won't be playing against Charlton, as Curbishley stresses, 'We weren't allowed to play Carlton Cole against Chelsea, so I can't see why we would let Scott play against us.'

Veron is expected to be out for three months following a back operation. 'He's OK, thank God,' his father Juan Ramon Veron says. 'Everything went well. He is in the hands of professionals who are keeping close tabs on him.' Veron Senior dispels the notion of any threat to his career. Veron will remain in Argentina during the initial stages of his recovery. He is under armed guard after a spate of kidnappings in Argentina and a robbery suffered by his family in their home town of La Plata three years ago.

FRIDAY, 30 JANUARY

Scott Parker is unveiled at Stamford Bridge as a new £10m signing. 'I know I'm not going to play as many games as I did at Charlton, but I want that challenge. I'll try my hardest for Chelsea – but if you're not playing you're still a part of it. I'm not going to be used to all the games Chelsea will play, so maybe not playing every week will help me out.

'I don't want to get into a war of words with Alan [Curbishley] – I can't speak too highly of Alan, he gave me the chance, I took it and I haven't looked back. I can understand some people at Charlton won't be happy, but in life there are some opportunities you can't turn down – and this is one of them.'

Parker cannot play against his old club at Stamford Bridge, and he accepts that is a wise move for all concerned. Ranieri has been interested in signing Parker, who agrees a four-and-a-half-year contract, for two years. 'We are looking for young champions and Scott is one of them. I believe in him and now I am very happy. I like the young English players and he has shown the last two years some fantastic performances. Like Frank Lampard, he is up and down, strong, works hard and has good quality. He shoots for goal very well and defends very well.

'Scott gives me a lot of options. I can now check if midfielders like Frank and Claude want a rest – although I know them very well and they don't want a rest. I like to change my system and he can play in every position. Of course he likes to play in the middle but when we play a diamond he can play anywhere. When we play 4-4-2 he can play in the middle or wide positions. It is very important to me we have good young English champions. I like this.'

Parker waives a £1m golden handshake from Charlton. But the new number 19 has every right to be pleased. He moves up from £15,000 a week to £45,000.

SATURDAY, 31 JANUARY

Ranieri is down to 11 fit senior outfield players for the game against Blackburn. 'It's not a problem when I have all 22 players. My problem is when I don't have players. The team grows up at times like this because they have to come together. Scott will be playing; he will have to because so many other players are out at the moment. The trip to La Manga was good for us because we were able to recharge our batteries even though we have had some more injuries.'

Duff is missed at Chelsea, but, perhaps, even more so by Blackburn Rovers. Manager Graeme Souness says, 'Certainly our two strikers haven't been presented with the same opportunities since he's gone. And he's the sort of player who can change a game with one piece of creativity and he's great at creating space for himself. We never intended to sell Damien. We originally put a £17m price tag on him to scare off Arsenal and Manchester United. When Chelsea came up with the money, it was unrefusable.

'He was changing in the last six months of his time here. At first he just sat in the corner laughing along with everyone else's mickey-taking. Towards the end he was instigating one-liners himself and I saw that as a sign of maturity. It's important for the good players to carry around a great big ego that follows you everywhere. You must have that if you're going to be a top man.'

When Souness became Rangers manager in 1986, he found himself with more money at his disposal than at any other British club. 'I've no envy of Chelsea whatsoever. There's pressure everywhere and we all handle that differently. You have to get on with what you have. Chelsea have made great signings and buying players is the hardest thing in football; you never know what you've truly got until you start working with them. It would be hard not to field a strong team but the difficult job is how to handle them. What goes hand-in-hand with being a top player is that you have an enormous ego because you believe you are the best. It is how you handle that which is the difficult one.'

Four young reserves are loaned out: centre-half Valerio di Cesare joins Serie B club Avelino; Joe Keenan goes to Westerlo in Belgium; Kevin McKinlay to Ross County and Kneissl to Dundee.

Geremi is among four players to have his possessions rifled as he is helping Cameroon to beat Zimbabwe, while Celestine Babayaro is thrown out of the Nigeria camp for staying out all night. Babayaro, Yakubu and Victor Agali, of Schalke 04, leave the squad's camp in Tunisia. 'They did not respect the rules of the camp,' Taiwo Ogunjobi, general secretary of the Nigerian FA, says. 'They were supposed to be in quarters with the rest of the squad. They only returned to the hotel Friday morning. It was decided that discipline must be maintained and the players involved leave the camp immediately.' They are accused of sneaking three women into the team hotel in the early hours at the five-star Kuriat Palace Hotel in Monastir, Tunisia; an allegation all three strenuously deny. Dr Rafiu Ladipo, president of the Nigeria Supporters Club says, 'I'm proud of the decision of the FA to decamp those players.'

February

ARSENAL DELIVER A DOUBLE BLOW BUT THE CHAMPIONS LEAGUE
DREAM LIVES ON

Ranieri predicts that the Champions League might not be won by one of the usual suspects this season. He adds, 'The favourites are the perennial names like Real Madrid, Juventus, AC Milan, Manchester United and Arsenal. Chelsea? We are there or thereabouts. We are working hard towards that aim.'

The club are already looking ahead to next season with eight new signings in mind: an A-list of world-class stars including the likes of Andrei Shevchenko, Ronaldo and David Beckham. Brazil defender Lucio is also wanted by Juventus and Roma but says, 'Chelsea's offer is the most concrete I've received so far. London would not be a problem for me.' Dortmund's Tomas Rosicky and Atletico Madrid's teenage strike sensation Fernando Torres top both Chelsea's and Manchester United's wish list, along with Real Betis winger Joaquin. Bayern Munich's Owen Hargreaves wants to join Chelsea. 'It's no secret that I would

Pos	Team	P	W	D	L	GF	GA	GD	PTS
	THE PREMIERSHIP – FEBRUARY								
1	Manchester United	23	17	2	4	43	17	26	53
2	Arsenal	22	15	7	0	42	14	28	52
3	Chelsea	22	14	4	4	40	17	23	46
4	Charlton Athletic	23	10	7	6	32	25	7	37
5	Liverpool	23	9	7	7	32	24	8	34
6	Newcastle United	23	8	10	5	31	24	7	34
7	Fulham	23	10	4	9	36	33	3	34
8	Bolton Wanderers	23	8	8	7	28	34	-6	32
9	Birmingham City	22	8	7	7	20	26	-6	31
10	Southampton	23	8	6	9	23	21	2	30

love to move to the Premiership. Who would not listen to Chelsea in the position they are in now?'

A profusion of departures is mooted: Hasselbaink, Desailly, Melchiot, Babayaro, Gronkjaer, Stanic and, of course, Winston Bogarde are prime candidates. Chelsea have managed only one January signing – Scott Parker. Ex-Charlton team-mate Paolo di Canio believes Parker could be better than Roy Keane. 'Scott is the best English midfielder on the scene – and I am not exaggerating. He plays every match and gets nine out of 10. He is another Roy Keane but with an even more complete understanding of the game.'

SUNDAY, 1 FEBRUARY

BLACKBURN 2, CHELSEA 3

Frank Lampard finds himself sharing the front pages of the tabloids with Jordan, who has recently caused a stir in TV's I'm a *Celebrity – Get me Out of Here!* Lampard scores a first-half double. Those two goals and a magnificent last-minute strike by Glen Johnson give Chelsea an eighth win in 12 Premiership matches away from home, which keeps them six points behind Arsenal, who enjoy a narrow home win over Manchester City.

Asked if Lampard is the best midfield player in the country, Ranieri replies, 'I think so. I'm very pleased with him. He's a strong midfielder – quality, long passing, good vision, strong in the tackle. Now, I think he has scored 10 goals. That's unbelievable, very, very good. Frank deserves to play for England because he is the complete player. I am not Sven-Goran Eriksson but I think the way Frank is playing must make him very happy. This league is amazing. It is so strong on midfield quality but Frank is right up there with the very best.'

Chelsea line up in a diamond formation, with Petit, starting his first game since September, shielding the back four, Makelele on the right, Parker making his debut on the left, and Lampard at the front. Initially, the quartet look like strangers but they settle down and eventually dominate, although in typical 'Tinkerman' style they are rotated a few times during the game. It is the first time Lampard has played for the entire match at the apex of a midfield diamond and he relishes the opportunity to get forward more. Lampard last scored twice in a game for West Ham against Bradford four years ago.

After going a goal behind to a Garry Flitcroft strike in the third minute, and then being dealt the sucker punch of a Paul Gallagher equaliser in the 88th minute, Chelsea show their self-belief as Johnson thunders home a magnificent half-volley from the edge of the box. It's a contender for goal of the month, and maybe even goal of the season. Johnson, who is slightly injured during the raucous congratulations, will be happy to settle for second place in both categories after Henry's latest wonder goal just two hours later.

Lampard joins Hasselbaink and Crespo as Chelsea's joint leading scorers in the Premiership with seven goals. He has scored 10 in all competitions. He is the only Chelsea player to start all 23 Premiership games.

Ranieri says his team have shown tremendous character. 'When Blackburn scored so late, I thought the match was finished but my players showed how much they want to win. We must be more clinical. When we have the chance, we must kill the game off. We had two or three chances to finish the match. If you don't, the other team can win or draw. We must improve in this way.'

Team

Cudicini, Terry, Bridge, Gallas, Johnson, Makelele, Lampard, Parker (Gronkjaer), Petit (Melchiot), Hasselbaink, Mutu (Gudjohnsen).

MONDAY, 2 FEBRUARY

Chelsea's new chief executive Peter Kenyon begins work, while Bruce Buck becomes the new chairman of Chelsea Village. Buck says, 'We see Manchester United with a very good brand that is reasonably well recognised around the world and we think we can do that or better, largely because we are a London club.

'If Manchester United was sold today, it could yield £500m, £600m or £700m depending on how the stock market is on any given day. That's the kind of thing we want to achieve. You have got to have a whole new approach to marketing and brand recognition.' Buck stresses Chelsea will continue to be run as a cost-efficient business, despite the vast wealth on tap from its owner.

Meanwhile Ken Bates is shunted even further to the periphery after a shock call from Buck. He is told that space is required in the next programme for an introductory interview with Kenyon. No room for Bates's column! Bates's programme notes are renowned for their hard-hitting attacks on the FA, journalists and other figures within the game and have always made compulsive reading.

Bates informs me of the precise content of his conversation with Buck. 'Bruce Buck didn't want me to write my notes. I asked him, "Why Not?" He explained there was a big spread by Peter Kenyon and they wanted to give him a clear run. I said, "What's that got to do with my programme notes?" He said I can write them for the next game. But I was not going to be buggered about so I suggested we call it a day. I probably said it in my usual way, "You can shove it." I won't be doing them again.'

Away from the boardroom politics, Ranieri is hopeful of an early Veron recovery, with the player back in the country later this week. Meanwhile Southampton disclose that the £6m sale of Wayne Bridge has kept the south coast club in profit. West Ham have sold Jermain Defoe to Tottenham for £7m, but their debts of £44m could have crippled the club if Abramovich had not bankrolled summer raids for Glen Johnson and Joe Cole. Manager Alan Pardew says, 'In all honesty if Abramovich hadn't gone into Chelsea you would have had to seriously worry about the future of West Ham because a lot of those deals kept us from a Leeds United situation. One of the big, big problems of the last six years was that money on players went abroad to other clubs never to be seen again. But the Abramovich money has come to us. It's been fantastic. We certainly spent it in the British market and it filters down.'

TUESDAY, 3 FEBRUARY

Omitted from the World Cup party two years ago, there's little doubt Frank Lampard will make the Euro 2004 squad this summer. England Under-21 coach David Platt says, 'Frank has always been a good passing player who got from box to box, but the move to Chelsea has put his game on a different level. Going to Chelsea has made him realise that he can compete successfully at a higher level. Frank holds his position well and still looks capable of scoring 15 goals a season. Every serious championship side needs a striker who's going to get 20-25 and then a back-up goalscorer. Well, that's the job Frank does so well for Chelsea.'

England's assistant boss Tord Grip says, 'Our younger players should look at someone like Frank and see just how hard he has worked at his game. Frank always had vision and technique but now he has the strength too.'

WEDNESDAY, 4 FEBRUARY

Scott Parker wants to match the example set by another major Chelsea signing who also made his debut at Blackburn Rovers – Gianfranco Zola. Parker says, 'I know that Zola made his debut at Blackburn as well, so I'd love to follow in his footsteps.' Chelsea abandon plans to unveil Parker at the Bridge before the Charlton game for fear of antagonising the visiting fans. But Danish midfielder Claus Jensen insists, 'I don't think there's bad blood between the sides. The millions that Charlton have got for Scott are going to make the club go even further. The main point is we'll miss a great player, a great personality and a good friend of mine. I hope the fans remember Scott for being a great player and for what he did here. Scott was always 100 per cent loyal. Let's be positive.

We've got a lot of money for a player who came through the youth system and Scott will get to play Champions League football.'

THURSDAY, 5 FEBRUARY

Ken Bates interrupts a speech by Claudio Ranieri to call agent Pini Zahavi a 'dickhead' at a £35-a-head supper club at the Bridge. The ongoing internal rows are heating up. The remark is heard by the 100-plus diners; it is also filmed by Chelsea TV, although never broadcast.

Speaking at Bates's monthly Chairman's Supper Club in a question-and-answer session with supporters, Ranieri says, 'I'm the "Tinkerman", but many other managers also change tactics during the games. I love being called the "Tinkerman". It's also very close to "Thinkerman", which would be even better! Now, if I work hard, maybe I can change the word to "Thinkerman". That would be good.'

Claude Makelele admits he put money first when he moved from Real Madrid to Chelsea. 'I don't regret a thing. I took the decision for the good of my financial future and my health. I'm not an egotist but a moment came when I had to be – because other people were only thinking of themselves and nothing more. It's dangerous when a club pays so much for you because, with this amount, you are not given much time to demonstrate your game. But the truth is, I have adapted very quickly. I have got my head round it and am giving my all. I'm very professional.'

Adrian Mutu has cut down on the partying in a bid to improve his sharpness. 'At the moment, I'm reading Dostoyevsky's *The Idiot* – in translation. There are a lot of temptations and, if you try and mix work and pleasure too much, you will never succeed. I only go to a club after a game and there's nothing wrong with that. My price tag was not up to me but, when someone pays so much for you, expectations are very high. For me, the job is to play football and that is the most important thing.'

FRIDAY, 6 FEBRUARY

Peter Kenyon warns that anything less than a major trophy this season will be 'a failure', but he is adamant he is not adding to speculation surrounding Ranieri. 'If you leave the investment aside, it will be a huge disappointment if we don't win anything and I'm sure the fans would agree with that. If you include the investment, however, it will be a failure if we don't win something. That's the way the manager will see it and the way we see it because we're expected to win things – that's what we do.'

Kenyon insists his parting with Manchester United was 'amicable' despite their official complaint to the Premier League. 'I wasn't looking to move, but this job represents the single most exciting challenge in European football over the next five years.' Kenyon speaks about his working relationship with Abramovich. 'He's involved in the business, but I am there to run it. He's passionate about it and we have to move away from this perception that Chelsea is his hobby or his plaything. This is a serious commitment by a very serious businessman. He wants Chelsea to achieve European status, to be number one, and while we are prepared to invest we also want, over a period of time, to get a return for that investment.

'I first met Roman Abramovich when he came to Old Trafford for the Champions League quarter-final against Real Madrid. We met again shortly after he took over at Chelsea. I was approached and nothing happened then because the summer is a particularly busy time, both with transfers and the end of the football year. The next time we got together was in August and that led to me resigning on 7 September.'

As part of his job with United, Kenyon had to tell David Beckham he was being sold. Now he'd like to buy him back for Chelsea. Kenyon says, 'Any club would like to see David Beckham wearing their shirt. The end for David at United came following a lot of discussions. I wasn't nervous of delivering that news. It was my job, it had to be done. I wouldn't say he was shocked. There was a recognition that a long relationship at the club probably was not going to continue. That was the tone of the conversation – not that he had never heard such a thing was possible before.

'I didn't feel sorry for him. He's a professional, as were we. I like David a lot. He was a huge part of United's success. He contributed immensely to the image of Manchester United. I wished him very well and I think it was the right move for him. He has settled in so well and I think his football has moved on. I think he needed the change and we haven't fallen out at all. He appreciates why it happened.'

Claudio Ranieri can feel the wind of change blowing at the club. 'I know that when the owner and chief executive change it's normal to change the manager also. It's unusual for a club to keep the manager. It's the story of football and I'm trying to work against the story – and I knew that before I met Roman Abramovich and he met Sven-Goran Eriksson. You ask if I'm scared about losing my job. I'm not, because all I can do is wait for what happens.'

Pretending to hold a gun to his head, Ranieri adds, 'I work and then if somebody wants to kill me, I'm here. I am waiting for it. What can I change? Nothing. I can only work well for my conscience. That's my motivation, so that at the end of the day I can look everybody in the face. This is nothing new to me. I am happy with myself.

'The new man [Peter Kenyon] has arrived, seen that Mr Abramovich has spent a lot of money and declared we must win. That's normal. I have a contract here to 2007 but I am not the owner and I am not Peter Kenyon. I am only Claudio Ranieri... I could be sacked even if I win something. It's part of the show. Everything is a show in football and I accept it. I have met Mr Kenyon and we agree on most things. Everyone will be disappointed if we don't win things. Mr Abramovich, Mr Kenyon and myself. But I will continue to do it my way.'

Kenyon explains his position. 'Changing the manager is a big, big decision for the directors of Chelsea. It would be a combined decision, which is as it should be. Of course the speculation would not have been as high if there had not been a picture of Sven walking into Roman's house. I know that. The picture is there... the picture is history. We aren't going to change the picture, are we?

'Will the manager be changed if we don't win something? We review all these positions. It's an ongoing process. It's like speculating in March who we are going to buy in the summer. We will sit down and have those discussions at the end of the season.'

Elsewhere Eriksson is quoted as saying that 'something may happen' at Chelsea if he fails with England at Euro 2004. He later denies it.

SATURDAY, 7 FEBRUARY

Peter Kenyon spells out what is now expected at Chelsea. 'We must start winning sooner rather than later. You can't get away from the quality of the squad we've got and the investments that have been made. We've got to start winning pretty quickly. There's not a time frame that says if we don't do it this year we must do it next year, but it is pre-eminent to everything we are doing here that we start to get the success Chelsea deserve. There's nothing planned and Claudio has got three years on his contract. I've lived through the speculation surrounding a manager and it's destructive. It's not right that every time we lose a game he is looking over his shoulder.'

Asked whether Eriksson is their number one target, Kenyon says, 'I have no comment to make. All I can guarantee is we will do what is best for Chelsea at the time. I am not going to give any guarantees as to where we start next season. I am a week into the job and have got a lot of work to do. We are trying to build for long-term success.'

The next game up is Charlton. Alan Curbishley's men have beaten the Blues five times in seven meetings and Parker says, 'They are going to get all 11 players committed and they are going to work hard. When I was at Charlton, we were told to close Chelsea down because it was felt they were not the fastest of sides. The top teams had the personnel and the quality to probably beat Charlton nine times out of 10, but Chelsea have always struggled.'

Ranieri says, 'I haven't even spoken to Scott about ways to beat Charlton. Besides, I know Charlton very well and I hope we can show that we have learned well from the defeat in December. Sometimes bad defeats like that and the one at Aston Villa in the Carling Cup are as big steps as those wins against Manchester United and Lazio. You can learn so much from them.'

SUNDAY, 8 FEBRUARY

CHELSEA 1, CHARLTON 0

The Charlton fans goad Ranieri by chanting, 'You're being sacked in the summer.' Ranieri turns round waving his finger at them and replies, 'No, no. In May.' With such humour, the charming Italian is beginning to win the hearts of the fans, if not their minds. Ranieri explains, 'They all laughed and I had a giggle as well. But that's all it was: a joke. What is not a joke is the incredible mix of injuries, suspensions and forced absences that have seriously stretched our squad in the past few weeks. When I said that I had two players for every position last summer, I thought I was well covered in every department. Who would have thought that I would have to call upon a youngster such as Alexis Nicolas – who played very well, by the way – at this stage of the season?'

Some fans notice the Bates programme notes are missing. A furious Bates says, 'Reports of my death have been greatly exaggerated. I don't know if it is the end of an era but it is the end of something. I still get my seats and I still entertain in the boardroom but I am not involved in the day-to-day running.' Ron 'Chopper' Harris, an old adversary, is glad to see the back of Bates, who criticised the team he played in in the 1970s. Harris gloats, 'He called the team a bunch of lager louts. He banned me because I had the nerve to respond. He's history now.'

With his usual impeccable timing, Eriksson is at Stamford Bridge as another chink appears in the Ranieri armour with the impending demise of Bates. Chelsea have 11 players absent due to injury or suspension. A team full of internationals is missing handing Nicolas a Premiership debut in midfield.

The game is decided by a single goal. Defender Mark Fish escapes punishment when he pushes Mutu in the box, but he is finally caught out by Hasselbaink. The Dutch striker uses all his know-how as he backs into Fish and, rather than just stand up to him, Fish wraps both arms round the Chelsea striker. Down goes Hasselbaink and ref Steve Bennett points to the spot. Charlton are furious and coach Mervyn Day argues with fourth official Graham Poll. Hasselbaink stays calm to side-foot past Dean Kiely. After Hasselbaink's 28th-minute penalty winner, his 99th goal in the Premiership, Chelsea trail Arsenal by six points and Manchester United by four.

Scott Parker is introduced to the crowd at half-time; the new signing sheepishly waves from his position in one of the corporate hospitality boxes. The Charlton fans let him know what they think. 'Judas' is one of the more polite terms. Alan Curbishley is angry that Charlton do not have a single shot on target. Charlton come close in the second half only when Huth toes a clearance a foot wide of his own post. Ranieri says the team is missing the influence of Makelele. 'We are used to playing with Claude Makelele in central midfield. He gives us a good tempo. Without him, it's a little bit more difficult.'

Team

Sullivan, Melchiot, Bridge, Gallas, Huth, Johnson, Lampard, Nicolas, Gronkjaer, Mutu, Hasselbaink (Gudjohnsen).

MONDAY, 9 FEBRUARY

Eriksson begins to fear he will receive the same treatment as Don Revie, who took the England job in 1974 but quit three years later to manage United Arab Emirates – a decision seen as treachery by the fans. Eriksson knows he could earn more at Chelsea – £5m a year, rising to £8m depending on success – compared to the £3–4m per annum the FA are offering for a new contract. Asked if he could turn down a massive offer, he says, 'Oh yes – without any question. I don't think of money in that way. I am NOT for sale. I have been working in Europe for many years and earning a lot of money. I could retire any day and still be able to eat a meal every day. If I take a club in England, it must be a challenge. I want to be a winner.'

Perfectly aware of Chelsea's interest, he maintains he did not talk with Abramovich about replacing Ranieri when they met. Eriksson insists, 'Absolutely not and I repeat NOT. We were talking football in general. When I say that, you must believe me!' The FA have offered him an extension until 2008.

Beckham hints a Chelsea move could happen when he is ready because of the enormous respect he still has for Kenyon. The England captain says, 'He is a really nice man. I worked well with him when I was at Manchester United and would have no problem doing it again.' He will never forget how Kenyon confirmed his worst fears about his irreconcilable feud with Sir Alex Ferguson and made it clear he had no future at Old Trafford. But Beckham insists he is in no rush to quit the Bernabeu.

The fee for Parker turns out to have been £11.25m. Parker waived a £1m 'loyalty bonus' for not asking for a transfer. However, Charlton still paid it and were reimbursed by Chelsea.

Craig Rocastle, 22-year-old midfielder, gets his first taste of the first team as an unused substitute against Charlton. His cousin is the late David Rocastle.

Like his relative, Rocastle is an attacking player who can boss the midfield with an impressive range of passing. He is capable of unpicking the tightest of defences. With 15 midfielders in front of him in the pecking order, it would be easy for him to despair of his first-team chances, but he is just pleased to be at Chelsea. He also hopes to graduate from pupil to teacher by acting as an inspiration to David's 11-year-old son Ryan, who was mascot at the 2002 FA Cup final between Arsenal and Chelsea, weeks after his father's death.

TUESDAY, 10 FEBRUARY

Peter Kenyon tries to shift attention from Ranieri back to the title chase. 'I know some of the comments I made with regard to winning a trophy have been linked directly with whether Claudio has to win a trophy or be out. Those links have not been made by me or anybody at the club. The issue is that there isn't a deal with Sven-Goran Eriksson and Claudio has a contract to 2007.

'We're third in the league and really in contention for the title, still in the FA Cup and further along in the Champions League than many people expected. The squad has definitely come together more quickly than most outsiders expected it would. So we're in a great position. It's time we closed ranks and there will be no more discussions on the subject from me, Claudio or anybody else. What we should now be concentrating on is maximising Chelsea's position at the most critical part of the season, which is the run-in.'

Kenyon confirms that Bates will accompany him – not the other way around – to Premiership chairmen's meetings. 'The first thing I would acknowledge is Ken's contribution to Chelsea. Equally, he sold the club last summer and, as a consequence, he ceased to have any executive responsibilities. Ken remains as chairman of the football club and, as a key responsibility, he will accompany me – the representative of the club – to Premier League meetings and will continue to do that until he takes up his life president position.'

But Bates's power base is again being eroded and Pini Zahavi reacts to the Bates 'dickhead' jibe. 'This revolting character is not worthy of a response. If I was in his shoes, I would wake up every morning praying to God and thanking him that Pini Zahavi saved him from bankruptcy and put £19m in his pocket. He is history as far as English football is concerned.'

Damien Duff declares himself fit but confesses that if his shoulder goes again, it could become a regular occurrence, as it did for former England captain Bryan Robson. He also states his wish that Ranieri should stop tinkering with his starting position. 'If I was the manager I would play me on the left wing every time. Everybody knows it's my best position, but football doesn't work that way. I am moved around all the time at Chelsea.'

Jesper Gronkjaer suggests he too should be on the left. 'I'm more comfortable on the left wing because I've got more options. It's easier for me to go inside and be a threat for scoring a goal. I'm a left-winger first and foremost but I have never been played there regularly at Chelsea and I certainly haven't had a look-in since Damien Duff arrived in the summer, and that has been very tough. I don't know if you could say I've gone backwards in my time at Chelsea, but I've certainly gone sideways. I'm definitely not the same player as when I came here. I was seen as a great player at Ajax, but perhaps that is because the Dutch League is easier. It's difficult to say.'

Frank Lampard hands the captain's armband back to John Terry for the game at Fratton Park, insisting the senior players back the coach. On current form, Lampard must be rated the best midfielder in the country according to Pompey manager Harry Redknapp, who brought Lampard up through the ranks at West Ham. Redknapp says, 'Frank is a great professional and a terrific player. He has a great attitude, works hard in training and deserves all the success he has got. He has been the best midfielder in the country this season, and he is certainly competing with Paul Scholes and Steven Gerrard for the two central midfield places for England.'

Alexei Smertin, who was once transferred between Siberian clubs Barnaul and Novosibirsk for a winter's supply of fuel, admits his move to Chelsea and then on loan to Portsmouth was even stranger. 'My journey to England was a rather complex one but I'm glad I made it. I've only met Mr Ranieri once. I had a chat with him in the summer before I came to Portsmouth but we haven't spoken since. I've met Mr Abramovich but only as the president of Chelsea and I do not know him personally. I consider myself a Chelsea player but at least Portsmouth play in the same colours. It's a shame I can't play against Chelsea but that's life. I will be at the game but can't tell you who I'm supporting.'

WEDNESDAY, 11 FEBRUARY

PORTSMOUTH 0, CHELSEA 2

Scott Parker's first goal in only his second game and Crespo coming off the bench to score are encouraging signs as the Blues move to within a point of second-placed Manchester United who lose at home to Boro. Seven games unbeaten and Chelsea's 14th clean sheet are impressive stats. Parker becomes the 17th different player to score this season.

The cacophony of abuse which greets Wayne Bridge's every touch confirms the former Southampton man is never going to win any popularity contests on the south coast. Accepting Bridge's short ball, Parker exchanges passes with Mutu, kills the ball with his first touch and drills an unstoppable shot into the roof of the net with his second. Portsmouth deserve to draw level in the 25th minute when Sullivan makes a pig's ear of Terry's back-pass, boots the ball straight against his own skipper then watches in relief as Yakubu smashes his shot over the bar. Patrik Berger comes even closer six minutes later when his low left-footer smacks off Sullivan's far post. Finally Chelsea kill the game off through Crespo in the 78th minute. Hasselbaink beats Shaka Hislop in a race for Lampard's through-ball and lifts his shot expertly over the advancing Pompey keeper. Only the crossbar prevents his 100th Premiership goal but the rebound falls perfectly for Crespo, who is suddenly all alone to chest the ball back into the unprotected net.

Next up are Arsenal twice in seven days, with the Gunners still undefeated in the league. 'Stop Henry!' That is the mantra. Ranieri says, 'I am happy to catch up Manchester United and now we would like to catch up Arsenal. I watched them on Tuesday and they were fantastic, but so are we. We are in good condition now, though. I am very happy that I am getting some of my injured players back. It should be a good match against Arsenal.'

Lampard climbs on to the team coach after another job well done and says, 'The next couple of weeks is why I joined Chelsea. It's all up for grabs.'

> **Team**
>
> Sullivan, Melchiot, Gallas, Terry, Bridge, Gronkjaer, Lampard, Makelele, Parker (Cole), Gudjohnsen (Hasselbaink), Mutu (Crespo).

THURSDAY, 12 FEBRUARY

Abramovich distances himself from a £285m bid to buy Roma as Ranieri announces he knows exactly what to expect from Arsenal. Wenger is less sure what to expect from Chelsea. Ranieri has used 30 players in first-team matches this season. 'We don't speculate much about our opponents,' Wenger says. 'We focus more on how we play.' But Wenger still selects Lampard as the key man for Chelsea. 'Lampard has been absolutely outstanding. I always thought he was a good player but he has improved in every respect. He has always had that ability to shoot from outside the area but now there is a lot more to him. The important thing is he often gets them a goal when it is most needed. He was young when he went to Chelsea and now he has played every week at a better level.'

FRIDAY, 13 FEBRUARY

This is an appropriate day for Veron, nicknamed 'The Little Witch' in Argentina, to declare, 'I feel I've had a lot of bad luck since I came to England. Maybe I'm cursed. It's very hard for me to take, but I must not risk my career.'

Ranieri responds to a prediction by Ashley Cole that the Italian may be out of a job if Chelsea lose to the Gunners twice in a week. 'In one hour I could cross the road and get run over by a bus. It's true these two games against Arsenal could be make-or-break for us, but I'm not scared about that. Why should I think that we'll lose these two games? I prefer to think we will win them.'

John Terry has three Thierry Henry shirts hanging on the wall at his home. 'The last time we played Arsenal, in October, I was out with a hamstring injury. But before the game I made a point of asking for his shirt. He kindly gave it to me afterwards and even signed it for me. He wrote, "To John, keep up the good work, Thierry". Thierry has given me a couple more of his shirts on previous occasions. But this one is my favourite. He is the best striker in the world. He is almost superhuman. If you come off the pitch with a half-decent result and he hasn't scored, you can take so much confidence from that.'

The first game in the double-header is in the FA Cup. In last season's quarter-final between the clubs, Terry scored at both ends in a 3–1 replay defeat. 'It's a painful memory which I have worked hard to erase from my mind. I really feel we owe Arsenal one and I am right up for this game.'

Rumours of dressing room dissatisfaction with Ranieri's regime are growing. Gudjohnsen feels a settled strike force is required. 'Maybe a run of a few games would benefit me … It is difficult because you don't play with the same player all the time. At this moment, we haven't really been firing. Not one of us has really found great goalscoring form even though we might be opening defences up for the midfielders to run through and get their goals. Jimmy and I have played together a lot of times, but this is the least amount of games in the last three years that Jimmy and I have played together. Our styles complement each other. Jimmy is very strong at going in behind the defence and I prefer the ball to my feet.'

At the beginning of the season with the profusion of midfield signings, Frank Lampard looked the most vulnerable, but he has become a regular all the same. As he explains, 'Claudio's rotation policy can affect the players and they get angry. If he did rest me for a few games, maybe I'd bang his door down. I love to play every game and, if you don't, you get frustrated.'

SATURDAY, 14 FEBRUARY

Ranieri discloses how close he came to signing 'the Muhammad Ali of football'. The story is sparked off when he explains how he was at Highbury on Tuesday to watch another outstanding Thierry Henry show against Southampton. 'I watched him a long time ago when I was manager of Fiorentina and he was playing for the French Under-21 team. I said to my chairman, "Please buy him because he is one of the best," but it did not happen for some reason. I said to my chairman, 'He is the Muhammad Ali of the football pitch because he has such elegance, such speed. He does everything with such style and grace.'" How does Ranieri intend to stop him? 'With a gun,' he smiles. 'But seriously, I have my players and we will do our best to stop him.

'I've heard some Chelsea fans singing, "We don't need Eriksson!" I'd be lying if I said I did not enjoy that, because I see it as a show of affection from our fans and I thank them for it. They must understand, however, that the club and I are on the same page. Our strategy all along had been to help the newcomers blend in with the old guard and, at the same time, rotate players so that the bulk of the squad would be fresh in March, when the legs start to tire. I expect there will be less rotation between now and the end of the season... although that may mean that the press will have to find a new nickname for me because I might not be tinkering quite as much!'

Under Ranieri, Chelsea have been knocked out of the FA Cup by Arsenal every season – including the 2002 final. Ranieri has a ready response to such statistics. 'In Italy we say, "There isn't two without three'. We lost three. Now it is time for a win. It is a big rock in front of us, but we are ready.'

SUNDAY, 15 FEBRUARY

ARSENAL 2, CHELSEA 1

Former Chelsea target Jose Antonio Reyes grabs a superb second-half double leaving Ranieri to criticise his Chelsea side. 'I expected more fight from my players after the interval but, maybe, we lost the plot. It wasn't just one or two it was the whole squad.' As Eriksson watches on from the directors' box, Ranieri confesses he does not know what has gone wrong. 'At 1–0 up at half-time, I was positive we had a great chance of winning this game. So of course this was a wasted opportunity.'

With Thierry Henry sitting it out, Reyes is starting only his third game since he was snatched from Seville right under the noses of Chelsea. His first is a cracker. He cuts across Parker before unleashing an unstoppable 25-yarder into the top corner. Wenger says, 'I always felt we'd win after that. But, for me, his second goal was even better because of the quality of his movement and the magnificent pass from Patrick Vieira. I always expect my players to deliver the goods but I didn't expect Jose to have the courage to take the ball and do something special like that.' Reyes departs to a standing ovation when he is substituted seven minutes from the end.

At one stage, though, Chelsea have the Gunners on the rack and are playing with all the confidence in the world. Mutu's superb goal on 39 minutes gives them the advantage. With Parker – omitted from this week's England squad – running the midfield, Arsenal are chasing, with no hint of what is to come. Reyes turns a pulsating tie on its head in the 55th minute. Chelsea never properly clear an Edu corner and, when Reyes picks it up, they retreat to the edge of the area. He switches to his left and unleashes a thunderbolt which flies into the top corner. Six minutes later, Reyes is celebrating another. Sullivan comes on for the injured Cudicini on the hour and immediately has to pick the ball out of the net. Vieira's pass with the outside of his right foot is perfectly weighted to beat Melchiot and Reyes takes it in his stride. He side-foots wide of Sullivan, who can't prevent it trickling over the line despite getting a hand to it.

The Chelsea supporters at the Clock End had been chanting, 'We don't want Eriksson,' but Reyes's winner must make them think twice! Ranieri sends on Gudjohnsen and Cole but, despite much frantic effort, Chelsea can't break Arsenal. Wenger insists, 'The teams have always been close but I hope we have shown that they have not caught us yet.' What's Arsenal's secret? 'I don't know,' replies Ranieri. 'But I do know we play them again on Saturday.' Thierry Henry should be back for that one.

> **Team**
>
> Cudicini (Sullivan), Melchiot, Terry, Gallas, Bridge, Parker, Lampard, Makelele, Gronkjaer (Cole), Hasselbaink, Mutu (Gudjohnsen).

MONDAY, 16 FEBRUARY

Makelele does not hold back on his frustration at losing to Arsenal. 'This is a match that is going to stick in our throats. We simply stopped playing and I can't understand why. Now our hopes of winning the FA Cup are at an end; all we have left to play for are the Premiership and the Champions League. It is always Arsenal who are the winners when we play them, and we are sick and tired of it.'

Ken Bates is linked with a bid to take control at Sheffield Wednesday. He recently met with the directors but he claims it was only in an advisory role as a favour to close friend and former Owls chairman Dave Richards. However, chairman Dave Allen reveals Bates is serious about becoming involved in the debt-ridden Second Division club and urges him to show them his money.

TUESDAY, 17 FEBRUARY

Glen Johnson is named captain of England's Under-21 team. Coach David Platt remarks, 'When I told him, he looked me in the eye as if he expected it. But that's the way he is. It's confidence, which is not arrogance, and I like his demeanour. If you look at where Glen is in terms of international football, he is above the Under-21s and slightly below the seniors. Sven has decided it is better for him to play in this game than sit on the bench for the senior team in Portugal. He is still improving, technically gifted and has pace to burn. He could do the decathlon and beat Daley Thompson. To me it is this status that says, "You deserve the armband." Glen has a presence about him; if he walks in a room everyone will turn their heads.'

Jimmy Floyd Hasselbaink is left out of Holland's provisional 28-man squad for Euro 2004. He says, 'I have two aims for the season – to win the title and to win a place at the European Championships. Holland will take five strikers to Euro 2004 and we've got loads of strikers – Van Nistelrooy, Kluivert, Makaay, Van Hooijdonk, Van der Vaart and me. But I want to go and I want to finish my international career there.' After being left out of recent friendlies, he admits, 'I didn't get an explanation from the boss and I'm not the kind of guy to ring and ask for one.'

WEDNESDAY, 18 FEBRUARY

Brazil are in Dublin for a friendly. Ronaldo says, 'I know there is interest from English clubs though, as yet, there's nothing concrete. Right now I'm happy at Real and love the club but I'd be foolish to dismiss any interest in me. Chelsea? I am not moving from Madrid; I am very happy there.'

Chelsea are interested in Uruguayan teenager Jorge Garcia, 17, to farm out to Belgian partner club, Westerlo. Peter Kenyon was at Manchester United when they formed a similar alliance with Royal Antwerp and his old employers use the Belgian side for youngsters who would not be given British work permits through lack of caps.

THURSDAY, 19 FEBRUARY

Most Arsenal players have come through the midweek internationals without injury. Thierry Henry, Freddie Ljungberg and Kanu are back, but Gilberto Silva was carried off after twisting his ankle in Brazil's goalless draw with the Republic of Ireland in Dublin, while Joe Cole limped out of England's clash with Portugal after jarring his back.

Looking forward to the game with Chelsea, Vieira says, 'It is fantastic for Chelsea to have players like Claude Makelele and Frank Lampard. But only 11 players can be in the team. To be honest, I don't understand how they cope with not playing every week. Footballers want to play every game. It is difficult to have so many top-quality players around.'

Top: Veron's season was wrecked by back problems and criticism that he failed to live up to his reputation.

Bottom: Crespo, left, showed, when he played, that he has a genuine goal-scoring gift.

Top: Damien Duff, middle, in Champions League action. He was one of the big successes until he dislocated his shoulder, robbing Chelsea of his £17 million match-winning presence.

Bottom: The goal by Robert Pires (far right) at Stamford Bridge. Arsenal thought it would take them through to the Champions League semi-finals.

Claude Makelele, left, tussles with his French colleague Thierry Henry in the Champions League clash.

The Tinkerman can never quite make up his mind!

Top: Frank Lampard's goals were the big bonus of the season. He enjoyed the one against Arsenal!

Bottom: The moment of the season. Wayne Bridge scores the winner in the Champions League quarter-finals against Arsenal.

Tears: losing to Monaco was hard to take.

Top: Cheers: glory in the Champions League took Ranieri to the height of his career.

Bottom: Abramovich (third from left) and Chelsea supporters. Behind them, one of Abramovich's luxury yachts.

Ranieri beats Wenger at last – one out of 17 is not so good.

It is not just Chelsea who get linked to the world's great players. And Makelele is being as provocative as ever when he suggests, 'I don't understand why Henry would not want to move. Real Madrid is Real Madrid.'

There's no let-up in the 'Eriksson for Chelsea' headlines, but Ranieri remains focused on the challenge of Arsenal. As he says, 'We cannot make any mistakes against them – I want to see us show great will and fantastic mentality. We have to face Arsenal again and this is our chance for revenge. The title race is alive because, if we win, the gap is very close.'

Bridge returns from England duty in Faro and says, 'We don't want to let it slip now. We have to fight right to the end of the season but, if we lose again to Arsenal, it's going to make things very much harder. It's strange that there is always so much speculation about the manager's job considering what a good season we're having. But Claudio is dealing with it very well and isn't showing the pressure at all.'

Lampard knows Ranieri's head really is on the block over the next few days, with the Arsenal game and a trip to Stuttgart. 'It would be hard to sack someone who has just won the Champions League, wouldn't it? We want to do well in the Champions League for the manager. But every step you go in this competition becomes more and more difficult and Stuttgart will be a major test for us.'

FRIDAY, 20 FEBRUARY

Ranieri is aware that failure over the next four days will mean the sack. 'It is a very important week for our futures – both the club's and mine. I am not stupid. My satisfaction at beating Arsenal would only be to see us close the gap to three points. We cannot afford to let Arsenal build a gap of nine points.'

But Chelsea suffer three major blows. Duff, whom Wenger admits he admires as much as anybody in the Blues line-up, has still not recovered from an Achilles tendon injury; Crespo has been struck down with a high temperature; Cudicini is still suffering with the groin injury that forced him off in the second half at Highbury.

John Terry observes, 'When the final whistle went last Sunday I just wanted the ground to eat me up and it was the same with the other boys. We were just deflated. Honestly, it's doing my head in not being able to beat them.'

Defiantly Ranieri insists, 'This is another match and another competition. I am sending a team out telling them to play like they did in the first half at Highbury.' So why can't he ever beat Arsenal? 'I don't have a block, honestly, and I hope also my players don't have. Maybe there are some stadiums that are good for you and other stadiums that are not. I believe sometimes a team are good for you or not good for you. Look at Liverpool. Every year when we go to Anfield we lose and, when Liverpool come here, we used to win. That changed this season. Now it's Arsenal. It's very, very strange. Sometimes we play very well, but without winning.'

Ranieri tries to be positive by introducing ex-Chelsea striker Bobby Tambling, who once scored four against Arsenal at Highbury, to the assembled media. He is also reminded of a story he heard on a coaching course he attended in Italy, when he was told how 'being a manager is like parachuting – sometimes the chute doesn't open and you splatter on the ground'. He observes, 'Maybe it will open tomorrow but break another day.'

Celestine Babayaro is the only current player to have experienced victory over Arsenal, a 5–0 League Cup success back in November 1998 that meant little as Wenger fielded a virtual second team.

SATURDAY, 21 FEBRUARY

CHELSEA 1, ARSENAL 2

Ranieri's reign instantly seems untenable as Arsenal surge seven points clear at the top, nine ahead of Chelsea, stretching their unbeaten Premiership run to 26 matches, thanks to goals from Patrick Vieira and Edu. The Gunners blew an eight-point lead to Manchester United in last year's run-in but they won't be making the same mistake again. It is over for Chelsea, anyway, according to Ranieri. 'Yes, for us it looks like it's over. It may not be too much for Manchester United but nine points for us is too much.'

Arsenal are together in their approach, Chelsea divided. Yet, it is a promising start. Vieira uncharacteristically loses possession, Geremi races on to the mis-control and his cross is headed on by Mutu before being despatched by Gudjohnsen at the far post. Driving forward after one of Makelele's catalogue of errors, Vieira atones with his first goal of the season, crafted by Dennis Bergkamp's exquisite pass. Then Sullivan flaps at Thierry Henry's corner, the ball deflects off Gudjohnsen and is smashed in by Edu.

During the last 32 minutes, Chelsea fail to create an opportunity. The dismissal of Gudjohnsen on the hour contributes to that – but it cannot fully explain Chelsea's lack of willpower in front of goal. Gudjohnsen is booked for a pathetic dive in the penalty area and then sent off for clipping the heel of Gael Clichy. It might all have been different had a Geremi free-kick in the 35th minute fallen to anyone other than Terry with only Lehmann to beat, but the finish explains why he plays at centre-half. When Gallas misses the chance to flick a Geremi free-kick goalwards after 58 minutes, the chances dry up. Cole – again used in the substitute's cameo role – is becoming a caricature. Wenger says,

'Even when we were 1–0 down and the tackles were flying in we never got nervous and kept our heads. We focused on playing.'

Ranieri's assertion that Chelsea can run Arsenal close and that the difference is down to finishing does not hold much water. Looking ahead to the make-or-break European tie against Stuttgart, the lovable Italian says, 'Champions League is like a game of bingo, you can win, you can lose, it's in the lap of the Gods.'

Adrian Mutu reveals how Abramovich's mood has changed. 'Roman came into the dressing room after the game to talk to us. This is not unusual. We were all sitting there wondering what he was going to say. They'd ended our chances in the Cup and now maybe the league as well. He looked around at all of us and told us straight, "Arsenal are better than you." He then told us the title was gone. We didn't expect that, but he is entitled to his opinion after all the money he's spent this season.

'He was, obviously, disappointed. But for us, the players, it is very important he remains patient. It will not be good for him to be furious with us. When a team like Arsenal is far better than you, then you have no right to be upset. You must only go and congratulate them because they are the best team out of all the competitors in the Premiership this season.'

Abramovich shows a sense of humour as he responds to the inevitable question about Ranieri's successor. Asked by a Russian journalist about a change of manager, he replies, 'For Who? For Gazzaev!' Valeri Gazzaev is the under pressure coach of CSKA Moscow. The Russian journalists attending the game laugh at the Abramovich wisecrack, as he treats their enquiries with the same disdain as Ranieri himself.

Team

Sullivan, Melchiot, Terry, Gallas, Bridge, Geremi (Cole), Parker (Gronkjaer), Lampard, Makelele, Mutu (Hasselbaink), Gudjohnsen.

SUNDAY, 22 FEBRUARY

The sniping intensifies. Crespo has made just seven Premiership starts and a Sunday paper reports hearing 'whispers that several stars are increasingly unhappy with his attitude' after he cried off from training for two days last week with a cut toe. He also missed Friday's final session when he turned up with a high temperature and was immediately withdrawn from the squad. He was sent home by Ranieri in the morning and told to report for training when he felt better. The striker hasn't played since coming on as sub and scoring in the win at Portsmouth.

Chelsea plan to cut the playing staff to a manageable size, so a dozen or so could eventually go. Gronkjaer, Cole, Desailly, Melchiot, Bogarde, Petit, Hasselbaink. Geremi, Babayaro, Sullivan and Stanic are all on the list. Gronkjaer is wanted by Werder Bremen, while Ruud Gullit, the new Feyenoord coach, offers Melchiot the captaincy. Melchiot makes it clear that he is determined to stay and 'win trophies'.

Makelele irritates his bosses, who are paying him £82,000 a week, with his moaning about having to play too many games, despite having turned out 53 times for the Spanish champions last season.

The Chelsea hierarchy compare Ranieri's huge squad with the smaller ones at the disposal of Arsene Wenger and Sir Alex Ferguson and the conclusions they draw are to the detriment of Ranieri. Those in power believe that a first-team squad of 25 is more than enough. Chelsea are determined to build the new team around the English core of Parker, Lampard and Terry, players who have demonstrated a genuine commitment to the cause. Even the club's official yearbook discredits Winston Bogarde, who now trains with the youth team, labelling the former Barcelona man 'the unfortunate face of the post-Bosman era'.

On-field changes will be reflected off the pitch as well, with the continuing search to identify a suitable 100-acre state-of-the-art training ground near Cobham, while in the meantime there will be major refurbishment of the training ground which the club rents from Imperial College. Sven-Goran Eriksson and Fabio Capello remain the top candidates to replace Ranieri, but even Boro's Steve McClaren is suggested along with Juventus boss Marcello Lippi. Ranieri, who has not coached in Italy since leaving Fiorentina for Valencia in 1997, is linked with a return to his boyhood idols, Roma, an additional sweetener to the £6m-plus pay-off he stands to collect.

Meanwhile Scott Parker is deciding whether to buy Bobby Davro's house in Oxshott, Surrey, for £2.95m. It boasts seven en-suite bedrooms, a huge conservatory, fitness room, pool with sauna and parking space for a fleet of cars.

MONDAY, 23 FEBRUARY

Abramovich attends a crisis meeting with a number of his aides at the training ground. Terry reveals that the players have also had a 'positive' meeting. 'None of us were in the mood to give up. We've got this big match and then it's time to focus on the league.'

Emmanuel Petit provides a rather different assessment. 'With the means at our club's disposal and the squad we have here, it will be a failure if we don't win anything. People want success and we have to give it to them. It's true we are doing better than last year but that won't be good enough. We will be better but so will Arsenal and United.'

Ranieri doubts whether his team can make the last four of the Champions League. 'AC Milan and Real Madrid are the teams. They just change one player each year, I have changed ten. How could we be equals? We can't. Everybody talks about us as being a very good team, but we are not yet a team. I had to blend ten new players with ten older. They don't really know each other and, among the new players, none of them did pre-season training. I'm discovering the team little by little. Obviously the further we go, the happier we will be. But I can't say I see Chelsea in the semi-final or the final.'

Stuttgart have recharged during a six-week winter break and he adds, 'It is one of the most difficult ties of the knock-out stage. So then the most important thing is the physical condition of the team. We have got this problem, as we didn't have a winter break. In England, you play much more during Christmas time. During the same time, Stuttgart, had 40 days break and as a result they are in better shape for the Champions League.'

But Stuttgart have also gone off the boil since a flying start to their Bundesliga campaign and are now third – the same as Chelsea.

TUESDAY, 24 FEBRUARY

Roman Abramovich and Peter Kenyon make a scouting trip to Real's Champions League clash at Bayern Munich. Kenyon flies out with the squad to Stuttgart, then immediately travels on to Munich where he meets Abramovich ahead of Real's 1–1 draw with Bayern. They return to Stuttgart in time for the game.

One absentee from the official party is Ken Bates, prompting speculation that his position has been further eroded. Bates is missing a match in Europe for only the second time during his tenure at the club, the other was against Bruges in 1995. He has been angered by a succession of snubs. He used to put up mottos on walls around the office. One, in the reception at Stamford Bridge, said, 'The Romans didn't build a great empire by organising meetings. They did it by killing anyone who got in their way.'

One of Roman's men has proved just this point – Bates's mottos have been taken down. Bates is also annoyed that major renovations could include knocking down the main hotel which could mean that Bates will also lose his penthouse home. Bates says, 'I have no intention of moving out.'

Ranieri predicts a 'Premiership-style game' against Stuttgart but he needs a Champions League-style performance after six defeats in his last 16 games. 'We have arrived in good condition and we are confident,' says Ranieri as he touches down in snow-sprinkled Stuttgart. 'The Arsenal defeats have not affected us but it is important for us to show that rather than to just say it. It is very important not to concede a goal.'

When Felix Magath's side beat Manchester United in the group phase last October, the coach was applauded into his post-match press conference by German reporters acknowledging a home defence which had gone 735 minutes without conceding a league goal. However, Magath embarked on some Ranieri-style tinkering with his back four and, when they lost to Kaiserslautern last Saturday, it was the third time in three weeks they had failed to beat a team at the wrong end of the table.

They are now 10 points behind leaders Werder Bremen and tomorrow's match at the Gottlieb-Daimler stadium is a much less daunting task for Chelsea than it might have been four months ago.

WEDNESDAY, 25 FEBRUARY

STUTTGART 0, CHELSEA 1

Here's a quiz question – which team won away in Europe without a shot on target? Ranieri's men cannot muster one shot on target in the 90 minutes and win by an own goal! For once Ranieri's reaction is subdued. Despite his assurances that all the talk about his future does not affect him, he is weary of it all. Even success in Europe's most prestigious club competition might not be enough. 'If Mr Abramovich has decided to change the coach at the end of the season, I surely can't change his mind. I told him I would leave when he arrived last summer and he said, "No, I believe in you." But I don't know if he said that out of conviction or necessity because he hadn't been able to find a coach to put in my place. My players don't believe the newspapers, they believe in our project. I am today the manager and we work together.'

Fernando Meira's 12th-minute own goal gives Chelsea their fourth successive away win in Europe without conceding a goal. John Terry claims the goal resulted from part of the manager's master plan. 'The boss had said all afternoon, "Get wide and whip balls in. They don't like it."'

Crespo leads the line magnificently, while Johnson shows the adventure and composure which lit up his early games for the club. He carves Stuttgart open to set up the killer goal. Collecting Cudicini's throw, Johnson exchanges passes with Geremi and continues his run deep into enemy territory. His low, angled cross is aimed for Crespo lurking menacingly at the far post but it is intercepted by Meira who misjudges his attempted clearance and belts the ball straight past Timo Hildebrand and into his own goal.

Chelsea should add a second in the 31st minute. Geremi's pass down the line enables Crespo to work the ball behind the defence and into the path of the advancing Gudjohnsen. With only Hildebrand to beat, he smashes the ball over the bar. After the game, Magath admits, 'I am very disappointed because we had great plans to inflict Chelsea's first away defeat in Europe. We know that Chelsea are strong away and sometimes show weakness in their home games. We must hope to make more of our chances in the return game in London. When you spend over £100m on players and produce a performance like the one Chelsea did against us, you have to be disappointed. You wonder if Mr Abramovich will want to buy more players and spend a lot more money – perhaps another £100m!'

Chelsea have now gone 411 minutes without conceding a Champions League goal away. Lampard is back to his best, while Parker is kept waiting for his Champions League debut as Ranieri goes back to his tried and trusted formula. 'We had good balance,' says Lampard. 'We were doubly determined to bounce back. The pressure was on us and the lads reacted very well.'

It's now possible that, if they beat Stuttgart, Chelsea could be drawn against that team from North London again, and Lampard's reaction to that possibility speaks volumes. 'We could be drawn against Arsenal? Oh, fuck it,' he says.

> **Team**
>
> Cudicini, Johnson, Gallas, Terry, Bridge, Geremi, Lampard, Makelele, Gronkjaer (Duff), Gudjohnsen (Hasselbaink), Crespo (Cole).

THURSDAY, 26 FEBRUARY

Ranieri confesses to feeling like a manager on death row and the superb success in Stuttgart has only 'prolonged the agony instead of easing it'. In a remarkably frank assessment of his predicament, Ranieri says, 'I do not feel easier now. Instead I believe the agony will continue. You see, at the first defeat, and it could be in the Premiership this weekend, they will start again talking about me getting the sack.'

Ranieri could be the only Italian coach in the last eight if AC Milan and Juventus fail to recover from first-leg setbacks. Jimmy Floyd Hasselbaink demands to know about the future of his coach and himself. He suspects his days are numbered after being left on the bench in Stuttgart. 'There has been a lot of talk about everything at Chelsea, the boss and the players. It has been like this the whole season. Maybe it would be helpful if the club told us what is going on.

'I still prefer it when people say things straight to my face rather than having things going on behind my back. But what does that mean in football? Today they say, "Don't worry, your job is safe." And then tomorrow...? When they start saying your job is safe, that is the time to worry.

'But Ranieri is hard – hard to a lot of players. When we play bad, he can go over the top. He doesn't do the Alex Ferguson thing, but he has lost it. The last time was a while ago, at half-time at the Bridge. The joking is on the training pitch. But on the day of the game he is serious.'

Claude Makelele has bought a stake of under 10 per cent in Servette, the Swiss club based in Geneva which escaped bankruptcy when the player's agent Marc Roger purchased the majority shareholding from its president Christian Luescher.

FRIDAY, 27 FEBRUARY

Two directors of Moscow club Torpedo Metallurg will be at the City of Manchester Stadium on Saturday as part of plans to forge links with Manchester City. Kevin Keegan observes, 'Chelsea have become the easiest club to criticise these days. Chelsea are the new kids on the block, and it is much easier to criticise a club when a Russian guy nobody knew about comes in and wipes off the club's £90m debt and invests in new players.'

The Chelsea players back their besieged boss. Eidur Gudjohnsen says, 'It's time that people get off his back. If he was allowed to do his job, it would make things a lot easier. We're all in it together.'

Keegan admires the way Ranieri handles the pressure. 'I don't think any manager has ever had to endure as much speculation about his future as Claudio has. But it is the way of the world and he lives with it very well. I like the man and I like his responses. He is doing a good job.'

Could there be a trophy for a Chelsea player this season? Bolo Zenden is looking forward to the Carling Cup final with Middlesbrough. 'I could have stayed and played once in a while like others did. But the most important thing was to play, to do well and to improve myself. I am still owned by Chelsea, so I don't want any negative energy going that way. I have friends at Chelsea who I still speak to. As for going back there in the future? That, is for later. I won't be going down the route of saying I have won something and you have not. Anyway, the job is not done yet.'

SATURDAY, 28 FEBRUARY

MANCHESTER CITY 0, CHELSEA 1

Eidur Gudjohnsen's 11th strike of the season eight minutes from time lifts Ranieri's team above Manchester United into second place. Ironically, he has been a long-term target for City, first under manager Joe Royle and then Kevin Keegan. Less than 20 minutes after coming on for a miffed Hasselbaink, he times a deep run to perfection to sprint on to a pass from Bridge and chip calmly over David James with just about his first touch. City complain about offside but Gudjohnsen keeps his cool. Keegan says, 'Claudio Ranieri's English is better than mine and at the end he said, "You fantastic, we poor, you lose, we win, that's football, eet's crazy." Then he walked off.'

Gudjohnsen is in no mood to surrender the chase. 'The gap between ourselves and Arsenal remains the same but nobody at this club has given up. There are still 11 games to go and, who knows, maybe in four or five matches the gap will be much narrower than it is now. But to finish second would be a great achievement as well. It would be a measure of our progress under Claudio. I like working with Claudio. All this speculation about his job has not affected him; he has not changed. I can't tell Chelsea what to do but perhaps it is time people got off his back and let him get on with it.'

Ranieri is in such a rush to begin a 10-day break that he fails to attend the post-match press conference, which leaves Keegan to sum up the game. He says, 'Robbie Fowler could have broken the record of three in 140 seconds set by James Hayter earlier this week – he had three chances in a short space of time. We totally outplayed a very good team.'

On the flight back to London, Ken Bates finds himself seated 15 rows from the players and officials. As he takes his seat in row 24, it is another reason to believe it's time to go.

Team

Cudicini, Johnson, Terry, Gallas, Bridge, Cole (Makelele), Parker, Lampard, Geremi (Huth), Hasselbaink (Gudjohnsen), Crespo.

SUNDAY, 29 FEBRUARY

Sven-Goran Eriksson issues a denial to reports that he has told Pavel Nedved to join him at Stamford Bridge after the Euro 2004 finals. 'This is simply not true,' he says. Nedved's agent Zdenek Nehoda is quoted as saying, 'Mr Eriksson phoned Nedved and said, "I will be taking over Chelsea this summer, would you be interested in signing for me?"' Eriksson coached Nedved when both men were at Lazio.

Chelsea are in talks with PSV Eindhoven to act as their nursery club. As part of the proposed agreement, Chelsea are helping to finance a big-money move for Santos defender Alex to join PSV. 'Nothing's been properly finalised just yet but there are clear advantages for everyone concerned,' says PSV chairman Harry van Raaij. 'It is true Chelsea are behind this signing of Alex for PSV. Everyone's hopeful we can continue to work together for the good of both clubs.'

Brazilian Alex, 21, would spend a maximum of two years with PSV before joining Chelsea. It would also enhance Chelsea's bid for PSV's brilliant young winger Arjen Robben.

Bolo Zenden picks up the man of the match award at the Millennium Stadium for his superb display in Middlesbrough's 2–1 Carling Cup final win over Bolton. 'I've really appreciated the way the people treat me here,' says Zenden, who makes the first goal for Joseph-Desire Job with just two minutes gone and then slots home a seventh-minute penalty. Zenden is delighted to be part of the team which finally carries a major trophy back to Teesside after a 128-year wait.

March

THE KEN BATES ERA COMES TO AN END AS THE CHAMPIONS LEAGUE QUARTER-FINAL DAWNS

Roman Abramovich announces he is taking Chelsea to his homeland for a friendly against Lokomotiv Moscow. The Russian Railways company, a state monopoly, is ultimately responsible for Lokomotiv. 'We will definitely accept the offer,' says Lokomotiv head coach Yuri Syomin. 'It's very pleasant to receive such an invitation. The match will be a real holiday for all football-lovers in Russia.'

The Moscow-Chelski fan club numbers around 500. They make and sell their own shirts, scarves, clocks and drums. Chelsea's game in Stuttgart was screened live in trendy bars in the centre of Moscow, and a group of fans visited London to watch the Arsenal game. There is even a Russian Chelsea magazine.

Abramovich remains a mystery to outsiders, but the Chelsea players have seen quite a bit of him now. Frank Lampard says, 'If we've won, he shakes your

PREMIERSHIP TABLE – MARCH

Pos	Team	P	W	D	L	GF	GA	GD	PTS
1	Arsenal	27	20	7	0	53	18	35	67
2	Chelsea	27	18	4	5	48	21	27	58
3	Manchester United	27	18	4	5	51	25	26	58
4	Newcastle United	27	10	12	5	38	28	10	42
5	Charlton Athletic	27	11	7	9	38	34	4	40
6	Liverpool	26	10	9	7	38	29	9	39
7	Aston Villa	27	10	7	10	32	32	0	37
8	Fulham	27	10	6	11	39	38	1	36
9	Birmingham City	25	9	9	7	25	28	-3	36
10	Tottenham Hotspur	26	10	4	12	39	42	-3	34

hand and, if you've lost, he is the same. He's always there and he has never shouted, bawled or complained that he has spent all of this money. He comes to the training ground and sits in on meetings with a translator. It's great for the lads to see that he is not just a figurehead who doesn't care about the players or the results. He speaks to you. For instance, if you have an injury or a gash, he will come right up and see if you're OK and other times he will say, "Shit result". His English is very broken but he can say a few words. I've heard him say, "Shit game" a few times!'

MONDAY, 1 MARCH

Chelsea snatch outstanding Dutch forward Arjen Robben from under the noses of Manchester United. Robben agrees a five-year £10m contract even though Sir Alex Ferguson met Robben and his father, Hans, on 2 January at United's training ground and convinced them that the player's future lay at Old Trafford. Robben Senior was then made aware of Chelsea's interest but in mid-January he declared, 'Arjen will only play for PSV or Manchester United.'

Ferguson gave the Dutchman a personal tour of the club's training ground but negotiations broke down a month ago when United refused to pay more than £8.6m. Peter Kenyon masterminded Chelsea's links with PSV and, through him, Robben met Abramovich and Ranieri in London two weeks ago. Robben says, 'It was a very nice personal touch for me. It was very important to know how much Chelsea wanted me.'

The formalities don't take long. Robben is flown to Stansted Airport by private jet at lunchtime, with PSV technical director Frank Arnesen and his agent Ton Smit, then whisked to the Chelsea Village Hotel, arriving at 1.45pm and undergoing a medical at a west London hospital in the afternoon. Robben says, 'I was attracted to Manchester United. But Chelsea have proved the better option for both me and PSV. At first, I was not so keen on Chelsea. United were very much in the driving seat and I know their manager Alex Ferguson has a very good reputation. I did not have such a positive image of Chelsea, because of the way they have been buying a lot of players. But the conversations I had with Peter Kenyon and Claudio Ranieri made up my mind. Peter is an impressive man; he wants to make Chelsea great. Maybe if he'd been at United, I'd have gone there but I'm happy with my choice.'

Dutch national boss Dick Advocaat, who has hailed Robben as a massive talent, endorses the move to Chelsea. 'I am delighted for him. It is great he is going to such a big club. I just hope he gets enough minutes on the pitch at Chelsea, as I feel he is currently one of the best players this country has. I feel England is a good place for him to develop as a player.'

Chelsea will pay a percentage of the fee now for what is effectively an option to buy the 20-year-old in July. Abramovich also hands PSV £7m to sign Brazilian youngster Alex, who will now spend a maximum of two years in Holland – earning European citizenship before joining the Blues.

PSV president Harry van Raaij is still furious with Sir Alex Ferguson for allegedly 'tapping up' Ruud van Nistelrooy and accuses him of similar tactics over Robben. He is also angry that United agreed a £10m fee and then tried to change it to £6m. Van Raaij says, 'Because United were first in the queue, we kept Chelsea waiting. But when we had our second discussion with United over a fee, we were very disappointed over how low they believed they could push us. They seemed to think he was worth a lot less than Chelsea were willing to pay. That was a massive letdown and it was only then we opened negotiations with Chelsea.'

Kenyon has outbid his old club and manager. Van Raaij adds, 'Peter is an honest man. When you make a deal with him, the deal remains a deal. Kenyon was very important in the deal and I've dealt with him in the past in negotiations with Ruud van Nistelrooy and Jaap Stam. He is a fine negotiator.'

Robben becomes the 13th signing of Abramovich's reign and the fee takes the owner's total outlay on players to £134m. The deal was effectively sealed nine days ago when Kenyon and Ranieri made a secret trip to Robben's flat in Eindhoven. Van Raaij admits, 'Peter Kenyon had originally made us a very good offer for Robben when he was still working for Manchester United, and I never worried when Manchester United changed their mind and made us an offer that was nowhere near our valuation of the player. Peter and I keep in very good contact and talk regularly about things together. The close friendship we have was the key factor in the transfer going ahead. I knew when he took over at Chelsea he would come to me with a fair offer from them.'

The club wined and dined Arjen's dad and agent by inviting him to the tie in Stuttgart. Hans was obviously more impressed with that than with the tour of cold and rainy Old Trafford with Sir Alex justafter Christmas.

Since moving to PSV in the summer of 2002, Robben has broken into the Holland team, scoring the winner against the United States last month. Ranieri adds, 'Arjen will be a fantastic addition to our squad. He is quick, strong, scores goals, makes goals. He can do everything. His style is perfect for the Premier League and I am very happy that he wanted to come to us.'

Joe Cole becomes the centre of intense media speculation that he is about to seek a summer transfer. It is officially denied, even though his father George gives the impression, on the trip to Stuttgart, that his boy is disenchanted. Cole has started just 11 Premiership games and been substituted in every one. Everton, with their tight budget, want him on loan for next season. Cole, who practises shooting with Jonny Wilkinson's kicking coach Dave Alred, confirms, 'I have certainly not asked for a transfer and am determined to win a regular place in the Chelsea first team. Mr Ranieri has assured me I still have a big future at Chelsea.'

Ranieri hints for the first time that he might consider letting Cole go out on loan. 'I understand that Joe needs to play but I must think of what is best for the team. Sometimes I change the system like against Manchester City. He was playing well but I needed another defensive midfield player. I would prefer to keep him here but if he comes to me and says, "I would like to play," I would understand that.'

It is difficult to see Cole wanting to go anywhere other than his beloved West Ham. Manager Alan Pardew says, 'Joe was loved by the fans here. If he wanted to come here we would welcome him back with open arms as you would any player of his ability.'

TUESDAY, 2 MARCH

I attend Ken Bates's last Chairman's Supper Club in the Charles Kingsley suite in the West Stand as he announces his resignation. Unsurprisingly, he fires a broadside at Abramovich. 'Certain things were agreed when I signed the contract that handed the club over to Abramovich. A gradual fade-out is what I planned but things have not gone the way I anticipated. It has been a clash between Eastern and Western cultures. Roman Abramovich now owns the toys – let's hope he respects the toys we brought into the club. We have to have patience and build brick by brick, not overnight.'

Bates also blasts Peter Kenyon. 'What a great appointment! Kenyon must have thought all his Christmases had come at once. I was asked not to write anything for the programme that introduced Kenyon. They insisted – and I decided to call it a day. With Kenyon now here, it's better he operates the club his way without me being on the sidelines. I don't want to go the same way as Matt Busby at Manchester United. He never retired and intimidated many of his successors.'

Bates is seeking a £2m pay-off. Under the terms of a contract agreed following Abramovich's takeover, Bates was to remain as chairman until 2005 and then become life president. Bates was entitled to generous expenses to cover the work he would do on behalf of the club. The contract does not provide for a salary, nor does it contain a notice period or pay-off clause if it is terminated. Talks have been going on over the terms of his departure and Bates is now considering legal action. When asked about any potential settlement, he adds, 'Mind your own business.'

Bates has removed his possessions from his office and it has now been taken over by Kenyon. Bates also criticises new chairman Bruce Buck for his failure to attend the Supper Club. Buck bought three tickets but no one from the Abramovich camp turns up. Bates concludes, 'The King is dead, or at least is retired, long live the King. We will continue to live in the penthouse and see you all. I live on top of the hotel and am not moving. I would not accept half of Siberia for the penthouse. In the meantime, I'm going to spend my money on wine and song.'

Bates has 'one more challenge' left... perhaps Sheffield Wednesday! Lord Dickie Attenborough urges the Russian hierarchy to make peace with Bates. The renowned film-maker, a lifelong supporter and vice-president, sits at Bates's top table. Attenborough, 80, says, 'Ken Bates is a colossus; he's the major figure who transformed this club from a good club into a great club. Like tens of thousands of other Chelsea supporters, I am very disappointed that he's going. But I think the decision is typical of his own self-respect and dignity, he doesn't just want to be at the club in name only. I hope that Mr Abramovich, Peter Kenyon and Bruce Buck will perhaps do him the honour of asking him to be life president.' But Abramovich and his aides are simply glad to see the back of Bates!

WEDNESDAY, 3 MARCH

Arjen Robben's capture leads to new questions. Did he know whether Ranieri would still be coach next season? He says, 'I like Mr Ranieri's temperament. It would be a shame if he is not there next season. For me it's a pity he's going away. I had a meeting with Mr Ranieri and he came over as a very good coach with lots of temper and hunger.'

But Damien Duff is stunned by the signing of another left-winger. 'I must admit it was a bit of a kick in the teeth after two months out to hear about it. I hear Robben is a left-winger but I don't play there very often so maybe I'll get a game somewhere else in the team!' Duff, who has played a full 90 minutes for the reserves in a 2–1 defeat by West Ham, continues, 'I'll struggle with the Achilles for the rest of the season but I'll just have to grind it out. It has been the worst two months of my life.'

Robben observes, 'I'm not only a winger. I can play inside or just behind the two strikers. So this doesn't bother me. Damien can play inside too.'

Frank Lampard adds his opinion on the subject. 'You can wither, fade away and not be up for the challenge – or you stand up and fight for your place. That's what everyone at the club has to do. Damien is being honest. You are always thinking that new players are going to come in and take your place – but that's the challenge of being here. I know how he feels because I think Chelsea signed about eight midfielders last summer!'

Lampard is only two games short of a century of Premiership appearances. He is in talks about a new £70,000-a-week, five-year deal worth £18.2m. Discussion is at an early stage but the club have been encouraged by a positive response from Lampard's advisers.

Meanwhile Bates's adversaries are celebrating his departure. Ron Harris says, 'He has shit on a few people over the years and what goes around comes around. He should have gone a couple of years ago. He won't be missed and life goes on.' Scottish firebrand David Speedie says, 'He is a tosser who has no respect for anyone and he treats people like a piece of shit. He always has to be one up on you. If I told him I'd been to Tenerife, he'd say he'd been to Elevenerife.'

Peter Osgood says, 'He certainly put my nose out of joint. He wasn't a nice man at times and he got lucky getting Abramovich to buy him out. But he has left the club much healthier than he found it so you've got to say well done to him.'

Ronaldo signs a two-year extension with Real. His and Beckham's coach Carlos Queiroz confesses that he doesn't know whether the England captain will stay next season. Chelsea are the only club in the Premiership that can afford him, and from a family point of view a move to London would be ideal.

If Eriksson is to be enticed to the Bridge, then there is no doubt that interest in Beckham will intensify. Eriksson and Beckham have forged one of the closest relationships in international football as coach and captain, and the Swede would love to replicate that union at club level. Ranieri says, 'It would be fantastic for Chelsea to bring back the England captain. Nothing has happened yet, but it would be fantastic to sign Beckham.' The buy-out clause in Beckham's Real contract is an incredible $140m – around £100m!

Belgium's youngest international, 17-year-old centre-half Vincent Kompany is a £15m target from Anderlecht, so too is Belgium central defender Daniel van Buyten, currently on loan at Manchester City from Marseille. As for outgoings, Valencia are interested in signing Mario Melchiot on a free in the summer.

THURSDAY, 4 MARCH

Claudio Ranieri plus an assortment of pre-Roman stars turn out as the staff give Bates an emotional guard-of-honour send-off. Bates hits out again at the Abramovich regime, claiming they blocked video tributes to him on the club's television station. 'I didn't realise that Vladimir Putin had taken over Chelsea Television. He runs the television stations in Russia as well, you know.'

Ranieri pays his tribute to Bates. 'He brought the team to a higher level,' but he then puts it into perspective, 'and now there is a new era, everything has changed and it is time to look forward. The future of this club is Mr Abramovich.'

Ex-Owls director Joe Ashton backs Bates to take the Sheffield club back to the big time. 'He is definitely interested in Sheffield Wednesday. I can't think of a better candidate to do the job.' Owls chairman Dave Allen wants an injection of

£30m. 'Does Ken Bates have that kind of money?' he asks. 'This has been going on for six weeks – many businessmen I know would have made a decision by now.'

FRIDAY, 5 MARCH

Marcel Desailly believes Chelsea are strong enough to profit from any slip-ups at Highbury. 'Arsenal are the strongest team right now but we have not rolled over yet.' Desailly has made only 10 starts in the Premiership and has not featured in the first team for over six weeks. He is doing extra training to convince his manager he deserves another chance.

Yet, Desailly and Gus Poyet of Spurs have been spotted en route to the Middle East, perhaps with a view to joining Frank Leboeuf, Gabriel Batistuta, Steffen Effenberg and the Brazilian Romario playing in Qatar. But Desailly says, 'I have an exciting season to finish at Chelsea and another one to follow next year. At my age, I am not going to turn everything upside down. I went to the Gulf to check on a property deal.' Not so, according to Philippe Troussier, the Qatar coach, who suggests Desailly flew to Doha and met Sheikh Hamad bin Khalifa al-Thani, the Emir.

SATURDAY, 6 MARCH

Seba Veron is suffering from a major disc problem that has produced secondary symptoms. He explains, 'It prevents you from performing the most basic exercises, let alone playing football. Part of my disc has been removed and has to regenerate. It was a very delicate and tricky operation. Now I have the problem with my leg. The wrong exertion at this stage could mean further surgery.'

Midfielder Emmanuel Petit has had no discussions over a new deal. He has played just seven games this season because of a persistent knee injury. He says, 'I don't believe they want me to stay. It's not a shame – it's a business these days. I hope to come back by the end of the season but I don't think my future will be at Chelsea. I love London and there is life in me yet.'

Jesper Gronkjaer is optimistic about a new contract. 'There could be another 100 games for me at Chelsea. Since I came to the club I've become more of a team player.' Meanwhile Bolo Zenden says he would like to go back to Spain if Chelsea don't want him any more.

SUNDAY, 7 MARCH

Take your pick of the Sunday papers and there is a different rumour in each one. Almost anyone could be coming to Chelsea: Figo, Walter Samuel, Rio Ferdinand in a swap for Duff, or perhaps another Dutch star who Manchester United are trying to sign – Sir Alex Ferguson urges his board not to allow Ajax's Rafael van der Vaart to go the same way as Robben.

Chelsea continue their quest for Joaquin, determined not to miss out again after Reyes escaped their clutches. Fergie reckons the Blues are stalking every one of the players he wants. He expresses his anger at losing Robben. 'I can't believe this is the last one they know about. They can probably buy everyone they're looking at. Losing Robben is not a blow to us. Our scouting system is good. When we identify a player we try to get him as quickly as possible. We made an offer which PSV refused and they used that to jack up Chelsea's offer. If you're asking us to pay €21.5m for a 21-year-old, you must be joking. We won't be held to ransom by anyone. It's a disappointment but we have one or two players in the pipeline so we'll be OK, don't worry about that.'

MONDAY, 8 MARCH

Ranieri's patience finally snaps when he is asked once again about his future. 'I cannot look too far forward and you know why better than me. I have to work day by day. I can only look as far forward as tomorrow. If you are writing every day – "Arriving Eriksson, arriving this, arriving this" – then how can Claudio Ranieri look forward?'

The word is that Ranieri's fate is sealed, but whether his successor will be Eriksson is less certain. Ranieri refuses to answer questions about Robben, fuelling speculation in certain quarters that the transfer was made without his knowledge.

Damien Duff can still have a huge impact this season, according to Ranieri. 'Damien is the man who can open every door. It's not been easy for him recently because he has been injured and frustrated. Damien can bring a lot of quality to the team. He is an amazing player. He gives great ability, speed and dribbling. I want him to play against Stuttgart like I know he can.'

Stuttgart hold a three-hour crisis meeting to restore their season in time for the return at Stamford Bridge. Players and staff meet for a clear-the-air dinner after achieving only one victory in 12 matches. Felix Magath says, 'We would have preferred to have won at home but we came close to scoring and the tie is still very much alive. Chelsea are a good team and have an impressive away record, but at home, perhaps, they are not quite so good. We will see.'

TUESDAY, 9 MARCH

CHELSEA 0, STUTTGART 0 (Chelsea win 1–0 on aggregate)

Before kick-off Ken Bates issues a writ for £2m claiming breach of contract and threatens to subpoena Abramovich into giving evidence in what will be a sensational case if it ever goes to court.

Ranieri axes top scorer Hasselbaink and uses Crespo as a lone striker in an unadventurous formation. He insists he is playing an attacking 4-3-3 system, but it looks far more like 4-5-1. Wide players, Duff and Gronkjaer, are mainly employed to keep Stuttgart's adventurous full-backs quiet. By far the biggest cheer comes after the final whistle, when the result from Old Trafford is announced and Porto have won. At least Chelsea are through to the quarter-finals, which is more than can be said of Manchester United.

Parker, making his first Champions League start, begins well in his favoured central midfield role, but looks far less happy when he is moved to a wide right position as Ranieri changes to a 4-4-2 system. Chelsea live on their nerves as Stuttgart pin them back in the second half – but Ranieri insists he always believed his side would go through. Ranieri, who sees full-back Johnson stretchered off with a badly sprained ankle, says, 'I was not nervous – but it was not easy. But I like these emotions! I was only scared in the first half when they had a chance but they did not give us too many troubles and we had three great opportunities at the end.'

Incredibly, Chelsea hold on to a 1–0 lead for 168 minutes over two games, an own goal at that! The European campaign has been about excellent away days and only one win out of four matches at home. Terry helps sub Desailly and his creaking joints through the final hour. It is only in the final four minutes, when sub Mutu is twice denied by the otherwise unemployed Hildebrand, and Gronkjaer shoots against his upright, that Chelsea threaten. Magath says, 'I'm very disappointed particularly as we are out thanks to an own goal. I think it's fair to say that Chelsea had a little bit of luck.'

Team

Cudicini, Johnson (Desailly), Gallas, Terry, Bridge, Gronkjaer, Makelele, Lampard, Parker (Geremi), Duff (Mutu), Crespo.

WEDNESDAY, 10 MARCH

Hasselbaink may be the team's top scorer but he has started just two of Chelsea's last six games and didn't even make the bench against Stuttgart. He says, 'I have stated that I prefer a move away. I want to play every week but Ranieri makes a lot of changes and, if you play well, you can very well be on the bench the next game. The result is you cannot get into a rhythm and you see that now. However, they don't want to co-operate.'

Mutu is also a victim of Ranieri's tinkering but urges Hasselbaink to reconsider. 'Jimmy is a very good player and I hope he is here next season. It's not difficult changing the strikers and it's normal. The manager decides who to play.'

Both Milan clubs are linked with goalkeeper Carlo Cudicini. AC, with whom Cudicini began his career, and Inter will fight for his signature if there is any sign Chelsea will sell. Despite Ranieri insisting that he wants Cudicini to stay, the keeper will not settle for being Petr Cech's number two.

The Bates row rumbles on. He says, 'The case will be determined in the High Court and not by any spin-doctors briefing newspapers. I'm amused at the way in which they are trying to rewrite history. Mr Buck has been quoted as saying that "the owner decides everything". That will all come out in court. Unless I get my £2m then, yes, it will end up in court. I have no idea if that would be an embarrassment to Chelsea but, if it is, then it won't be of my making.' Chelsea intend to 'vigorously defend' the legal action.

THURSDAY, 11 MARCH

Cudicini cracks a bone in his right hand diving for a ball in training. He also suffers severe bruising around one of his fingers. Ranieri awaits the doctor's report as Cudicini is sure to be out of the Champions League quarter-finals. With Sullivan also crocked, Marco Ambrosio, on the bench against Stuttgart, is set to play.

John Terry leads the pro-Ranieri campaign. 'Claudio has been great for Chelsea and it wouldn't hurt for the club to come out and support him. Hopefully, they will do that soon – so everyone can just concentrate on the football. Everyone is fed up with the constant rubbish about Sven-Goran Eriksson taking over in the summer. It's getting all the lads' backs up. Everyone in that dressing room is 100 per cent behind Claudio.'

The draw for the quarter-finals takes place on Friday. Arsenal's Patrick Vieira says, 'It would be sad if we drew Chelsea. We don't want to play them.' However the Arsenal skipper also stresses that such is the confident mood at Highbury that they fear no one.

Abramovich can pocket £5.6bn from the sale of his stake in Sibneft. He has been liquidating his assets but the Sibneft deal would dwarf these other disposals. Sibneft hold talks with Shell, ChevronTexaco of the US and France's Total. A Sibneft spokesman says, 'At the moment we are focusing on the de-merger with Yukos and it's too early to comment on what might happen in the future.'

Abramovich is still bubbling with enthusiasm for Chelsea. The intention is for the club to become financially secure independent of the Russian's billions. Kenyon says, 'Nobody wants a Leeds experience. That's not good for the club or the game. Financially Chelsea are already much more secure than before and that is a positive thing. Ultimately Abramovich wants the club to be able to do without a sugar daddy. Roman is very committed to rebuilding Chelsea in the medium and long term.'

FRIDAY, 12 MARCH

Would you believe it? The Champions League draw throws up the worst possible scenario. For the historians it is great news, as it guarantees the presence of a London side in a European Cup semi-final for the first time since Tottenham Hotspur were beaten by Benfica in 1962.

This is the biggest London derby of all time, with £10m at stake in prize money, gate receipts and revenue from television. But it is pride and prestige that drives on Ranieri and his team as he says, 'My English players are fighters, gladiators. They are players who never surrender. If an English person has an adversary in front of him, he goes on straight and tries to throw him down. They always continue to fight and do their best.'

Ranieri insists his men are not frightened. Mario Melchiot says, 'My first reaction was to start laughing. It's like the *Groundhog Day* movie that repeats itself. We always seem to draw Arsenal in cups.' Lampard reveals how the draw went down in the dressing room. 'We thought, what a surprise! At first there was a bit of a groan from all the lads, but it's a case of focusing on the task ahead and getting up for it. We have played them three times this season and been in front three times, but still lost three times, and now we come up against them in what is probably the biggest British game in this competition. Now is the time for us to stand up and be counted to show what we are made of, to roll up our sleeves and fight like never before. We have to play to the best of our ability and match them in every department.'

Neither Chelsea nor Arsenal have ever reached the semi-finals of Europe's elite competition. It is the first time two English sides have faced each other since Nottingham Forest knocked out Liverpool on their way to winning the trophy in 1979. The happiest man at Highbury is Dennis Bergkamp. His fear of flying usually rules him out of away games.

Ken Bates will sit on the Bolton side of the directors' box for the upcoming game at the Reebok Stadium. Bates's column in the Bolton programme has been censored by chairman Phil Gartside and Wanderers' legal advisers. Several paragraphs about Kenyon and Abramovich have been removed or toned down.

SATURDAY, 13 MARCH

BOLTON 0, CHELSEA 2

John Terry suggests on *Football Focus* that the title race isn't over, and he makes sure it is still alive with a superb volley which opens the scoring. Two weeks ago in the Northwest, Chelsea jumped up off the canvas to KO Manchester City and they continue to grind out results. But Arsenal win at Blackburn to maintain a nine-point gap.

Bolton manager Sam Allardyce rages at referee Graham Poll for 'bottling' a nailed-on, first-half penalty shout which he describes as 'GBH', as Desailly fouls Kevin Davies. Bolton also deserve a penalty after Stelios Giannakopoulos robs Gallas. TV replays show the defender losing control and felling the Greek. Only Giannakopoulos's over-reaction saves the visitors. Bolton's best chance is their first one, and if Henrik Pedersen's shot had sneaked past Ambrosio instead of hitting his post, there may have been a different outcome.

Four times in the first half and once in the second, Jay-Jay Okocha has the chance to score after initially being denied by a fabulous one-handed save from Ambrosio, who is outstanding on his Premiership debut. The Italian keeper makes another key save with his chest to deny Davies as half-time approaches. It is Davies who does most to unsettle Chelsea, using his aerial aggression and direct running to give Desailly a torrid time.

Without the suspended Mutu and Gudjohnsen, Chelsea have only a couple of chances. The first falls to Crespo who makes a hopeless attempt to turn in Duff's pass in the box. Then Crespo and Gronkjaer go clear only for Crespo to play his header forward for an offside. Ranieri sends on Cole for Crespo and he pushes forward with more purpose. Terry breaks up an attack and keeps going, sneaking in at the back post to volley a sweet finish after Duff's cross is flicked on by Hasselbaink. Moments later Cole plays a superb pass to Hasselbaink who finds Duff steaming into the six-yard box to bundle the ball past Jaaskelainen and secure Chelsea's fifth successive away win.

'Sloppy finishing cost us the lead, sloppy defending cost us the match, and the referee has cost us a penalty,' blasts Allardyce. He adds, 'Chelsea have a knack at the moment of picking up points when they're not playing well. If they carry on doing that, God knows what they'll be like when they start playing well.'

Terry agrees, 'Everyone was disappointed because they were causing us problems, but we sorted it out. We don't care if we play crap for the rest of the season if we keep picking up points. I'm not sure about Roman Abramovich. You'd have to ask him. But from a player's point of view there's nothing better than playing badly and winning.'

Ambrosio is narrowly beaten to the man of the match award by Terry. The keeper says, 'This is the first big chance of my life and I want to do the best so I can change my career. My biggest game before now was an Italian League Cup quarter-final for Chievo against Roma. Everyone will have been looking at me to see if I was ready to play for a big team like Chelsea. Well, I kept a clean sheet.'

Team

Ambrosio, Gallas, Desailly, Terry, Bridge, Gronkjaer (Huth), Geremi, Lampard, Duff (Parker), Hasselbaink, Crespo (Cole).

SUNDAY, 14 MARCH

Beckham emphatically denies that he is seeking a move. 'I'm happy. I'm playing great football; everyone can see how much I am enjoying my football. Why leave? I will be a Real player next season.' Regarding a move to Stamford Bridge, the England captain says, 'I can categorically deny I've had any meetings with Roman Abramovich, any official from Chelsea, or any other club to discuss a move back to England.'

As for any Eriksson-Chelsea link-up, he adds, 'I've not spoken to Mr Eriksson about this. For a start, I don't want to get involved in anything else that's going on or any other stuff that's said about the England manager. As far as I'm concerned he's the England manager and that's it.'

Manchester United turn down flat Chelsea and Real's moves for Rio Ferdinand. Chelsea make it clear to Ferdinand's adviser Zahavi that they have the money and desire to tempt him back to the capital. Peter Kenyon retains close links with Zahavi, but the Israeli agent also has strong ties with Ferguson and has reported back to Stamford Bridge that the United manager will not be budged. Arjen Robben is likely to be out for three months after suffering a serious injury to his right leg during PSV's 1–1 draw against Auxerre in the UEFA Cup. A scan reveals his hamstring is torn in several places.

MONDAY, 15 MARCH

As chairman of the FA's Challenge Cup committee, Ken Bates challenges Sven-Goran Eriksson to come clean about his intentions about the England job. Bates reports, 'I said to Eriksson, "You keep banging on about wanting a winter break to help the England team, and that's all very well and good, we are ready to help you, but will you be here to lead us in Germany?"

'Eriksson replied, "I have a contract until 2006." But we know all that; he has said that many times before, but I told him, "That's fine, Sven, but you have not answered the question I put to you, will you be here for the World Cup in 2006?"

Our eyes met across the room and reluctantly, I felt, he finally gave me his answer: "Yes, I'll be leading England in 2006."'

However, Sven's affirmation of his commitment to England does little to curtail the belief that Ranieri is still living on borrowed time. But if he can pull off a miracle in the Champions League he might just survive...

TUESDAY, 16 MARCH

Chelsea deny they offered Ranieri's job to Bayern Munich coach Ottmar Hitzfeld, who claims he has been approached. Hitzfeld was quoted in German daily newspaper *Bild* as follows: 'I have received an offer [from Chelsea], but I will fulfil my contract until 2005.' Hitzfeld has come under pressure recently after Bayern's exits from the domestic cup to second division opposition and in the Champions League to Real Madrid. His side are also nine points behind runaway league leaders Werder Bremen in the Bundesliga and his once steady seat with the Bavarians is beginning to wobble after six years of success. The German media have reported that Hitzfeld is in danger of losing his job and that Bayern have approached VfB Stuttgart coach Felix Magath.

WEDNESDAY, 17 MARCH

Jimmy Floyd Hasselbaink is supposed to be appearing at a misconduct hearing for allegedly elbowing Scarborough's Mark Hotte in January's FA Cup clash. But the hearing is called off because the referee has not been invited! Hasselbaink, Hotte and Chelsea secretary David Barnard gather at Heathrow and it is only then that it is realised the FA has failed to summon referee Barry Knight. While Hotte was flying down from Scarborough to speak on Hasselbaink's behalf, the Orpington official has been preparing for the Premiership clash between Liverpool and Portsmouth.

THURSDAY, 18 MARCH

Abramovich's Moscow-based Sibneft pay CSKA £30m over three years for exclusive rights to the club's name, trademark and image both in Russia and abroad. The deal could placate those Russians who have been angered by his takeover of Chelsea.

Chelsea's challenge to Manchester United moves to another level with the announcement of a tour to the United States this summer. The Old Trafford club have been targeting North America as a major growth area which is why they went on a high-profile summer trip there last year. That move was the brainchild of Peter Kenyon and he clearly now sees the US as a route to expansion for Abramovich's club. Chelsea and Liverpool will join United, Celtic, AC Milan, Roma and Bayern Munich in the seven-team Champions World series. Chelsea will play three matches in total: against Celtic in Seattle, Roma in Pittsburgh and Milan in Philadelphia.

In Argentina, Juan Sebastian Veron surprisingly appears in a practice match for local side Estudiantes. The run-out lasts 40 minutes. Veron features alongside youth-team players, with senior players banned from taking part. Team-mates and onlookers reveal that Veron plays 'within himself' and players are told not to tackle him, and definitely not to foul him.

Claude Makelele responds to newspaper stories that he wants to quit. 'These reports were absolute lies and malicious. I didn't speak to those who wrote them and they made the story up. I don't know why they do things like that. Perhaps they are trying to unsettle us ahead of the most important part of the season. It has never crossed my mind to leave. I have no problems with Claudio or his tactics.'

FRIDAY, 19 MARCH

Claudio Ranieri knows how elusive the truth can be as he follows stories of the chase for a new coach with changing headlines every day. 'Maybe it's agents who say, "Chelsea want you, do you want to go?" Agents cause a lot of confusion.'

Ken Bates launches a series of attacks on Abramovich's spending. Unknown to Bates, there are moves to spend even more! Kenyon and Zahavi are in Italy discussing a variety of options with Roma sporting director Franco Baldini. Walter Samuel is the most likely acquisition, and the centre-back says, 'If I leave Roma it will be to play in England, I love the atmosphere at English matches.'

Bates blasts back, 'We spent nearly £40m on Hernan Crespo and Adrian Mutu yet the top Chelsea scorer in the Premiership is Mikael Forssell who is at an average club, Birmingham City. We had four strikers – Jimmy Floyd Hasselbaink, Eidur Gudjohnsen, Carlton Cole and Forssell – so we didn't need any more strikers. There's indigestion in the dressing room. They've bought 11, 12 or 13 players on top of the players we already had and you can't keep all of them happy. Abramovich has been taken to the cleaners on a number of occasions because. But at least he can afford it.

'Claudio and I sat down and discussed things in 2003 after we got into the Champions League. We had options on Scott Parker and Joe Cole for a total of £12m. But Roman Abramovich was advised they were not good enough for Chelsea and not to buy them. He then went out and spent £17m on them in

January! Claudio's the man to do that job. He blooded John Terry, brought young players in and has been prepared to give them a chance.'

Bates also criticises the way Trevor Birch was ousted from his position as chief executive. 'The day after the summer transfer deadline after Trevor Birch had signed eight players, Bruce Buck and Eugene Tenenbaum went into Trevor's office and told him they had just signed Peter Kenyon. Birch just burst out laughing. The acting chief executive Paul Smith had no experience of running a football club at all. He was brought in by Kenyon to act as his locum and that was a problem. I've never got on with Peter Kenyon. We have different values. He only seemed to want what was best for Manchester United; I wanted what was best for the whole of football. A lot of Premier League votes were 19–1 with Manchester United the one.'

Bates warns Abramovich he is not guaranteed success. 'If you take Arsenal, Manchester United and, in the old days, Liverpool, their directors never put their hands in their pocket. They achieved everything with good business and planning. You have to admire them more than people who just throw money at it. People have done that in the past and not been successful.'

Meanwhile Abramovich pays for a group of 50 children from Chukotka to come and watch his team as the highlight of a five-day trip to London for a party of elite athletes and students aged eight to 17. The group has been hand-picked by Abramovich's advisers to demonstrate his continuing commitment to his homeland. Interest in Chelsea is spiralling throughout Russia and has even reached Outer Siberia. A Chelsea fan club is established in Chukotka and many Russians are adopting the Blues as a second team.

Carlo Cudicini could be back in goal in time for the Champions League semi-finals if the Blues get there. Meanwhile, from enjoying gentle work-outs with coach Giorgio Pellizzaro a week ago, Marco Ambrosio has been plunged into the most important game in Chelsea's history. Despite a 10-year career in Italy, his big-match experience is virtually non-existent, with just 25 of his 114 career appearances coming in Serie A. Ambrosio says, 'My whole world has changed since last week. I know Chelsea's season is in my hands but that is the role of the goalkeeper. We have a lot of extra responsibility and there's even more responsibility because I'm playing for one of England's biggest teams.'

Ambrosio doesn't even play for the reserves, with coach Mick McGiven preferring to use youngsters. Tomorrow's derby will be only his third game of any description this season. But Ranieri speaks highly of him. 'For a second choice, it is important to liaise with the first-choice goalkeeper and always give 100 per cent, which isn't easy. Ambrosio is perfect for this because he is always in good form and ready.'

Fulham manager Chris Coleman points out one of the major problems when you play against Chelsea. 'I find it hard to plan because they change their formation all the time. I'm not a big fan of rotation. There are cases when you need to rest certain people but overall throughout the season you pick your best team. You get a good team, get it settled and play them every week and that is what gets you results. When you have 25 or 30 international players that is not always a good thing. Chopping and changing all the time is not ideal.'

Hernan Crespo is struggling, despite all the earlier hype about how well he was settling in. 'I didn't think it would be so hard to settle into this society. The biggest thing is the cultural difference and I'm finding it very hard at a social level. The differences between the Latin and Anglo-Saxon way of life are huge.'

SATURDAY, 20 MARCH

CHELSEA 2, FULHAM 1

On this evidence, victory against Arsenal is improbable. Damien Duff, the best player on the field, is visibly angry when he is substituted after 70 minutes. 'No, look,' Ranieri pleads in that inimitable style, 'I was just protecting Damien ahead of Wednesday. He is OK with that.'

Naturally, there are changes from the outset too. Gudjohnsen starts for only the tenth time this season after being benched for the previous three games. He takes just seven minutes to stake his claim for a regular place. Desailly wins a 50-50 ball in central midfield, picks him out and Gudjohnsen takes a few steps, jinks to his left and thunders in a shot from 25 yards. Fulham equalise after 18 minutes when Mark Pembridge's free-kick from the edge of the box takes a wicked deflection off Gronkjaer's shoulder and spins into the net. Duff first forces a great save from Edwin van der Sar with a shot from a tight angle and then after half an hour he puts Chelsea back in front. Lampard opens up the defence and drills in a low shot which is parried. The rebound flies to Duff, just inside the area, and he controls neatly to make space for the shot to score for the second successive week.

Inevitably, Ranieri makes a change at the break. At first, the crowd assumes he has removed Gronkjaer, who has had a very good first half, because the Dane is injured. But it soon dawns on them that containment is the motive. Ranieri pushes Lampard, who has been running the show in central midfield, out wide on the right to accommodate Parker and, in so doing, disrupts the rhythm that has been found towards the end of the opening period. Later, Duff, who has been playing in a free role, shakes his head as he trots off to be replaced by serial substitute, Cole. Geremi, who comes close with a free-kick that needs a one-handed save to tip it over, struggles in midfield. So why does Ranieri leave him on and take off the impressive Duff? Ranieri explains, 'I took Gronkjaer and Duff off because, although we were doing well on the wings, we were also leaving too much space when we defended. Lampard and Geremi had four players around them all the time in midfield.'

Ranieri feels that his team have played well, when they clearly have not. 'It was difficult against Fulham because they are well organised, but we played very, very well.' Well enough to beat Arsenal? 'Sometimes all that matters is making the net bulge. The three points are important...We are ready for the Champions League game and I expect all of my players to be fit.'

Chelsea's record would make them a strong bet for the title in most years. Their points haul of 64 would have made them leaders in three of the last five seasons – and in another they would have been second to Manchester United only on goals scored. Wednesday night is the biggest game in Chelsea's 99-year history but the Gunners' scouts can't possibly be worried as Ranieri's men stumble to their ninth league win at home. Coleman believes the 'stars' in Chelsea's dressing room must step up a gear. 'I'm sure they'll be better on Wednesday night – they'll need to be to get a result. You have a big game coming up and you're not quite there for the one before. If we'd had a bit more bottle and guile, we could have come away with a different result.'

Team

Ambrosio, Gallas, Desailly, Terry, Bridge, Gronkjaer (Parker), Geremi, Lampard, Duff (Cole), Crespo, Gudjohnsen.

SUNDAY, 21 MARCH

All today's newspapers suggest Ranieri will lose his job even if the Blues win the Champions League. Peter Kenyon lets it be known he feels Ranieri is incapable of establishing the club as a long-term European superpower for the following reasons: he is far too cautious and negative; he chops and changes the team too much; he is not able to bring out the very best in players.

According to a pre-weekend briefing with Kenyon and new publicity chief Stuart Higgins, it is made known that Abramovich wants to bring in a 'team-builder' rather than a Tinkerman, to take Chelsea 'on to the next level'. Eriksson is now established as firm favourite, with Steve McClaren to be his number two. The suggestion is that Abramovich first became disenchanted with the lack of adventure in the home tie with Stuttgart. Abramovich is prepared to ride out any 'emotional' backlash. If Sven stays with England, others on the short list are Juventus coach Marcello Lippi or AC Milan's Carlo Ancelotti.

But Ranieri vows not to be deflected by the predictions. 'I can only do what I've done ever since the beginning of the season and that is to concentrate on Chelsea and try to do as best as I can.' Ranieri is tipped off that Kenyon has held an informal breakfast briefing with Sunday paper journalists, and greets the latest twist with resigned amusement. 'What's new? What is news? I've been in this situation since July when Eriksson visited Abramovich. So, I can't see what changes there are in that situation.'

Kenyon tells journalists Chelsea will not become another Blackburn Rovers, when, financed by Jack Walker's millions, they won the title in 1995 and then quickly faded. Kenyon says there will soon be a change of emphasis away from spending money like it is going out of fashion. 'That all led to "Dream Team" headlines, and stories that we were emulating Real Madrid, but that's not what we're about. There won't be the same amount of activity this year. Players will come and go but we'll put more stress on building up our academy and training facilities than on a transfer spree. We have identified that as an area of weakness within the club. If you want to build a world-class side, to attract the very best young players from around the world, you have to have world-class facilities. We want to make Chelsea a sustainable success story, not a one-off. Gearing everything up to buying a Champions League spot doesn't work.'

As for the big clash, Kenyon says, 'We've got to believe we can get the right result. The significant thing is that two English teams are meeting in the quarter-final of the Champions League, something which wouldn't have happened five years ago.'

MONDAY, 22 MARCH

Ranieri calls a meeting after training. He thanks the players for all their hard work during his reign and wishes the team every success for the future. But when Ranieri later looks at a back page headline that says, 'Goodbye Boys', he laughs. 'I didn't say, "Goodbye boys", I said it is not important if Claudio goes or no. It is important now – not important in a couple of weeks – now is important.'

Months of frustration boil over in front of the Sky News TV cameras when Ranieri says, 'For me everything is rubbish. I don't believe it is the club. Of course now the club should say something. I continue to work for Chelsea. The club could say something to defend the coach and the players – the squad. If they don't want to say this I cannot say anything more.' Later, Ranieri declares that he will not ask the club to issue a statement backing him.

Four hours after the transmission, Chelsea respond with a statement that actually does not contain any backing for the coach. Kenyon says, 'This wave of unprecedented and continuous media speculation about Claudio's future and false links to other managers is unhelpful to our manager and the players in the build-up to an important match in the Champions League. We will not add to this speculation by responding and only wish to reiterate that Claudio Ranieri has over three years to run on his contract.'

John Terry restates his unflinching support. 'Everyone is behind Claudio and we support him 100 per cent. With all the rubbish being said about him, it does get on your nerves. But we're staying together as a team. We'll work as hard as we can for Claudio and get the results.

'This first leg against Arsenal will be the hardest, even though we should know what they are about by now – we seem to play them every week! But we don't have to be afraid of Arsenal. They are not invincible – so let's stop worrying about them and go out and beat them.'

Fans are paying up to £700 for a pair of tickets to the game. Old-fashioned street touts are holding on to batches of tickets until the last minute, confident of getting at least £1,000 a pair – with a face value of £42 each – at the gates. Arsenal's official allocation of 2,934 tickets is snapped up in minutes. With just 2,800 Chelsea tickets for the away leg at Highbury only available to those who have attended the last six Champions League away games, the scramble is guaranteed to intensify.

The two games are worth £3m in prize money and gate receipts for the winning club. Qualifying for the last four would be worth at least another £2m from television. Add to that a potential £4.3m prize for winning the competition and the two games open the way for a windfall of more than £10m.

A reminder of how much money the club might have saved on strikers arrives from the Northeast. Mikael Forssell's double at Middlesbrough takes his tally for the season to 16 goals. Forssell's 14 goals in the Premiership are as many as Crespo and Mutu have managed between them.

TUESDAY, 23 MARCH

Ranieri wears a navy blue suit and an open-neck shirt for the media conference in the bar of the Imperial College training ground at Harlington, venue for his latest interrogation by the hundred-plus journalists crammed into the small area. His back is only protected by a tiny Champions League sponsors' blackboard.

Ranieri insists he will only talk about the match. But being so angry at his treatment, he finds this promise impossible to keep. He has been living with speculation about his position since July and his sense of helplessness now comes through. 'I see I am known as "dead man walking". And that is how I will continue. Step by step, day by day. That has always been my philosophy.

'I am an Italian manager and have been brought up in a world where you win one game, draw the next, lose the third... and then you are sent home. I was asked when I first came here if it worried me that Chelsea had had so many managers. I said that in Italy we sometimes have six or seven managers in one season! That is the culture. For me, I look only at tomorrow, tomorrow and tomorrow. The pressure on me is not important. But I am an emotional man and it's important for me to feel the support of my players and the fans. It is not so important to have the support of other people within the club.

'Right from the very beginning, from the first of July, I have known that, even if I won everything this season, I could still be going home in the summer. That will not be a surprise for me. I first heard the rumours on 3 July. There is nothing I can do about them but continue in my job. A manager in my position must continue to work and not listen to anything else.' He laughs recalling how he said you need time to build. 'You must build very quickly now – everything, the foundations, the first floor and the roof garden! All in 24 hours. But it all takes time. I know that because I am a man who works with his feet on the ground.'

Asked if he has considered resigning, he smiles, 'I'm not stupid, I'm not crazy – I'm like my boys. I'm a gladiator. I have some of that English spirit too. And when I fight, I do it face to face.' He continues with his jokes. 'Until a year ago I watched the Champions League on television and sometimes I went to Highbury. I went by Tube, among the Arsenal fans. It was good but now it i s better. Now I can hear the sound of the [Champions League] music on the pitch.

'AC Milan and Arsenal are the best teams in Europe. But if we can prevent Arsenal scoring we will go to Highbury with a good chance. I am looking forward to seeing what destiny has in store for this club. By the law of averages, we have to beat Arsenal sooner or later. I just hope it is sooner, otherwise it may be too late.'

Talking about the vote of confidence from his players, he adds with emotion, 'They are my blood, my strength – their support is fantastic. But what's important is not Claudio Ranieri. It's the players, it's Chelsea FC.

'Before I came here I knew English football. But it is different to smell something and then taste it for real. I love the culture, the respect. Would I like to stay here whatever happens. Yes, why not? When you meet a team like Arsenal, you dare not make a mistake otherwise they will kill you. In the three games we have made just subtle little mistakes but we have paid. We will be positive this time but it is important we do not concede an away goal. Will I be calm? Yes I think so. We have nothing to lose and everything to gain.'

WEDNESDAY, 24 MARCH

CHELSEA 1, ARSENAL 1

The fans began by chanting, 'One Ranieri, there's only one Ranieri' along with a clear message that Eriksson is not wanted. 'We love you, Claudio' is one banner in the Shed End. 'Kenyon no clue – Claudio true blue' is on another towards the bottom of the Matthew Harding Stand.

Yet, despite the hype, the football suggests Ranieri is not the man to bring his expensive assembly of stars to a point where they can challenge Arsenal. The players respond well enough with a powerful and committed performance. But once again it all falls flat. The Gooner supporters soon remind their hosts, 'You'll never beat the Arsenal.'

In the dressing room, Ranieri's half-time talk heralds Chelsea's best moment. Lampard plays a teasing ball over the top of Lauren. Gudjohnsen chases a lost cause as he wrestles his way clear of Kolo Toure to close down the advancing Jens Lehmann. The keeper smashes his clearance against Gudjohnsen, the ball falls nicely back into the striker's path, and he keeps his balance to convert his 13th goal of the season brilliantly from wide out on the edge of the penalty area. Lehmann redeems himself with a double save four minutes later that proves crucial. First he dives to keep out Lampard's drive and then recovers to block Duff's follow-up.

With the Gunners wobbling, and with chances for a second or even third, Ashley Cole finds room on the left, Lampard fails to track Robert Pires and the Frenchman nips in ahead of Terry to glance a header home from six yards inches inside the upright. Terry then heads off the line as Chelsea lose their grip. They have to play the last seven minutes with ten men after Desailly is dismissed for two yellow cards. First he pushes away Lehmann's attempted throw-out with his hand and within minutes he brings down Vieira as he advances on goal. A second caution is not a great shock and Desailly only has himself to blame for the deliberate handball.

Wenger is confident for the return. 'We have the psychological edge now and it was a big blow for Chelsea when we scored. Chelsea made life difficult and you could see it was a European tie because they were playing not to concede. They were quite cautious in their approach and tried to suck us in and score on the break. But that didn't surprise me because in our games this season they chased us all over the pitch and we always won. Tonight we conceded a goal at an unexpected moment and for 10 minutes after that we needed to show a lot of character to survive. But 1–1 is a good result for us. We know we can win at Highbury and now we have a good opportunity to go through to the semi-finals.'

It is the third successive match between the two sides when Chelsea have taken the lead and then surrendered it. Scoring against Chelsea is no mean achievement. It is the first goal they have conceded in 560 minutes of European football. The players cite the relentless speculation over Ranieri as a motivating factor. Frank Lampard says, 'I don't think all the talk about the manager has affected us players. In fact we've rallied round. We've got closer together and turned the negative stuff into a positive. Everyone has been against us and trying to cause problems in the camp and that has only made us more strong.'

Arsenal have to play Manchester United twice before the second leg – a Premiership match on Sunday before their FA Cup semi-final three days before the return. Ranieri believes his side are still in contention. 'After this performance my players are happy. I am happy, but Arsenal is Arsenal – no?' In Madrid, Real beat Monaco 4–2 after going a goal down and are deemed favourites to go through and face the winner of this tie.

Team

Ambrosio, Gallas, Terry, Desailly, Bridge, Parker (Cole), Lampard, Makelele, Duff, Mutu (Crespo), Gudjohnsen (Melchiot).

THURSDAY, 25 MARCH

The failure to finish Arsenal off when they were wobbling will be the end of Chelsea's ambitions, fears Desailly. 'We had a really good 15-minute spell and we needed to put a bigger distance between ourselves and Arsenal. But we didn't do that – and now Chelsea have missed the bus. The two sides cancelled each other out in terms of skill and tactics but Arsenal showed they know how to stand up in the face of our passion. It's at times like that when you see what truly great teams are made of and Arsenal equalised at the worst possible moment.'

Mario Melchiot insists the away record is the key. 'It's not a problem that we have to score at Highbury because we always score there. We have been playing better away, especially in Europe where we have won every away game. We have players like Claude Makelele and Marcel Desailly who have the experience of winning the Champions League and can pass that on. And I was in the Ajax squad that reached the final when I was just a kid. We know what it takes.'

Melchiot feels the calls for Ranieri to keep his job have distracted the players. 'There's been too much talk about the manager's position and it does not help.

It's disrespectful to the supporters if our minds are focused on who is going to be in charge next season.'

On Saturday, Chelsea have a much more comfortable afternoon against relegation favourites Wolves.

FRIDAY, 26 MARCH

Claudio Ranieri might be the Tinkerman, but not when it comes to Frank Lampard, who will clock up 100 consecutive Premiership appearances. Across London, Eriksson, is giving a Sunday paper briefing ahead of his England squad announcement at which he tells reporters he has 'had no offer from any other club'. He adds, 'Nothing has changed, absolutely nothing.'

Chelsea plan to defend Bates's £2m breach of contract claims as details of his deal leak out. Bates was given a deal to remain as chairman of Chelsea Village until the company's next annual general meeting, and to stay on as chairman of Chelsea Football Club until 30 May 2005. All Bates's privileges, such as continued use of the chairman's office at Stamford Bridge, are also guaranteed for the rest of his life. Although Bates's position is not salaried, his expense package is worth £200,000 a year. As well as paid-for use of his office, a PA and mobile and home telephones, he was given £2500 a month towards the rent of a prestige motor vehicle and chauffeur. His contract also guarantees him: match-day dining for himself and three guests in the chairman's dining room in the West Stand, six directors' box tickets – two of which are in the front row – two directors' box tickets for every away game, with travel on the executive club coach or team plane, and six VIP tickets should Chelsea reach a domestic, or European cup final.

Bates is permitted to represent Chelsea at Premier League and FA meetings alongside the chief executive. In return he is expected to 'act in accordance with the directions and policies of the board' and 'undertake such tasks as the board shall from time to time reasonably delegate to him'. The contract includes a £2m severance clause if Chelsea terminate the deal. There is also a clause prohibiting any involvement in a Premier League club for two years after leaving Chelsea, which perhaps explains the interest in Sheffield Wednesday.

Later in the day, word spreads that the *Sun* will publish photographs of Sven-Goran Eriksson in a secret meeting at Kenyon's £5,000-a-month rented apartment in Kensington, west London, for two hours of talks in company with Stuart Higgins, a former editor of the same tabloid that will publish the pictures, who is engaged as a public relations consultant.

An exasperated FA makes contact with the Swede and next morning bookmakers slash the odds against him becoming manager of Chelsea. Zahavi, charged with acting as the intermediary, confirms, 'This meeting was business.'

The pictures of Eriksson leaving Kenyon's flat in a silver chauffeur-driven Mercedes supplied to him by the FA are to be published under the headline 'Sneaky Sven'. Early next morning the FA makes contact with Eriksson again, so too do Chelsea. Eriksson refuses to comment as he leaves his London home for a match at Charlton or when he arrives home again later that night.

The FA tells the Swede it is time to make a decision: either he agrees to their offer of a new contract, extended to 2008, or he gives notice of his intention to quit, allowing his employers time to identify a replacement. He is warned that otherwise his position with the FA is 'untenable' and he clearly feels this is a veiled threat that he might not be allowed to stay in charge for the European Championship. 'What's the big secret?' Zahavi shrugs. 'This has all been going on for months. What has Sven done wrong by meeting Peter Kenyon? I can't see what the fuss is all about.' Zahavi adds, 'The first meeting was purely social, I can guarantee that. But Thursday's meeting was business.'

On BBC Radio Five Live, Peter Kenyon says a two-year-old picture has been 'doctored', a claim which is subsequently withdrawn.

David Mellor turns on Ranieri in his newspaper column. 'I am afraid I am still one of those who thinks he should go. Chelsea haven't won anything under him and are unlikely to do so because of his ingrained eccentricity.'

Mellor favours Eriksson as successor and is also impressed by Abramovich. 'Some people have complained about Roman, but I think he's fantastic. Friends of mine know Roman and he's not doing this for ego. He's doing it for business. He sees it like this: if he puts in £230m, and he looks at what Manchester United are worth, it's only a quarter of that. So, if he gets there with Chelsea, it's a good deal. Europe is worth £28m plus TV rights. If you bung £200m in a bank you are lucky to get four per cent. People say he won't get a return on his money. I think he will.'

SATURDAY, 27 MARCH

CHELSEA 5, WOLVES 2

Abramovich is still enjoying the hospitality in his executive box 30 minutes before kick-off when the half-full stadium greets Ranieri with a standing ovation as he ventures on to the pitch to supervise the warm-up. The owner is present, though, in the front row when the first chorus of 'We don't want Eriksson' breaks out 90 seconds into the game – closely followed by 'There's only one Ranieri'. Ranieri's popularity has increased, and Abramovich knows it.

Hasselbaink celebrates his birthday in style with a second-half hat-trick to keep alive any slim hopes of catching Arsenal. Hasselbaink has turned 32 but comes off the bench with a three-goal blast inside 13 minutes. The first is his

100th in the Premiership, while Lampard scores a vital goal on his 100th consecutive Premiership appearance. Yet, incredibly enough Wolves, at one stage, look like earning their first away win of the season. Within four minutes, a fine passing move allows Melchiot, making his first start in more than a month, to score only his second goal of the season. Bursting forward on the overlap as Cole finds Lampard, Melchiot latches on to a through-ball and drives a low shot past Paul Jones. But on 23 minutes Wolves are gifted an equaliser as Ambrosio, Babayaro and Terry contrive to tie themselves in knots on the edge of the area. Ambrosio throws the ball out to Babayaro, who is closed down immediately by Henri Camara. Babayaro lays the ball back to Terry but the speed of Camara catches them out, and he intercepts as the central defender attempts to slip the ball inside to Makelele. Camara bursts forward and his low shot flies in off the keeper.

Chelsea lose their composure. Two minutes later Camara is allowed the freedom of the right wing to cross perfectly for the unmarked Mark Kennedy but, with only Ambrosio to beat, the winger side-foots his effort the wrong side of the post. Wolves sense an opportunity and on 57 minutes take a surprise lead. Kennedy's corner from the right reaches Jody Craddock, who has the easy task of heading home with Ambrosio rushing out in no-man's land. Chelsea sort themselves out despite the second-half introduction of Duff, who strangely replaces Gudjohnsen who has looked bright in the first 45 minutes. Hasselbaink, finally recovered from a neck injury, comes off the bench to replace Geremi but it is Lampard who finds the equaliser on 70 minutes with a trademark drive from 25 yards. Eight minutes later Hasselbaink shows his class to hold off Craddock's challenge and unleash an unstoppable shot into the top corner. He adds a second when he races on to Duff's superb defence-splitting ball to shoot into the bottom corner. He performs cartwheels and has Abramovich on his feet celebrating. Seconds before the final whistle, he blasts past Jones with the defence appealing vainly for offside. Hasselbaink deservedly strolls away from Stamford Bridge with the match ball under his arm. 'Now we can relax and sit and watch Arsenal play Manchester United. If we keep on winning, hopefully Arsenal will slip up.'

In the tunnel afterwards, Paul Ince is furious at what he feels is gloating from Babayaro and a tussle turns into an incident due to heavy-handed stewarding. A total of 1,070,048 fans have watched the games so far at the Bridge, beating the previous all-time best four years ago.

Team

Ambrosio, Melchiot, Terry, Gallas, Babayaro, Geremi (Hasselbaink), Lampard, Makelele, J Cole (Parker), Crespo, Gudjohnsen (Duff).

Ranieri rushes away from the Bridge to Heathrow, avoiding the post-match press conference, to catch a flight to Rome to attend his daughter's birthday party. En route he is in contact with his representative Jon Smith to quell the rumour that Spurs are talking to him. Privately, Ranieri is chuckling over Sven's remarkable U-turn to stay with the FA and snub Chelsea. When told he is back in the frame to keep his job, he jokes to friends, 'Why? Can't they find someone better than me!' Eriksson has left a message on Ranieri's answer machine – but only to inquire about the fitness of certain players. 'I would never talk to him about the possibility of me coming to Chelsea,' Eriksson says. 'I met him at Highbury once and he said to me, "When are you coming, Sven?" He has a very good sense of humour.'

SUNDAY, 28 MARCH

Following 48 hours of intensive talks with the FA and Chelsea, Eriksson finally agrees that he will sign a new contract until 2008. Kenyon issues a statement which includes the following admission: 'I did have informal discussions with Eriksson to talk about his future intentions. He made it very clear that he misses the day-to-day challenge of club football.'

Feelings are running high inside the Bridge that Arsenal's David Dein has played too prominent a role in the talks to deflect Eriksson from becoming Chelsea manager. As vice-chairman of Arsenal, as well as the FA, he has pulled off a coup ensuring the FA do not look towards Wenger, while keeping Eriksson from the clutches of one of his club's biggest rivals. When Zahavi sees Dein at the Arsenal game, he suggests that Chelsea might gain revenge by going for Wenger! Is he joking, or is he serious?

MONDAY, 29 MARCH

In his first *Sun* column, Ken Bates savages Eriksson. 'In fact, the question you want to ask is: Would you buy a second-hand Saab off this man?' He also turns on Kenyon and Zahavi.

TUESDAY, 30 MARCH

Roman Abramovich and Peter Kenyon hold clear-the-air talks with Ranieri, accompanied by Jon Smith. Ranieri feels humiliated by the Eriksson saga and at the hour-long meeting the Chelsea power-brokers pledge their support until the end of the season but there are no guarantees beyond that. Ranieri shakes hands with the pair after Kenyon apologises for the way Eriksson was courted.

Ranieri accepts he will be replaced even if he wins the Champions League. Ranieri's agent Vincenzo Morabito says, 'All that's important to Claudio is to achieve the best possible position and results for Chelsea and then just wait and see. Then he will find a lot of clubs interested in him. Claudio is in a very good position, to be honest.'

Privately Ranieri remarks, 'Don't bet on me staying!' Ranieri knows that the club are searching for an alternative to Eriksson. 'It is an intolerable position to be working under and Chelsea are coming out of it so poorly,' says John Barnwell of the League Managers' Association. Barnwell also slams Eriksson, honorary president of the LMA, for being prepared to walk out on England. 'Here we have the national coach wanting to get out of a contract. We don't agree with that. We won't support a manager walking out whether he's with England or a club in the lower divisions.'

Meanwhile Chelsea are ready to discuss new contracts for Melchiot and Gronkjaer.

WEDNESDAY, 31 MARCH

John Terry now has the confidence, stature and experience to take on Thierry Henry in Euro 2004, despite England's 1–0 defeat in a friendly in Sweden. Terry and Jonathan Woodgate start an international together for the first time, and Terry's defensive contribution bristles with purpose and determination. 'He's like a young Tony Adams,' says Eriksson. 'He's got spirit and he's strong. He's not the quickest in the world but he's difficult to beat, very difficult.'

Scott Parker accepts his dream of making Euro 2004 could be as good as over. He is only used as a late second-half substitute. 'It will be tough to get in now. All I can do is keep playing well for Chelsea and hopefully something might come up.' He is still optimistic of club honours though. 'The league is still in our sights and we all feel we can do well in the Champions League. The game on Tuesday is a massive one. All we can do is keep putting the pressure on Arsenal. But Arsenal have been brilliant this year, unbelievable. Any other year we would probably be top of the league.'

On the subject of Ranieri, he adds, 'The speculation over the manager never fazed me and it did not seem like a big issue for the rest of the players. We just got our heads down and tried to play well. It has bonded us together.'

April

*REVENGE ON ARSENAL AT LAST SETS UP THE BIGGEST GAME IN
CHELSEA'S HISTORY*

Abramovich splashes out £72m on his third stunning custom-made
yacht with a helicopter landing pad which lowers inside to hide the aircraft.
He names the 282ft yacht *Ecstasea* and will take delivery this summer. He owns
two other yachts, *Le Grand Bleu* and *Pelorus*, and will have to spend upwards of
£25m a year keeping all three afloat.

Roma coach Fabio Capello is out of the running to succeed Ranieri after talks
break down over his demands: an annual salary of £5m, plus enhanced training
facilities, along with backroom staff and key team targets which are too
restrictive. Capello refuses to lower his demands in a second meeting and
insists there will be no short cuts if they want him in charge. It is also felt he
cannot work harmoniously with Peter Kenyon.

Even though some say Chelsea have signed too many players, they run out of

	PREMIERSHIP TABLE – APRIL							
Pos Team	P	W	D	L	GF	GA	GD	PTS
1 Arsenal	30	22	8	0	58	20	38	74
2 Chelsea	30	21	4	5	57	24	33	67
3 Manchester United	30	19	5	6	56	30	26	62
4 Liverpool	30	12	10	8	42	31	11	46
5 Newcastle United	30	11	12	7	41	31	10	45
6 Birmingham City	30	12	9	9	37	36	1	45
7 Aston Villa	30	12	7	11	38	35	3	43
8 Charlton Athletic	30	12	7	11	41	39	2	43
9 Fulham	30	11	7	12	42	40	2	40
10 Southampton	30	10	9	11	30	28	2	39

goalkeepers and have to borrow Paul Nicholls from Chelmsford, a former trainee, along with Sittingbourne's young keeper Kevin Fewell!

THURSDAY, 1 APRIL

Jimmy Floyd Hasselbaink is cleared of violent conduct against Scarborough in the FA Cup, which means he is now available for the rest of the league campaign as Chelsea bid to cut Arsenal's seven-point lead.

Damien Duff confesses he wants to blow Arsenal away to set up a clash with Real Madrid and his hero Luis Figo. 'I love watching Figo. He and Pires are my favourite players. But I don't think Pires can take people on as much as Figo, so Figo is my favourite. I like to study both and learn from them. Pires is certainly a class act: pace, goals – he's got everything, hasn't he? It's a dying breed, a player who can take on a few players with the ball at his feet. But I'd like to think I'm one of the players that can do that.'

Talks are ongoing with French Second Division club Chateauroux to set up another nursery club.

FRIDAY, 2 APRIL

Ranieri is named Barclaycard Manager of the Month. He gains my vote as a member of the voting panel. Ranieri says, 'I'm pleased with the new award and want to say thanks to my players as I've won this award because of them.' He tells friends privately, 'This could be the last chance for them to give it to me!'

Victory over Tottenham will guarantee Champions League football next season, but Ranieri says, 'I am an ambitious man and to be ambitious you always have to go one better than the last year. I won't be happy if we only match last season's fourth place.'

Asked about the pictures of Eriksson with Kenyon, he jokes, 'I was disappointed when I saw the pictures in the *Sun* because I always prefer looking at Page Three!

'Look, I'd like to explain my philosophy, my strength,' adds Ranieri as he leans forward, scattering the journalists' tape recorders before him and then hastily rearranging them in a straight line. 'The best way from here,' he says pointing in front of him, 'to here,' gesturing at the end of the table, 'is the straight way. But you cannot win every time three points, three points... only Arsenal. Fucking Arsenal.'

He utters another expletive and waits for the laughter to die down. 'Sometimes you have to go around here,' he says, swinging his arm in a circle. 'I try to take... the best route I can. 'Sometimes you have to go around here,' swinging his other arm in and out. Everything else I don't worry.'

Despite Chelsea having an even stronger hold over Spurs (undefeated in 27 league meetings) than Arsenal have over them, questions about the merits of the opposition are few. There is only one topic: Ranieri's future. Or lack of it! This is the first time he has been quizzed since Kenyon confirmed speaking to Eriksson.

Ranieri, who has been linked with a move to Tottenham, knew he was in line for the Barclaycard Manager of the Month award, and the news has leaked out, as usual. 'I picked up the paper and saw the headline 'Ranieri's Revenge' and a nice picture of me. Now I have won the Treble – the Malaysia Cup, Manager of the Month for September and now for March. Mr Kenyon has not congratulated me yet for my award but we had a lovely meeting in the week.'

Mikael Forssell is the top scorer on Chelsea's books with 16 Premiership strikes – all while on loan with Birmingham – and six goals last month earned him Player of the Month. More talks are planned to extend his loan period for another season. Hernan Crespo has been passed fit after returning from international action in midweek when he was Argentina's goalscorer in their World Cup qualifier against Ecuador. Seba Veron has splashed out around a week's salary on another luxury car, a spanking new silver Bentley coupe, which costs around £90,000 – but he still isn't fit!

Tottenham's caretaker manager David Pleat tempers his sympathy for Ranieri's position with a series of generalisations about foreign coaches. 'They have a different philosophy. They come for a period of time, they sign an agreement – they are gypsy-like in their mentality. He has had a chequered history and in Spain he went from one team to another after a cup final. They don't get involved in the politics; they don't get involved in the transfer of players; they don't ever go to watch Scunthorpe on a wet, windy night. They are a different breed of coach. Whether that is good in the long run for the British game I don't know. And the biggest problem is that they serve their contract and then go – Arsene Wenger is an exception – to a different country or whatever and leave the remnants behind them. But in Italy that is the acceptable thing – it is like musical chairs.'

Pleat also reckons Chelsea's spending is unfair. 'They have a bought team. Apart from John Terry at the moment, they are a team of immigrants. It is a morality issue. I like a level playing field.'

SATURDAY, 3 APRIL

SPURS 0, CHELSEA 1

Arsenal lose their lunchtime FA Cup semi-final to Manchester United and blow their Treble chance. Sir Alex reckons the Gunners will now succumb to Chelsea.

'Chelsea manager Claudio Ranieri's due a bit of luck after everything he's been through. I wouldn't bet on Arsenal on Tuesday night.'

Things get even better when Hasselbaink's first-half goal puts the Blues within four points of Arsenal. It is his 11th league strike against Spurs, his 17th goal of the season, and Chelsea haven't lost to Spurs now in 28 league meetings, going back a full 14 years! On their own ground they have not won for 17 years – no wonder Chelsea fans call it Three Point Lane.

Ranieri wisely makes few changes, keeping faith with Hasselbaink up front. As for the goal, Lampard and Gudjohnsen exchange passes before Lampard releases the ball down the left-hand channel for Duff to flash in an accurate low cross to the far post, where Hasselbaink is lurking to score. Jamie Redknapp, playing his first game since September, goes off with a badly gashed lip after a clash with Lampard, his cousin. Pleat says, 'Jamie has gone for plastic surgery. He was desperate to get back on the pitch – so he could kick Frank!'

Mauricio Taricco gets involved in scuffles with Parker and Lampard, and sends Duff to the floor with a right jab to the chin. Taricco then brings down Hasselbaink. Ranieri turns to his bench, saying, 'That's red,' but the referee shows yellow. At the final whistle, the importance of this win is clear as the players hug each other and Ranieri marches down the tunnel looking highly satisfied.

Ranieri refuses to discuss the gap at the top of the league. 'We don't see Arsenal. We are looking only at ourselves. Everything is in our own hands. Tuesday's game is a gamble for us. A 1–1 draw was not a great first-leg result, but we always score away in the Champions League and haven't conceded yet. If we continue, it will be good for us – but we have no illusions.'

At any other club, Hasselbaink's winner a week after his hat-trick would normally guarantee his place. Ranieri, though, is making no promises and laughs, 'I am the Tinkerman. Anything could happen.'

Team

Ambrosio, Bridge, Melchiot, Terry, Gallas, Duff, Lampard, Makelele, Parker (Cole), Gudjohnsen, Hasselbaink.

SUNDAY, 4 APRIL

John Terry reveals his long list of superstitions. 'I was offered the chance to be Chelsea's number 5 in the summer but turned it down. My number is 26, so that's why I have kept it. I do have loads of rituals before every game.

'Stupid things like always rotating tape round my shin-pads three times and never going to the two toilets on the left of the dressing room. I also don't have anything to drink, not even a cup of tea, once I wake up on the morning of a game, and I always count the number of lampposts on the journey between home and Stamford Bridge. I don't know why I do them, other than it is something I have always done and always will.'

For his part, William Gallas makes sure he is one of the last to leave the dressing room and always enters the tunnel with his shirt in his hands. 'I don't use shin-guards during the warm-up, so it takes me a bit more time to get ready when I go back in, and that's it. Titi [Thierry Henry] knows me. Before a game he will always give me one of his looks and try to make me laugh because he knows I'm trying to stay focused.'

The parallels between Gallas and Henry are fascinating. Their parents hail from the same Caribbean island (Sainte-Anne, Guadeloupe). They were born in the same city (Paris), on the same day (the 17th), of the same month (August), of the same year (1977). They learnt the game in the same way (on the streets), honed their skills at the same academy (Clairefontaine) and played in the same World Youth Championship (Malaysia 1997). Gallas wears number 13. 'Superstitious? Not at all,' he says. 'I took that number because I didn't know if I was going to play right-back or centre-half. I thought, "Well, if I take number 5 and play right-back, that won't look great. And I abhor the number 2, so I decided to take a number that would go well in the centre and well on the right. I feel better playing in the centre. They play me at centre-half and I'm in my element. They take me out of my element and put me on the wing and the reaction straight away is, "I prefer him in the centre." Why? "Because he didn't look great on the wing."

'I didn't play well in the last game with Arsenal. A winger should cross the ball at least 10 times during a game and I think I crossed it twice. Okay, so I've provided a good service for the team but now I'd really like to progress playing in one position.'

Right now he just wants to turn the tables on his friend, Henry. 'We were disappointed in the dressing room after the first leg, but we have every chance at Highbury. We've always scored there. I think we'll score again.'

MONDAY, 5 APRIL

Hasselbaink arrives with Claudio Ranieri for the pre-match press conference and the Chelsea manager says, 'Come and sit next to me, Jimmy, on the bench.'

Hasselbaink laughs and rolls his eyes but he will not be in good humour if he loses his place. He has started just one Champions League game in his career, scoring in a first-round win over Besiktas last December. 'Every player wants to play in the Champions League. If you asked 100 players if they wanted to, 101 would say that's where they want to be. When you cannot play and you feel you should be, you get upset.'

Ranieri calls the forthcoming battle 'the moment of truth' but tries to insist the pressure is now on Arsenal. 'For us, anything is a bonus because the players have worked hard and for us it is normal to lose to Arsenal. If we lose, what has changed? Nothing. In 18 games it has been this way. We are the underdogs but I am fed up with that. I want to be the owner – not the dog.

'Arsenal are one of the best teams in Europe, not just this country. They are ahead of us and the league says this. But my players are confident and are full of beans, as you say.'

Ranieri is playing the kind of psychological mind-games that have spiced up the rows between Wenger and Ferguson. He adds, 'It is not important what I do because the players know everything. They know Pires will cut in from one side and Ljungberg from the other. I am calm because my players are full of confidence. This is the moment of truth because this is the last match of the season between Chelsea and Arsenal.'

Hasselbaink reckons Arsenal may not recover if Chelsea progress. 'It would not be very nice to lose the game and be out of two cups within the space of a week. We believe we can beat them and it is just a matter of time before we have a victory over them. You can see that in all of our eyes.'

Chelsea follow the same travel routine as if they were playing on the Continent, training on the Highbury pitch, staying in a hotel – the White House in Regent's Park – and even holding their pre-match press conference at Arsenal. Ranieri, it seems, will go to any length to finally overcome Arsenal who, he insists, are still red-hot favourites.

Both managers, Wenger and Ranieri, identify Duff as the player to watch. The Arsenal manager says, 'He adds something offensively to their squad, without a doubt, and he's a major danger. He can run at you with the ball; he can provide crosses; he can score goals. He is one we have to keep quiet.' Ranieri agrees, 'He is an amazing player. Duff is the man who can open every door.' Ranieri also points out that no one, not even Henry, has amassed as many assists, 15 so far this season, to add to his six goals. Half of Chelsea's eight defeats were inflicted when Duff was absent from the team. Because he has made 35 appearances and missed 13 games, that is a noteworthy return.

Ranieri is urged by many to ignore the price tags and bank on a front pairing which dates back to pre-Roman times – Gudjohnsen and Hasselbaink. In their nine starts as a partnership, Chelsea have won eight and drawn once.

Here's a new twist... on the day before the club's biggest match, there is speculation that Chelsea have offered Ranieri a 12-month contract extension. However, the truth is that talks are ongoing but no offer has been made.

TUESDAY, 6 APRIL

ARSENAL 1, CHELSEA 2 (Chelsea win 3–2 on aggregate)

Ranieri masterminds the greatest result in Chelsea's history. But will it save him? Wayne Bridge's 87th-minute winner seals a sensational victory, making Ranieri's position even more fascinating. It is 10.30pm on Highbury's famous old clock by the time Ranieri emerges from the stadium's innards to make the short walk down one side of the pitch to the corner exit, where the Chelsea team bus waits. At the pleading of reporters he stops for a word. 'How do I feel?' he smiles. 'I was… I am… how can you say it?' Say it in Italian, somebody suggests. 'Also in Italian,' laughs the manager. 'I don't remember in Italian either, ha, ha…'

Ranieri begins a night of surprises with the first – he announces an unchanged team. He gets his game plan spot-on, squeezing the life out of Arsenal in the middle of the park and never giving Thierry Henry or Robert Pires any room.

In the first half, Arsenal still look a class act, though Duff ends a dribble with a shot wide from eight yards. Pires almost produces a headed goal from Cole's cross like the one from the first leg but directs it into the side-netting. With virtually the last kick before the break, Jose Antonio Reyes puts Arsenal ahead. Pires sweeps the ball out to Lauren and, when his cross is headed down by Henry, Reyes slams home from close range. Arsenal are in command.

Parker is swiftly removed at the interval after Chelsea have been skinned too often down the right flank. There may be a few sighs when he is replaced by the more lightweight Gronkjaer, not everyone's idea of a big-match performer, yet it proves the master stroke. Gronkjaer gives new width and enterprise and keeps Ashley Cole in check. His threat so changes the game's momentum that, after the equaliser, Arsenal are deflated, while Ranieri's late double introduction of Cole and Crespo is perfectly timed to help set up the killer blow. 'I thought it was important that we didn't allow Cole to come forward so much in the second half,' explains Ranieri.

On 51 minutes Chelsea equalise. Edu's clearance is superbly volleyed by Makelele from 35 yards, Lehmann spills it and there is Lampard to roll it coolly into the net. Chelsea's tails are up. Lampard, who seems to get faster and stronger as Vieira wilts, whips in a 30-yarder which strikes the side-netting. Then Ambrosio rises to the occasion, diving to his right to push away a drive by Reyes and springing to tip Kolo Toure's 35-yard effort over the top. Then comes the sight of Henry being substituted with a hamstring injury.

The superstitious Terry is outstanding at the back, Lampard outbattles Vieira in midfield and Gudjohnsen is a handful up front. Ashley Cole's desperate clearance off the line from Gudjohnsen's close-range shot denies Chelsea but it is only a stay of execution. Arsenal are on their knees by the time Bridge scores. The full-back exchanges passes with Gudjohnsen, bursts into the box and raps a left-foot shot into the far corner. Bridge is engulfed by joyful team-mates. Bridge wears 18 – the number of games it has taken Chelsea to beat their adversaries.

There is a newfound belief that Ranieri could yet have the last laugh. Chelsea have continued to win every match on their travels in Europe, and he has taken Chelsea further in the Champions league than ever before. 'It's difficult to kill me,' he says. 'I may be dead but I will continue to work. Can we win the Champions League? Why not? Anything is possible now. This can transform the season and we want to catch Arsenal in the league. Describing my joy at the final whistle is difficult, but I was mad, it was 30 seconds of delirium. Roman Abramovich was mad afterwards as well; everyone was going crazy in the dressing room as we have made history. People have said I am a dead man walking. But I'm not. I am still moving and I will continue to fight.'

When shown his exuberant celebrations at the goal, punching the air, waving his arms like pistons, he jokes. 'It's a crazy man!' There are tears in his eyes as he applauds his team before heading down the tunnel. Those tears are to provoke a national debate about grown men crying à la Gazza. It endears him to football fans, not just Chelsea supporters, and indeed to anyone who witnesses his show of pure emotion.

Watching from the stands is Sven-Goran Eriksson. In the press box, an Italian journalist who is close to Ranieri smiles. 'Now,' he says, 'Peter Kenyon is crying too.' Abramovich is said to have looked a touch more subdued, sitting next to wife Irina, perhaps because he has to wear a tie in the Highbury directors' box, or more likely because he is not far away from David Dein, so instrumental in keeping Eriksson from his clutches. Later he makes a rare comment. 'Chelsea played great and I think the team showed the Russian character to hold on, to fight, to win. This is a great result.'

In the privacy of the dressing room my spy tells me, 'There were big hugs from Abramovich with everyone, but Claudio felt there was only a little hug for him.' There are massive celebrations inside the dressing room. There is also shock at another major surprise: Monaco have eliminated Real.

Wenger looks aghast at the suggestion that Arsenal would now have to rescue their season by merely winning the Premiership. Merely? 'I'd sign for 20 years if you could guarantee me the Premiership every year,' he replies.

In the hour of his most crushing disappointment, Wenger is asked whether he can feel just a touch of pleasure for Ranieri. It says much that he just smiles ruefully. 'You will understand if I cannot jump to the roof because he is happy.'

Team

Ambrosio, Melchiot, Terry, Gallas, Bridge, Parker (Gronkjaer), Lampard, Makelele, Duff (Cole), Gudjohnsen, Hasselbaink (Crespo).

Immediately after the game, the mobile of Vincenzo Morabito, Ranieri's Italian agent, rings. One of Real Madrid's Mr Fixits is calling. 'Tell Claudio, that if Chelsea don't want him I can make it happen at Real. I've spoken to Florentino about Claudio and he has asked me to arrange a meeting next week, Queiroz is out.'

Suddenly, Ranieri's stock is rising, and it is time for his advisers to act. For Ranieri, there is a quiet dinner date to wind down. 'Straight afterwards I was thinking about Middlesbrough. They say, "Oh Ranieri, champagne and loads of women." You saw me going crazy and you think I am a lucky man. You thought I would celebrate with supermodels but I had dinner with Gary Straker [Chelsea's first-team administrator and translator] not Claudia Schiffer – and all we talked about was Middlesbrough!'

WEDNESDAY, 7 APRIL

Ranieri prepares for a second summit meeting in a fortnight with another dinner date, this time with agents Jon Smith and Morabito at La Famiglia just off the King's Road. One week earlier, Smith, Morabito and Ranieri had gathered for a similar meeting at Smith's house in Hertfordshire. Then an effort to persuade Kenyon to back Ranieri publicly before the Arsenal match had failed. As Smith and Kenyon plan to meet, this dinner is a critical briefing.

Ranieri strolls to the restaurant and is approached by well-wishers every step of the way. Smith tells me, 'People wanted just to shake his hand and tell him, "You're a star." And when we got to the restaurant, there were 20, probably 30 people who came up to him at the table and they all said, "Please don't go."

'Claudio seemed angry to me; he says he is doing everything he can but without much credit from those who run and own the club. It hurts him when he gets calls from colleagues in Europe who ask him, "How can you stand for it?" The question is whether he should stand such a battering to his personal pride, and he wonders whether he is being taken for a mug.'

Privately Ranieri is now thoroughly exasperated by the constant speculation. Publicly he says in a TV interview, 'It is my first time in the Champions League and I am in the semi-final. It is a great achievement of my career. But I am used to thinking about the club, not Claudio Ranieri. I am one man inside a big club. The players are writing history in Chelsea.'

Meanwhile it emerges that Bates 'emigrated' to Monte Carlo on 1 April. So, just imagine the scenario: there he is, enjoying the view from his balcony getting an update on the Blues score, discovering that there was an even bigger upset on his own doorstep against Real. But if he isn't going to Chelsea these days, then Chelsea are coming to Ken! Bates tells me, 'It was like a West Indian wedding here when Monaco went through, the celebrations went on for more than two hours; everyone went mad.'

Will Bates be going to the big match in Monte Carlo? 'Only If I can get a ticket! I opened a fine bottle of Pouilly-Fumé, sat back and thought about Claudio and how he had won the greatest battle of his career. I had spoken to him earlier in the day, wished him all the best and reminded him he was a Roman.

'The king of Monaco, though, is Didier Deschamps. We had him for a season at Chelsea and, though he was very quiet, he was a brilliant captain. We didn't want to sell him but he had to move because he and Vialli didn't get on. The great thing about him was he had no ego. But he did have charm. In fact he was so charming he reminded me of myself! Eric Cantona described him as a water-carrier. It was meant to be a slight but in fact it was a great compliment. If you don't have water you die of thirst. Not that there is much evidence of H_2O in my apartment here right now.'

Deschamps reckons he made a mistake playing for Chelsea in the twilight of his fabulous career. 'It's true I had a few problems in my relationship with the coach Gianluca Vialli. It wasn't the Gianluca I knew at Juventus, and my wife and I found it difficult to adapt to London. But I did play 49 out of 61 matches and we won the FA Cup.'

His young team have been Champions League underdogs all season. 'My priority is the French championship but the players are obsessed by the Champions League. I have the feeling sometimes that it's the only thing for them.'

Deportivo La Coruna's sensational 4–0 second leg victory knocks out holders AC Milan and Chelsea are immediately installed as Champions League favourites.

THURSDAY, 8 APRIL

Chelsea put forward proposals for a broader job description should Ranieri stay, but have also been asked to make an offer for an amicable settlement if they are going to bring in a new coach. That is the outcome of talks between Smith and Kenyon. There are proposals for Ranieri to meet face to face with Kenyon next Wednesday.

Chelsea tell Ranieri, via Smith, that they are seeking a coach to take a far more global view of the club in order to take it forward. Kenyon outlines his blueprint for a Sir Alex Ferguson/Arsene Wenger style manager who also develops the youth academy and brings in outstanding young continental talent besides just shelling out on big transfer fees.

Although Ranieri is entitled to £6m for the remaining three years of his contract, his advisers are seeking around £8–£9m for him to go. Smith tells me, 'We don't know what the final outcome will be, but there was no new contract offered, only the terms of reference over the existing one. But it was a good meeting, a chance to clear the air that has been hanging over Claudio since the Eriksson situation. We have all agreed that the only mention now of Eriksson will be in connection with mobile phones!'

Smith's sense of humour masks the bitterness felt by Ranieri over the way Chelsea have attempted to woo Eriksson. Smith goes on, 'We have discussed various options and there will be another meeting. They want answers from Claudio, and Claudio wants answers from them. It should be resolved within the next week or 10 days.'

However, Smith knows that Chelsea would like to run a little longer to see how Ranieri fares in the Champions League. Ranieri is linked with Real, Roma and Spurs, and it is clearly in his interests to be allowed to talk to other interested cubs if he isn't going to be retained. The players have realised for some time that their coach is on the way out. Duff says, 'The gaffer's been brilliant with us all season and we all love him to bits. Hopefully we can win something for him this season because the victory over Arsenal was as much for him as it was for the players. Everyone knows he hasn't been treated very well but what we can do now is let our football do the talking.'

Frank Lampard admits that even winning the Champions League won't save Ranieri's job. 'I don't know how they can fire him but, then again, they can do anything they want. He's been very supportive of us and we all have a great feeling for him. He's a very dignified man and that's why he has so much public support.'

Ex-Chelsea star Frank Leboeuf believes Ranieri's recent upturn in fortune is just reward for his dignity. 'I guess the players are a little bit appalled at the situation. The man is great; he's got good communication with the players and is somebody who wants to succeed. I speak to Marcel Desailly, Emmanuel Petit and Celestine Babayaro sometimes on the phone. They are very supportive of the manager. They stick to his ideas and don't understand why anything should change.

'He deserves some credit because he has done a very good job, even if he hasn't won anything yet. Instead of speaking about him in the middle of the season, the board should have waited until the end of the season.'

There's also a vote of confidence from Ranieri's mum Renata, 'It was about time Chelsea beat Arsenal, they are always such a lucky team. After the game I spoke to Claudio and he was so happy, the happiest I'd heard him in a long time. What this win does is put an end to all this idle talk about Claudio and that he will lose his job at the end of the season. He is a good manager and he has the backing of the players and the fans and they are the people that count above all. I don't understand where the problem is at Chelsea. Can you imagine what would happen if Claudio wins the Champions League and he is sacked?'

Gianfranco Zola believes Chelsea will be making a huge mistake if they get rid of his fellow Italian, 'He is doing well despite all the problems he has had to deal with. I don't know the politics, but talking about Claudio you have to say he is doing a very good job so far. I was ecstatic when Chelsea beat Arsenal, it was a great night for them.'

FRIDAY, 9 APRIL

How did Chelsea outplay Arsenal? 'The preparation was very good,' says Frank Lampard. 'We were in the hotel for a day and a half. We watched videos and remained determined. We were very focused.'

The videos included Arsenal's FA Cup defeat by Manchester United, a game that became something of a blueprint for the Blues. United had struck a balance between cautious defence in the face of Arsenal's forward power, and free-flowing attack, to exploit a perceived weakness of the Gunners under pressure.

In a variation of this strategy, Ranieri ordered his defenders, the pacy Gallas in particular, to retreat at top speed whenever Arsenal threatened, and yet he boldly fielded two strikers and a winger. The result was that Henry was unable to break behind his opponents.

United also launched a physical assault on Arsenal, so did Ranieri's players – particularly after Lampard had equalised. 'You sensed Arsenal wilt,' says the midfielder. 'They're such a machine, but they weren't quite working the way they normally do. I wouldn't say we thought they were there for the taking, because we've been there against them so many times and lost, but they certainly didn't come again like we thought they might. We grew stronger from that, and believed. We had a plan, we were determined and we deserved it.'

Chelsea were much fresher, which makes you begin to understand the purpose of Ranieri's squad rotation. But Ranieri is still feeling far from fulfilled. 'The best moments in life are when you win trophies. This is like a little station; I still want to arrive at the final destination.

'For us, the Champions League is still a gamble. You can win or lose but the Premiership remains our main target. I said to the players that everything could happen now over Easter. Both teams are playing twice and we must wait and see. Before Arsenal's game against Manchester United, they were very strong mentally. But after that game, there were maybe a few doubts that crept in and now there are maybe even more doubts. Having seen the game at Highbury again on video, my Chelsea players were relaxed and the Arsenal players – although not nervous – seemed maybe too focused.'

Wenger hits back and insists that the best team is the one which wins the Premiership, 'I still think the championship is a real reflection of the quality of a team because you need consistency and I don't think Monaco would be ahead of Real Madrid if they were playing in the same championship. You see big upsets in the cup. The team that wins the European Cup is not necessarily the best team in Europe.'

Melchiot reveals how the players held a meeting where they vowed not to let Arsenal destroy their season. 'When we drew them in the Champions League, we laughed and we knew this was our chance to make sure Arsenal didn't ruin everything for us. I've been at the club for five years and we'd never beaten Arsenal before. I played in most of those 17 games but none of them was as important as this one. We chose the right moment to beat them. I have never felt more joy after a game. Now we have to keep up the pressure on Arsenal because the title race is not over.'

However, Arsenal twice come from behind at Highbury to beat Liverpool 4–2 with an Henry hat-trick. Ranieri holds the usual media conference after training. Despite Arsenal extending their Premiership lead to seven points, he insists the pressure is still on Arsenal not to lose the title. 'This is my first title race and it is very important for my career now. The league is your character during one season. It's your ability, your everything. I am very focused on this. Now we must work harder than before. After Tuesday night I said, "Well done, great performance, but now let's clean everything up because Boro want to test us."'

SATURDAY, 10 APRIL

CHELSEA 0, MIDDLESBROUGH 0

The fans rise to their feet, hailing the dark-overcoated Ranieri as he emerges to oversee the pre-match warm-up. 'There's Crazy Man on the pitch,' declares the PA announcer as Ranieri responds with a discreet wave. 'A welcome back to Claudio Ranieri.'

Ranieri enjoys more than a hint of told-you-so in his programme notes when, talking of his rotation policy, he stresses that his players had 'more power, more stamina, more vitamins' than Arsenal in the second half. 'I said at the beginning of the season it is important to rotate all the players so we arrive in good condition in March, April and May,' he writes.

Before the game, a group of fans meet in the upmarket Sofa Bar near the Bridge to plot their 'Save Ranieri Campaign' – they need not have bothered. By the end, it is enough to make Claudio cry again! A display like this, where only Terry emerges with any credit, virtually ends the title race.

Ranieri rests his first-choice left side, Bridge and Duff. Cole, Desailly, Babayaro and Gronkjaer all start. The Middlesbrough camp cannot believe their luck when they see Duff's name is not on the team-sheet. Gudjohnsen has the chance to nudge Chelsea ahead but pops his shot against a post. Geremi, the former Boro star, makes an appearance for the second half in place of Gronkjaer. Then Makelele is carried off with a serious-looking knee injury after a challenge by Gaizka Mendieta, providing the first glimpse of Veron in over five months. Veron poses a couple of threats to Mark Schwarzer – one free-kick and one first-timer skimming the bar.

Crespo remains uneasy on the bench, even though Hasselbaink and Gudjohnsen are misfiring. Ranieri uses his full quota of changes, though his third one is unexpected: Huth for Babayaro. At the end, there is a handshake from Ranieri for Steve McClaren. Fascinating – had Eriksson accepted Chelsea's overtures, the Boro boss may well have arrived here as the Swede's assistant.

On Good Friday, as Arsenal trailed Liverpool 2-1, the Chelsea faithful were dreaming of being one point behind the Gunners. Now the gap is six and Arsenal have a game in hand as Boro become the sixth side this season to leave Stamford Bridge unbeaten – too many for championship contenders. Chelsea may have won eight out of nine Premiership matches before this one, but Arsenal have won ten and drawn one out of 11. That's consistency.

Yet, the dropped points do not dampen the feel-good factor around Stamford Bridge. Reaching the last four of the Champions League is something special. The fans still chant Ranieri's name. The party atmosphere continues in full swing.

Team

Ambrosio, Gallas, Terry, Desailly, Babayaro (Huth), Gronkjaer (Geremi), Lampard, Makelele (Veron), Cole, Hasselbaink, Gudjohnsen.

SUNDAY, 11 APRIL

Not everyone has sympathy with Ranieri's plight. Take Swindon goalkeeper Rhys Evans, once of Chelsea, who claims he was promised a new contract by Ranieri that didn't materialise. 'I am not Ranieri's number one fan. I wasn't too happy with the way he treated me when I was there. In fact I was pretty disgusted really. I don't think it takes a genius to pick a winning side at Chelsea with the squad they have.'

Sven-Goran Eriksson hints that Scott Parker can still make England's squad for Euro 2004. 'I am counting on John Terry, Frank Lampard, Wayne Bridge and probably Scott Parker.' Eriksson's reference to Parker could be bad news for Joe Cole, who is conspicuous by his absence from Eriksson's list of favoured Chelsea stars.

In Holland, Arjen Robben is carried off with a recurrence of a hamstring injury 17 minutes into his comeback for PSV but he is expected to make it to Euro 2004 and turn up at Chelsea fully fit next season.

Nearer home, Villa boss David O'Leary is awaiting the latest Ranieri team sheet with interest. 'We can all learn something from him. Claudio is a man of dignity and competence who just wants to get on and do his job right. There has been an enormous amount of speculation concerning his job and the way he has coped is remarkable.'

MONDAY, 12 APRIL

ASTON VILLA 3, CHELSEA 2

The feel-good factor surrounding Ranieri disappears along with any lingering hope of miraculously winning the title. When Kenyon catches sight of Ranieri in the dressing room, he merely shrugs his shoulders and moves on, according to eye-witness reports.

Ranieri makes eight changes but again defends himself against the charge that he has over-tinkered. Chelsea have not beaten Aston Villa on their home patch for five years, yet they start brightly and, after a long injury break for treatment to Huth's bloody nose, Bridge supplies the left-wing cross, Mutu steers a header against a post and Crespo collects his first goal in ten games – his tenth of the season.

Villa look about to crumble but get a break after 37 minutes when Melchiot inexplicably shoves Gareth Barry in the area under no pressure. Melchiot can only watch in dismay as Darius Vassell converts the spot-kick. The equaliser turns out to be the catalyst for a much-improved Villa show. But two goals in three second-half minutes exceed even the most optimistic expectation. Thomas Hitzlsperger eases away from Melchiot and buries a low shot past Ambrosio after 49 minutes. Then Jlloyd Samuel's 52nd-minute throw-in is touched on by Vassell for Lee Hendrie to finish.

Crespo scores a superb consolation goal three minutes into extra-time, curling a shot into the corner, but the travelling fans are mostly already on their way home. One point from the holiday programme leaves Chelsea seven behind Arsenal and watching Manchester United over their shoulders. Ranieri denies his players have been distracted by involvement in the Champions League. 'Our focus is very much on the league. Villa were better than us. And when your opponents are better than you, then you lose. Now is the start of a big challenge with Manchester United.'

> **Team**
>
> Ambrosio, Mutu (Cole), Lampard, Duff (Gronkjaer), Geremi, Melchiot (Gallas), Bridge, Parker, Crespo, Terry, Huth.

TUESDAY, 13 APRIL

Barcelona vice-president Sandro Rosell says he is worried Abramovich will swoop for Ronaldinho. Rosell, who deals with all Barça's transfers, says, 'I refuse to answer the question of whether we have received a bid for Ronaldinho. I have a degree of fear concerning Chelsea because, if it is true that Abramovich is willing to invest further hundreds of millions of pounds in the transfer market, then his aim will be to buy one of our best players. With Abramovich you know he has the money whereas with, say, Real Madrid you don't know it to the same degree. Barcelona remains a 'sick club' because we still owe £164m but I promise you we are imposing financial control and that we are on the road to recovery.'

Ronaldinho says: 'With his money, Abramovich can buy almost everything. I would prefer to make less money and not to live under as much pressure as the Chelsea players do. I had a chance to go to Manchester United last summer, rather than Chelsea, but as a team I don't like them. I would not turn my back on Barcelona for all the gold in the world, or the money in Abramovich's pockets. I like to live well and be in control. I am very happy here.'

Former superstar Diego Maradona believes Ronaldinho's 'speed with the ball at his feet, his tricks, his dead-ball skills and his speed of thought put him a little bit ahead of Ronaldo and Totti.' Peter Kenyon, then at Manchester United, spent most of last summer chasing Ronaldinho. Sir Alex has already blamed some of his side's failings this season on Kenyon's failure to sign him from Paris Saint-Germain.

Meanwhile, Jose Mourinho emerges as the key candidate to replace Ranieri. Porto president Pinto da Costa is aware of Chelsea's machinations. 'I know there are some clubs interested, but if anyone wants him they will have to wait another two years and hope to God that he does not renew his contract.'

Chelsea want to defer any definite decision on Ranieri's future until May, because, should the Italian coach win the Champions League, then there might have to be a hasty rethink. Wouldn't it fit neatly with the amazing events all season if Porto were to clash with Chelsea in the Champions League final!

WEDNESDAY, 14 APRIL

Kenyon rings Gary Straker to pass on a message to Ranieri that a midday meeting is now on after the papers again turn on the chief executive, accusing him of snubbing his coach. But a 40-minute meeting resolves nothing. 'Pissed off' is how Ranieri is feeling, according to insiders. A close associate tells me, 'The suspicion in Claudio's mind is that Abramovich and Kenyon have decided that, no matter what, they will sign a new coach.' Publicly both parties play down the significance of the meeting.

John Barnwell, head of the League Managers' Association, believes Ranieri could take Chelsea to an employment tribunal if he resigns over his treatment, arguing, 'Claudio has handled the situation with professionalism, massive dignity and some humour. But he has been put in an intolerable position and could have a case for constructive dismissal. Chelsea appear to be openly looking at other managers. If Claudio was looking for another job and doing the same thing, he would be sacked.' But Ranieri has no intention of resigning. As he says, he is not idiotic enough to walk out on a massive pay-off.

His time does seem to be up though, as Mourinho hints he is on the move. 'I would like the chance to manage in the Premiership. I have had several agents and third parties contact me from clubs and now we will see what happens. But the chance to coach a big club in England would be very attractive.'

The agenda switches to David Beckham – a neat move by Chelsea to deflect attention away from Ranieri. The capture of the England captain would be a spectacular coup for Abramovich and Kenyon and heal any perceived rift with the fans. Beckham insists he is happy in Madrid and intends to see out his four-year deal at the Bernabeu. Yet there are continuing, but unconfirmed, reports that he met Abramovich in a Madrid restaurant in the last week of February. The fact is that Florentino Perez faces a presidential challenge from millionaire entrepreneur Enrique Sobrino, a Madrid lawyer who heads a group of 18 influential Real members. Sobrino has one major promise in his manifesto: 'Beckham has to change. I would listen to offers for him.'

THURSDAY, 15 APRIL

Ron 'Chopper' Harris enjoys an unexpected audience with Abramovich, after an appearance on Chelsea TV. 'They asked me to wait in this plush office. I was gobsmacked when in walked Mr Abramovich. We spoke for about an hour and a half, through an interpreter, and he wanted to know all about my time at Chelsea.

'We also spoke about the current players and, although I'm not the manager and I'm not telling Claudio Ranieri how to do his job, he wanted to know who I thought were the best pairing up front. We both agreed it was Jimmy Floyd Hasselbaink and Eidur Gudjohnsen, who one season scored over 50 goals between them. We also talked about the size of the squad and how Damien Duff's been used. He gave me the impression he felt the side had chopped and changed too much. I asked him who he felt were Chelsea's best two players this season and he came up with the same names as me: John Terry and Frank Lampard, who have played regularly. He wanted to know my views on the rotation system. I told him it was all double Dutch to me. He seemed switched on. I was impressed. Chelsea supporters can look forward to a long period of success under him.'

Ranieri accepts an invitation to be the PFA's guest of honour at their annual awards night.

FRIDAY, 16 APRIL

Three hundred Russian tycoons will watch the Everton game as guests of Abramovich. The businessmen, bankers and politicians have paid up to £575 each for their visit. They will meet Chelsea's owner while in Britain for a top-level economic conference. The organisers of the conference, the Russian Economic Forum, have paid for two suites in Chelsea's Millennium Stand.

Ranieri apologises for his late arrival at the media conference at the training ground with a disarming smile and jokes, 'I'm a busy man – too many meetings!' Ranieri refers to Rudyard Kipling's stirring 1910 poem, 'If', which advises you to treat defeat and victory the same and to 'keep your head when all about you are losing theirs'. He could still be about to lose his. 'All Englishmen know the poem by Rudyard Kipling. I read this poem when I was young and the words are so true. In England there is stress. But if you go out and give everything and don't win, the fans say, "Don't worry, next week we will do better." In Italy if you draw or lose they say, "Don't worry," and then they stone you. It's a different philosophy.

'I am still in love with English football despite everything that has happened this year and it will always be that way. I want to stay in this country.'

Next up in the Premiership are Everton and their manager David Moyes knows Chelsea are probably the only club in England that could afford Wayne Rooney, but they aren't selling and Chelsea appear to have lost interest.

SATURDAY, 17 APRIL

CHELSEA 0, EVERTON 0

Top managers Louis van Gaal, Sven-Goran Eriksson and Didier Deschamps are all in the VIP seats. It is assumed Van Gaal is a candidate to replace Ranieri particularly as he is pictured next to Peter Kenyon. But the Ajax director of football is actually there to negotiate a feeder-club link and advise Kenyon on academy issues. Kenyon wants Chelsea to have a similar system to Ajax.

Chelsea enjoy most of the play yet Rooney curls a superb free-kick around the wall, forcing Ambrosio into a flying save. Parker picks out Lampard in the middle, he drags the ball under control before sweeping in a right-foot shot that beats Nigel Martyn but hits the bar and bounces over. When Gallas limps off after 24 minutes with a hamstring injury Ranieri is forced to reshuffle his team. It is a big worry for Tuesday's game against Monaco.

Chelsea fail to clear a long ball into the box and Rooney finds himself free in front of goal. He unleashes a quick-fire shot but Ambrosio saves the day by throwing out his right leg to make a terrific block. Everton are roaring for a penalty in the 40th minute when Tomasz Radzinski goes flying after competing with Huth. Referee Graham Poll is not impressed. In fact, he penalises Radzinski for pulling Huth. And TV replays prove the match official is spot-on.

With 10 minutes to go, Hasselbaink thinks he has created Chelsea's winner with a cross to the unmarked Mutu. But astonishingly the Romanian heads wide. Story of his season. The fans have been vocal in backing their manager, but the Tinkerman's decision to replace the impressive Parker and Cole with Gronkjaer and Filipe Oliveira when the team are chasing a late winner is greeted with a chorus of boos.

After Manchester United's lunchtime defeat at Portsmouth, this is yet another wasted opportunity. Monaco manager Deschamps, who leaves five minutes from the end, will fancy his side's chances if Chelsea play like this, as they end the Easter week with a defeat and two draws. But Ranieri says, 'The Monaco game will be really different.'

Team

Ambrosio, Gallas (Melchiot), Desailly, Huth, Bridge, Geremi, Parker (Oliveira), Lampard, Cole (Gronkjaer), Mutu, Hasselbaink.

SUNDAY, 18 APRIL

Abramovich is named the wealthiest man in Britain, with an estimated fortune of £7.5bn. He heads the *Sunday Times* Rich List of the 1,000 wealthiest people in Britain. Abramovich is the sixth-richest person in Europe and the 22nd-richest in the world. In the UK, he has knocked the Duke of Westminster off top position.

One of football's enduring friendships began in a hostel for aspiring young footballers in Nantes. 'He had these patchwork jeans, and roll-necked jumpers, knitted by his mother,' as Marcel Desailly remembers it. They were both 15, Desailly the older by five weeks. Even then, recalls Desailly, Didier Deschamps had 'this great maturity'. So they went on, colleagues as juniors, seniors, internationals, always room-mates. Now, one of them will make the final. Again. Of the 12 European Cup finals from 1993 to 2004, Deschamps or Desailly, or both, will have been involved in eight.

Does Didier Deschamps expect Monaco to defeat Claudio Ranieri's men? 'I respect Chelsea,' Deschamps says, 'but we have no reason to fear them. There will not be a favourite for the tie and it is wide open now. It will be a special evening when I go back to Stamford Bridge.'

MONDAY, 19 APRIL

Chelsea depart for Monaco and Ranieri knows they cannot be underestimated. 'Only a good team would beat Deportivo La Coruna 8–3 and then Real Madrid in the quarter-finals,' he says, 'and that is what Monaco have done.'

Ranieri decides his team after a training session in the Stade Louis II, but he is already without Duff and Gallas who failed to travel because they both have a fever. Gudjohnsen and Crespo will spearhead the attack; Hasselbaink is left out, while Mutu is suffering from an alarming dip in form and confidence. Deschamps has been getting tips on how to beat Chelsea from his former Stamford Bridge club-mate Frank Leboeuf, now playing in Qatar, who says, 'I have told Didier he has to watch out most for Gudjohnsen and Lampard.'

Meanwhile Cudicini will fly on from Monaco to Paris tomorrow morning to have the wires removed from his hand which were inserted to immobilise a broken bone. If there are no complications, Cudicini is due to resume full training and could be back in time for the second leg.

Monaco's Louis II stadium could give the hosts a major advantage, as Petit warns, because it is so compact. He developed a special affinity with the Monaco supporters during his 12 years there. 'Monaco's population is about 40,000 and there are hundreds of fans who follow the team every week. We used to say that at bigger clubs all the fans know the names of the players. At Monaco, it is the players who know the fans! When there was a break in play for an injury or something I used to see people I knew in the crowd. We would sometimes talk and arrange to meet up later! But although the stadium only holds about 20,000 people, they can create a good atmosphere.'

Now is the time for the big name imports to deliver. Their records are scrutinised. Veron: 12 games, 2 goals, 4 yellow cards; Crespo: 28 games, 9 goals, 1 yellow card; and Makelele: 41 games, 0 goals, 6 yellow cards, 1 red card.

Ranieri continues to back them all, even Veron, 'the Little Witch', now taunted 'because he only plays in spells'. Ranieri says, 'Veron is in good shape. He could play in any country. He's an amazing player but of course I need him 100 per cent fit.'

Marcel Desailly has the opportunity to become only the second man, after Clarence Seedorf, to win the European Cup with three different clubs. Desailly has been talking tactics with Deschamps. 'Yes, we talk quite often. He has played in France, Italy and England and has moulded the collective cultures of these three countries into his Monaco team. He has given them confidence. He now has four big players and the rest are young. He has them playing as a team. It will be a big mistake if, because we are playing Monaco, we think we are already in the final.'

Ranieri is tipped off that Abramovich and Kenyon have travelled to Vigo in Spain for talks with Jose Mourinho's representative. Mourinho, himself preparing for the Champions League semi-finals, backs out of the meeting at the last minute. Mourinho leaves his side of the negotiating to Portuguese agent Jorge Mendes. The visit lasts seven hours before Chelsea's power-brokers arrive in Nice at 7.00pm. That leaves time for talks with another agent Paulo Barbosa about £8m-rated Deportivo centre-half Jorge Andrade.

Mourinho is suddenly Europe's most wanted manager after winning the Treble of the Portuguese league and cup plus the UEFA Cup last season, and taking Porto to the last four of the Champions League this. He is on Real's wanted list, which is why Chelsea so desperately want to ensure they tie up his services. A fluent English speaker and former assistant to Bobby Robson at Barcelona, Mourinho would have no difficulties settling in London. Porto president Pinto da Costa is fuming after learning about Abramovich's bid, but Ranieri is pretty cut up about it too on the eve of such a vital tie.

More eve-of-game headaches as Spanish newspaper *Marca* publishes a Q&A interview in which Ranieri says Abramovich knows nothing about football. Ranieri is quoted as saying, 'Ever since he arrived at the club Abramovich wanted Eriksson. From the very start! They even met in the summer. But Eriksson said he couldn't leave the England team and so the next day Abramovich met me and told me, "Okay, you've done a good job these last few years and you are going to carry on, and take them into the Champions League."'

Ranieri also says that even victory in the final will not save him. 'Look, I already have the Abramovich sword embedded in me. I'm convinced that even if I win the Champions League I will be sacked. Abramovich knows nothing about football. That's the real shame. If he had understood what my side had achieved that season he would have valued me more highly. We did it all without any money.'

He also accuses Abramovich of having no appreciation of how difficult it was going to be to make the team gel. 'It was a very tough job to sign so many players and get them to play together. Abramovich didn't realise that. He thought I'll sign that one and that one and then we will win. Since he arrived he has signed 11 players, it's crazy. Moreover, Abramovich's people are not yet convinced about me and for this the public are on my side, but I haven't had any time to digest it all, I have only had time to work, work and work.'

Having been interviewed on 8 April, Ranieri is shocked at the timing of the publication and feels his words have been grossly misinterpreted. One wonders.

TUESDAY, 20 APRIL

MONACO 3, CHELSEA 1

Abramovich plays host to Ranieri and the players aboard his yacht moored in Monte Carlo harbour in the afternoon, but Ranieri is all at sea with his substitutions on the night, his reputation sinking to an all-time low.

The small group of Chelsea fans in the stadium are determined to make themselves heard. They chant, 'Are you watching Arsenal?' But it ends up a big let-down with Ranieri's status nose-diving from its recent dizzy heights. Ranieri has been trying out Veron on the left in training but plumps for Gronkjaer in the absence of Duff. He wants the Dane to get at the opposition early on and try to rattle them.

Instead his team are the ones rattled from the start. Jerome Rothen gets away down the left, Melchiot takes him out with a scything challenge and the full-back cannot argue about the yellow card. Monaco score from the 17th-minute free-kick. Rothen whips the ball in, Crespo tries to clear but misses with an elaborate diving header and, as the ball bounces, Dado Prso climbs above Melchiot to head firmly into the top-left corner.

Within five minutes, Lampard fools the defence with a delightful ball over the top and Parker collects on the right. He plays it in to Gudjohnsen, who falls over but manages to push the ball on to Crespo, who shoots low into the bottom corner from eight yards. Crespo is there again to meet Lampard's cross minutes later but, at full stretch, he puts the ball just over the bar. Chelsea are in the groove, with Lampard pulling all the strings, and Crespo proving a point. But Ranieri's tinkering from the start of the second half costs them a winning position.

Ranieri hauls off Gronkjaer at half-time and replaces him with Veron; it is a hopelessly wrong decision. It gets worse. Fernando Morientes is fuming when he goes down in the box, having been elbowed in the face by Desailly off the ball and told simply to get up by the referee. Julien Rodriguez has a header well saved by Ambrosio and, seconds later, Morientes produces a bicycle kick which Desailly manages to hack off the line.

Then there's a turning point, which should be in Chelsea's favour but ends up being an advantage for Monaco. After 52 minutes, Makelele holds off Zikos, allowing Ambrosio to slide out to collect. Makelele touches his opponent on the side of the face; Zikos reacts by slapping him gently on the top of the head. Makelele has time to glance around for a split-second before going down theatrically. Referee Urs Meier is straight out with the red card and, to Monaco's fury, Chelsea instantly look like getting a second. Gudjohnsen is denied by the legs of the keeper and also puts a free header over the top from Veron's corner.

Sensing more goals, Ranieri gets all excited, takes off defender Melchiot, and replaces him with Hasselbaink. Puzzlingly, Huth is sent on for Parker. The 10 men of Monaco subsequently seize two goals through Morientes in the 78th minute and substitute Shabani Nonda on 83 minutes. Hasselbaink fluffs a headed chance at the far post from Bridge's cross, the keeper plays the ball out swiftly and Morientes races away down the right to smash a half-volley beyond the despairing Ambrosio. Substitute Nonda scores at the near post but Ambrosio helps it in.

Ranieri confesses that his players lost the plot in the last 15 minutes. But what exactly is the plot? No one knows from the moment Veron comes on. Deschamps says that coaches get ten per cent of the credit when their team wins and 90 per cent of the blame when it loses. Ranieri gets 100 per cent of the blame on this occasion. Makelele is suspended for the second leg after being booked for his part in the bust-up with Zikos. Desailly will also be punished after TV cameras capture his elbow on Morientes.

The Russian billionaire invites Ranieri on to his yacht, *Le Grand Bleu*, to discuss the game. Ranieri declines and tells Abramovich he is going back to the hotel to talk with his team. But the manager has little to say as the players discuss reasons for the defeat.

Team

Ambrosio, Bridge, Terry, Desailly, Melchiot (Hasselbaink), Lampard, Makelele, Parker (Huth), Gronkjaer (Veron), Gudjohnsen, Crespo.

WEDNESDAY, 21 APRIL

There is no mistaking the discontent now within the dressing room. As one international makes plain, 'Claudio makes a complete cock-up.' Texts from others are even more derogatory. 'What a dickhead' reads one message back home.

Abramovich, who was cheered by the fans in the stadium, is said to have endured a sleepless night. He had tears in his eyes as he walked across the pitch for a post-match meeting with Ranieri but recovered his composure by the time he entered the dressing room. Abramovich returned to his yacht for an informal gathering with friends but after they had left he found himself unable to sleep. So at 2.00am he went to the team hotel, La Port Palace, for a meeting with Kenyon, Bruce Buck and Eugene Shvidler. Abramovich had a drink in the hotel bar and discussed the match with several players, including Hasselbaink, Lampard and Desailly, before returning to his yacht in the small hours.

Ranieri jokes, 'It's not true that he was crying. Roman Abramovich was a fantastic man after the defeat. He invited me on to his yacht – because he wanted to use me as his anchor!'

The fall-out for Ranieri is devastating. One star demanded, 'What the fuck was that all about?' in an otherwise silent dressing room after the match. Ranieri did not respond and stood with his head bowed. When Ranieri told Veron at half-time to replace the ineffective Gronkjaer, Veron said he was not fit to take part in such an important match after five months out injured. Ranieri shocked his players by instructing Veron to play left-side midfield. It was the first in a series of tactical mistakes. His blunders leave even his staunchest supporters in the squad questioning whether he is still the right man for the job. 'Inept' is how the hierarchy describe the coach's performance.

Hasselbaink confesses, 'I don't think a single one of us slept on Tuesday night. We are all disgusted about what happened. We can't believe it. It is a massive missed opportunity and everybody is feeling shit. Roman Abramovich spoke to us after the game and what he said is private. But he felt the defeat just like us. I bet he feels as shit as we do. Maybe we feel a little bit worse, because it really was the chance of a lifetime.'

Terry is determined to remain upbeat. 'It's only half-time and we're not out of it yet – not by a long way. There were some big comebacks in the quarter-finals and that gives us inspiration. When we get them back to Stamford Bridge, with the support of our own fans behind us, anything is still possible.'

But team spirit is dipping as some stars get the vibes they will not be wanted for next season. Crespo, Veron, Makelele, Desailly, Gronkjaer, Hasselbaink and Melchiot are among those earmarked for the exit door according to relentless media speculation.

Perhaps Ranieri suffered a brainstorm during the game because he was under so much stress. He had to prepare for the biggest game of his career and Chelsea's history dogged by a series of distractions. Ranieri was tipped off that Abramovich and Kenyon had travelled to Vigo before the game for talks to recruit Jose Mourinho. To find out 24 hours before the semi-final that talks are going on face to face, if only with Mourinho's Portuguese agent, must have affected him even though he will deny it. Could he truly be totally focused on the game?

Jon Smith tells me, 'Claudio was very emotional when he found out the day before the game, perhaps more emotional than I have ever seen. It would be fair to say he was disturbed. Word had got out in Spain and Italy and he had been told. He said he would try to remain focused on the game, on the football, and despite what occurred in the match he had no intention of using those talks as an excuse. But of course it affected him, how could it not?'

Porto complain to FIFA about Chelsea 'tapping up' Mourinho. Kenyon is asked if Mourinho has been offered Ranieri's job. He laughs, before adding, 'We were in Spain. We do a lot of things. Have Porto complained? Why would they complain? You are telling me that – but I don't know that it has happened.'

The Chelsea hierarchy launch an 'internal security review' aimed at stopping details leaking out of Abramovich's movements as he and Kenyon are perturbed at how the paper discovered their whereabouts and travel details.

Manchester United closed the gap to one point with a 2–0 win over Charlton on Tuesday but Kenyon is determined to finish above his old club. Finishing second would guarantee the group stages of next season's Champions League and is worth £3m in prize money alone. Kenyon says, 'We've got a massive game against Newcastle on Sunday and have it all to do.'

THURSDAY, 22 APRIL

Pundit Ron Atkinson resigns from ITV Sport after calling Desailly a 'fucking lazy, big, thick nigger' in what Big Ron assumed was an off-air conversation with fellow commentator Clive Tyldesley during the Monaco game. But several countries in the Middle East, including Egypt and Dubai, were still receiving the ITV feed. A spokesman for ITV Sport says there is little option but to accept Atkinson's resignation.

Meanwhile, Roy Bentley, star of the 1955 championship-winning side, is critical of Makelele's dive to get Zikos sent off. 'When players dive it makes me sick. They're cheats. Makelele's dive was pretty blatant, Zikos tickled him under the chin and he went down straight away. We had one or two players who tried it on in my day but, if one of my team-mates cheated to win a penalty, I felt very rough about it. I don't like to see it and there's no credit winning games like that.'

Supporters have finally had enough of Ranieri's tinkering. A fan writes on the club's official website: 'I've really tried to be supportive of our manager over the past few years. But Monaco is the last straw. It proves he is just not good enough to manage at the top level. The team changes were an embarrassment.' Another says, 'Ranieri has been exposed for what he is – a bloke trying his best but tactically inept at this level. He has got away with his tinkering in some games and been lucky.' The criticism continues: 'Maybe now the 'Keep Ranieri' brigade will shut up. I was in Monaco and the second half was embarrassing.'

Frank Lampard's demands for pay parity with his celebrated overseas team-mates stall after the fourth meeting between the parties in London. Steve Kutner, Lampard's agent, confirms, 'The ball's in Chelsea's court. We would like to get it done. If Frank had his way he would sign a long-term contract and stay at Chelsea. Inter love him. They think he's great.'

For their part, Inter have targeted Veron and Roma's Emerson, although Inter believe Emerson is on his way to Stamford Bridge in a £15m deal. The Brazilian plays the same central role as Lampard, but his arrival could throw Makelele's future into doubt more than the Englishman's.

FRIDAY, 23 APRIL

Claudio Ranieri borrows a line from Ol' Blue Eyes. 'I did it my way, just like Frank Sinatra. I cannot change my ways now. If I do not tinker then people will have nothing to write about. I learn lessons from every defeat and, yes, it was all my fault but you cannot always win. I told the players everything I did in the Monaco game was wrong. I changed things to win the match – but we lost and I was thinking, "Oh fuck, Claudio, why, why? Bad Tinkerman!"

'There were specific reasons why I made certain decisions. The lads were telling me, "We can win this; we can beat these guys tonight!" But Monaco were well organised defensively and I felt that we needed something different to break them down. Hugo Ibarra, their right-back, was having an excellent game against Jesper Gronkjaer. Gronkjaer's strength is running at people and creating width, but, on this night, Ibarra was shutting him down. So I replaced him with Juan Sebastian Veron.

'Veron is a different sort of player from Gronkjaer. He is capable of providing the defence-splitting pass and creating chances from deeper positions. I thought that, by putting him in, Ibarra would have to adjust to a different type of threat and this could cause Monaco problems. He needs ten more days' training to improve his stamina. It was a mistake to play him. Every change was made for the right reasons. But when you lose a game no one is interested in that.

'The sending-off of Akis Zikos a few minutes later changed the game. All of a sudden we had the man advantage, and it felt as if the pendulum had swung in our direction. That's when I made the decision to go for it, to try to close out the tie that night. I thought that by sending on another striker we could pin them back and create the chance for a winning goal. Yes, it was a gamble, but a calculated risk. I had two strikers on the bench, Jimmy Floyd Hasselbaink and Adrian Mutu. I picked Hasselbaink because Mutu was not 100 per cent fit and I thought that, by playing him on the right of the front three, he could use his superior physical presence against Patrice Evra, their left-back, who is small and quick. Of course, this meant I had to take somebody off. It was not an easy choice, but the logical candidate to me seemed to be Mario Melchiot. I knew that Scott Parker had the intelligence and versatility to fill in as an emergency right-back and I was a little concerned because Melchiot had already been booked, and I could tell the referee was watching him closely.

'The plan worked for a while. We created two good chances for Hasselbaink and he was unlucky not to score. But Parker was struggling. I wasn't sure if it was a muscular problem or if he had picked up a knock, but he was not 100 per cent. With William Gallas and Glen Johnson injured, I had to ask Robert Huth, a central defender, to come on at right-back.

'I don't need to remind anybody that Monaco scored twice in the last 12 minutes. My strategy had backfired. We spent too much time on the ball, everybody tried to do too much and they took advantage. That's football. You make a decision, you formulate a strategy and everything can go wrong.'

Ken Bates targets his arch-foe Pini Zahavi over the Veron deal. 'A £16m transfer fee, five per cent levy to the Premiership, £20m wages over four years, bonuses, 13 per cent National Insurance contributions plus £2m or so as Pini Zahavi's cut. Something tells me there may have been a few medical expenses as well. And what have they got in return? A player who has made just nine starts this season. From his attitude on the pitch against Monaco you got the impression he wasn't interested. It is also perfectly reasonable to ask just how he passed his medical. If indeed he did. Further, is it true that, at the time, doubts were voiced within the club about his fitness? And that they were overruled from above?

'I raised my own doubts when I heard he was coming. He was a bloody disaster at United and I firmly believed the club didn't need him. In fact, former chief executive Trevor Birch held the deal up as he tried to talk Roman Abramovich and his advisors out of it. Well, chickens came home to roost. And turkeys. Okay, Claudio Ranieri cocked up by playing Veron. But even if he wasn't fully fit, he could have still pulled his finger out. There is no doubt the decision to send him on after the break cost us the game. He didn't make one tackle, he hardly completed a pass, he gave the ball away and he got caught in possession. Money can buy you success, but only if you buy wisely over a period of time. To go out and spend £120m on 11 or so players, though, is bloody madness. Before the revolution, we brought players in slowly and helped them adapt.

'As for Claudio, I find it strange that when he beat Arsenal he was acclaimed one of the best managers in the world. We lose to Monaco and, suddenly, he has to go. When you are under pressure – as he has been all season – you make mistakes. Okay, he didn't call it right against Monaco but there were enough internationals to sort it out themselves.'

Marcel Desailly's future is under threat as Argentina centre-half Walter Samuel admits he wants to leave Roma for Chelsea. UEFA find Desailly guilty of violent conduct, while Makelele escapes with a warning. Desailly will now sit out the second leg and the final – if the Blues get through. UEFA are also unhappy with

Makelele. Their spokesman says, 'We noted the unsporting behaviour and provocative attitude of Makelele, who dived and feigned injury after the incident.'

Enrique de Lucas is suing for £2.78m in lost earnings. De Lucas was the only close-season signing the year before Abramovich's takeover, but despite mounting debts at the time he was still handed a generous pay packet. Manchester United offer a new contract to Rio Ferdinand to fend off growing interest from Chelsea. Ferguson's willingness to secure Ferdinand's future stems from the knowledge that Zahavi also has close ties with Abramovich as well as Kenyon, and that, along with Real Madrid, they are probably the only club in Europe with the riches to prise him away from Old Trafford.

SATURDAY, 24 APRIL

Confusion or Confucius? Ranieri says, 'I have been through worse, this is nothing. I am a lucky man because I love this job. My relaxation is football. I was reading Confucius a few days ago and he says something along the lines of, "The man who works and loves his job, is not working at all." Why would I want to remember my bad moments? It's like racing drivers – if they crash, they get straight back into their car and race again. That's what I do in football. I continue to work. I am not an actor. If I'm angry you know it by my face. If I'm happy you will see me smile. I am smiling right now. There are always bad moments, but being at Chelsea now is a great moment for me.

'Ninety-nine per cent of people expected Chelsea to get to the Champions League final and maybe 70 per cent expected us to win the whole thing. But I kept saying that there was only a 20 per cent chance that we would do so. I was talking into the wind. I am always optimistic, but I still say that we only have a 20 per cent chance of winning. We must produce our best performance, and they must produce their worst.'

But has Ranieri lost his team? The growing fear among senior Stamford Bridge personnel is that he no longer commands the respect of key players.

SUNDAY, 25 APRIL

NEWCASTLE 2, CHELSEA 1

Alan Shearer finally ends Chelsea's lingering title dreams with a stunning winner that keeps the Toon in the chase for the fourth Champions League spot, and Arsenal finish the job with a draw at White Hart Lane to be crowned champions.

It has been a terrible two weeks for Ranieri – they have not won for five games. Ranieri makes only two changes, Gronkjaer and Parker making way for Cole and Geremi. Cole puts them ahead after just five minutes, latching on to

Lampard's brilliant through-ball to toe-poke the ball through Given's legs. It is Cole's first Premiership goal for Chelsea. He then has the chance to wrap it up; once again he is put clear in the inside-left channel by Gudjohnsen but after cutting on to his right foot he fires well wide.

Shola Ameobi changes the game two minutes before the break, turning Desailly and drilling an unstoppable drive past the despairing Ambrosio. Then comes the stunning winner. Picking the ball up 25 yards out, Shearer holds off Desailly before turning and hammering home an unstoppable shot. Desailly is substituted after being over-powered by Shearer for the winner. Terry hits the post in the last minute when it looks easier to score from four yards. Then substitute Robert Huth treads on Shearer in a very delicate place a couple of minutes from time and Shearer is in agony. Huth, already booked, is fortunate not be sent off. Hasselbaink, who blatantly kicks Bernard as he sprints past with the ball 15 yards away, is lucky not to see red too.

Ranieri says, 'I was very pleased with the reaction of the players after the Monaco defeat. We deserved a point, but if we had stayed out there for another two hours I do not think we would have scored. We have a few days now to get together and we need a change of luck because without luck you cannot do a thing.'

Team

Ambrosio, Melchiot, Desailly (Huth), Terry, Bridge, Geremi, Makelele, Lampard, Cole, Gudjohnsen, Crespo (Hasselbaink).

Thierry Henry is named PFA Player of the Year and Scott Parker is Young Player of the Year, beating John Terry to the honour. Ranieri presents the award to Henry, who says, 'I remember everyone saying at the start of the season that we wouldn't be able to do anything as we were down and Chelsea had bought a lot of players and United were as strong as ever, but when you give stick to Arsenal, we always answer.' He points out that Chelsea are 10 points better off and United four superior than this time last season, a measure of Arsenal's remarkable unbeaten run to the championship.

MONDAY, 26 APRIL

Ranieri publicly announces the club's interest in Ronaldo and Beckham. Ranieri has not only lost patience but also the art of discretion in an interview with *Tuttosport*, the Turin newspaper. 'There is only one person in the world who can try to take them from Florentino Perez and he is called Roman Abramovich.'

Real are angry at losing out on Roma's centre-back Walter Samuel to

Chelsea. Perez thought the transfer was in the bag after offering the centre-half £40,000 a week. But Chelsea soon doubled that. Another of the many names that the London club have been linked with is the exciting young Spanish international Joaquin. Normally, a player of his promise would be guaranteed to be snapped up by either Real or Barça. Not any more. Even though a deal has yet to be done for Beckham, the Spanish press are treating a transfer as inevitable, and the Madrid interest in Ruud van Nistelrooy has come about because the club want Ronaldo to leave. Barcelona are paranoid they will lose Ronaldinho and president Joan Laporta as good as admits that their only defence against Chelsea is to persuade the player he could get lost amid the Stamford Bridge All-Stars.

Chelsea are still considering selling Mutu because of his poor recent form. Reports that Kenyon has been made aware that Mutu is unpopular with the rest of the players because of his surly attitude are denied. Mutu protests that he counts Hasselbaink, Melchiot and Terry as close friends and has been invited on holiday with Desailly this summer.

Mikael Forssell agrees to stay on loan for a further year at Birmingham. His 17 goals in 30 Premiership games have kept Bruce's side in contention for a place in Europe. Birmingham will pay another £500,000, the same loan fee as for this season, and Kenyon remarks, 'Mikael has improved so much this season with constant games. At this stage of his career, the club felt it was best for him to continue getting that experience.'

TUESDAY, 27 APRIL

Jose Mourinho asks his assistant Baltemar Brito and goalkeeping coach Silvino Louro to follow him to Chelsea. Mourinho breaks the news to his two pals in an Oporto restaurant as they celebrate winning a second consecutive Portuguese title. Porto accuse Chelsea of illegally approaching Mourinho, threatening an official complaint to UEFA. Yet, Porto are already sounding out Real coach Carlos Queiroz as Mourinho's replacement.

Porto president Pinto da Costa is demanding £2m in compensation, 'I want to make it clear that we will go to war with Chelsea over Mourinho. We will bring in UEFA, FIFA – whoever we need to. The attitude of the Russian is the worst I have seen in the football world. He thinks that, after buying Chelsea, he can do what he wants and skip all the established rules.

'I have spoken with other European clubs and they are also fed up with the style of Abramovich since he arrived at the club. Mourinho has two years left on his contract and I know that he is an honest and professional person. Chelsea are putting him in an uncomfortable position. I will continue to trust him that he will fulfil what he has signed with us.'

At Chelsea, Mourinho wants the final say over signings and developmental policy, which Ranieri has either been denied or deliberately not sought. He is comfortable with the media, multilingual, with a naturally communicative style. He will come down heavily on those who anger him in the media and, as employees of Porto will testify, he is not the sort to be silenced if he wants his say.

His transfer dealings at Porto provide a stark contrast with recent happenings at Chelsea where inflated fees have become the norm. Mourinho has proved himself in the market by buying low and transforming a succession of players into multi-million-pound transfer market commodities. Benni McCarthy, Carlos Alberto, Derlei, Paulo Ferreira and Maciel have all benefited from a Mourinho makeover. He is also a stickler for discipline, ensuring that players know exactly what is expected.

Ranieri accepts the inevitable parting of the ways with Chelsea. 'I've never spoken about it before because of the respect towards those who pay me. Sure, it's difficult thinking I will stay with Chelsea, so I'm thinking about what I'll be doing next year.'

Chelsea appeal to UEFA over the three-match ban on Desailly. They will find out on Friday if they can include him for the second leg. Huth faces trial by video over his stamp on Shearer. The FA's compliance unit decide not to take the matter further after referee Rob Styles confirms he had seen the incident.

WEDNESDAY, 28 APRIL

Didier Deschamps is said to be in the frame for Ranieri's job... not a day goes by without Chelsea dominating the media agenda and most of it is pure speculation.

Chelsea are negotiating to secure first option to sign Belgian wonderkid Vincent Kompany in a year's time. The Anderlecht centre-back has attracted interest from Arsenal, Manchester United and Internazionale, but Chelsea are first in line. Abramovich will pay a seven-figure option. Manchester United want Kompany and, in a repeat of the Robben capture, Peter Kenyon is delighted to put one over on his former club.

Although it appears a huge risk to shell out such a vast sum for the right to buy a teenager with less than 50 career appearances, such deals are becoming increasingly common. Kenyon has stated that the club's transfer policy is based on securing the best young players from home and abroad.

Kompany made his debut in a Champions League qualifying game in July but has quickly established himself as a first-team regular. He became Belgium's second-youngest international in February's friendly defeat to France. The son of a Congolese father and a Belgian mother, Kompany has been described as the 'Belgian Desailly'.

THURSDAY, 29 APRIL

Damien Duff suffers a second dislocation of his shoulder after a training-ground collision with Glen Johnson. He has just returned to full training after a virus. Duff will miss the remaining three Premiership games along with the second leg against Monaco.

FRIDAY, 30 APRIL

Ranieri knows his days are numbered and accepts the inevitable. 'Maybe the pressure is less now. The pressure started for me on 3 July, when Roman Abramovich bought the club. I want to do a good job until the end. I believe I have done that and it is very important to me. I have not written my will yet. I am the dead man walking but also the dead man working. Please wait a little longer before deciding I will be leaving Chelsea without a trophy. I am very focused on the Champions League. I still want to achieve my maximum.

'Now there is only two weeks to the end of the season and all the pressure will be over. After that, we will see what happens. My Chelsea career could finish or I could continue. Nothing would surprise me. But whatever Mr Abramovich decides, I will know very well I have given my best. I can look in the mirror and know that I have done a good job for Chelsea. And that is very important for me.'

Chelsea are seeking to end a run of five matches without a win. Ranieri says, 'There is a big challenge between us and Manchester United and I hope to win.' Real indicate that, if they do sell David Beckham, they will drive an extremely hard bargain, while Chelsea have earmarked 'around £20m' for the fee. A stand-off is pending. Wenger admits he would be interested if the England captain decided to return to London, but simply cannot compete with the spending power of rivals Chelsea.

Desailly's European ban is reduced from three games to two by UEFA's appeals body as 'Desailly did not commit an act of deliberate assault.' He still misses the second leg and the final should they get there. However, Ranieri receives a small ray of hope as Monaco suffer a double injury scare in a 2–1 win over Nice. Rothen has hurt his groin and Prso has injured a foot.

Ranieri has failed to win a significant trophy in his managerial career, let alone his four years at Stamford Bridge but he is not giving up yet. 'Just wait. I can wait. I know it is difficult but I am still positive. All I have on my mind right now is Southampton. We need to beat them because it would be a very good three points which we need to give us a little more confidence. That is never bad.'

May

THE CHAMPIONS LEAGUE DREAM – SO NEAR AND YET SO FAR

Chelsea's interest in David Beckham dominates the front and back pages. Other spectacular transfer coups are mooted, involving the likes of Ronaldinho, Spanish football's outstanding player in his debut Primera Liga campaign. Speaking at a business lunch in the Catalan capital, Barcelona vice-president Sandro Rosell admits, 'The club and the player have made it very clear that they must continue together. We have to fight to keep the player but if someone comes in with the money to pay his transfer clause (€100m – £60m), then it will be a personal decision. From a business point of view, perhaps the decision would be different but I believe he must stay. He has surprised us all and I believe that, without any doubt, he is the best player in the world.'

It looks increasingly likely that Real will sell some of their *galacticos* – one

PREMIERSHIP TABLE – MAY								
Pos Team	P	W	D	L	GF	GA	GD	PTS
1 Arsenal	34	24	10	0	69	24	45	82
2 Chelsea	35	22	6	7	61	29	32	72
3 Manchester United	35	22	5	8	61	33	28	71
4 Liverpool	35	14	11	10	49	36	13	53
5 Newcastle United	34	13	14	7	47	34	13	53
6 Aston Villa	35	14	10	11	46	41	5	52
7 Fulham	35	13	9	13	49	44	5	48
8 Charlton Athletic	35	13	9	13	44	45	-1	48
9 Birmingham City	35	12	12	11	42	44	-2	48
10 Bolton Wanderers	35	12	11	12	42	52	-10	47

or more of Ronaldo, Luis Figo and Beckham – to raise the money to table a bid for their new signings. But Chelsea dismiss reports they are interested in signing Ronaldo either separately or as part of the Beckham deal.

As Chelsea prepare for the biggest game in their history, deep feelings of hurt linger on at Highbury. Freddie Ljungberg confesses, 'I'm really, really happy that we won the Championship and we're unbeaten in the league which is really good, but then I think all of the players are a bit down because of the Champions League. It's not every year that you have that chance, and to get beaten like that by Chelsea still hurts. I watched the game between Monaco and Chelsea and you're left thinking, "We had a big chance." That's life sometimes, but it still hurts.'

SATURDAY, 1 MAY

CHELSEA 4, SOUTHAMPTON 0

Monaco coach Didier Deschamps doesn't bother showing up to watch as Ranieri selects both Cole and Gronkjaer and leaves Crespo and Veron on the bench as he tests out the formation for Monaco. With this win, Chelsea hit 75 points to equal their highest-ever Premiership total as Southampton are handed their biggest defeat of the season. The home team also pull further clear of Manchester United, beaten at Ewood Park. They can now afford to lose at Old Trafford and still finish second for automatic qualification to the Champions League. But a point at Manchester United will confirm them in second place.

The game turns when Terry's headed back pass is woefully underpowered and Kevin Phillips is on it like a flash, but weakly clips a shot which Cudicini catches comfortably. Chelsea immediately break and win a corner. Gronkjaer's delivery is aimed towards Gudjohnsen at the near post, but young Saints debutant Martin Crainey heads past Antti Niemi's despairing dive. An own goal is Chelsea's first score in three games at the Bridge since Hasselbaink's hat-trick against Wolves back in March. As the Blues celebrate, the teenager is withdrawn.

Next Hasselbaink squeezes a pass through to Gudjohnsen and, although his shot is blocked, the ball falls kindly to Lampard, who strikes the rebound on the run. He poaches his second goal when Hasselbaink's cross-shot is punched right to his feet. Ranieri throws on Veron ten minutes from time but the Chelsea faithful clearly haven't forgotten his contribution in Monte Carlo. The boos that greet his arrival are unmistakeable.

Glen Johnson, on as a sub for Gronkjaer in midfield, finishes the Saints off with a late strike, marking his return from an injury lay-off by side-footing into the corner after more good work from Gudjohnsen. With Makelele suspended, Duff out, Veron short of fitness and Parker shaking off a hamstring injury, the door is suddenly open for Cole against Monaco.

Paul Sturrock, the new Southampton manager, sums the game up. 'They'd been struggling in their last few games but everyone turned up to the show for them. I'm very hopeful Chelsea will do well on Wednesday. It's vital for British football and I've got a sneaking feeling they'll do it.'

Team

Cudicini, Melchiot, Huth, Terry, Bridge, Gronkjaer (Johnson), Geremi, Lampard (Makelele), Cole (Veron), Gudjohnsen, Hasselbaink.

SUNDAY, 2 MAY

Apart from Beckham, Chelsea are being linked with a profusion of players yet again and are reported to have made a 'huge' offer to lure centre-back Walter Samuel away from Roma; he would be an ideal replacement for Desailly. He is eager to join compatriots Veron and Crespo in west London. Roma are holding out for £17m.

Chelsea want midfielder Emerson from Roma too, but he is also on Inter's wish list. So much for the Milan club having their eyes on Frank Lampard! Chelsea are still interested but not willing to pay as much for Emerson's services as they would have done last year. The fact that he has only one year left on his Roma contract must increase the sense of urgency for the club to sell up so as not to lose him on a free transfer.

Emerson is ranked among the finest holding midfielders in the world alongside Vieira and Makelele, ironically already at Chelsea. Francesco Totti, a longstanding Abramovich favourite, is keen on Real. 'Only Real Madrid is on my mind. I would never join another Italian club. As far as English soccer goes, it doesn't fascinate me.'

David Trezeguet has been linked with a swap deal involving Crespo but Chelsea sources rubbish that idea. Ronaldo is supposedly 'on the way to Chelsea', but the club have cooled their interest. When Ronaldo visited London in January and met incoming chief executive Kenyon and Pini Zahavi, no formal offer was made.

Ronaldinho knows he is wanted by Chelsea but he says, 'It makes me happy if clubs are watching me and want me because it means that what I am doing is being recognised. Spain is the most appealing for me because of the contrasting styles and tactics, plus stars such as Zinedine Zidane, Ronaldo, Luis Figo, Raul and, of course, David Beckham.'

Frank Lampard is upset that his contract talks have stalled. 'Yes, it riles me because all I'm asking for is parity with other players here at the club. I think I'm a top player at this club and I am not asking for outrageous wages. I just want what I feel is just reward for my hard work. I really hope we can sort something out before the end of the season. I don't know if Peter Kenyon is messing me about but, hopefully, I will get that parity in the end.'

Claudio Ranieri has had job offers according to his agent Jon Smith. 'Juve are an option but other clubs want to speak to him. We've had nine firm approaches so far from clubs in England and elsewhere in Europe, but Claudio can't talk to them while he is under contract. The bottom line is that he would prefer to stay at Chelsea.'

MONDAY, 3 MAY

Lifelong Spurs fan Simon Greenberg is appointed Chelsea's director of communications. Greenberg, 34, was assistant editor of the *Evening Standard* and will head up a new communications team to work closely with Peter Kenyon. Kenyon says, 'Chelsea will continue to be one of the most exciting stories over the next few years and Simon will play a key role in communicating our aims and ambitions, both on the field and off, both domestically and further afield.'

Discussions as to whether Ranieri will stay on with the club continue. 'Probably, yes, he should stay,' argues Eidur Gudjohnsen, 'because he knows the players that are here. Even though our results have not been so good recently, we seem to be getting to know each other. We have to take that forward. But it's not up to me to say whether he'll be here next season or not. I think we've all backed the manager, and we'll continue to do that until something different happens.' It sounds like a typical response from a player. In reality, the players were destabilised by Ranieri's multiple substitutions in Monte Carlo. They feel the blame lies with him.

Jimmy Floyd Hasselbaink declares, 'If we do not reach the final with the great team we have here, you can say we have failed.' He believes he is the man to deliver the goals against Monaco. 'It will be very hard on me if I don't play. The most important thing is that we need to score goals and I have shown this season that is what I do best. I am not criticising my team-mates, just pointing out facts. My goals are like my business card. This game could be my match of the season and it would be an enormous blow not to be given the chance to help Chelsea reach the Champions League final.'

Being top scorer with 18 – and having notched 88 goals in four seasons since his £15m move from Atletico Madrid – won't be enough to keep him at the club. 'I have had several propositions from other clubs. But Wednesday is the key day for many questions to be answered.' At Celtic, Martin O'Neill could offer Hasselbaink around £40,000 a week and might be able to persuade Chelsea to make up the rest of his £60,000-a-week wages by loaning him out for his final season or paying him off.

Didier Deschamps knows his club must make a good start at Stamford Bridge. 'We have to concentrate for the first 20 minutes of the match. They have players who are very comfortable with the ball and they will battle very hard. Every Chelsea player will think it is still possible to qualify – that's normal. Myself and my players, we thought the same when we lost 4–2 to Real Madrid in Spain. The fact that we are leading 3–1 is not going to change anything.'

TUESDAY, 4 MAY

Ranieri's press conference contains its regular dose of gallows humour. 'Welcome, sharks, to the funeral,' he remarks with a beaming smile as he greets an even larger media contingent than usual. 'Will a win change anything?' he repeats in disbelief to the usual question about his future. 'Really! Come on, my friend. My destiny is already decided. I don't think it changes anything if I win. For me, it's important to build the strong foundations. I knew this from the start. Then, I didn't know the name of the next coach. Now I know also the name, but then everyone knows. And the winner is...!'

He continues, 'I don't want to put myself out of Chelsea. But I *am* out. Then again, I am still in.' Can it get more bizarre?

One thing is clear. 'It would be a very good thing to stay in England. I don't think I have a bad reputation. I believe that everyone can make mistakes but very few men can say that they did make a mistake. My main mistake was I gave Monaco too much respect for their away record in the competition. That is why I went for the win on their own ground.

'Monaco will want to counter-attack. Monaco are used to playing this way because they have good speed. If I thought we could not beat Monaco, I would stay at home and watch the game on TV!'

The conference draws to a close with Ranieri acknowledging the support he has received from those present. 'Yes, I am aware of it. I thank you. You do a good job. Before you kill me, you call me the "dead man walking", then you call me this fantastic man. I should buy you all an espresso. But only a little one – I am Scottish!'

Before the first leg, Monaco enjoyed the benefits of a ten-day break, whereas during the past two weeks they have been fully occupied sustaining a challenge for the French title. An excellent 2–1 victory in the Riviera derby at Nice on Friday night keeps them in contention. But, tellingly, Deschamps selected a full-strength team. Unlike Chelsea, Monaco do not have enough bodies in the squad to tinker.

Emmanuel Petit continues his rants against his club. 'Abramovich needs to realise money doesn't buy success. Maybe he feels that running a football club is just like running an oil company, but it is not the same. He could spend a billion pounds on another 40 new players but that would not guarantee success.'

Fortunately Ranieri believes he still carries the dressing room's support. 'I think the players still believe in me. They show me that. Ask them – I feel we have a good relationship.' Privately, though, some have been questioning his selection policy, and now Hasselbaink goes public with his thoughts in Dutch newspaper *Algemeen Dagblad*. 'Before a match, we don't know who he wants to play. It's always a surprise. Until he announces the team two hours before a game we know as much as anyone else. Even if you are playing well and have found the right rhythm, you still don't know if you are in the squad.'

Fifty-six matches into the season and still nobody can be sure Ranieri knows his best combination. Ranieri's next substitution will be his 150th of the season.

Monaco train at the Bridge, after which Ludovic Giuly sings the praises of their on-loan striker. 'Morientes is a great idol for Monaco; he has taken our club up to the next level. His technique is awesome. He's hardly missed a chance since he arrived but what sets him apart is his humility. He has come here from the biggest club in the world to play league matches in front of 3,000 people and he has not complained once.'

Morientes reckons his 'heart still beats for Madrid', despite how it was clearly trampled on by the club's hierarchy in their clamour to sign Ronaldo. But he is still single-mindedly focused on Monaco's Champions League challenge. Morientes says, 'We want this with all our strength and we have nothing to lose.' He describes Deschamps as phenomenal, and is then asked about his best goal of the year. 'The one against Chelsea, because it was important, and very beautiful.'

In the other semi-final, Porto edge through thanks to Derlei's 60th-minute penalty and then their manager Jose Mourinho insists he is not worried about angering Ranieri by watching Chelsea take on Monaco at the Bridge. 'I have my ticket and I have one bodyguard – and I have to go. I go there because I'm professional, because what I want more than anything in my professional life is to win the final. I don't feel the pressure of being linked to Chelsea and I don't speak with other clubs.'

Mourinho claims he has had no contact with Abramovich because he leaves all negotiations to his agent Jorge Mendes. 'I don't speak with directors, presidents or owners because I concentrate on my work at Porto and we have the final to look forward to. There is a person who controls that situation for me.'

The odds could be stacked against Chelsea. Decades have passed since an English club overturned a two-goal, first-leg lead in the European Cup. Tottenham Hotspur did it in 1961.

WEDNESDAY, 5 MAY

CHELSEA 2, MONACO 2 (Monaco win 5–3 on aggregate)

A good two hours before kick-off, the man much touted as Ranieri's successor, Jose Mourinho, is signing autographs for eagle-eyed Chelsea fans in front of the directors' entrance. 'I am only here for the game,' he informs interested observers. Yet rumours spread that Mourinho has been seen in conversation with Peter Kenyon. In the programme, under the headline 'Mission Impossible – We Can Do It', Ranieri virtually banishes any optimism with his opening words, 'After the bad defeat in Monaco, we have a very, very little hope. But we'll try.'

The line-up suggests that Ranieri does not trust many of his new recruits either. In making five changes from the first leg, he fields a team which features only three of his dozen recent signings: Bridge, Cole and Geremi, worth a mere £20m. Of those available, Crespo is on the bench while Veron does not even manage that – he is replaced by the rarely seen Mario Stanic.

At first, Chelsea rock Monaco with their pace and power. Goalkeeper Flavio Roma has to make two outstanding saves, the first from Hasselbaink and the second from Lampard. Gronkjaer supplies the early lead, albeit a fluke, with an intended cross that flies into the top corner, his first goal since he scored the winner against Liverpool on the final day of last season to earn Champions League qualification. Lampard then puts Chelsea firmly in control just before the interval with a superb goal carved out by a powerful Melchiot run and a neat Gudjohnsen pass, with the midfielder rampaging into the box to finish the move.

The team are buzzing, the crowd roar. Fans hold up their 2–0 posters. But at the very moment Chelsea take charge of the tie – just when they need to retain possession, consolidate their advantage and take the sting out of the game – they forget the basics. Hugo Ibarra's infamous 'handball' goal in added time at the end of the first half changes the game, hands over to Deschamps the motivational ammunition he needs in the dressing room and, ultimately, costs Chelsea their place in the final.

But had Cole scored, instead of slicing his shot after 15 minutes, or Gudjohnsen headed in instead of hitting the bar from close range, the match would have been over at half-time. These and other missed opportunities are to prove costly. Instead, within seconds of Lampard's goal, they face a new reality when the tricky Jerome Rothen crosses from the left on to the head of Morientes. The ball loops to the back post where Ibarra supplies the finishing touch. Cudicini claims handball but Swedish referee Anders Frisk is having none of it.

Like Maradona before him, Ibarra is unrepentant; he insists the ball ricocheted off him after Morientes' header struck the woodwork. 'It was an accident because I thought Morientes had already put the ball in, but it came back off the post and hit me. I didn't realise it had gone in off my hand until after I saw the TV replay.'

Lampard can't maintain the same level of commitment once Monaco begin to exploit the space between Chelsea's attack and defence. Gudjohnsen and Gronkjaer squander wonderful opportunities soon after, but the goal Morientes scores in the 60th minute puts recovery beyond Chelsea.

An angry and frustrated Hasselbaink is substituted midway through the second half by Crespo and the Dutchman damages a bone in his foot kicking the dressing room door. Later he limps out of Stamford Bridge on crutches.

Terry and Gudjohnsen are in tears at the final whistle, while Ranieri stands impassively in front of his dug-out as Monaco's most famous supporter, Prince Albert, is waving his scarf at the travelling fans and punching the air.

Later Abramovich visits the dressing room, throws his arms around Ranieri and, through an interpreter, promises he will buy more players in the summer. Ranieri reveals, 'He said it will be better next time.'

Where did it all go wrong? It was quite simple really, as Deschamps explains, 'Chelsea expended a huge amount of energy putting us under pressure in the first half.'

Team

Cudicini, Melchiot (Johnson), Gallas, Terry, Bridge, Gronkjaer, Geremi (Parker), Lampard, Cole, Hasselbaink (Crespo), Gudjohnsen.

THURSDAY, 6 MAY

The soul searching goes on next day as Melchiot says, 'Nobody spoke in the dressing room after the match and it was very quiet at the training ground the next morning. Everybody is feeling down because to come that close to the final then let it slip through our fingers really hurts.'

But the real activity is taking place in a far less sweaty environment than the training ground. Agent Pini Zahavi meets Jose Mourinho plus his agent Jorge Mendez at Les Ambassadeurs, where photographers are barred. Mourinho is scheduled to be installed after the Champions League final.

Forced to work within a tight budget at Porto, Jose Mourinho will have almost unlimited funds at Chelsea. Abramovich will sanction a £50m bid for three Porto players: right winger Costinha, right-back Paulo Ferreira and the brilliant Brazilian, now a naturalised Portuguese star, Deco... and Beckham, of course! Mourinho will have a €150m budget (around £110m).

The hugely ambitious 41-year-old Mourinho refuses to deny that he is joining

Chelsea – although sources in Portugal indicate that he is not yet convinced that a move to Stamford Bridge will be his wisest option. Mourinho is acutely aware of how much in demand he is and wants to hold on for the best offer. 'Porto's president knows that at the moment I'm thinking only about Porto but he also knows there's a lot going on around me,' insists Mourinho. 'If I leave Porto, I can't guarantee it will be England but if the alternative is Italy then England will be my choice. I can guarantee my future will not be in Spain.' His comments come in an interview published in the Portugal sports daily *O Jogo*.

Mourinho did not enjoy the most distinguished of playing careers. His fortunes rose when he was employed as a translator for Sir Bobby Robson when he was coach at Sporting Lisbon during the early 1990s. Robson was impressed. 'Jose was a very good student of soccer, very intelligent, ambitious, enthusiastic and curious.' Mourinho followed Robson to Porto and then on to Barcelona, where he stayed alongside Louis van Gaal after Robson left.

After spells at Benfica and Uniao Leiria he returned to Porto as head coach. Mourinho – a qualified PE teacher with a degree in psychology – has a reputation as a shrewd tactician and motivator. Mourinho also has a will of iron and an eye for the theatrical. He adds, 'People are saying I am going to leave my team. But if that is the case I have to do something big before I go. I want to win the Champions League final. It is what I have been dreaming about. It has been a season of upsets so no one should be surprised any more. It's been a great competition and, of course, whoever wins it should be regarded as the best team in Europe. It would be my greatest achievement.'

Ranieri now has one goal left in his remaining two games: to finish second above Manchester United. He was spotted in Scallini's, just behind Harrods in Walton Street, immediately after the Monaco game, dining with family, friends, his agents Jon and Phil Smith, and Vincenzo Morabito. At the upmarket Italian restaurant, which specialises in spicy lobster spaghetti and where the walls are adorned with photographs of famous footballers, Manchester United's biggest shareholders JP McManus and John Magnier were also dining.

At the adjacent table to Ranieri's was Daniel Levy's finance director at Spurs and his business partner Paul Kemsley. Inevitably, the subject of the vacant position at White Hart Lane came up, but it was clear that another of the Smiths' clients, Martin O'Neill, is the wanted man.

FRIDAY, 7 MAY

Abramovich watches Ranieri put his squad through their paces in training. In the media conference afterwards, Ranieri reckons his record will heap pressure on Mourinho, his successor. Ranieri says, 'The owner Mr Abramovich did not ask me to win a trophy for him but I was one hour away from getting the chance to do exactly that. This season we have done that, so next season there must be improvement again. It's not easy because football can be so unpredictable but I have laid the foundations. The ground floor is ready and now I'd like to put the windows in and finish with the roof garden.'

In four years at Chelsea, Ranieri has failed to deliver any silverware, but he insists, 'Second place in the Premiership and the Champions League semi-final is a fair return for the investment made in players. If you had said we'd achieve that at the beginning of the season, then everybody at Stamford Bridge would have been happy. Manchester United couldn't get a place in the Champions League semi-finals, so now they will be desperate to finish second. That's why it is such a big game at Old Trafford. If they beat Chelsea, they will be one point behind with one game to go, so it will be decided on the last day.'

Peter Kenyon will return to Old Trafford for the first time since leaving Manchester United as Chelsea seek to claim second place by taking a point off his old club, securing the club's best Premiership finish and guaranteeing Champions League football next season. United have lost three of their last four Premiership games and Sir Alex Ferguson is determined his players will not go into the FA Cup final against Millwall with a run of bad results behind them.

Ferguson defends Ranieri, 'The man has shown great integrity and nerve and he has made his team play. I believe they have had a successful season. He's done a great job at Chelsea. I don't think anybody can argue against that. I felt for them the other night against Monaco because they could easily have been 4–0 up at half-time. I felt for Claudio desperately. What happened is what has happened to Manchester United before in Europe. If you make mistakes, then you tend to get punished. Overall, they've had a successful season.'

Arsene Wenger also pronounces it a good season for his west London rivals. 'It's a bit ridiculous for Chelsea to be second in the Premiership, to reach the Champions League semi-finals and for people to call it a failure. But that is football nowadays.

'This season has shown that you can't buy success. There are big clubs waiting 50 years to win the championship, clubs who spend as much as we do. When you make mistakes by buying a lot of players who don't settle, it takes time to get over it. Because you can't just sell them on, you end up carrying those mistakes for several years. Of course, Chelsea don't really have that problem as they can afford to forget the mistakes of the previous year and change the team every year. At some point you'd imagine they might get it right.'

Confession time, and insult is added to injury as Monaco's Hugo Ibarra admits, 'The ball bounced on to the post and then on to my hand, and it was a goal. I didn't do it on purpose but I slightly pushed it with my hand and, if I had not, there would not have been a goal.'

For Ranieri, that goal could be the straw that breaks the camel's back.

SATURDAY, 8 MAY

MANCHESTER UNITED 1, CHELSEA 1

Ranieri delivers an automatic Champions League place and their highest finish since Chelsea won the title in 1955. Needing just a point to secure second spot, Chelsea survive a late bombardment after Ruud van Nistelrooy levels following a Cudicini blunder. The goal comes shortly after Robert Huth has been sent off for his second bookable offence – a fate Paul Scholes might well have suffered much earlier had Sir Alex not taken his midfielder off to preserve him for the FA Cup final after an initial caution for diving is followed by a crude lunge on Lampard.

Gronkjaer puts the visitors in front with a superb curling effort early in the first half after a strike by Gudjohnsen has rightly been ruled offside. Gronkjaer's beautifully struck shot from 20 yards leaves Tim Howard with no chance on 19 minutes. This is Gronkjaer's first Premiership goal since the one last May that enabled Chelsea to claim fourth place. Ranieri's leadership is then called into action when Huth is sent off. He eventually makes all three substitutions and changes the formation four times in 15 minutes... surely a record, even by his standards.

Ranieri's response to going down to ten men is to swap Melchiot for Johnson and play Gronkjaer at right-back. Then he brings on Cole for Parker, and moves Geremi to right-back and Gronkjaer to the left wing. Finally, he brings Gronkjaer off and Babayaro on. Lampard stands with arms outstretched, hands open in bafflement, epitomising the confusion caused in the players by Ranieri's changes. Lampard has witnessed most of the tinkerings, as this is his 57th match of the season (as well as John Terry's 50th and Wayne Bridge's 47th).

Cudicini makes a fabulous save to deny Van Nistelrooy from the penalty spot, then the keeper makes a complete hash of a cross on 77 minutes to gift the Dutchman an equaliser. Had Howard not reacted well after Gudjohnsen turned Brown in the 70th minute, it could have been three straight defeats for last season's champions.

The Tinkerman departs with head held high, while United set off on a slightly sheepish lap of honour. Old Trafford does not celebrate finishing third.

Later Ranieri urges Abramovich to give him and his players another chance to win the Premiership. 'This season it was important to close the gap with United and Arsenal and we did that. It was hard to lift the players after that defeat with Monaco; it was important to show our character and ambition and we showed that today. Tomorrow I will think, "OK, it is a good season," because it's not easy to achieve second place in England. I am an ambitious man and would have hoped for better, but the platform for this club is laid now and I am positive about the future.' Ranieri suspects Mourinho already has his job. His final public utterance at Old Trafford could be his epitaph. 'The Tinkerman,' says Ranieri of himself, 'used to tinker and change. OK, thank you.'

> **Team**
>
> Cudicini, Melchiot (Johnson), Huth, Terry, Bridge, Gronkjaer (Babayaro), Lampard, Makelele, Geremi, Cole (Parker), Gudjohnsen.

SUNDAY, 9 MAY

The plot thickens as Jon Smith, back in Spain, is called by one of Abramovich's top aides and told that Claudio is still the manager and that no decision has yet been taken. 'Uncertain' is how Smith describes their stance. There is a gentleman's agreement not to air the contents of the conversation and a further meeting will be arranged for the 'week after next'.

Ranieri says, 'After I leave Chelsea, I would like to stay in London because my wife and I are very happy here. There are lots of fantastic clubs in London; I would listen to any offers from other London clubs very carefully. I can't worry about what the Chelsea fans or players think after I leave Chelsea, I must do what is best for me. I like the dressing room culture in England; I don't have to change who I am to be a manager here. I can be myself. I love living in London and the English people, and their way of life. London is a fabulous city.'

Ranieri's agent Vincenzo Morabito switches the pressure back on to Mourinho. 'The important thing to say to Chelsea supporters is, "Will the new manager bring better results next season?" Don't forget that whoever replaces Claudio needs to win the Premiership and the Champions League because of what Claudio has achieved this season.

'Claudio has still got three years to go on his contract from 1 July, so we are just waiting for communication from Mr Abramovich and Mr Kenyon, although all the indications are that some guy called Mourinho will replace him on 1 July… so far we have no official confirmation so we will see what happens in the next few days.

'It is up to Chelsea now to tell Claudio if they want to keep him or not. Chelsea can talk to any manager they want but I would be disappointed if they used the word "sacked". It would be far better if they thanked him for what he has done for the club, for providing them with automatic qualification for next season's

Champions League, but said they had other plans. Claudio doesn't deserve to be sacked. It may only be playing with words but "replaced" would be far better because it would indicate they have done him some respect.'

Enrique Sobrino, contesting the elections at Real Madrid, says, 'Claudio Ranieri is a manager that we like and we do not rule out the possibility of contacting him if he finally leaves his current club.' Then again, he is also keen on Jose Mourinho. 'We know Chelsea are also interested but we will make every effort to reach a formal understanding with him.'

Arsene Wenger says he is looking forward to locking horns with Mourinho, 'It should be fun. Jose seems to like a bit of sparring – and so do I. Jose seems to like having his say. But that is good. Alex and I have become too quiet and it will be nice for someone else to join in.'

Ranieri leaves for Paris with his wife for a three-day 'romantic break', and will return on Wednesday.

MONDAY, 10 MAY

Sven-Goran Eriksson praises Ranieri. 'It has been a difficult season but I must say he has done a great job. But I think he is used to this [speculation]. He is Italian and every day in Italy there are rumours. I think he is handling it very well.'

Peter Kenyon and director Eugene Tenenbaum are in Monte Carlo to meet Abramovich aboard his yacht and to discuss a move for Ronaldinho. Geannot Werth, Didier Deschamps' agent, hopes the pair are there because they haven't made up their minds on a new coach, but of course the deal for Mourinho is already sealed.

Mrs Beckham bumps into Kenyon at Heathrow Terminal One's VIP lounge and they spend 20 minutes together before each leaves for their respective flights without making a comment. Victoria is off to LA for talks about her new single, while Kenyon is jetting off to the south of France. The meeting is purely coincidental. No one can tell me whether the conversation gets round to a move to Chelsea.

At the Laureus World Sports Awards in Estoril, Marcel Desailly thanks Ranieri for what he has achieved and warns the new man that the Italian will be a hard act to follow. 'We know the mistakes we made and so does the manager. The reality is that Chelsea definitely have to win the Premiership title next year and go further than the semi-final in the Champions League otherwise there will be big trouble. Next season will be a big season for the club.'

Desailly suggests prospects will be harmed by another influx of players. 'If the chairman decides to change half the team, then it'll be another season when we can't expect great things. If we change three or four players maximum, then we can win something, definitely. Four or five will leave, three or four will come in and the objective must be to win the Premiership. We can speculate on all of the players coming in – Ronaldo, Beckham and the like. But this is not just a toy for Mr Abramovich; he likes his football but he also wants success.

'You cannot win things straight away. We had the right guy, Ranieri, who managed to keep everybody focused on their job and we did not reach Arsenal's level collectively. But it was a good season overall for Chelsea.'

Desailly also insists he has not received an apology from Ron Atkinson (see 22 April). 'I have seen in the newspapers that he tried to talk to me but I haven't had any contact with him. I don't forgive. If he has done a mistake, he's going to pay for it. I don't have anger and I will continue my life.'

Gianfranco Zola wants to say goodbye to Chelsea fans in a testimonial match against Cagliari on 18 May but his plans are scuppered by Eriksson, who has written to every Premiership manager requesting that no members of his European Championship squad take part in any testimonial games after the final day of the season. Yet, Eriksson relaxes his ban after agreeing to be guest at Martin Keown's testimonial at Highbury on 17 May – the day he will name his 23-man party for Portugal.

Zola has the opportunity to return to Stamford Bridge in a possible coaching role. He says, 'Chelsea still have a special place in my heart. It will be a difficult decision. On one hand I want to carry on with what I've been doing for 15 years but I may have the chance to do something new. When the promotion [for Cagliari] is complete I will decide. There are five games left and we can still win the league.'

Joe Cole regrets splashing out on shares in Millwall, 'I heard a rumour Chris Evans and Danny Baker were going to buy the club but the shares just plummeted. I didn't get the best advice. They're worth a quarter of a penny now. They cost me a penny each, so I'm on a 75 per cent loss!'

In the latest edition of *Loaded* he reveals he also harbours a daring ambition. 'I do a lot of mad stuff in my spare time and would still like to go scuba diving so I can go in a cage and come face to face with a shark. I want to get in there with a big old Great White. They're the perfect killing machine. Just make sure you jab one right in the eye if they sink their teeth into you.'

TUESDAY, 11 MAY

Fans fork out £40 a head for a three-course dinner with speeches from Peter Kenyon and Bruce Buck who hold court in the Charles Kingsley suite at Stamford Bridge. In front of a group of 200 fans at the Supporters' Night Out dinner, Kenyon thanks the players and staff for their efforts but does not praise the manager, or back down from his 'no trophy equals failure' remark when he first took office. 'I'm on record on this and you should look at what John Terry said. He as club captain feels the players have failed. Finishing second in the league and reaching the semi-finals of the Champions League is a good achievement and we've had a good season but we are not where everyone at Chelsea wants us to be. We want to do better than this next season and better than that the season after.'

A voice from the floor asks, 'What about the manager? Don't ignore that.' Kenyon replies, 'I didn't ignore it. We've had a good season, but we're not where anybody at Chelsea wants us to be and that's what we're all planning and working hard to achieve.' Cue applause, then Buck says, 'Of all the people who didn't win, we were first.'

The next question is the most predictable. 'Is Claudio staying?' 'Claudio has a three-year contract,' comes the response, with a pause for sarcastic laughter. 'There has been no new manager appointed.'

'Hang on,' says master of ceremonies, Neil Barnett. 'There is a follow-up question: why has the club treated Claudio Ranieri so appallingly?' More applause.

'What happened on Roman's yacht?' someone yells.

'That's none of your business,' snaps Kenyon. 'All throughout this process we've conducted discussions on an ongoing basis with Claudio. If you don't believe me, that's unfortunate, but there's not been a decision taken on Claudio Ranieri. Those decisions will be taken over the forthcoming weeks and that is the fact of the matter.'

Buck adds, 'There has been a lot of press coverage suggesting that we have already agreed a deal with this or that manager but it is not true.'

Kenyon looks particularly uncomfortable when Buck refers to Eriksson as 'Peter's friend Sven'. Kenyon promises that Chelsea will bring in several new players, but declines to reveal the size of the club's transfer budget. Frank Lampard has been linked with Manchester United, but Kenyon dismisses the possibility of him leaving and raises the possibility of a Zola return in a non-playing capacity. Kenyon says that he wants to start up a fans' forum but that there is no prospect of Chelsea appointing a fans' representative to its board.

Ken Bates arrives, unannounced. The subject of the lawsuit is raised by a question to which Bates immediately responds, 'I didn't ask that question, I promise you. But where's your cheque?'

Buck takes it all with commendable good humour. 'I hope we can reach an amicable solution. I was talking to Ken the other day and he said he was in his doctor's office. "The doctor reckons I have another 25 years to live," he tells me, "so I am increasing my claim."'

Bates is underwhelmed by some answers. 'He's talking bollocks,' he mutters on one occasion, 'and that's a technical term.' His sharpest riposte, and one which draws laughter and applause from the audience, comes when Buck asks Bates if he can talk to him afterwards about 'knocking down the hotel'. 'No,' bellows Bates from the back of the room. 'You can fuck off. Take that as a no.'

At the end, Ron Hocking hands Kenyon a book he has written on the history of the club, saying, 'Seeing that you are United and know nothing about Chelsea, here's a history of the club for you.'

In a Sky TV interview afterwards, Bates says, 'The way Ranieri has been treated is quite shameful, and he doesn't deserve it. The job he's done this season... could you do your job if you were being vilified every day in the press and media? And not lose your temper, but smile and make a joke? He's a gentleman – the Russians don't deserve him. I speak to Claudio and he's a proud man and I think he's done a great job.

'I've sacked a few managers in my time but I've done it – bang, out. I haven't done it by death of a thousand cuts. If you want to change your manager, you change the manager. Some of the players signed this year are only highly paid mercenaries. They don't give a damn about Chelsea, they just give a damn about their wage packets and it's interesting that not many of the new players, the foreigners, have made it into the team successfully.

'Chelsea are losing the reputation that was built up over the last 20 years. I treated the staff well and got an extra ten per cent out of them but they're in danger of losing that, if it hasn't been lost already. It's a great pity, the staff and the fans are what makes the club.'

Asked if that is down to Abramovich, Bates replies, 'It's his henchmen. Remember, if you're aged under 80, you've only ever lived under communism and the communist way of life is very different from the Western way of life. It's not the way of doing things in England and they are learning that the hard way. They will end up losing all the good people because they'll be headhunted elsewhere.

'Claudio's done a good job here. I would keep him. He would've done better [under me] as he would not have been under the pressure he has had for the past nine months.'

WEDNESDAY, 12 MAY

Barcelona president Joan Laporta is ready to listen to proposals for Ronaldinho, providing it brings in the level of cash to buy three new stars. Frank Lampard observes, 'Ronaldinho is the one player in Europe who really makes me excited to watch every week. He has skills and character. He plays with a smile and always tries something different on the pitch. He would be a great entertainer. I'd love to play alongside him.'

Roberto Carlos warns Real that, unless they offer him £125,000 a week and a four-year contract instead of two or even three years, he will quit them for Chelsea. With only one year left on his current deal, he believes he is in a powerful bargaining position. But at the age of 31, this is his final big contract. He says that his advisers have been contacted by Chelsea. Real sporting director Jorge Valdano flatly denies the club will be listening to offers for either Beckham or Ronaldo.

THURSDAY, 13 MAY

Seba Veron formally requests a transfer in a meeting with Kenyon. Because of his back injury, Veron has made just 14 appearances at a cost to the club of over £1m per game. 'He met Kenyon and told him that he wants to be sold,' says Veron's agent Fernando Hidalgo. 'He would love to return to Italy where he has his best memories as a player.'

Inter value Veron at £8m and will propose a swap with Vieri or Nigerian striker Obafemi Martins. Veron says he is satisfied with his three-year spell in the Premiership. 'It took time for me to adapt to the way of playing in England. I played much better in the second season with Manchester United and at Chelsea I had no chance to show what I can do because I suffered too many injuries. I had to live with a hernia for three months. Now I've solved my problems and I feel good. But, unfortunately, the season is ending.'

The midfielder is in line for a large windfall because, with three years left to run on his £90,000-a-week deal, he will be due a £2m pay-off should he be shipped out.

Chelsea insist John Terry is not for sale at any price following reported interest from Internazionale. Reports in Italy claim that Inter have inquired about Terry's availability during discussions about Veron, but Chelsea will resist any attempts to poach one of their key players. Terry is so well thought of by the club's Russian owner that he is referred to by his team-mates as the 'son of Abramovich'.

Adrian Mutu is training with the youth players, having turned up late from international duty two weeks earlier. After recovering from a knee injury he is assigned to training with the youngsters, alongside that other outcast, Winston Bogarde, whose huge contract is finally about to expire.

Meanwhile Real prepare to offer Roma centre-back Walter Samuel a £4.5m-a-year contract despite the Blues proposing a £20m deal with Roma. Madrid match the offer and are ready to up the ante with their seductive personal terms.

Frank Lampard insists he wants to stay on at Chelsea for the rest of his career – but wants to resolve talks over his future before the European Championship in Portugal. He tells Chelsea TV, 'I'm not going to Manchester United. I'm very happy here and I'm hoping we'll get it sorted out. It's much deeper than money. I feel very at home here and my family have all converted to being Chelsea fans.'

Lampard is the front-runner to be voted Chelsea's player of the season after coming second in the PFA nominations behind Thierry Henry, although he insists there other candidates, such as Terry. 'It would be a great honour for me but JT has had a great year and so have other players, including those who don't get as much credit, like Wayne Bridge. Obviously, I want to win things but coming second to Thierry Henry was like coming second to Gianfranco Zola in the player of the season awards at Chelsea last year.'

FRIDAY, 14 MAY

Ranieri is tipped off by agent Jon Smith that the Leeds United match will be his last and that he will indeed be replaced by Jose Mourinho. One of Ranieri's close Italian friends tells me, 'You could feel it from his voice, that he was depressed as this was now the eve of his execution.'

Ranieri had been hoping for a reprieve after word reached him in the middle of the week that Abramovich was having second thoughts. In the absence of the usual Friday press conference, Ranieri gives an interview to Sky Sports News where he delivers a withering assessment of the man Abramovich has chosen to succeed him as coach at the Bridge.

'Mourinho is new to club football, having only been a trainer for the past four years and, yes, he is a good manager. He trains well and last season he won the UEFA Cup. This year he has reached the final of the Champions League – that is good. But we will have to see how he does in another league; we shall see if he is the same. You know it is very different in other leagues, and we shall see how he manages when he moves to England.

'In the Portuguese league he is the best, fine. Porto are the best but it is not like leagues in Italy, Spain and England, where there are five or six teams that are very strong. The Portuguese league is Porto and Benfica, but maybe not now Benfica, although they are improving.'

When asked the perpetual question about his future, Ranieri hides the fact that he already knows his fate. He replies, 'I am sure Roman will choose!' He adds that he hopes it will be officially resolved sooner than the scheduled end of Porto's season, the Champions League final, because everyone needs to plan ahead to next season.

Marcel Desailly sums up Ranieri's achievements. 'The atmosphere that Chelsea have in the group has been great. It has not been difficult for me, as captain, to keep everyone together. The mistakes he made were tactical. Because of the type of players here, he started off using a diamond formation. But all the teams who have won the Premiership here play 4-4-2. He switched to that, but we only had three or four months to try out the new tactics. Christmas was a terrible period. We lost silly points against Middlesbrough and Villa and maybe that cost us the title. We lost twice – that's six points – but still finished close to Arsenal. That's not a lot, so let's be positive.'

The row with Lampard rumbles on, stoked up by his agent, Steve Kutner, who says, 'The way things stand, Frank doesn't feel that he will be able to stay. All he wants is parity with the club's best-paid players but Chelsea aren't prepared to give him that. After the kind of season he has had, you wouldn't think there would be a problem. Now they risk losing one of their best players because everyone knows that Juve and Inter want him – and they clearly want him more than Chelsea do.'

Peter Kenyon amends his initial offer, but the money on the table is still nowhere near what Kutner's man expects. 'They offered him a five-year deal and made it clear what they think Frank is worth – but that is nowhere near our valuation,' adds Kutner. 'Frank would sign for life if he could, but Chelsea aren't prepared to pay him the same as some of the foreign players. Maybe he should change his nationality!'

Several stars are on the way out. Talks are ongoing to find a buyer for Hernan Crespo who has made just 19 Premiership appearances, including six as substitute. Crespo has scored just ten Premiership goals and the signs are that he will be on his way back to Italy. Yet he is top earner along with Juan Sebastian Veron on £4.9m a year, £93,750 a week.

The final game of the season looms, where debt-ridden Leeds will bow out of the top flight against a club at the opposite end of football's financial spectrum. Caretaker boss Kevin Blackwell says, 'It's unbelievable to think that three years ago we were a club who could go out and buy any player we wanted. Yet now we have nothing. It was Chelsea who were struggling for finances not so long ago – but our situations have completely changed around. They are the haves and we are the have-nots. But, if it hadn't been for Roman Abramovich, then where would Chelsea be now?'

SATURDAY, 15 MAY

CHELSEA 1, LEEDS 0

Ranieri leaves the field draped in a Chelsea scarf with his palms together in thanks to the fans. The players form a guard of honour. The fans chant his name throughout the second half and the lap of honour. 'One Ranieri, there's only one Ranieri', they chorus. Abramovich and Kenyon applaud politely.

The banners reveal the fans' views on the matter: 'Claudio, you may lose your job, but you've kept your dignity'; 'Don't tinker with the Tinkerman'; 'Claudio, we thank you with all our hearts'. The Shed End make their feelings known with a rendition of 'Stand up if you hate Kenyon'. As you'd expect, Sven-Goran Eriksson is there to witness affairs, his final spying mission prior to naming his Euro 2004 squad.

Out on the field, Ranieri can't resist one last shuffle of his pack. He opts to play a lone striker in Gudjohnsen and hands Cole a rare opportunity in central midfield. Leeds' rookie keeper Scott Carson twice reacts well to tip shots from Cole just over the bar. Chelsea finally take the lead on 20 minutes as Gronkjaer notches his third in three games. Gronkjaer will be on his way at the end of the season as well as Ranieri and, fittingly, he scores the winning goal (for the second year running). Lampard releases Johnson down the right and he delivers the ball on a plate for Gronkjaer to power a diving header into the net. Gudjohnsen then heads over from six yards before sending a shot from the edge of the box curling inches wide of target.

Leeds then throw on Jermaine Pennant and he almost makes an impact in the 70th minute when he curls a free-kick against the post. But Chelsea are a class apart from their opponents and, had it not been for another wonderful save from England Under-21 star Carson, Cole would have sealed his impressive display with a deserved goal. Chelsea achieve a 30th clean sheet of the season, but again fail to provide the exhilarating football Abramovich apparently craves so much.

Ranieri is set to leave with an £8m pay-off but no amount of cash can make amends for his anger and frustration at being denied the opportunity to reap the rewards of his hard work. 'It's not important to be rich or not rich, it doesn't change your life. It will change my life if I leave Chelsea.' He also hints it was Abramovich and his associates who were responsible for many of the superstar signings who failed to deliver. 'At the beginning, people were saying it was Sven-Goran Eriksson who chose the players. But me and the owner know everything.'

Now Ranieri just wants to be put out of his misery after being kept dangling all season. Still, the reaction of the Stamford Bridge crowd has cheered him up. Ranieri says, 'It was fantastic because all the fans shouted my name. The scenes will stay in my memory for all my life. There were no tears this time. I was very brave! But it was very emotional, especially when my players clapped me off the pitch. I will miss you lot [the media] too; you attack me like sharks and now you clap me. Only in England.'

He climbs into his car with members of his family and they head for the airport, for a big shopping spree in Rome in an early attempt to start getting rid of his multi-million pound pay-off.

> **Team**
>
> Cudicini, Melchiot, Gallas, Terry (Huth), Bridge, Gronkjaer, Makelele, Lampard (Nicolas), Johnson (Stanic), Cole, Gudjohnsen.

SUNDAY, 16 MAY

Frank Lampard's form guarantees him a place on the plane to Portugal when Eriksson names his 23-man squad for the Euro 2004 finals. He says, 'I didn't go to the last World Cup so the fact I'm there and challenging makes me happy. Everyone wants to play in their favourite position and I'm no different. I want to play in the centre – but with a diamond it's not always possible. I have had the benefit of playing in a diamond formation for Chelsea, both right, left and at the front and I like to think I can play in all of them.'

It looks as if he will be staying on at Stamford Bridge after Chelsea indicate they want to keep him at all costs. And Lampard is setting himself higher targets for next season with Chelsea, as he believes they have finally beaten their demons and no longer fear Arsenal. 'They were overcoming us mentally whenever we played them, however well we played against them. We broke that and hopefully we can carry on breaking it next year. The Premiership title is the goal.'

MONDAY, 17 May

Veron is flattered by the advances of Inter Milan and is expected to return to Italy. 'I have spent three years in England. Maybe they were good from a personal point of view, but not from a footballing perspective, even though I won a title with United. I am excited by the prospect of playing for a big club like Inter.

'Inter have qualified for the Champions League and, although it is extra motivation, my stance in wanting to join them is based on far more than just that.'

Crespo wants to head in the same direction. 'I am delighted AC Milan are showing interest. I am ready to have a reduction in wages and start as a reserve.' But this may not be enough to convince vice-president Adriano Galliani, who insists, 'He would be too expensive for a fourth-choice striker.'

TUESDAY, 18 MAY

Chelsea are ready to make a British-record, £30m-plus bid to take Steven

Gerrard from Liverpool. Abramovich has approved more big spending for the right players. Peter Kenyon is free to offer as much money as it takes to tempt Liverpool and their captain.

There is talk of a contract worth more than £100,000 a week. The 23-year-old recently signed a new deal at Liverpool and was also made captain by Gerard Houllier, but the club's resolve to keep him will be tested as Chelsea embark on the second stage of their attempt to become one of world football's major powers.

Liverpool rebuffed Chelsea 12 months ago when Abramovich picked Gerrard out as an initial target. They were willing to pay £20m-plus because his contract was running out, but now he is worth double that since Liverpool persuaded him to commit to a long-term deal.

Abramovich will open the bidding at £30m, but could go as high as £40m. Liverpool may find such an offer hard to resist. After all, the Anfield club are short of funds to compete at the top level, as has been proved by their talks with the Thai Prime Minister and local millionaire Steven Morgan. Selling Gerrard would be a big blow to the team, but they know that there will be more offers for him soon because of his form this season.

Ronaldinho joins the likes of Henry and Vieira in declining a move to the Bridge. Fernando Morientes is interested in a move to England and has been linked with a £17.5m transfer to Arsenal or Chelsea, but he is way down Chelsea's wish list of superstars.

WEDNESDAY, 19 MAY

A personal favourite of Abramovich, the Ukrainian Andrei Shevchenko remains a top target. His 24 goals in 24 league games were instrumental in taking Milan to the Serie A title. At 27, Shevchenko is at the peak of his career.

One thing is certain: Chelsea will revamp their attack, with Hasselbaink on his way out and Crespo seeking a return to Italy, but Milan are not going to sell Shevchenko on the cheap, certainly not for the £20m touted in the press.

As other top targets prove elusive, Morientes becomes more attractive. He confirms he has accepted an offer and that a move is close to being finalised, but he refuses to name the club. This only fuels speculation that it is Chelsea. 'We're slowly coming to an agreement and we can say the deal is 90 per cent done,' he says. 'I really like the idea of joining.'

In this situation Mutu looks vulnerable, but he has been given assurances about his future and says, 'It has been a tough year, a real test of character and a new experience for me, but I would like to stay at Chelsea and Roman

Abramovich has assured me I will. I am not tempted to leave but then you never know. Anything could happen.'

Mutu has been criticised over his private life since his divorce. He feels there is nothing wrong in having a healthy sex life. 'My name is not being associated with bank robbers or people like that. To be associated with sex is not a problem for me.' As for being banished to the youth team after arriving back late from international duty, he says, 'In everybody's life there must be some bad points. It has been hard, but I will learn from it.'

Slowly but surely Chelsea are losing the race for Walter Samuel as Real match their £15m offer and the 26-year-old Argentine looks like opting for Madrid, even though he could well earn more at Stamford Bridge. Roma need to sell players to ease their financial problems and still hope Chelsea will come back with an increased bid.

While Samuel and Crespo are in Argentina's squad to meet Brazil on 2 June, Veron misses out on the 2006 World Cup qualifier in Belo Horizonte. The midfielder is still not fit after his back surgery.

New signing Arjen Robben is in Holland's 23-man squad for Euro 2004 after recovering from a hamstring injury, but there are no places for Melchiot and Hasselbaink.

Rumour has it that Joe Cole may be on his way out. Everton manager David Moyes is interested in a loan arrangement for next season. However, Cole, selected for England's Euro 2004 squad, says, 'I've enjoyed my time at Chelsea, I've broken into the team now and I want to stay and establish myself both for Chelsea and England.'

THURSDAY, 20 May

Victoria Beckham announces she will move to Madrid, putting an end to Chelsea's immediate aims of bringing the England captain back to the Premiership next season.

Rebecca Loos, though, suggests the switch is 'a touch too late', declaring that her alleged affair with Beckham would never have happened if Victoria had moved to Spain when he first signed for Real. Beckham himself says, 'I have a long-term commitment to Real and to my life in Spain. I've been here for one season and it feels like the job's not done yet. The support that I have received from the fans has been amazing and I would like to see them repaid with success. Victoria shares my vision of our life here together.'

Speaking at the British Embassy in Lisbon, Sven-Goran Eriksson gives Jose Mourinho the thumbs-up when he says, 'Jose has the quality to triumph anywhere.

It could be at Chelsea, Liverpool, or Madrid. His career in charge of Porto leaves no room for doubt.'

At Porto's training HQ, Mourinho puts the finishing touches to his Champions League preparations, and outlines his football philosophy. 'To win the Champions League, it is necessary to have a great team, and we are a great team. You can't just buy players and make a great team. We and Monaco have constructed good teams without having the money to sign the great players, but the end result is better because we are both in the final.'

His words prompt renewed speculation that he is having second thoughts about joining Chelsea. It's all wide of the mark though – the Mourinho deal is already in the bag.

FRIDAY, 21 MAY

Chelsea are bitterly upset as Real agree a five-year deal with Samuel, who is to join them on 1 July. Chelsea feel they have been stitched up after being told by Real that they would not enter the bidding for Samuel. They also resent handing Real the money to pay for the deal if they buy Morientes!

Thierry Henry defends Desailly after the France captain faced a hostile reception from home fans during the friendly against Brazil. The defender was much criticised in France for elbowing Morientes during the Champions League semi-final and he was jeered when his face appeared on a huge TV screen before the prestigious clash at the Stade de France. Desailly later suggests the booing came from Brazilian fans in the crowd.

SATURDAY, 22 May

Abramovich buys a Boeing 767, normally a 360-seater, to run alongside his Boeing 737 private jet. The new aircraft is rumoured to be equipped with missile-jamming technology comparable to that used on the US presidential jet, Air Force One.

Arsenal celebrate their title triumph, as vice-chairman David Dein takes a sideswipe at Chelsea. 'There are two kinds of directors. There are those, like Arsenal's, whose money follows their passion and there is a new wave whose passion follows their money. The latter buy into a club, then suddenly become a fan of that club. But I don't want to criticise Chelsea; they will get success, I'm sure, because they are acquiring talented players, however much it costs them. It's not a level playing field, but there's nothing we can do about that, except try to be more astute in other ways.'

Chelsea issue a statement on their website, 'to make it clear that, unless a story is broadcast or published by one of our official outlets, it should not be assumed to be happening. Summer is the media "silly season" and we are already seeing stories unfolding. So when you read or hear about things like Joe Cole moving to Everton, please give them no credence.'

SUNDAY, 23 MAY

On a day out at the Monaco Grand Prix, Abramovich is caught on camera beside Formula One supremo Bernie Ecclestone as ITV's Martin Brundle conducts interviews on the grid before the start. Brundle takes the opportunity to ask Abramovich about his F1 interests and the Russian reiterates that he has no business plans for the sport. Abramovich talks through one of his chief aides, although I am told he now understands English perfectly but prefers to answer questions in Russian.

Liverpool make an audacious bid to snatch Mourinho in place of the axed Houllier. Even though Liverpool were told Mourinho had committed to Chelsea, they wanted to put their proposals to him. Mourinho will now confirm he is to become Ranieri's successor after the Champions league final as Abramovich's aides contact Ranieri's agent Jon Smith to call a Tuesday meeting with the Russian owner present.

MONDAY, 24 May

Ranieri returns from his holiday break and meets up with Jon Smith at his Parsons Green home prior to tomorrow's summit with Abramovich, who is supposed to be flying in from Monaco. Smith tells me, 'I went around to Claudio's home. He was sad as we expected the inevitable outcome, but at least tomorrow he will know where his life is going, if he didn't already know.'

Real are anticipating a £20m bid for Roberto Carlos. The club's director of football, Jorge Valdano, says, 'He's confirmed it. We are waiting for a fax from Chelsea, confirming they will pay the £20m fee in order to complete the deal.' Chelsea would be paying a great deal for a player now in his 30s with just one year left on his contract. The player's wage demands have been turned down by Real and it's claimed he will take up an offer from Chelsea that will more than double his salary to £120,000 a week.

When president Florentino Perez is asked if some of the *galacticos* might now leave, he issues a warning that could have been intended for Beckham – and, indeed, Roberto Carlos. 'I don't like the phrase *galacticos* because it can be used as a weapon against us. I don't know if they will all stay, but all I can say is that Samuel came here for a lot less money than was offered by Chelsea. If anyone here wants to go to Chelsea, we'll be delighted to listen, because we don't want any players who have doubts about Madrid.'

Frank Lampard, who appears in a new Sainsbury's TV ad with celebrity chef Jamie Oliver, is on the point of accepting an £80,000-a-week offer for a new extended contract, just short of his £90,000-a-week asking price.

Adrian Mutu concedes he has had a confrontation with the English contingent at Chelsea. 'I'm fed up with rumours about how I affect team morale. Somebody said I am unpopular in the squad, especially with the England lads, so I went into the dressing room and asked my team-mates if I'd upset them. I insisted on a private talk with the Englishmen to sort this out. They told me that things are fine and that they have no problem with me and I hope this is the case.'

Chelsea take another step towards rivalling Manchester United and Real Madrid as a global football brand by appointing marketing group TWI to handle their overseas TV and new media rights. Abramovich has been seeking to accelerate the process of making the club an international force on the world stage. TWI, the sports agency, has agreed a three-year deal to sublicense all the non-UK rights to the club's content from its Chelsea TV channel, Chelsea Broadband and Chelsea Mobile services.

The deal gives TWI the rights to a wide range of Chelsea content, including delayed rights to Premier League and Champions League matches, official club news, live reserve matches, exclusive interviews and classic archive moments outside the wider deal for overseas live rights, which is negotiated centrally by the Premier League.

Ruud van Nistelrooy criticises Arjen Robben's decision to reject Manchester United. 'It's very stupid to choose Chelsea when United are interested in you. I don't understand that boy. He came to United for a day and was very enthusiastic. It was his dream to play for United. But while United and PSV were trying to reach an agreement, he suddenly chose Chelsea. He is very young but he is a big talent and has years ahead of him. Money should not be the most important thing in your life at that age. He can earn a lot in the future.'

TUESDAY, 25 MAY

Jon Smith is shocked that Abramovich isn't at the summit meeting and that the talks are with Tenenbaum and Kenyon. Smith gets his files ready to negotiate a compensation package and asks, 'Where are we at?' Kenyon replies that there is no decision. Abramovich is delayed in Russia. Smith puts away his files immediately.

A two-and-a-half hour discussion follows about which players should leave and Ranieri is asked for his recommendations for new signings. He suggests

Steven Gerrard from the club that still harbours hopes of deflecting Mourinho from the Bridge.

Ranieri had been expecting to pick up his P45 but he leaves Stamford Bridge still expecting to be fired within days. Why the delay? Ranieri is left to make an educated guess. Perhaps problems with recruiting Mourinho... Maybe second thoughts about hiring the man if he turns out to be a loser in the Champions League final... Could it be the late intervention of Liverpool to snatch Mourinho? These are a few of the wild questions going through Ranieri's mind.

Peter Kenyon arrives in Gelsenkirchen for a UEFA function, prompting speculation that a deal with Jose Mourinho will be announced after the match. Preparing for the final in the AufSchalke Arena, Mourinho fields a barrage of questions about his future – as expected. When asked if he will move to Stamford Bridge after the final, he says, 'That's a private question, that's only between me and Porto because I am still involved with Porto. It's my club and I have a contract with them for two more seasons.

'I don't know if it's my last match but I do know it is the most important match of my career and something I've worked on for two years. I said a few weeks ago, I don't want to know anything about other clubs, presidents, agents. If you ask the players they will say exactly the same. Everyone is fully concentrated on this match. It deserves one hundred per cent from us and I must be an example to the players.

'We must make it a good game because this wasn't the final everyone expected. No one would expect two teams like us to be here and we want to show the world that outsiders are capable of playing well. I hope the game will be a tribute to football and the fans watching around the world. The Champions League is much more important than my future. And my future could be Thursday.'

Mourinho, who refuses to discuss whether he has signed a pre-contract agreement with Chelsea, leaves no doubt that team affairs will be his business. 'I can't imagine a successful club without a very good relationship between the manager and the board. Porto is a very good example of a successful club and the success was built with everybody having the same motivation and everyone fighting for the same objective.'

Asked whether he can ever work for a club where he is not calling all the shots, Mourinho insists, 'That is a wonderful question to ask me on Thursday. I will have an answer then. It happened to me only once before in my career, at Benfica – and I walked out.'

Asked why he would want to leave the Champions League finalists for a club which has not won a championship for almost 50 years, Mourinho simply shrugs and replies, 'Successful people are headhunted in every profession in the world. When you take a team to the European final, it's natural that other clubs are interested. It's the law of the market, the law of life.'

Mourinho has a reputation for being a control freak. 'You don't win major matches without controlling your emotions. If you don't keep calm and cool, it's very difficult to achieve anything. My players don't need a psychological whip to be motivated. There will be no brainwashing or emotional speeches. I know them well and I know they're not afraid.

'They are ready for everything that Monaco can throw at us and there is nothing they can do to surprise us. I want happiness in my football club. I want players who I trust and who trust me. The greatest thing in my life is when, after I have lost, my children say, "You are the best daddy!" But then I also like to win football maches.'

Mourinho's man-management methods are endorsed by experienced Porto defender Carlos Secretario. 'Jose has an excellent relationship with all his players and his success is based on his human qualities. He doesn't try to control us. He gives us all the freedom in the world and the squad have responded to that responsibility.'

Mourinho has held court for 45 minutes and is cool under intense questioning. He switches effortlessly between Portuguese, Spanish, English and French. Mourinho is proud of his side's attacking prowess, though, and he is promising to provide a platform for the inventive Brazil-born Portugal international Deco Souza to win the final for his side. 'I know Deco's ability and what he can do for us. The Monaco coach will be trying to find ways to block him, while I find a way for him to play to his full potential. We like to have the ball and when we don't have it we go and look for it. I'm not saying I'll have an open-door policy and try to win 5–4.'

Victory will make Porto only the second team after Liverpool in 1976 and 1977 to win the UEFA Cup and European Cup in successive seasons.

Ranieri may be able to take advantage of the managerial merry-go-round to be reunited with old pals at Valencia. Liverpool, who were also interested in Mourinho, are heavily linked with Valencia's current boss, Rafa Benitez. If he leaves, Ranieri is already being tipped to rejoin his former club.

Ranieri will be named Man of the Year on 2 June by the Variety Club of Great Britain. Awards night chairman Jarvis Astaire says, 'It's a special award for a special man who always carried himself with dignity no matter what the circumstances.'

Abramovich is currently in Milan to indulge in his car-racing hobby and to meet AC Milan vice-president Adriano Galliani at the club's headquarters. Galliani insists the Serie A champions, who have just won their 17th league title, will not be talked into selling Shevchenko. 'Milan will not sell their top players. Thus, we will not sell Andrei Shevchenko,' says a defiant Galliani on the club's official television channel. 'I have already let him [Abramovich] know that Shevchenko is not for sale. If he makes this request he will get only one answer.

I will reiterate that Shevchenko is not on the market. I will receive Abramovich as a courtesy but we will speak about other things.'

WEDNESDAY, 26 MAY

John Terry is a notable absentee as the England players watch the European Cup final in their Sardinian training camp. As he explains, 'The semi-final wasn't a nice night for any of us and it was difficult to take. It's painful enough getting knocked out, so I'm not going to sit there watching it, knowing it should be us in the final. We were very disappointed to lose because we believed we were the better side and deserved to go through.'

Meanwhile Frank Lampard warns Chelsea against making too many summer changes as he urges the power-brokers to put everyone out of their misery and name the new manager. 'I can't say enough about what Claudio has done for me. I'm much more of a developed player and character now, but the club is the be-all and end-all and the sad fact is that managers and players all move on in time.

'It's lingered over us all season and made it a little bit difficult though. A good thing would be to get it sorted either way now. We've done very well this year without winning anything, but there is already a core of the team. There will be changes, we all anticipate that. But I don't think there should be wholesale changes because we have got to know each other this year. New players have come in and the majority have fitted in very well. Hopefully, we can add to that core and come back even stronger than we were.'

As for his new contract, he adds, 'I want to stay. Things have to be right and I hope they will be. And the sooner the better, because I'm going to Euro 2004 and I would love to have it tied up before I'm starting to play games. I wouldn't personally like to be in the position of sitting out two years.'

Trevor Birch is about to land his third job in a year when he is appointed as Everton's new chief executive at a board meeting. A former Liverpool player and unused substitute in the 1978 European Cup final, he starts in June after taking over from Mike Dunford. The new role will involve bringing new investment into a club that has a debt of around £30m and is struggling to give manager Moyes funds for new players.

Andrei Shevchenko signs a new deal with the Italian champions which ties him to Milan until at least 2009. Marseille striker Didier Drogba moves up the pecking order as an alternative target for Chelsea. He is also wanted by Manchester United.

With a 3–0 win over Monaco, Mourinho's Porto show why he is the most coveted young coach in Europe. He leaves Porto after two Portuguese championships, the Portuguese Cup, the UEFA Cup and, now, the European Cup. He feels confident he can meet the challenge at Chelsea. 'As a manager I want to do more. I want to win more. I want to remain ambitious and to grow as a manager. There are things I can improve in my performance.

'I would now like to leave Porto. I have a contract with Porto but I have other options. Tomorrow I will look at them in detail. The country I want to work in is England. There is a club there I have given my word to but I do not want to say any more. We have done something unforgettable tonight. Let me enjoy the moment.'

A watching Peter Kenyon has been relaxing and appreciating the fruits of his headhunting during the final. He gives a fence-sitting interview at half-time to ITV, where he says that Ranieri is still the coach and stops short of confirming that Mourinho has consented to work for Chelsea. 'This isn't a holiday period for us, this is about preparing for next season. Claudio Ranieri is our manager. We're fully involved in that process and that's what we'll be getting on with next week. I think we've got to get things resolved next week and start planning for next season. Claudio and I had a good meeting this week on players.'

In a tribute to Mourinho and Deschamps, he adds, 'I think what you've got in this game are probably the two best young coaches in Europe. These guys are going to continue their careers, they've done tremendously well to get here as we know first-hand from one of them.'

As Kevin McCarra writes in the *Guardian*, 'The obvious comparison cannot be shirked, cruel as it is. Ranieri vandalised Chelsea's chances in the semi-final with Monaco through his ham-fisted mid-match alterations. Mourinho, an artist of strategy, destroyed Didier Deschamps's team with his canny adjustments.'

Mourinho has shut out opponents who have scored 27 times on their way to the final. After the match, Mourinho is halfway across the pitch, heading for a celebration with his players, when he doubles back towards the touchline. In the tunnel entrance, he locates his small son and daughter. He sits quietly on the bench, flanked by his children while his players continue their celebrations.

The night belongs to Mourinho. Once an early injury deprives Monaco of captain Ludovic Giuly, the efficiency of Mourinho's methods become obvious in his final match in charge of the Portuguese champions – there is organisation throughout the team, coupled with the brilliance of the Brazil-born trio of Deco, Derlei and Carlos Alberto up front. Mourinho's final contribution comes on the hour, when he removes his goal-scorer, 19-year-old Carlos Alberto, and sends on Alenitchev. Within 15 minutes, the Russian has played a vital role in two more goals, making one and scoring the other.

Lifting the European Cup after only four seasons as a manager is the standard Mourinho expects to maintain at Stamford Bridge. 'It is a great feeling to win the European Cup at 41,' he says. 'When you look at the great managers in the world who worked for 20 years at the highest level, some never had the chance to win the UEFA Cup or the Champions League. I've had great success in winning the UEFA Cup and the Champions League so quickly but if you tell me that in ten years I will just have the same medals, I will be very sad.

'As a manager, I have got to do more. I want to be ambitious, to become better and better. I believe a lot of things can grow in my performance. When I say that I know many good managers can go 30 or 40 years without this kind of success. I'm aware of this and because of it I want to enjoy this night with my players before I discuss the future.'

He reveals the speech that helped to inspire Porto to their 3–0 victory. 'My last words to the players were: "We will not forget this day, not even when we are very old, so you had better have a good memory. It is better to have a good memory than sadness for the rest of your life." You always play to your strengths, you look at your players and it doesn't matter what system you play, 4-3-3, 4-4-2, you have to be the same model, you always have to be true to your identity.'

The task now? To win the same trophy for Chelsea! 'Basically, they have got to win the European Cup next year.'

THURSDAY, 27 MAY

Ranieri is summoned to a meeting with Abramovich in Milan at 4.30pm local time expecting to be sacked – only to be asked again for his detailed plans for next season. As Ranieri is making the flight from Rome to Milan with his wife, his 'successor' Mourinho is already announcing on Portuguese TV that he is going to the Bridge.

Ranieri goes into the meeting with Abramovich, Tenenbaum, and Kenyon believing the axe is going to fall at last, but heads back to Rome just as confused as ever, still the Chelsea coach and with no clear pointers as to his future. He is told that there will be another meeting in a few days, when, no doubt, he will finally be put out of his misery, one way or another. But the stay of execution has been prolonged beyond the point of endurance for a man who has conducted himself with great dignity. The reason Chelsea are keeping him hanging on would seem to be simply that they are waiting to cement the 'deal' that is already in place with Mourinho. But the big mystery is about why Abramovich should want to see Ranieri personally! Theories abound. Is it merely to pick Ranieri's brains about which players to buy and sell or is there some credence in the eleventh-hour possibility of a U-turn to keep Ranieri?

Ranieri's advisers are trying to fathom the motives of Abramovich without much success. Italian agent Morabito and Phil Smith, brother of Jon Smith, are in Milan, sitting outside the meeting at the Four Seasons Hotel, a 15th-century converted convent. Inside room 444 in the 118-room luxury hotel, beside the exclusive designer shops and city finance houses on the Via Gesu, Ranieri is confronted by Abramovich, Kenyon and Tenenbaum.

When Ranieri is asked for his plans for next season he smiles and wonders if they are 'taking the piss'. But no, they are serious; there is no discussion about being sacked. They want to know what he has in mind for next season. After more than two hours of elaborate discussions, Ranieri and his wife join up with Morabito and Phil Smith to make the journey back to Milan airport. On the way to the airport Morabito tells me, 'Claudio said that the meeting was very pleasant. Until he is finally fired we cannot say anything, but actually there was no discussion about terminating his contract or compensation. All they talked about was the future, about players and Claudio was told there would be another meeting in a few days.'

Ranieri has been on tenterhooks for virtually a year, since the very first meeting between Eriksson and Abramovich. The most prolonged and agonising execution in football history has intensified since the season finished and become intolerable in the last few days.

Ranieri has no intention of forcing the issue, despite offers from other clubs because he does not want to jeopardise a £6m-plus pay-off for the remaining three years of his contract. Ranieri wants to remain in England, preferably in London. As yet he has not held talks with the most likely candidates – Spurs.

Reinaldo Teles, Porto's director of football, confirms Mourinho's exit. 'We will have a new coach, a big team and will continue to work towards winning more titles.' Mourinho has insisted he comes with his backroom staff assistant, Baltemar Brito, the goalkeeping coach, Silvino Louro, and the fitness coach, Rui Faria. He also wants the playmaker Deco, right-back Paulo Ferreira and the midfielder Costinha. The acquisitions will cost at least £50m and raise question marks over the future of Joe Cole and Glen Johnson. Officially Chelsea simply say, 'Watch this space.'

Despite asking Ranieri for his opinion on players, Abramovich meets Milan vice-president Adriano Galliani in the morning but, according to Kenyon, new signings are not discussed. 'We have known the Milan executives for some time and we respect them very much. It has been a general meeting and we have not spoken about any player,' says Kenyon. He denies Abramovich and he are due to meet Inter Milan executives later in the week. 'On this occasion, our only purpose was to meet [AC] Milan,' Kenyon says. Galliani adds, 'We have not spoken about any player, that is the truth.'

FRIDAY, 28 MAY

Ranieri remains manager of Chelsea this morning despite the club's very public attempts to recruit Mourinho, who flies into London to thrash out the final terms of a four-year deal worth £16m, making him one of the best-paid managers in the world.

Celestine Babayaro gives an insight into Abramovich's relationship with his players. The Russian's post-match visits to the dressing room have been the source of much intrigue, but Babayaro reveals, 'Abramovich is a very humble man and doesn't say very much. He comes into the dressing room and sits down in the corner with his hands on his knees. If you didn't know who he was you'd think he was a cleaner! He shakes the players' hands and observes what's going on but that's about it. He's very quiet and modest.'

Babayaro has been one of the casualties of the Abramovich revolution, making just 13 starts following the signing of Wayne Bridge. The Nigerian left-back has one year left on his contract. 'I'd like to stay at the club but what can you do if you're not wanted? It depends on the club but I'm in no rush to leave. There's going to be players leaving and players coming and it's not really up to me.'

Babayaro is confident of a real challenge next season. 'Chelsea did okay this season but we will be even better in the future. At the start of the season we couldn't even shout to each other in training because we didn't know each other's names very well but it will be different next season.'

SATURDAY, 29 MAY

Ranieri is amazed to think he might still have a chance of remaining with the club. After a debriefing from Ranieri, Jon Smith tells me, 'Claudio was pleasantly surprised when Roman put his arm around him and looked him in the eyes and told him he hadn't made up his mind.'

Ranieri says, 'I spoke with Roman. It was a lovely meeting and now I can only wait. We talked about players, we talked about the future. Was Mourinho mentioned? No, no, no, because I spoke only about myself and my plans. Roman said, "Okay, Claudio, next week I will give you the answer."'

A conclusive meeting between Abramovich and Mourinho is to take place at a neutral venue, mostly likely to be in Monte Carlo. This will be the third face-to-face meeting between Abramovich and Mourinho. A Chelsea insider tells me, 'We would expect to have everything in place by the middle of the week. Having come this far, it would be hard to believe that Roman will now change his mind.'

Interestingly, Abramovich was first attracted to the idea of Jose Mourinho when he inspected the AC Milan trophy room and was taken aback by all the gleaming silverware. It was hard not to compare the amount that Mourinho had won in just two years with Ranieri's record over his entire career, let alone the four trophy-free years at the Bridge.

Smith has made contingency plans for a press conference at a Park Lane hotel next Wednesday, just before Ranieri is scheduled to go to the Hilton Hotel to collect his Variety Club award.

Porto president, Nuno Pinto da Costa, a member of the G14 cartel of clubs, lines up Luigi Del Neri, coach to Italy's Chievo, as replacement for Mourinho. Meanwhile Richard Critzman accepts a new post with Swiss oil company BITOL and therefore leaves Sibneft and the Chelsea board.

Marseille insist Didier Drogba is not for sale as president Christophe Bouchet says, 'He won't be transferred for he's untransferable. Chelsea have contacted us about Didier but we want to build a team around him.' Drogba is one of the players put forward by Ranieri to Abramovich, and the forward is also wanted by Mourinho.

Chelsea defender William Gallas points out the problems awaiting Mourinho. 'Arsenal are better than us because they play together and they defend together. We can play together, but won't. We score a lot of goals, but we concede a lot of goals. Arsenal are playing for each other but we are playing for ourselves sometimes.

'Roman Abramovich should be buying players with the right personality. You can have some stars, maybe one or two, but they must work. Look at Real Madrid: they have a lot of stars and, yes, they are very good, but where are the results? We have big players but sometimes some of them don't know how to play for the team. If we had Arsenal's togetherness, maybe we could have won the Championship. But we did not fight together.'

SUNDAY, 30 MAY

Mourinho is determined to manage, not just coach. 'England interests me because the concept of manager prevails rather than that of coach. He takes charge of everything, from the 11 players on the field to the organisation. It would be a good move.'

Abramovich and Mourinho talk aboard the Russian billionaire's yacht, *Le Grand Bleu*, moored at St Tropez. The meeting progresses so well that Mourinho, who flew to Nice on Friday for the meeting, and Abramovich even draw up a list of possible transfer targets. Mourinho will sign his contract with Chelsea by tomorrow night, ahead of a formal press conference on Tuesday.

Costinha, the anchor midfield player who marked Fernando Morientes into submission at the AufSchalke arena, Deco, the Brazil-born Portugal international who scored Porto's second goal in the final, full-back Paulo Ferreira and Ricardo Carvalho, a centre-half groomed in Porto's youth system, are all on Mourinho's wanted list for Chelsea.

Mourinho, who agrees a deal at five times his current salary which will be the highest in domestic football, has all but secured Porto play-maker Deco for €20m (£14m) and midfielder Costinha for €8-10m (£5.5-£7m). A third deal, for right-back Ferreira, is being resisted, while midfielder Maniche may move instead.

Chelsea expect to land Deco even though Bayern Munich have also lodged a bid. Deco says, 'Of course I'd like to go to Chelsea as he's a coach I know well. He's won everything here and now has other ambitions. I've a preference for the English league because of the way they play.'

Porto midfielder Costinha, whose goal knocked Manchester United out of Europe, joins team-mate Deco in expressing a desire to follow Mourinho. 'I still have two years left on my contract at Porto but of course I'd love to go with Mourinho. I know if I go I will have more success. My agent is taking care of it and I know there will be developments over the next few days.'

Costinha is in no doubt Chelsea will be getting a manager of the highest quality. 'He is probably the best trainer I've ever had. He knows how to prepare the players and how to speak with them. He thinks about football 24 hours a day. He is always wondering where he can improve his team, where he can make better use of a player. He also likes to discuss things with the players. I can say, "Coach, I think you can play like this," and he is OK with that – it's better for the team.

'If he has to be harder with the players, he is. For instance, at half-time in the final he told me I was not playing very well. He is fair with everybody. He is not one way with the star of the team and different with a youth player. There are no superstars for him – the most important thing is the team.'

Mourinho's mentor, Sir Bobby Robson, is concerned about his move to English football. 'The fact is Jose is coming into an area he doesn't know. He won't find the Premiership anything like the Portuguese league. He is joining the big boys and the big teams, where every game is a potential blip. In Portugal, if you can defeat Benfica and Sporting home and away, you are likely to win the title. What he has done on five or six occasions in European competition over the last two seasons is beat the big teams. He has to do that 38 times in the league.

'I never thought of him as being a coach. I always felt his vocation would be in education because he had been a PE teacher.'

Mourinho says, 'I still see Sir Bobby as a father to me. My early times with Bobby were really important and the way he put faith in me gave me confidence and taught me to be strong in believing myself. Tactically and dealing with players I could not ask for a better teacher and I could not have learnt from anyone better. It was an experience that was invaluable and I still telephone and talk to him now. He is a leader to me and I will go on respecting him as a great manager. He is always close to the players and that is something, as a manager, you must always be. They are your blood and the most important thing of all. They have to respect you and that is something that I learnt from Bobby in the way they respect him and will always play for him. A little something from everything I achieve will always be dedicated to him.'

Reports from Spain reveal that Chelsea still want Ronaldinho, but Barcelona vice-president Sandro Rosell says, 'It's not our objective to sell him.'

Meanwhile Cagliari are on the way up to Serie A following a 3–1 win over Salernitana, which takes them back in the top flight for the first time since the 1999–2000 campaign. Sardinia-born Gianfranco Zola could not have asked for a better return home. 'This is the most beautiful moment,' Zola says. 'It was a very difficult game. We were coming from behind but we managed to get the result we wanted. I am extremely happy.' Zola could be lined up to return to Chelsea in a non-playing capacity. 'This is a time to celebrate. It has been a difficult and long season, but whatever decision I take, I would like it to be respected.'

MONDAY, 31 MAY

Peter Kenyon contacts Jon Smith to inform him that Claudio Ranieri has now been sacked. Smith contacts Morabito who in turn calls Ranieri in Rome. Finally Ranieri has been given the axe and, after another day of intense intrigue, a 62-word statement, prepared by Stuart Higgins in consultation with Kenyon, is released. Ranieri is dismissed with a few kind words, but there is a behind-the-scenes row about the terms of his compensation. Smith is trying to sort out the dispute.

The Chelsea statement refers to Ranieri's 'first-class job for the club [which] paved the way for future success'. But Roman Abramovich has taken the advice of Kenyon and other trusted advisors that Ranieri was not the man to actually provide that success. Abramovich told Ranieri that he had not made up his mind when they met in Milan last Friday but, when he met Mourinho again, it was decided to bring in the man who lifted the Champions League with Porto. A Chelsea insider tells me, 'We intend to honour the terms of Ranieri's contract.'

Smith, the Italian coach's UK representative, says, 'We read the tea leaves a few weeks ago or even a few months. He [Ranieri] is very proud of the job he has done but he is a little sad at not being able to complete the job. We are assured he is a man in demand. We heard the decision this afternoon and we are involved in an ongoing discussion regarding the terms of his departure.'

Ranieri has three years left on a £2m-a-year contract. Ranieri is claiming £8m with bonuses he might have earned, while Chelsea's opening offer is pitched under £2m.

The Chelsea statement wishes Ranieri 'all the best for the future', and, clearly if he does get another job, that would mean that 'honouring the terms of his contract' would no longer require the west London club to cough up the entire £6m. The lack of comment from Ranieri indicates a row brewing over the compensation. The Chelsea statement also hints that compensation is a sticking point when it adds, 'We are discussing the exact terms of his departure with him and his representatives.'

Out with the old, in with the new: Mourinho has already stamped his personality on Chelsea as he is not interested in spending vast fortunes on stars such as Ronaldinho or Roberto Carlos.

In another day of twists and turns, all the parties directly involved had agreed a pact to keep quiet for a further 24 hours, but because of Mourinho's expected unveiling at the Bridge it is decided close to 6.00 pm to formally issue a statement that Ranieri has been sacked. The main issue is the compensation. Chelsea argue that the enormous sum is 'mitigated' by the likelihood that the Italian will be re-employed at some stage, even if not this summer.

Kenyon and Abramovich want to part on good terms with Ranieri. After so many weeks, months – in fact, the whole year of turmoil – the club at least owe him a proper send-off and not a lingering dispute over the amount owed. But someone, somewhere, at some time, will have to account to Abramovich just how much he is spending at the Bridge. The huge amounts of money involved make this managerial sacking a one-off. Mourinho will be hired on a £4m-a-year salary for three years with a fourth-year option, Ranieri needs to be compensated, and then there will be the new coaches and players arriving from Porto.

Whereas Ranieri, in his two sessions of talks last week, recommended only three new players, Mourinho wants four or five. Ranieri put forward a short list of new players, including a striker, a central midfield player and centre-half. He suggested Gerrard for the midfield berth, Morientes of Real Madrid, Drogba from Marseille or Samuel Eto'o from Majorca as the new striker, and after his first-choice defender Walter Samuel signed for Real a number of alternatives were suggested.

Mourinho wants three of his Porto stars, plus another Portuguese player, and he wouldn't say no to Gerrard if he could be prised from Liverpool. Mourinho has not insisted upon either of the Brazilians previously mentioned in dispatches: left-back Roberto Carlos is only wanted if Real's asking price of £20m drops by half for a 31-year-old with just one year left on his existing contract; nor does he want Ronaldinho unless Barcelona halve their £60m asking price.

Ranieri did not want to be too hasty in off-loading players such as Gronkjaer, while Mourinho won't hesitate to kick out a dozen of the Italian's squad. Mourinho shares Kenyon's conviction that Chelsea are vastly over-staffed, and Mourinho's appointment will signal a mass clear-out. Three of the five players put forward by Mourinho come from European champions Porto.

While that means five new faces, it will also mean offloading as many as ten current players over the close season. Players such as Melchiot, Petit, Stanic and Bogarde, who have come to the end of their contracts will be informed that no offers will be made and they are free to go. Others, such as Hasselbaink and Desailly with a year left, will be told they can also go on free transfers and, if they cannot fix themselves up with clubs, then there is no place for them in the first team. Gronkjaer is already attracting a host of clubs including Birmingham and will now go at a reasonable price. Others on loan such as Zenden at Boro and Carlton Cole at Charlton will be sold off. But Chelsea will be looking to recoup around half of the fees paid out for Argentina internationals Crespo and Veron.

Ranieri's options are limited for joining a big club. The Real Madrid post, vacated by Carlos Queiroz, has been filled by former Spain coach Jose Camacho. Juventus swooped for Roma's Fabio Capello instead of Deschamps, who looks set to stay in France for at least another season. The Roma position was filled by Cesare Prandelli, ending a two-season stint with Parma. At least the Tottenham job is still available. Ranieri hopes the phone will start ringing with offers. If not, he is prepared to hold out for the right club, supplementing his compensation from Chelsea with media work.

Ranieri is preparing to fly to London from his home in Rome on Wednesday just as Kenyon and his entourage are on their way from Oporto with Mourinho to unveil him at the Bridge, with Abramovich in Moscow. Mourinho will be installed before he flies off on a family holiday to Brazil on Wednesday night.

The reaction to Ranieri's demise is predictably mixed. Frank Lampard breaks off from his preparations for the England friendly with Japan in Manchester to say, 'In the three years I've been at Chelsea, Claudio has done loads for me. He gave me a chance and, without that, who knows where I would be? I cannot say enough about him. The way I'm playing and how I've developed in character, that's got to be down to him. He is a very honourable and dignified man. I respect everything he's done and I will be talking to him and thanking him. There is some sadness. It's a difficult situation but the club is the be-all and end-all. Managers and players move on. What's made it difficult is that it has lingered over a whole season.'

Peter Osgood believes Ranieri has 'gone with dignity' but questions his Tinkerman approach. 'He has brought this upon himself and I am not surprised he has gone. He tinkered too much. We beat Lazio 4–0 and then we beat Newcastle 5–0 to go top of the league. It was the best football I had seen but, the following week, he changed his team. Roman Abramovich has put a lot of money into the club and he can do what he likes. I don't feel sorry for Claudio. He'll get another job.'

David Mellor agrees that Ranieri had to go. 'Chelsea spent massively last summer and they have two internationals for every position. He should have done better. If Roman Abramovich had been looking for a manager when he came in, nobody would have suggested Ranieri. I would love to say, "What a lovely fellow, he should have been kept on," but you cannot watch Chelsea without thinking there is something eccentric and unusual about how they manage their resources. It could have been better handled but I believe he had to go.'

Ron 'Chopper' Harris says, "He spent a lot of money and won nothing. Gianluca Vialli won five trophies in two years and got the sack. It seems to be part and parcel of football these days – if people don't win anything they're on the way.'

So, football's most drawn-out sacking is finally confirmed to no one's surprise, and the charade ends. Ranieri finished second in the Premiership and reached the Champions League semi-final but Peter Kenyon and Roman Abramovich did not regard him as a coach who could fulfil their ambitions.

The task of leading Chelsea forward instead goes to Jose Mourinho, fresh from winning the Champions League with Porto.

June

THE NEW MANAGER ARRIVES

TUESDAY, 1 JUNE

A shocked Ranieri suffers more humiliation and anger as he is forced to go to war with his 'old' club Chelsea over his right to compensation. Chelsea offer to pay in instalments until such time as he finds new employment. Ranieri demands he must be paid £6m but Chelsea insist he looks at the finer points of his contract where he must use his 'best endeavours' to find a new job. Chelsea's argument is that they should not pay him once he has found new employment.

With the Valencia chief executive flying to London for talks now that he has lost his coach, Rafa Benitez, to Liverpool, it might not be long before Ranieri is re-employed. Ranieri has consulted with employment experts, lawyers, the League Managers Association and the Premier League, who are keeping a watching brief. The whole issue of Ranieri's contract becomes a major battle ground. Close friends of Ranieri are appalled that, after being so badly

	PREMIERSHIP – FINAL TABLE							
Pos	Team	P	W	D	L	GF	GA	GD	PTS
1	Arsenal	38	26	12	0	73	26	47	90
2	Chelsea	38	24	7	7	67	30	37	79
3	Manchester United	38	23	6	9	64	35	29	75
4	Liverpool	38	16	12	10	55	37	18	60
5	Newcastle United	38	13	17	8	52	40	12	56
6	Aston Villa	38	15	11	12	48	44	4	56
7	Charlton Athletic	38	14	11	13	51	51	0	53
8	Bolton Wanderers	38	14	11	13	48	56	-8	53
9	Fulham	38	14	10	14	52	46	6	52
10	Birmingham City	38	12	14	12	43	48	-5	50

treated, in their view, for so long, there should be a final 'kick in the teeth'.

Simultaneously Valencia have stepped up their interest in Ranieri now that it is confirmed that their coach Benitez is heading for Anfield. Ranieri is still highly regarded in Spain and he is now free to talk to clubs after being sacked. And Chelsea would welcome a new club taking up part of their financial obligation.

Abramovich can afford to pay Ranieri whatever he wants, but the Russian owner has been advised that, under the terms of the ousted coach's contract, he is not entitled to the full amount. The row is still going on behind the scenes as Chelsea decide to delay the unveiling of Mourinho who turns up at the Bridge, but still has to go through some last-minute fine-tuning of his record £20m four-year contract.

Under a revised deal agreed by Ken Bates two years ago, Ranieri is entitled to be paid in full for whatever is remaining on his contract, if dismissed. But this is dependent on him not taking a new job during that time period. Under employment law he has an obligation to mitigate the losses of his former employer and so, if Ranieri does take a new job as seems likely, he does not get paid in full. The Italian's advisers dispute this. They argue that Chelsea are not honouring the deal and he should be entitled to the full pay-off regardless.

Ranieri could be a contender for the manager's post at Spurs but Valencia will be favourites unless chairman Daniel Levy acts decisively. Rafa Benitez resigned as Valencia coach yesterday just weeks after leading them to a first-ever domestic and European double to join Liverpool.

'This had been possibly one of the most difficult decisions I have had to take in my sporting career,' a tearful Benitez says at Valencia's Paterna training ground. The 44-year-old, who speaks English, had been offered a five-year deal by Liverpool. Valencia president Jaime Orti insists the club has done all it can to persuade Benitez to remain with the Primera Liga champions and that the coach's decision to leave has come as a shock, but he has still moved fast to talk to Ranieri.

Mourinho arrives with his family at Heathrow, to be met by Kenyon. Asked if he was the new Chelsea manager, he smiles and says, 'No comment.' Questioned about the stage his negotiations are at with Chelsea, he replies, 'It is not finished yet. You'll have to wait a little bit. You will know very soon.'

Kenyon spends all day in Portugal in talks with Porto executives to negotiate a compensation package for Mourinho and his back room team. This is agreed and is €2.5m (£1.75m).

As part of the deal Porto will act as a feeder club for Chelsea for the next five years as part of the deal that brings Mourinho to Stamford Bridge. Mourinho will have first option on the local talent developed over the specified period by his former club. Chelsea will pour money into Porto's academy to help them spot and coach players and, in return, will get preferential treatment if they want to bring Portuguese youngsters to Stamford Bridge. The deal is announced by Porto as they confirmed that they had agreed compensation for Mourinho.

'Porto agree with Chelsea Football Club Ltd the terms for the annulment of the contract of employment of head coach Jose Mourinho,' they say in a statement. 'As part of the agreement ... Porto announce the establishment of a partnership with Chelsea for five years, with exclusivity in the Portuguese market, with respect to the detection, training and promotion of young talent.'

Ranieri has a meeting at the Hilton Hotel, near Heathrow, to discuss the vacancy left at Spurs by Hoddle the previous September. Also present were Spurs vice-chairman Paul Kemsley, sporting director Frank Arnesen and Ranieri's UK agent Phil Smith. They spend nearly two hours in a basement meeting room discussing the finer details of the job at White Hart Lane. Ranieri and Smith are first to leave in the agent's turquoise sports car.

When quizzed about joining Spurs, the former Chelsea manager is in good spirits but only comments, 'I'm sorry, I can't say anything.' The pair are followed out of the Hilton's £90-per-hour meeting room by Levy, Kemsley and Arnesen. Levy interrupts a mobile phone conversation to say, 'It is pure coincidence. You are jumping to the wrong conclusions.'

Ranieri now has time to enjoy Euro 2004, 'I will be watching my Chelsea players.'

Ken Bates criticises the manner of Ranieri's sacking. 'Whatever happens I think the fans will be disappointed, if not disgusted, with the way he has been treated. I would have kept Ranieri. After all, somebody who gets you second in the League and into the European Cup semi-finals with so much turbulence, background pressure and public disloyalty, has had a magnificent season.'

After tomorrow's 10.00 am press conference Mourinho and his family are due to go on holiday to Brazil before returning for Euro 2004. He is contracted to do a newspaper column, for the sports paper *O Jogo*, throughout the tournament.

Nuno Pinto da Costa, the Porto president, says that he has already rejected an initial offer from Chelsea for Ferreira. However, Ferreira, 25, says, 'The president said that I was not for sale, but if the offer is good, it will be difficult to refuse. I would be honoured if Jose wanted me.'

WEDNESDAY, 2 JUNE

Mourinho delivered a message of intent at his unveiling at the Bridge. 'We have top players at Chelsea. And, I'm sorry if I sound arrogant, we have a top manager as well. I don't want to be compared with coaches from the past and nor do I want to be viewed as the face of young managers in the game. I have won the

Champions League. I'm not one who comes straight out of the bottle. I'm a special one.'

Kenyon admits, 'I don't think we'll need to work on his confidence. He has been charged with being arrogant but I don't think he is. He's very confident and self-assured and thoughtful about what he does. He's deliberate and has a gameplan.'

Mourinho asserts, 'I accept that if I don't win this year it will be a failure. If I am sacked, I can always find another job. But I have not come here to give myself nightmares. I have come here to sleep well.'

Mourinho had time to point an accusing finger at Ranieri, 'I didn't like what he said about the Portuguese league being an easy one to win. I prefer to use my head and not react to other people's opinions. But what I suggest is that if someone is Mr Ranieri's friend, or has contact with him, you should explain to him that if a team is to win the UEFA Cup or the Champions League it has to play clubs from other countries. I didn't win the UEFA Cup and the Champions League playing 20 Portuguese teams. I played and beat players and clubs from his country, Italy, from England and Spain. Porto beat everyone in Europe.

In a warning to his new squad, Mourinho says, 'I love players who love to win. And not just during the 90 minutes on the pitch. Players have to love to win every day, in every training session, in every moment of their life. When Chelsea players read this, they will know whether they are the ones for me. If we are to have success we can only do it together.'

As for Eriksson, Chelsea's first choice, Mourinho shrugs his shoulders. 'It is only natural they went for him. Mr Eriksson is a manager with a lot of prestige in the world. He also had a close relationship with Chelsea and, because of that, he was their number one choice.'

He moves on to Abramovich and the suspicion that he will be difficult to control. 'I don't have to control Roman Abramovich – he has to control me. But, as in any business, you have to communicate with the top man. I spent two days with him on his yacht and he never once mentioned what he expected from me. Instead, I gave him a four-page document about how I work and what I am.

'He is the owner and the first person in the club. But what I need to do I have already done. I have established clearly what my position is and my functions in the club. But at the same time I want a close relationship between all the different structures.'

At the Hilton Hotel in the evening, Ranieri is to receive his Variety Club award, but before the presention, he poses in with a Valencia scarf in anticipation of his appointment after two days of intensive talks with the club's general manager Manuel Llorente.

And the Spanish champs could end up meeting Chelsea in Europe next season!

Ranieri reveals he was given the boot while in Rome. 'I spoke with my Italian advisor, Vicenzo Morabito, and he told me the news by phone, after he had heard it from my English agent, Jon Smith. It will be the biggest regret of my career that I have not been able to say a proper goodbye to the Chelsea fans. I saw Gerard Houllier say goodbye live on television at Liverpool but for me that was not possible. I am very angry and have been all season. The death was not a sudden surprise. I was like a lamb to the slaughter. I was slaughtered and then roasted on the spit.'

Mourinho gets straight down to work, taking a private jet along with Abramvoich and Keyon to a meeting with Terry, Lampard, Bridge and Cole. Although England are busy preparing for Saturday's final Euro 2004 warm-up match against Iceland, the meeting has been approved by the FA and Eriksson.

Chelsea's players are scheduled to return for pre-season training on 5 July but Mourinho cannot wait to meet some of his new charges. Mourinho shares Ranieri's vision of a Chelsea team with young English players at their heart. Terry is likely to remain as captain, and Mourinho wishes his players all the best for the European Championship in his native Portugal, adding, 'I want to have many English players in the team and I hope England reach the final or the semi-finals.'

Terry is now relishing the chance of playing under Mourinho and maintains he is ready to rise to the challenge after watching his no-nonsense message to his new players on the televised press conference. 'I am here today in the England team because of one man and that man is Claudio Ranieri. All I can do is thank the man. But the club have made their decision. It will be tough and it will be interesting, you can see that from what the new manager says. It'll be good; there will be new competition and hopefully some new players and we will see what happens. It's a challenge I relish. It will be a new start for everybody. The new manager might not favour me, but I will just work hard and hope to be in the eleven at the start of the season.'

HOW THE TINKERMAN TINKERED

Claudio Ranieri simply couldn't resist tinkering. He called himself the Tinkerman and the description fits perfectly.

Analysing all of his team selections for the season, it is apparent he couldn't resist change, sometimes for change sake. Hardly ever did he field the same side twice and his policy of using the full range of his extensive squad for rotation sacrificed any semblance of continuity.

He argued from the very start of the season that the object was to ensure that his players were fresh come March and April and he was proved right, with results picking up in the latter stages of the season, but far too late to catch Arsenal in the league. Perhaps he thought about his tactics and deployment of his players too much.

Ranieri called himself a gladiator, Christopher Columbus, Rudyard Kipling and Michelangelo. He took Chelsea on a voyage of discovery like Columbus, won Champions League glory in Rome with his gladiators, quoted Kipling as he responded to endless questions about his future – or lack of it – and painted marvellous pictures with his tactics. He insisted he wanted an English backbone to his team, but he was never a Churchill in the dressing room. He failed to galvanise his players into winning a trophy. So Ranieri became accustomed to being dubbed 'dead man walking' by others and referred to himself in the same way.

It wasn't all bad. Twice 1–0 up against Arsenal in both Premiership games, had his team ran out two-time winners they might have won the title. Chelsea's total points were almost good enough to land the club's first title since 1955.

And, of course, Chelsea went further on their Columbus expedition in the Champions League, reaching the last four. However, the downside was pretty spectacular.

A complete mess of the second half substitutions in Monaco cost Chelsea a place in the final. Opportunities in a variety of Premiership games were wasted through bizarre tactical changes. Ranieri tinkered in such mysterious ways that fans even placed bets on the line ups. The positions in which he deployed players were unusual, to say the least. Having invested £17m in a left winger Damian Duff, he was often played on the right or behind the front strikers. It's a credit to Duff that he had a successful season, apart from the long absence with a dislocated shoulder.

The reality for Ranieri was that he was actually a dead man walking from the very moment the man who appointed him, Ken Bates, sold up to Abramovich. Abramovich has an inner circle of advisors, around five to six he trusts and consults. It was unanimous from the start that Ranieri was not the calibre of coach for New Chelsea, the one investing £250m in the best players available, £140m in the first season alone. Having also spent £6on buying up 100 per cent of the shares and taking on the £90m debts, the final bill amounted to £400m, surely sufficient to believe you are entitled to some tangible return.

Sven-Goran Eriksson went to tea with Abramovich in his London pad, but the England coach was not ready to leave his Soho Square posting so no offer was made. However, Eriksson clearly had some input into the 'committee' deciding how to spend Abramovich's millions in the transfer market. As Chelsea had to wait for Eriksson to decide on the optimum moment to dump on the FA, Ranieri was in situ and possession is always nine-tenths of the law. He began well and Abramovich warmed to the coach who was turning media and public scrutiny in his favour with some impressive results. He was reinvented by the media who had at first ridiculed him as clown for his broken English to the point where he refused to conduct after match press conferences. Then he was the media darling because he was the underdog who said he would like to be the dog for a change.

He was charming in the face of adversity and polite and self-effacing under a barrage of questioning about how long he thought he would survive. He affectionately called his inquisitors sharks before he began later press gatherings at the Harlington training ground.

But a dip in the team's performances over Christmas and the New Year, coupled with rows with players like Jimmy Floyd Hasselbaink behind the scenes, permeated the dressing room. Word reached Abramovich's men that the players had become baffled by the tactics, unsettled by the rotations system and mystified by the positional experiments.

While Liverpool plotted Gerard Houllier's demise by conducting discreet soundings with potential successors, newly-installed chief executive Peter Kenyon was followed by photographers ready to snap him in action talking to the England coach or accompanying Abramovich to Vigo for talks with Jose Mourinho's agent. Sympathy abounded for Ranieri – his tears when he finally beat Arsenal prompted backing from everyone in the country and he was named Man of the Year by the Variety Club of Great Britain. Football is a cut-throat world and Liverpool were only doing exactly the same as the Chelsea top brass, but without the media hordes that wanted to know every move of the mysterious Russian owner at the Bridge.

The sterile home draw with Stuttgart in the Champions League, coupled with Ranieri's inability to beat Arsenal until the 17th attempt, convinced Abramovich's courtiers it was time to ensure a new man was in charge for the following season. Kenyon started work on 1 February and instantly made it clear that, given the huge investment in players, lack of a trophy at the end of the season would be deemed failure. With that as the benchmark, Ranieri has not delivered, irrespective of how close he might have come.

The feeling has grown that another season, even with better players, would not be enough to enhance the team's chances of tangible success if Ranieri were still in charge. The verdict was reaffirmed – not good enough.

Eriksson expressed interest, only to change his mind when trusted allies such as Tord Grip warned him of the consequences of trying to work and live in the UK after being branded a traitor for deserting the England team. However, if he makes a hash of the European Championships, the same media who would have hounded him for walking out on the FA will want to hang him from the nearest pub sign and call for a new England coach. Having signed a new agreement with the FA, he burnt his bridges with the Bridge, so Mourinho became the target.

Ranieri had already pointed out that his successor is a novice in the big leagues of Europe, but won the UEFA Cup last season and has now reached the Champions League final.

He might have started as Bobby Robson's interpreter but he is speaking the eight language of success within Europe for New Chelsea.

ENTER JOSE MOURINHO

NAME: Jose Mourinho
DOB: 29 January 1963 (Setubal, near Lisbon, Portugal)
EDUCATION: Left school at 18, did a physical education degree
FAMILY: Married Tami in 1989 (two children: Matilde aged eight and Jose Mario aged four)

No manager has won the modern European Cup so young, or achieved so much on such a limited budget as at Porto. It is hard to believe that just three years ago Jose Mourinho was in charge of Uniao Leiria, a small Portuguese football club which struggles to attract 2,000 fans to its home games. In his two full seasons in charge of Porto, Jose Mario Santos Mourinho Felix has won all but one of the six serious competitions the club has entered – two Portuguese titles, one UEFA Cup, one European Cup, one Portuguese Cup – and lost only two matches of consequence: a Portuguese Cup final and the one-off European Super Cup, against Milan, last August.

In each of his close seasons he has sold Porto's most valuable player: centre-half Jorge Andrade to Deportivo La Coruna in 2002, and striker Helder Postiga to Tottenham Hotspur in 2003. The final 90 minutes of the Champions League final reflect particularly well on Mourinho, who made two contentious selections. Carlos Alberto, the Brazilian teenager, started ahead of Benni McCarthy, his leading scorer and conqueror of United. Alberto scored the first goal. The coach also picked Pedro Mendes ahead of Alenitchev, who came on to set up the second goal and to score the third.

It was some weeks beforehand that Mourinho picked his team for the final. 'I decided the line-up a month ago,' he reveals. 'I first had the idea when Porto played Coruna [in the semi-final] and I saw Monaco in Chelsea. I was very clear about it. I was also clear that, if we were not winning at half-time, I would put on McCarthy instead of [midfielder] Pedro Mendes, pushing Carlos Alberto back. But we scored and then had the chance to play in the style we prefer. I told

Alenitchev to be the most attacking part of my midfield diamond and that we mustn't lose the diamond shape.'

After landing the Champions League with such an emphatic victory over Monaco, striker McCarthy says, 'Mourinho is the best coach in the world at the moment because, to achieve all this with Porto, which is not a "great" club like the leaders of Europe's more powerful leagues, marks him down as someone special. He is brilliant at his job, certainly good enough to manage any side in the Premiership. It promises to be one hell of a ride at Chelsea – for the players and directors.'

To give you an idea of his character, Mourinho sometimes enjoys role-reversal games, swapping places with his players and sometimes carrying out their orders while they act as manager. That's what happened to former Manchester United star Karel Poborsky when he told Mourinho – then in charge of Benfica – what position he wanted to play. Mourinho, who saw Poborsky as a winger, called him in and said, 'Right, you're the boss, why do you want to be play-maker?' He listened, let Poborsky pick his own place in the next match – and took him off after half an hour. Poborsky, 32, says, 'Mourinho then told me, "Right, I'm the manager again. I gave you the chance to prove you were right and you proved nothing." You will play where I tell you from now on and, if you do not want to, you'll play in the reserves.'

Mourinho was determined to have his say when he was assistant coach at Barcelona. Louis van Gaal had to handle superstar Rivaldo and gathered his staff to seek advice. Mourinho, the last to speak, told Van Gaal, 'You don't know how to talk to Brazilians, you don't know how to talk to Rivaldo and you can't get the best out of his immense quality.' He feared the sack. Instead Van Gaal replied, 'Jose is the only one who told the truth.' Later Mourinho sent his Porto players personal letters that contained the uncompromising message: 'Every training session, every game, every minute of our professional and social life is centred on our aim to be champions.' He admits, 'Yes, I am arrogant. But only with people I don't like.'

'First-teamer is not a permitted word here,' he used to tell his players at Porto's Olival training centre. 'I need you all and you all need each other. We are a team. Everybody has the same chance to play and everybody contributes.'

One of Porto's squad players, Jankauskas, said of Mourinho's skill in managing a squad, 'He keeps your confidence going. He gives each player the respect and he does explain how he understands our role to us, lets us know we are a special player, that we have a lot of games in the season and some will play in the cup more, some in the Champions League, and so on. He does his rotating carefully like that. He's a great coach, and he made this team and instilled that confidence in his players.

'Three years ago, we did not have a great name in Europe. Now we've won the UEFA Cup and the Champions League. Of course he takes credit. He has his own tactics, his way of playing and a specific idea of how he wants us to play, and the key to that is the discipline, players keeping their positions. We are lucky to have him. He's a very modern coach, different from most coaches I've worked with. He's very modern and very passionate. He's a winner, and he transfers that spirit to us. He's a strong character. He's not scared to shout.'

Porto's ex-Monaco star Costinha, 29, says, 'Jose speaks the language of players. He treats everyone on the same footing whether he is experienced or an 18-year-old. But he speaks to each player differently. He can adapt to an extra-sensitive player or to an aggressive one. He understands what others, seen from the outside, cannot understand.'

Scout for Porto Gil Rui Barros says, 'I have never known a manager prepare his training sessions so thoroughly. Like Zidane with a ball at his feet, Mourinho has this thing that cannot be taught. He is the Zidane of managers.'

Mourinho, a deeply religious man, was struck by tragedy when his sister died in a diabetic coma during his spell with Barcelona. The experience reinforced his strong bonds with wife Matilde, his seven-year-old daughter of the same name and his son Jose, four. It was to see them that he left the scene of Porto's triumph in the AufSchalke Arena so hurriedly – on the way to Chelsea.

Mourinho's uncle Mario Ledo owned a sardine cannery and grew rich under dictator Antonio de Oliveira Salazar's regime. Ledo died in 1972 and Salazar was later ousted, leaving Mourinho's family on the wrong side of the political divide.

The canning factories were confiscated and Jose and his sister Teresa moved with Felix and mum Maria to a more modest home. He never talks of Ledo, whose death badly affected him as a nine-year-old. Teresa died in 1997, aged 37. The official explanation was diabetes. But others believe the drugs she began using after her marriage broke up caused the infection which killed her. Mourinho refuses to discuss it. Before every kick-off, he kisses a photograph of his two children, and a crucifix. But what will he find at Stamford Bridge?

Former Chelsea manager Claudio Ranieri was adored by the fans for his charming English, and the wonderful laugh that accompanied his sharp sense of humour. He also had a huge following among women football fans.

The Tinkerman will be missed. Replacement Jose Mourinho has a reputation for being a hothead on the touch-line and a disciplinarian in the dressing room. In the moments after the semi-final Champions League triumph over Deportivo La Coruna, though, Mourinho was seen trying to dial a number on his mobile telephone and it kept telling him he couldn't get through. Mourinho, surrounded by Portuguese television cameras, was surprisingly mellow for such a hard man.

'At moments like these,' he said, live and euphoric, 'you want to speak to your loved ones.' Next morning he took his loved ones – his wife and two young children – and his adviser to Francisco Sa Carneiro airport and boarded a flight to London to watch Chelsea versus Monaco in the second leg of the semis.

He took his family to Chelsea because, as he explains, he had not given them the attention they deserve while he had been concentrating on taking unfancied Porto to the Champions League final. Mourinho avoided any direct contact with Roman Abramovich or Peter Kenyon as they have had a habit of being caught on camera in talks with potential successors to Ranieri! Kenyon was snapped with Sven-Goran Eriksson, who most definitely was a candidate and with Luis van Gaal, who most definitely was not even considered, but both incidents provoked column inches in the papers none the less.

Gossip surrounding Mourinho's private life has been fascinating. When there was a campaign to oust former Barcelona President Josep Lluis Nunez, the assistant to manager Bobby Robson, who just happened to be Jose Mourinho, was targeted in the media and suffered gay slurs. Mourinho may feature on gay internet sites in Portugal, but someone close to the negotiations to bring Mourinho to the Bridge tells me, 'He is most definitely not gay.'

Mourinho's rise to the top had fairly inauspicious beginnings. When Bobby Robson arrived in Lisbon to join Sporting 12 years ago, an immaculately dressed young PE teacher introduced himself in perfect English as Jose – the translator. Mourinho was 29 years old when he greeted Robson at the airport and subsequently introduced the grand old man of English football to Portuguese football.

Now 41 but still impeccable, having risen from translator to the continent's must-have coach in the meantime, Mourinho is similarly likely to suffer from culture shock when he arrives in English football. Though he has been here for a while, Sven-Goran Erikssson has still hardly come to terms with the media's obsession with, and the public's fascination for, the personal lives of celebrities. David Beckham knows just how the England coach feels. It is hoped too that Mourinho will benefit from a more liberal introduction to polite society in England than some of his predecessors, including Arsene Wenger.

'Arsene who?' was by far the most polite jibe the Frenchman had to endure when he first arrived at Highbury from Grampus 8 in the J League. It was vice-chairman David Dein's inspired move to take on his longstanding friend Wenger, whom he believed would reshape Arsenal into one of the country's most powerful football clubs again. Wenger soon found himself standing on the steps of the Marble Halls, calling an impromptu press conference to denounce malicious mischief-making on the internet. Wenger looked so enraged that Dein feared his newly appointed Messiah might hop it back to Japan.

Of more concern to Chelsea fans than old rumours about their new manager, though, is whether it will be a good season in terms of trophies. These have not been seen at the Bridge for quite some time now. The rare thing about Mourinho is that he is one of the few top coaches who never excelled within the professional ranks as a player. His father, Felix, says that he announced his intention of becoming the 'greatest coach in the world' at the age of 15. Felix Mourinho was a goalkeeper who won international honours and who later became a first division coach. Jose Dos Santos Mourinho – Ze to his friends – sought to follow in the footsteps of his father.

He enrolled at the Sports University of Lisbon, combining academic work with a playing career in the Portuguese second division for Sesimbra. From the age of 14, he scouted for his father, by now a rising coach. By 23, Jose had realised his limits as a player. 'I'm an intelligent person. I knew I was not going to go any higher. The second division was my level.' He took courses in coaching, some under the auspices of the FA and the Scottish FA, where Andy Roxburgh, the former Scotland manager, would be an important influence, 'particularly on training organisation, the points and techniques you need to establish in practice sessions'. Roxburgh was impressed by his student's attention to detail.

The first step on the career ladder came when Mourinho was made coach of the youth section at Vitoria Setubal. He was later appointed as assistant at Estrela da Amadora. In 1993, Sporting Lisbon were looking for local men to support their new foreign manager, Bobby Robson. Mourinho was sent to Lisbon airport to meet Robson, the beginning of an enduring friendship and a career-defining professional relationship. 'I owe him so much. I was a nobody in football when he came to Portugal,' Mourinho says. 'He helped me to work in two clubs here [Sporting and Porto] and he took me to one of the biggest clubs in the world [Barcelona]. We are very different, but I got from him the idea of what it is to be a top coach.'

The Setubal-born Mourinho has an iron will and used Robson as his mentor. Mourinho followed Robson from Lisbon to Porto, where they won two league titles, and in 1996 went to Barcelona. Robson still insists that 'fundamentally his job was interpreter' but, astute and clever as well as a quick learner, Mourinho took on an increasingly active role, carrying out scouting missions, dealing with players such as Ronaldo and talking to the press. When Robson moved on, Mourinho stayed on under Louis van Gaal, winning two league titles. Offered the chance to go solo, he left for Benfica, only to fall out with the club's President Manuel Vilarinho, after which he joined Uniao Leiria, leading them to their highest-ever finish, fifth, in 2000/01.

When he joined Porto in January 2002, they were languishing in mid-table and yet he informed the press they would win the league the next season. He announced that Porto would 'do things my way' and promised, 'We'll qualify for the UEFA Cup and next year we'll win the league.' He was right.

A first-season treble has been followed by another waltz to the title, as well as a major European final. Against Celtic in last year's UEFA Cup final, Porto were accused of diving and play-acting, of failing to play the British game. Against Deportivo in the first leg of the Champions League semi-final, a Spanish commentator said, 'He looks like a gents' hairstylist but his teams boot you all over the park.'

After two desperate years on Celta Vigo's bench, the confidence of South African striker Benni McCarthy had vanished. Mourinho told him, 'If you were with me you'd be top scorer,' and told the press, 'I have three transfer options – the first is McCarthy, the second is McCarthy and the third is McCarthy.' Yet even Mourinho has been surprised by McCarthy's progress, as well as that of Porto. Last year he insisted, 'We can do nice things in the Champions League but we can't win it – that's just for the sharks, clubs that pay €20m (£13.5m) for one player.' Could he have meant Chelsea? Surely not!

However much of a disciplinarian he may be, he still manages to retain the full respect of his players. 'I've known him a long time, and he has this special way of organising his players and understanding how they want to play,' says Porto goalkeeper Vitor Baia, who first worked with Mourinho a decade ago.

'He stands out as the best in Portugal,' says the midfielder Costinha. 'He's young for a head coach, and that can be a good thing. He knows how players think.'

McCarthy's verdict is, 'An expert in developing a player's confidence.'

Portugal, though, is officially only the sixth-strongest league in Europe and already Ranieri and others have questioned whether Mourinho will cut it in a 'big' league like England. No Portuguese club has reached a European Cup final since 1987, when Porto won it; no club from outside the four richest leagues – Spain, Italy, England, Germany – has won the European Cup since Ajax in 1995. A Porto-Monaco final guaranteed that one would do so in 2004, namely Porto.

'After the Bosman ruling, Portuguese football lost some ground,' Mourinho says. 'We are up against clubs from bigger economies, who get three or four places in the Champions League every year. So this is a fantastic moment, not only for Porto, but for Portuguese football. These players are going to leave a mark.'

In west London, Mourinho's background as an interpreter means he will be able to converse with the broad spectrum of players inside the Chelsea dressing room. He owns up to finding German a little tough, but has mastered English, Spanish, French and Italian. 'I would find it completely impossible to work at a club in a country where I hadn't learnt the language,' he says. As Robson recounts it, 'He told me what the players were saying when they thought I couldn't understand.'

On the bench and patrolling the technical area, Mourinho chews gum, sometimes takes note and can get very excited; witness his jubilant leap and sprint down the line when Porto scored their late goal at Old Trafford to knock Manchester United out of the European Cup, or a notorious slanging match he became involved in with the Sporting player Rui Jorge in a League game in January.

Mourinho acknowledges his debt to Robson and Van Gaal. 'One of the most important things I learnt from Bobby Robson is that, when you win, you shouldn't assume you are the team and, when you lose, you shouldn't think you are rubbish.' He speaks to Robson often, 'about football, family. We'll talk about my Porto team, about his grandchildren, lots of things.'

After he left Barcelona in 2000, Mourinho was offered the job of Robson's number two at Newcastle with a view, his old friend told him, to Robson moving upstairs after a season and Mourinho becoming head coach. Mourinho says, 'He had forgotten I worked with him for many years. Bobby Robson will only leave the pitch when he retires. It is unthinkable. I didn't accept.'

Sir Alex Ferguson declined to shake Mourinho's hand after the match in Porto. 'I thought about how to put pressure on Ferguson and his club,' Mourinho told *France Football* magazine after that tie had been settled in his side's favour. 'He had said Vitor Baia was a clown and that Carlos Alberto and Deco were girls who could never play in England. I explained that the money earned by Ruud van Nistelrooy would be enough to pay the salaries of all my players. That can work towards the psychology of players.'

We can look forward to such hostilities being resumed in the new season. Arsene Wenger has already welcomed the needle which Mourinho can bring to the Premiership. But, for the media, there is one big snag about the new man. His English is near faultless. Journalists will almost be sorry that no more pigeon English is going to be spoken in Chelsea's press conferences. The language will never be as colourful again.

Days before the 26 May Champions League final, Mourinho said, 'My reputation is very important to me. I want people to remember me as one of the all-time great managers. I want to leave my mark in football history and be remembered like Bill Shankly, Bob Paisley, and Matt Busby. I loved the way Liverpool played in the 1970s and 1980s. I loved Kenny Dalglish, Graeme Souness, Phil Thompson, Ray Clemence and Ian Rush. now I want the same success.'

He recalled how he 'wound up' Ferguson, who called the players of Porto cheats after they won the first leg 2–1 in Portugal. 'When my team are involved I don't care about my image. Sometimes I make enemies because of my reaction, but when my players are under attack they are my family and I will protect them.

'I think Ferguson's comments were a strategy. He realised for the first time that United had lost their invincibility and I saw fear in his eyes. I think he was very disturbed. Afterwards I told my players, "He was surprised by our quality, he thought it was easy for them to beat us, but we beat them. Now he is afraid of the second leg and this is a ploy to unsettle us, so I need you to be with me in this fight... go to Old Trafford and play; don't be afraid, show your character."

'I had met Ferguson in the past and he was very polite, but at the end of that first leg he had an angry reaction when I went to shake his hand; he told me my players were cheating, so I had to use his rage to fire up my team.'

Once Mourinho tasted victory, the moment went to his head. 'When Francisco Costinha scored, I ran all the way to the corner flag. It was one of the best moments of my career and very emotional. It was like a golden goal. At that moment, I knew Manchester United were out of the competition. Man U are the biggest club I've knocked out in my two years at Porto.'

Despite the support of his players, Ranieri was not close to them. By comparison, Mourinho is almost attached at the hip. Striker Benni McCarthy explains, 'The manager has been world-class and inspired the whole team. He brings out the best in all the players and we all respond well to him. He's a great person and an excellent trainer with perfect manners and that's why he's working so well for Porto.

'He can do it at the very highest level. He's got a good mentality and if the players give him the right co-operation at Chelsea he can achieve anything he wants to. Mourinho can handle the big players. He worked with Ronaldo at Barcelona and gets on very well with the big players at Porto. He'll do very well at Chelsea and I wouldn't be surprised if they won the Premiership or Champions League next season.'